HANDICAPPED STUDENTS

AND

SPECIAL EDUCATION

THIRD EDITION

Published by
Data Research, Inc.
P.O. Box 490
Rosemount, Minnesota 55068

PREFACE

Federal law requires that school districts provide each handicapped child with a free appropriate education. This volume, *Handicapped Students and Special Education,* has been published in response to the need of school administrators and others involved in providing special education services to have a reference available when confronted with any of the multitude of problems in the special education area. The textual development of this new and revised Third Edition is based upon examination of state and federal appellate court decisions in the field of special education. In addition, the volume contains the full text of the Education for All Handicapped Children Act of 1975, as amended, as well as the four landmark U.S. Supreme Court decisions dealing with special education. The full legal citation is also given for each case, and all cases have been indexed and placed in the Table of Cases.

The intent of this volume is to provide professional educators and lawyers with access to important case and statutory law in the field of special education and handicapped student rights.

EDITORIAL STAFF
DATA RESEARCH, INC.

INTRODUCTORY NOTE ON THE
JUDICIAL SYSTEM

In order to allow the reader to determine the relative importance of a judicial decision, the cases included in *Handicapped Students and Special Education, Third Edition,* identify the particular court from which a decision has been issued. For example, a case decided by a state supreme court generally will be of greater significance than a state circuit court case. Hence a basic knowledge of the structure of our judicial system is important to an understanding of school law.

The most common system, used by nearly all states and also the federal judiciary, is as follows: a legal action is commenced in **district court** (sometimes called a trial court, county court, common pleas court or superior court) where a decision is initially reached. The case may then be appealed to the **court of appeals** (or appellate court), and in turn this decision may be appealed to the **supreme court.**

Several states, however, do not have a court of appeals; lower court decisions are appealed directly to the state's supreme court. Additionally, some states have labeled their courts in a nonstandard fashion.

In Maryland, the highest court is called the Court of Appeals.

In the state of New York, the trial court is called the Supreme Court. Decisions of this court may be appealed to the Supreme Court, Appellate Division. The highest court in New York is the Court of Appeals.

Pennsylvania has perhaps the most complex court system. The lowest state court is the Court of Common Pleas. Depending on the circumstances of the case, appeals may be taken to either the Commonwealth Court or the Superior Court. In certain instances the Commonwealth Court functions as a trial court as well as an appellate court. The Superior Court, however, is strictly an intermediate appellate court. The highest court in Pennsylvania is the Supreme Court.

While supreme court decisions are generally regarded as the last word in legal matters, it is important to remember that trial court and appeals court decisions also create important legal precedents.

TABLE OF CONTENTS

TABLE OF CONTENTS

CHAPTER THREE
PROCEDURAL SAFEGUARDS OF
THE EAHCA

TABLE OF CONTENTS

TABLE OF CONTENTS

TABLE OF CONTENTS

CHAPTER ONE

RIGHT OF THE HANDICAPPED TO AN EDUCATION

I. The Education for All Handicapped Children Act of 1975

A. Background

The Education for All Handicapped Children Act (EAHCA)* is an effort by Congress to assist the states in fulfilling the duties imposed upon them by the widespread recognition of the right of handicapped children to a free public education appropriate to their needs. The Act establishes requirements which must be complied with in order for states to be eligible to receive financial assistance. First, each state must have "in effect a policy that assures all handicapped children the right to a free appropriate public education" [20 U.S.C. section 1412(1)], and must develop a plan which details the policies and procedures which insure the provision of that right [section 1412(2)]. Each state must also establish the requisite procedural safeguards [section 1412(5)], and must insure that local educational agencies in this state will establish the individualized educational programs required by the Act [section 1412(4)]. The Act additionally requires that each state must formulate a plan for educating its handicapped children which must be submitted to and approved by the Secretary of Education before the state is entitled to federal assistance.

The EAHCA has remedied a situation whereby local school districts, prior to the Act, could lawfully exclude children whose handicaps prevented them from participating in regular school programs. Now, states receiving federal assistance under the EAHCA must prepare an individualized educational program (IEP) for each handicapped student and review the program at least annually. Both the preparation and review processes must be conducted with participation by the child's parents or guardian. The EAHCA, the full text of which is reprinted in the appendix, also requires that a participating state provide specified administrative procedures by which the child's parents or guardians may challenge any change in evaluation and education of the child.

---

*Sometimes referred to as the EHA (Education of the Handicapped Act).

B. Overview

The term *handicapped children* is defined in the EAHCA as any children who are "mentally retarded, hard of hearing, deaf, speech impaired, visually handicapped, seriously emotionally disturbed, orthopedically impaired, or other health impaired children, or children with specific learning disabilities, who by reason thereof require special education and related services" [section 1401(1)]. The public schools must provide all such children with a *free appropriate public education*, which means "special education and related services which (A) have been provided at public expense, under public supervision and direction, and without charge, (B) meet the standards of the State educational agency, (C) include an appropriate preschool, elementary, or secondary school education in the State involved, and (D) are provided in conformity with the individualized education program required under section 1414(a)(5) of this title" [section 1401(18)].

The above-mentioned *related services* are in turn defined as "transportation, and such developmental, corrective, and other supportive services (including speech pathology and audiology, pyschological services, physical and occupational therapy, recreation, and medical and counseling services, except that such medical services shall be for diagnostic and evaluation purposes only) as may be required to assist a handicapped child to benefit from special education, and includes the early identification and assessment of handicapping conditions in children" [section 1401(17)]. While medical services are excluded from the definition of related services, insofar as they may be needed by a child for diagnostic and evaluative purposes, medical services must also be provided free of charge.

Section 1401(17) states that psychological services are related services and thus are to be provided free of charge by school districts to handicapped students who require such services. While it is clear that not all services involving psychotherapy are related services, if the psychotherapy required by the child is of the type that could be provided by a social worker, school psychologist, nurse or counselor, it will be considered a related service. Where the required psychotherapy is of such a nature that it can only be competently administered by a licensed psychiatrist, then it will be considered a medical service and the school district will not be required to furnish it. Thus, a U.S. district court in New Jersey held that a school district was required to pay $25,200 for a child's stay at a day school which provided individualized psychotherapy, family therapy, group therapy, and individual and group counseling. The court held that the psychotherapy provided here was an integral part of the child's special education. See p. 52, *T.G. v. Board of Education*, 576 F.Supp. 420 (D.N.J.1983). It is important to remember that under section 1401(17), even medical and psychiatric services must be provided free of charge if such services are required for evaluative or diagnostic purposes. See p. 56, *Darlene L. v. Illinois State Board of Education*, 568 F.Supp. 1340 (N.D.Ill.1983).

Section 1415 of the EAHCA contains mandatory procedures designed to safeguard the rights of handicapped students. The safeguards emphasize, among other things, notice to parents and an opportunity for parental participation in the development of a child's special education program. Most important, the various subsections under section 1415 require that parents be informed of all available procedures and methods by which any grievances or dissatisfaction may be resolved. Written notice must be given to parents if a school proposes to change or refuses to initiate a change in a child's educational program, or if the school refuses to perform an initial evaluation and placement of the child [subsection (b)(1)(C)].

In case of any dispute over their child's IEP, section 1415 of the EAHCA states that parents have the right to an impartial hearing before a hearing officer who is neither an employee of the school district nor of the state education department [subsection (b)(2)]. If either the parents or the school are unhappy with the hearing officer's decision, appeal may be taken to the state education department [subsection (c)]. During pendency of a dispute over any aspect of a special education program, the child must remain in his or her "then current" program [subsection (e)(3)]. A lawsuit may be commenced in either state or federal court after a decision has been reached by the stated education department [subsection (e)(2)].

II. State and Local Responsibilities to Handicapped Children:
Board of Education v. Rowley

The U.S. Supreme Court case of *Board of Education v. Rowley*, 458 U.S. 176 (1982), is the definitive case dealing with the responsibilities of states in the education of handicapped children. That case arose when the parents of an eight-year-old child, deaf since birth, claimed the child was entitled to have a sign language interpreter in her classroom to enable her to have the same educational opportunity as her classmates. The district court held that the child was entitled to have a sign language interpreter in her classroom (483 F.Supp. 528). The case was appealed to the U.S. Court of Appeals, Second Circuit, which affirmed the district court (632 F.2d 945). The school board then made a final appeal to the U.S. Supreme Court, which reversed the two lower courts. The Supreme Court held that the Act is satisfied when a school provides personalized instruction with sufficient support services to permit the handicapped child to *benefit educationally* from that instruction. The court went on to state that the individualized educational program required by the Act should be reasonably calculated to enable the child to achieve passing marks and to advance from grade to grade. The Act does not require a school to provide a sign language interpreter as requested by a child's parents. The court stated that the Act was not meant to guarantee a handicapped child a certain level of education but merely to open the door of education to handicapped children by means of special educational services. Additionally, the decision notes, a school is not required to maximize the potential of each handicapped child, nor is it required to provide equal educational opportunity commensurate with the opportunity provided to nonhandicapped children. (The *Board of Education v. Rowley* case is reprinted in the Appendix of U.S. Supreme Court Cases of this volume.)

Other cases elaborating upon state and local responsibilities to handicapped children follow.

An Indiana case demonstrates the proposition that although state education departments are, under the terms of the EAHCA, the primary parties responsible for special educational services, states may require local school districts to assume responsibility for such services and related expenses. Here the parents of a mentally retarded boy sued their school board and the State Board of Education seeking reimbursement for the tuition and transportation costs involved in their son's placement in a private residential facility in Kansas. The boy was first identified in 1975 as being in need of special educational services, and in 1976 the school board concurred with the parents' decision to place the child in the Kansas facility. Pursuant to Indiana law the school board sought and was granted State Board approval for such placement. The school board therefore made transfer tuition payments to cover the cost of the boy's special education. State Board approval was similarly granted for the 1976-77 school year.

However, for the 1977-78 year the school board neglected to forward an application to the State Board but nevertheless assumed that it concurred in the school board's decision to continue the boy's placement at the Kansas school. When the school board forwarded its application for approval for the 1978-79 school year, the State Board rejected it and furthermore refused to meet with the parents' attorney to discuss its decision. The child's parents then sued the school board and the State Board of Education contending that under state law they were entitled to tuition and transportation expenses. An Indiana trial court ruled that the school district wsa liable for the boy's transportation costs and that the State Board was liable for transfer tuition fees. On appeal, the Court of Appeals of Indiana reversed the trial court and held that under Indiana law the local school board is primarily liable for all special education expenses. The case was remanded to the trial court to determine whether the State Board was obligated to reimburse the school board for the excess transfer tuition. *Weesner v. Baker*, 477 N.E.2d 337 (Ind.App.2d Dist.1985).

Three school districts in Pennsylvania brought suit against the state's Department of Education challenging a change in the special education plan of an "intermediate unit" which had been educating handicapped children. The unit proposed to suspend operation of classes for the educable mentally retarded (EMR). The unit's decision placed responsibility for operation of all EMR classes on each individual school district, with the unit providing support services and supervision for the classes. The adopted changes affected four school districts, one of which acceded to the plan changes. The remaining three districts argued in the Commonwealth Court of Pennsylvania that the unit had an obligation to continue to operate EMR classes in their districts unless each district consented to the cessation of the classes.

The court disagreed. "On the contrary," said the court, "the authorities establish overwhelmingly that the primary responsibility for identifying all exceptional children and developing appropriate educational programs to meet their needs is placed on the local school districts." Because the unit was not bound to continue EMR classes absent a showing that the districts could not "efficiently and effectively" provide appropriate educational programs for EMR children in the districts, the proposed changes were upheld. *Bermudian Springs School District v. Department of Education*, 475 A.2d 943 (Pa.Cmwlth.1984).

The Human Rights Authority of the State of Illinois Guardianship and Advocacy Commission appealed an order of an Illinois district court denying the enforcement of a subpoena issued by the Commission. Acting on a complaint which alleged that a local school district was not providing occupational and physical therapy for its students, the Commission started an investigation and asked the district superintendent to produce the students' educational program records. The records were to be masked so as to delete any information by which students could be identified. When the school district failed to turn over the information, the Commission issued a subpoena for the masked records. Again, the school district refused to comply. The Commission then sought judicial enforcement of the subpoena.

A trial court ruled that the Commission had no right to examine the records because it did not satisfy the access requirements of Illinois state law regarding student records. After the Commission appealed to the Appellate Court of Illinois, the school district argued that, along with the access provisions of the Student Records Act, the commission had no authority to investigate or review special education programs, and that the Commission's right to investigate does not apply to all of the handicapped students in a school district but is limited to individual cases. The thrust of the school district's first argument was that the Commission was somehow usurping the role of the State Board of Education by investigating the special education program of the school district. According to the school district, the Commission's inquiry was "tantamount to the control and direction of special education which makes local school authorities accountable to the [Commission] rather than the State Board of Education as required by the School Code."

The Appellate Court disagreed. The court held that the statutory authority of the Commission to investigate complaints concerning violations of the rights of handicapped persons, including the right to special education programs, was not subordinate to that of the State Board of Education. Further, the Commission's investigation of the school district's overall special education program and not merely individual students was within the bounds of the Commission's statutory authority. Finally, the Student Records Act did not bar enforcement of the subpoena issued by the Commission. *Human Rights Authority v. Miller*, 464 N.E.2d 833 (Ill.App.3d Dist.1984).

CHAPTER TWO

"FREE APPROPRIATE EDUCATION" UNDER THE EAHCA

I. Financial Contribution to Special Education

Under the EAHCA and the Act's implementing regulations, state educational agencies are charged with the responsibility to ensure that all eligible children within the state are provided with a free appropriate education. This duty is carried out by allocating federal funds to local educational agencies which in turn are to apportion the funds to educate handicapped children.

A. Financial Contribution by Relatives of Child

Courts will not allow schools to assess parents or other relatives for expenses incurred in educating a handicapped child, if such expenses were necessary in order to provide the child with an appropriate education.

Two Illinois cases illustrate the principle that any state statutory scheme which assesses parents or guardians or other relatives and requires reimbursement to the state for educating a handicapped child will not stand as valid law. This is due to the EAHCA's mandate of *free* appropriate public educations for handicapped children and the supremacy of federal law over state law.

In the first case the parents of a handicapped child appealed from an order of the Illinois Department of Mental Health and Developmental Disabilities assessing them a "responsible relative liability charge" for the care of their child. The department's decision was based upon its belief that this was mandated by the Illinois Mental Health and Developmental Disabilities Code. The Appellate Court of Illinois upheld a lower court decision reversing the department's order, ruling that the department's decision was in violation of the federal Education for All Handicapped Children Act.

The court observed that federal law requires maintenance by the state of "a policy that assures all handicapped children the right to a free appropriate public education." This education is to include both "special education" and "related services." The state's contention was that federal statute should not prevent the assessment of charges pursuant to state law. The court disagreed, observing that there is a strong insistence by federal law in the requirement that all expenditures of every kind for the education and welfare of the child are to be borne not by the parents but by the educational authorities of the state. The assessment was therefore prohibited. *Parks v. Illinois Department of Mental Health and Developmental Disabilities*, 441 N.E.2d 1209 (Ill.App.1st Dist.1982).

In the second case, a U.S. district court held that an Illinois statute requiring relatives to reimburse the state for payments made to support the residential placement of developmentally disabled children was contrary to the EAHCA and, therefore, invalid under the Supremacy Clause of the U.S. Constitution. The EAHCA requires that states provide handicapped children with a free appropriate public education, which includes both special educational and related services provided at public expense. The court characterized the Illinois scheme as anything but free and as a blatant violation of federal law. In overturning the "responsible relatives" statute, the court ordered that relatives who had paid prior assessments be reimbursed for the $100 monthly contribution fee they had paid (back to the year 1978) for the residential care of their developmentally disabled children.

On appeal by the state, the U.S. Court of Appeals, Seventh Circuit, affirmed the ruling that Illinois violated the EAHCA by requiring parents to pay any part of the living expenses of handicapped children who are placed in a private residential facility on the ground of developmental disability rather than of educational need. The court rejected the state's argument that the class of developmentally disabled children are placed in residential institutions for reasons other than education and, therefore, those children fall outside the protection of the EAHCA. It noted that "if the child is so far handicapped as to be unconscious, and is thus wholly uneducable, he falls outside the Act even though his handicap is more rather than less severe than that of the children protected by the Act." However, the court continued that "in light of the close connection between mental retardation and special educational need . . . developmental disability, far from being an exempted category, is an important subcategory of the handicaps covered by the Act." What Illinois had done, found the court, was to carve out a class of handicapped children and deny them the full reimbursement to which they were entitled under EAHCA.

The appellate court, however, reversed that portion of the district court's ruling which ordered the state to reimburse the parents for expenses they had paid back to the year 1978. It ruled that the parents were only entitled to reimbursement necessary to clear outstanding bills, thus preventing the expulsion of children from their residential placements. *Parks v. Pavkovic*, 753 F.2d 1397 (7th Cir.1985).

Neglect proceedings involving a New Hampshire child resulted in the child's placement in a residential school and a court order requiring the child's father to reimburse the city in which the school was located for the costs of her educational placement. The father brought suit seeking to terminate his financial liability for his daughter's placement. He argued that he was not financially obligated because his daughter should have been placed as an educationally handicapped child at public expense under the EAHCA. In support of his argument he pointed out that the child's former school district had formulated a special education plan for her. The Supreme Court of New Hampshire observed that the lower court which had ordered the child's neglect placement properly did so without considering the child's special education needs. The court then turned to the father's allegations that the state had violated the EAHCA by not placing the child in a special education setting. The court held that the judiciary was not the proper forum to decide, in the first instance, whether the child was entitled to special education. The father's complaint was dismissed until such time as he completed the administrative appeals process. *In re Laurie B.*, 489 A.2d 567 (N.H.1984).

A case dealing with the issue of whether parents should be assessed the costs for the educational care of their handicapped children was decided similarly by the Supreme Court of New Jersey. The guardians of a profoundly mentally retarded nineteen-year-old woman and the parents of a ten-year-old crib-confined child suffering from significant brain damage brought suit against the state of New Jersey challenging a New Jersey law requiring parents of institutionalized children to bear the costs of maintenance of the children in a state or county "charitable institution." Payment of expenses was made pursuant to an "ability to pay" scheme. The parents argued that under the New Jersey constitution their children were entitled to a free education to be paid for by the state. The Supreme Court of New Jersey ruled against them, holding that the parents were not constitutionally entitled to have the institutional care of their children furnished free of charge at public expense.

The court reasoned that, sadly, there exists a category of mentally disabled children so severely impaired as to be unable to absorb or benefit from education. The court noted that the mentally retarded woman in this case had received a curriculum consisting of the attempt to develop minimal self-care skills, for example, eating and dressing, and that the totally crib-confined boy was undergoing brief physical therapy and auditory reaction testing, but deemed these as only of secondary significance to the greater functions of residential institutions to provide care, custody and safekeeping. Therefore, the court rejected the parents' argument that the residual care provided to the children qualified as "education," and concluded that there was no state constitutional ground upon which the parents could be relieved of the costs of maintaining their children in a state institution. *Levine v. State*, 418 A.2d 229 (N.J.1980).

B. Financial Contribution by State Educational Agencies and Local School Districts

Parents or guardians of handicapped children sometimes assert that their children are not receiving a "free appropriate education" because of a state educational agency's or a local school district's failure to pay the educational and related expenses involved in educating the child. Generally, the school district of the child's residence is responsible for the educational expenses of a handicapped child. Disputes have arisen when a child is temporarily institutionalized within the boundaries of one school district and the parents reside in another school district.

The New York Supreme Court, Appellate Division, has issued a ruling which interprets section 4004(2)(a) of that state's Education Law. This section declares that "[t]he school district in which a child resided at the time the social services district . . . assumed responsibility for the support and maintenance of the child . . . [shall] reimburse the state toward the state's expenditure on behalf of such child." The dispute in this case arose when custody of a handicapped child was surrendered by his mother to a county social services department. He was later returned to the custody of his mother. At that time he began to attend school in the Brentwood school district, his district of residence.

When the mother once again surrendered custody of her child to the county social services department, the state sought reimbursement from the Brentwood district. Brentwood refused, arguing that the school district where the child resided at the time of his first placement with the social services department was his school district of origin for the purpose of section 4004(2)(a). This interpretation would mean that any subsequent residence was irrelevant. The state Commissioner of Education had previously ruled that "when a child is returned to the custody of his parents and then subsequently replaced with the Department of Social Services, the financial burden of such care falls on the school district in which the child resided at the time of placement, regardless of his residence at the time of any earlier placement." The Appellate Division agreed with the Commissioner, holding that section 4004(2)(a) requires that whatever school district in which a child resides at the time of his placement in a social services program must bear the financial burden. The five-judge panel concluded that the Commissioner's ruling that Brentwood reimburse the state was practical because it "relieves a [former] school district of the responsibility for underwriting the expenses of a subsequently relocated child with whom the district may not have had any contact for years." *Brentwood Union Free School District v. Ambach*, 495 N.Y.S.2d 513 (A.D.3d Dept.1985).

A Massachusetts town providing special educational services to a child brought suit challenging the burden imposed upon it to pay the child's expenses. The town sought reimbursement from another town in which the child's natural parent resided. However, the child was temporarily in the custody of the Department of Social Services (DSS) and the town from which reimbursement was sought argued that the DSS should assume the child's residential and educational expenses. The Supreme Judicial Court of Massachusetts found this argument without merit. The agency with custody, found the court, does have the power to determine the child's place of abode, medical care and education. However, quoting Massachusetts law, the court stated that an acceptance of a child into DSS custody "shall entail no abrogation of parental rights or responsibilities, [rather, it is] a temporary delegation of certain rights and responsibilities necessary to provide foster care . . . agreed upon by both and terminable by either." The purpose of the child's transfer to DSS custody was only to aid him in obtaining appropriate residential care and educational services, not to place full legal responsibility in the agency. The DSS, therefore, was not a parent for purposes of Massachusetts law and thus was not liable for the child's expenses. *Town of Northbridge v. Town of Natick*, 474 N.E.2d 551 (Mass.1985).

The Supreme Court of New Hampshire decided that a child committed to a youth center for the duration of his minority, where the youth center was located outside of the parents' legal residence, was entitled to have the school district of his parents' legal residence pay the educational expenses incurred during his incarceration at the center. The school district contended that the youth center was the place of the child's residence, residence being the place ". . . designated by a person as his principal place of physical presence for the indefinite future . . .," and therefore the school district where the youth center was located should pay the expenses. The court disagreed, however, saying that since the child was committed to the youth center for the duration of his minority only, this was not "physical presence for the indefinite future," and that since his parents retained legal custody of him, the district in which the parents lived was the place of residence for purposes of payment of expenses. Consequently, the school district in the town in which the parents lived was responsible for the child's special educational expenses. *In re Bryan L.*, 462 A.2d 108 (N.H.1983).

In another New Hampshire case a declaratory judgment action was brought to determine which school district was liable for the special education expenses of an educationally handicapped child. The child had lived for nearly one year with a married couple who wished to adopt him. However, later the couple decided not to adopt him and the child then became a patient at a New Hampshire state hospital. He later lived at a group home and at a training center in Massachusetts. A New Hampshire trial court placed all responsibility for the child's educational expenses on the school district in which the child had lived with the couple who had wished to adopt him. The school district appealed to the Supreme Court of New Hampshire, which affirmed the trial court ruling, saying that a state statute which obligated "the district in which the child last resided" to pay his special education expenses referred to the place where a child actually lived outside of a facility. Because the evidence was sufficient to support a finding that the child's residence for nearly one year with the couple who had wished to adopt him was bona fide, that district was liable for his special education expenses incurred after his leaving the couple's home. *In re Gary B.*, 466 A.2d 929 (N.H.1983).

In a Pennsylvania case involving a dispute over who was to pay the educational expenses of a handicapped child, the Pennsylvania Secretary of Education declined to approve an exceptional child's special education program and placement at a private residential school located in a district other than that of the parents' residence. The secretary concluded that the child was a "low functioning educable retarded child who required a highly structured special education program," but rejected the private school placement because of a Pennsylvania statute requiring the school district in which a child was institutionalized to assume responsibility for a public education, regardless of whether the child was a legal resident of the district. The parents appealed the secretary's decision to the Commonwealth Court of Pennsylvania, which held that the school district had failed to meet its legal responsibility to provide an appropriate program of education and training for the child. The court based its ruling on the fact that the district, instead of making an initial recommendation, merely provided the parents with a list of "approved private schools" and took twenty-one months to make an official recommendation of appropriate educational placement. Further, the statute protecting the rights of institutionalized children did not preclude the secretary from recommending a private school as an appropriate placement, nor did it relieve the school district of the child's legal residence from responsibility in providing an appropriate education. *Pires v. Commonwealth*, 467 A.2d 79 (Pa.Cmwlth.1983).

A federal court has held that the Illinois State Board of Education was not relieved of its obligation to provide an education to a handicapped child by the possibility of financial assistance from another government or private agency. The mother of an exceptional child placed him in a residential school in Kansas after a hearing officer exonerated an Illinois school district from liability for all but "purely educational" expenses of the severely multiple handicapped child and determined that residential expenses should be borne by another agency. The mother then brought suit against state educational officials seeking an injunction to prohibit the district from adhering to its policy of distinguishing between "educational" and "noneducational" components of "related services" needed to enable handicapped children to perform adequately in school. The state argued that the Kansas placement was not "appropriate" because it was inordinately expensive. The court upheld the residential placement saying that the school district had the sole responsibility for providing a special education to the child and, further, that the allegedly inordinate cost of the placement did not preclude it from being the appropriate placement. *William S. v. Gill*, 572 F.Supp. 509 (N.D.Ill.1983).

An Oregon school district and the state of Oregon clashed over which was to pay the educational expenses of handicapped children attending a residential school located in a school district other than that of the children's legal residence. The school district in which the school was located refused to continue educational services to those children whose legal residence was not within the district. The parents of those children sought education expenses from their own school districts which also refused to assume financial responsibility saying that they did not place or enroll the children in the residential school or refer them to it and they did not contract with that school district to provide a free appropriate public education for them. The school districts of the children's residences argued that it did not make legal sense to hold them financially responsible for services provided to the students by state agencies or other school districts that have voluntarily assumed those duties.

After the Oregon Department of Education also denied responsibility for the children's education, the parents brought suit in a U.S. district court, which held that under the EAHCA, the Oregon Department of Education had the responsibility to insure that educational programs required by the Act for handicapped children were funded. In addition, Oregon law placed the financial responsibility for funding free appropriate public educations for handicapped children upon the state, which in this case had not provided the funds necessary to supplement the federal funds received under the Act. The state of Oregon was ordered to finance the children's educations. *Kerr Center Parents Association v. Charles*, 572 F.Supp. 448 (D.Or.1983).

II. Evaluation of Handicapped Students

Section 1412(2)(C) of the EAHCA requires states to assure that all children residing in the state who are handicapped are identified, located and evaluated. Parents or guardians of handicapped children sometimes take issue with the procedures by which schools identify and classify handicapped children.

A. Identification and Classification of Handicapped Children

The problems surfacing in identification and classification cases involve methods of assessing the intellectual ability of mentally or emotionally handicapped children, determining whether cultural, social or economic deprivation or emotional disturbances constitute handicaps for purposes of the EAHCA, and determining whether proper classification procedures have been utilized.

In a Rhode Island case a federal court ruled that a school district, faced with a hostile set of parents, acted properly in attempting to provide a learning disabled boy with an appropriate special education. The parents had enrolled their child at the age of six in the Scituate, Rhode Island, public school system. He received remedial reading instruction during first grade. The following year his parents placed him in a private Catholic school, but eighteen months later they concluded that he was learning disabled and once again enrolled him in the Scituate public schools. Eighteen months after this the parents placed him in a private day school, and later at the Linden Hill School in Northfield, Massachusetts, which specializes in the education of learning disabled boys. The child never returned to the Scituate public school system.

Three years later, in April, 1981, the parents sought future financial assistance under the EAHCA for their son's placement at Linden Hill. In May, 1981, they met with the special education multi-disciplinary team (MDT) and expressed their dissatisfaction with Scituate's past education of their child. When the MDT said that due to flawed and dated prior tests, a new evaluation of the child would be required, the parents objected and withheld consent until June, 1981. A partial evaluation was then performed by the MDT, but due to parental resistance it was never completed. At a September, 1981, meeting with the MDT, the parents were advised that the MDT would recommend placement in a Scituate self-contained classroom. Due to delays caused by the parents, an IEP meeting was not held until October 20, 1981. They attended this meeting with their attorney and later contested the resultant IEP (which provided for Scituate placement) at a due process hearing. The hearing officer ruled in favor of the school district, but the parents appealed and a review officer reversed. The Scituate school district then appealed to a Rhode Island federal district court.

The court examined the issues presented by the case, beginning with the parents' allegation that Scituate's letter notifying them of the October IEP meeting had failed to state who would be in attendance and that other individuals could attend. The court excused this failure due to the fact that the parents had attended one IEP meeting previously (in 1978) and thus were probably aware of their rights. Also, the individuals present on October 20, 1981, were the same individuals who had attended the September meeting. No one was a surprise attendee, nor was anyone absent whom the parents expected to attend. Also, there was no evidence of bad faith on the part of Scituate. The parents' second allegation was also dismissed by the court. They had correctly pointed out that the EAHCA places great emphasis on parental involvement in the formulation of an IEP. They alleged that at the October 20 meeting, an IEP was presented to them which read "Independent Education Program," to be effective from "October 20, 1981 – October 20, 1982." The parents argued that this was an attempt to steamroll them into accepting an "immutable, unchangeable, completed plan," which was subject only to their acceptance or rejection—not their participation. The court, however, held that the parents were aware of their right to offer input and make suggestions at the IEP meeting, noting that their attorney had written a letter to school officials after the meeting which stated: "they [the parents] will then inform the school what, if anything they feel must be added, eliminated, or changed. . . ."

Finding that Scituate was innocent of any procedural violations, the district court then proceeded to determine whether the proposed IEP was adequate. Rhode Island law requires that a school district "shall provide such type of education that will *best satisfy* the needs of a handicapped child" (emphasis added). This educational standard is incorporated into the federal EAHCA by reference. The district court, ruling on an issue of first impression, held that this standard was identical to the federal standard set forth in *Rowley v. Board of Education*. The U.S. Supreme Court held in *Rowley* that, at a minimum, an IEP must be designed to allow a handicapped child to "benefit educationally" from his or her instruction. The district court based its ruling on the fact that the Rhode Island statute using the language "best satisfy" was decades old and could not correctly be interpreted to give handicapped children the right to the best possible education. All that was required under Rhode Island law was that a child derive educational benefits under the IEP. Examining all the evidence, the court concluded that Scituate's proposed IEP was adequate. The testimony of the parents' expert witness, Dr. Edwin M. Cole, a renowned language disability expert, was discounted. It was the court's opinion that he was insufficiently familiar with the case, having met with the child for only one forty-minute period. At trial, Dr. Cole was unable to say whether the child wore glasses. These factors caused the district judge to give greater weight to the opinions of Scituate personnel, who were more familiar with the child. Finally, the court noted that the desirability of mainstreaming also supported placement in the Scituate public classroom. Reimbursement for the child's placement at Linden Hills was therefore denied to the parents. *Scituate School Committee v. Robert B.*, 620 F.Supp. 1224 (D.R.I.1985).

The New Jersey Superior Court, Appellate Division, struck down two regulations promulgated by that state's Department of Education as being contrary to the EAHCA. The first regulation defined a preschool handicapped child as one who possesses "a condition which seriously impairs a child's functioning and which has a high predictability of seriously impairing normal educational developemnt." Children without a "serious" condition were excluded from receiving special education services by the plain and unambiguous language of this regulation. Noting that section 1412(2)(C) of the EAHCA requires that services be provided to all handicapped children "regardless of the severity of their handicap," the court struck down the regulation.

The second regulation at issue, which defined the circumstances in which special educational services may be terminated for any child, read as follows: "The child study team, after parental notification, shall terminate a pupil's eligibility when sufficient written documentation is presented to indiate that the pupil no longer requires special educational and/or related services." The court held that "[t]he authority to terminate services when 'sufficient written documentation is presented' runs against the grain of every other enactment on the subject." Section 1415 of the EAHCA sets forth elaborate procedural safeguards as a precondition for the termination of special educational services. Although the Department of Education stated that the regulation in question was interpreted to reflect all federal requirements, the court held that it was invalid because its plain language was contrary to the EAHCA. *Matter of Repeal of N.J.A.C. 6:28*, 497 A.2d 1272 (N.J.Super.A.D.1985).

The U.S. Court of Appeals, Second Circuit, has held that a New York law requiring that a learning disabled child "exhibit a discrepancy of 50% or more between expected achievement based on . . . intellectual ability and actual achievement" in order to qualify as handicapped under the EAHCA was not contrary to the EAHCA's "severe discrepancy" standard. In reversing a U.S. district court ruling in favor of a group of parents of handicapped children who objected to the 50% standard on the ground that it was inconsistent with the federal standard, the Court of Appeals stated that the parents had failed to show that the 50% rule was more restrictive than the "severe discrepancy" standard. The court was not persuaded by the parents' argument that the Commissioner of Education intentionally sought to reduce the number of children classified as learning disabled in New York through application of the 50% rule, and that the 50% standard was quantitative while the EAHCA standard of "severe discrepancy" was qualitative, resulting in a significant undercounting of handicapped children because some might be suffering a severe discrepancy even though they do not meet the 50% standard. The court said no such conclusions could be drawn as the rule had yet to be tested. Because the court found the parents' attack on the 50%

discrepancy standard premature it upheld the rule. *Riley v. Ambach*, 668 F.2d 635 (2d Cir.1981).

A U.S. district court in Michigan was asked to decide whether special education services should be provided to children whose learning difficulties are caused solely by cultural, social and economic deprivation, and not because of a handicap. In this case fifteen black school children sued the Michigan Board of Education and other officials alleging that the process of determining student eligibility for special educational services violated their civil rights and constitutional rights. Specifically, the students claimed that the school board failed to determine whether their learning difficulties stemmed from cultural, social and economic deprivation and that the board failed to develop programs to deal with these problems. The district court held that the Michigan Special Education Code Rules were designed to allow school officials to identify children with handicaps. These rules did not require officials to provide special educational services for children whose learning disabilities stem from cultural, social and economic deprivation, and are not classified as handicapped. There is no law or clause of the Constitution of the United States which explicitly secures the right to special education services to overcome unsatisfactory academic performance based on cultural, social or economic background. The court went on to say that the classification of those needing special education as handicapped did not unconstitutionally stigmatize the students. The court, however, said that the students did state a claim upon which relief could be granted where the state failed to provide means of overcoming language barriers where so-called "Black English" rather than a foreign language was the language barrier. *Martin Luther King Junior Elementary School Children v. Michigan Board of Education*, 451 F.Supp. 1324 (E.D.Mich.1978).

Also in Michigan, the state Court of Appeals was asked to decide whether there was liability on the part of a school district for the alleged misdiagnosis of a handicapped child. In this case the parents of a handicapped child brought suit against their local school district alleging that the school had misdiagnosed the child's language impairment. The parents claimed the school had failed to use reasonable care in maintaining diagnostic procedures and had failed in its diagnosis of the child's language impairment. The school district's motion for summary judgment was granted on the ground that the school, in its operation of a speech therapy program, was involved in a governmental function and thus entitled to governmental immunity. In handing down its decision the court outlined the guidelines it used in deciding whether a particular function is entitled to immunity. The court stated that it examines the precise activity giving rise to the plaintiff's claim rather than overall department operations. In this situation the examination and diagnosis of students in a public school was "intended to promote the general public health and [was] exercised for the common good of all." The court held, therefore, that the school district was immune from liability in performing that function. *Brosnan v. Livonia Public Schools*, 333 N.W.2d 288 (Mich.App.1983).

A school district can be liable for failing to timely and properly classify a child as handicapped as the following cases illustrate.

A father of six children in Louisiana sued a local school board for actions taken between the years 1976 and 1978 in which the board allegedly misclassified each of his six children as mentally retarded in violation of the Rehabilitation Act. The father alleged that one of his children who was not mentally retarded was placed in a class for mentally retarded students without parental consent; two who were tested as normal or having no exceptionality were also placed in such a class without parental consent; and the other three were so placed without testing or the consent of the parents. He brought suit in a U.S. district court seeking an injunction prohibiting the school board from placing any child in classes for the mentally retarded without parental consent, the correction of his children's school records and $15,000,000 in compensatory damages. The court dismissed the suit, saying that the Rehabilitation Act does not grant a private cause of action for money damages.

On appeal, the U.S. Court of Appeals, Fifth Circuit, affirmed the district court ruling but for different reasons. The Court of Appeals held that the Rehabilitation Act does afford a personal cause of action not only to persons who are excluded from federally funded programs because they are handicapped but also to those who are excluded because officials have incorrectly classified and treated them as being handicapped when they in fact were not. However, because the children no longer remained in classes for the mentally retarded and because the father failed to allege that they would likely be placed in such classes again in the future, the father was not entitled to injunctive relief under the Rehabilitation Act; the claim was moot. Further, the father was not entitled to recover damages where he failed to allege that the misplacement was a result of intentional discrimination. *Carter v. Orleans Parish Public Schools*, 725 F.2d 261 (5th Cir.1984).

The parents of a handicapped child brought suit in a U.S. district court against the New York State Commissioner of Education and a local school board alleging that the district failed to timely and properly classify their child as handicapped and to provide him with an appropriate education. The child suffered from an emotional disturbance first observable when he was in third grade, and which eventually became serious enough to warrant his identification and placement as a handicapped child. However, the child was not so identified. When he reached the tenth grade, he was enrolled in a public high school and his behavior deteriorated steadily. For the last quarter of the academic year he did not attend classes at all, but was nevertheless permitted by the administration of the high school to qualify for his final examination. The parents requested the school district to identify their son as handicapped and to assume the costs of his placement at a private residential facility for handicapped children. The school district refused. The district court held that the school district had failed its duty to identify the child as handicapped and to provide him with an appropriate education. The court stated that the EAHCA "requires states to assure that all children residing in the state who are handicapped are identified, located and evaluated." The school district was ordered to place the child in a special education program. *Frankel v. Commissioner of Education*, 480 F.Supp.1156 (S.D.N.Y.1979).

Pennsylvania and New York courts have held that a school district and private school were not liable for the alleged failure to identify two children's disabilities.

The mother of a public school student in Pennsylvania alleged before the Commonwealth Court of Pennsylvania that her son suffered from a learning disability which was not identified by school officials who had a statutory duty to identify exceptional children and provide them with a proper education. The mother claimed damages for the alleged mental and emotional suffering and loss of earnings which she and her son had experienced as a result of the school district's failure to follow the statutory provisions of the Public School Code. The court held that the school district was not liable for money damages for failure to identify the boy's disability. The Pennsylvania School Code reflected the intent of Congress in enacting the EAHCA, i.e. to improve the educational opportunities of exceptional children. Since the EAHCA afforded no private cause of action for money damages, no such remedy could be inferred from the Pennsylvania Code. *Lindsay v. Thomas*, 465 A.2d 122 (Pa.Cmwlth.1983).

A private school in New York brought an action to recover tuition expenses from the mother of a student. The mother counterclaimed against the private school for breach of contract, fraudulent/negligent misrepresentation and negligent infliction of emotional distress. The private school moved to dismiss the mother's counterclaim for failure to state a claim for which relief could be granted.

The mother's counterclaim alleged that the private school's agents represented to her that they possessed a specialized faculty that could identify and individually treat children with learning disabilities. She claimed that these representations were fraudulently and/or negligently made, and that, to her detriment, she relied on the representations in entering into her agreement with the private school. She also claimed that the school did not provide the stated services and therefore breached their contract. Finally, the mother alleged that psychiatric intervention was necessary because her son received services which proved to be inappropriate and harmful when the school failed to diagnose or misdiagnosed his learning disability. This, she claimed, constituted negligent infliction of emotional distress.

The court granted a portion of the private school's motion and denied part of the motion. The court held that the mother's breach of contract claim alleging that the school agreed to detect her child's learning deficiencies and to provide the necessary tutorial and guidance services but failed to do so was permissible. However, the mother could make a claim for fraudulent misrepresentation only if she could show that the private school knowingly made the misrepresentations to her. Thus, she could only maintain an action based on intentional misrepresentation, not negligent misrepresentation.

Finally, the mother could not recover under her claim for negligent infliction of emotional distress. The court noted that it is well established that physical contact or injury is no longer necessary for such a claim. However, the courts have unanimously held that monetary damages for educational malpractice based on a negligence theory are not recoverable. Therefore, the mother could not sue for alleged mental distress caused by negligence in educational practices. *Village Community School v. Adler*, 478 N.Y.S.2d 546 (N.Y.City Civ.Ct.1984).

How schools evaluate children to determine whether they are handicapped is sometimes a source of litigation between schools and parents or guardians.

A U.S. district court in Ohio was asked to rule upon the alleged invalidity of one school's identification procedures. In this case the parents of an autistic and possibly mentally retarded child brought suit against an Ohio school district alleging that the procedures utilized by the school district to identify and classify their child were inadequate. Specifically, the parents claimed the district failed to provide a publicly-financed medical evaluation of the child, that the school district conducted some evaluations without obtaining parental permission, that the information provided to parents when parental permission was sought was inadequate, and that the use of standardized tests to evaluate an autistic child was improper. The parents claimed that had a medical evaluation been completed in 1974 prior to the child's placement in the school district's Severely and Multiply Impaired unit, as required, his allergic reaction to certain foods would have been discovered a year earlier and would have prevented a troubled first year in the program due to improper diet. The district court held that the school had not improperly failed to conduct a medical evaluation. The applicable standard in 1974 merely stated that "[a]ll children being considered shall be examined by a licensed physician for initial placement . . ." The court noted that the parents had to take their son to Chicago in order to obtain the allergy treatment outlined by the child's doctor. Thus, because the treatment was not available locally, the court was persuaded that a standard medical examination by a local physician would not have uncovered the child's condition.

As to the parents' allegation of lack of parental consent to conduct an evaluation of their child, the court found that the evaluations in question were conducted pursuant to the school's application for federal funding and did not involve placement decisions for any specific child, including the child in this case. Thus, the court found no legal necessity to obtain permission of the parents prior to conducting these assessments. Finally, the court held that the application for permission to do an evaluation submitted to the parents, although substantially in compliance, failed to give a "[g]eneral description of procedures and instruments that *will be used*" in evaluating the child, but instead provided merely a list of "possible" procedures and instruments. To this extent, the court found the application or permission to conduct an evaluation inadequate. To the parents' argument that standardized tests should not be used to evaluate their child, the court pointed to the testimony in the case that despite the problems associated with standardized tests, they can be used to gain certain information and insight into the capabilities of autistic children and, in addition, provide an objective criterion for comparison in the future. *Rettig v. Kent City School District*, 539 F.Supp. 768 (N.D.Ohio 1981).

The following two cases address the issue of whether an emotional disturbance is a condition rendering a child "handicapped" under the EAHCA.

In the first case, the Court of Appeal of California found that merely because a child's emotional disturbance is related to his home environment does not preclude a finding that a child is in need of special services. In defending its failure to formulate an individualized educational program (IEP) for the child, the school district submitted that since the child's emotional problems were not related to educational disabilities, but rather to his home environment, the child suffered from no such disability as would require an IEP. The district relied on a federal regulation [35 C.F.R. § 300.5 (b)] which states that the term "specific learning disability . . . does not include children who are having learning problems which are primarily the result of . . . environmental, cultural or economic disadvantage." The California appellate court, in overturning a lower court decision which had set aside an administrative determination that the child required a residential treatment program, said that substantial evidence supported the administrative hearing officer's determination that the child's emotional problems were so linked with his learning disability as to justify and require that he be provided with an IEP. The court was persuaded that the child's emotional problems adversely affected his ability to learn and thus interfered with his educational progress. *San Francisco Unified School District v. State*, 182 Cal.Rptr. 525 (Cal.Appl.1st Dist.1982).

In the second case, the father of an emotionally and physically handicapped child brought suit against a New York school board alleging that the board had denied his son's constitutional and statutory "rights to a decent education." At the time the child, a gifted student, was to enter the tenth grade, he was given a choice of which high school he wished to attend the following year. The boy chose a particular school over the wishes of his father. When the father learned of the child's assignment to the school of his son's choice, he brought suit in federal district court contending that the district's failure to consider the child's emotional and physical handicap in placing him at the chosen high school was a denial of a free appropriate education to handicapped persons.

According to the father the boy had been severely burned in his early childhood and as a result suffered emotional and physical handicaps. The father claimed that because of this, the child's emotional development has been so stunted that compelling him to attend the school "with its rampant crime, violence, drugs and social behavior that is sexually and emotionally far more open than [he] has experienced" would allegedly make it impossible for him to obtain an education as guaranteed by state and federal law. Thus, the father sought an injunction compelling the school district to enroll the child at one of two other schools of the father's choice.

The district court held that there was no constitutional claim and that the father did not have a claim under the EAHCA because of the failure to prove that the child was "seriously emotionally disturbed" within the meaning of the Act. The court was persuaded that if the child was troubled in any way, it appeared that he was only "socially maladjusted" and this problem alone does not render a person handicapped. *Johnpoll v. Elias*, 513 F.Supp. 430 (E.D.N.Y.1980).

B. Post-Placement Evaluations

The appropriateness of evaluation procedures is an issue which has arisen in post-placement situations as well as in the initial stages, i.e., the identification and classification stages of placing handicapped children in suitable programs.

Due to its failure to follow proper post-placement evaluation procedures, a California school district was ordered to pay the tuition and related expenses for a learning disabled boy whose parents unilaterally placed him in an out-of-state private residential facility. In November, 1976, the boy's first individualized educational program (IEP) in which he was classified as suffering from a mild learning disability was formulated by school district officials. The boy progressed and by June, 1977, he had successfully been partially integrated into regular classes. A new IEP was formulated at this time which provided that he continue in regular classes with minimal supplementary educational services. Three months later, in September, 1977, another IEP was developed which noted the boy's progress and recommended continued regular placement with some special education assistance. However, his performance and behavior suffered greatly during the ensuing 1977-78 school year. School officials observed increased anger, hostility and rebelliousness during this period.

The boy's parents were contacted in February, 1978, and a review session was held at which it was agreed that the September 1977 IEP would remain in effect. At the close of the 1977-78 school year the boy was removed from school after slashing the tires on a teacher's car. He also ran away from home in August, 1978, and consequently he was made a ward of the juvenile court. His behavior was described as "self-destructive" with "poor impulse control." In the fall of 1978, the boy was enrolled in the local high school where school officials, with the concurrence of his parents, tentatively decided that his September 1977 IEP would remain in effect. He was thereafter truant from school on numerous occasions and ran away from home again for a week in September, 1978, at which time he committed the offenses of joyriding and marijuana possession. He spent the remainder of the school year in juvenile hall and various youth residential facilities. The school district made no effort to reevaluate the boy or develop a new IEP during this period.

Due to the school district's failure to properly evaluate their son the parents decided to enroll him in a private residential facility in Utah in March, 1979, and asked that the school district pay the cost of his placement. The district, however, stated that it would pay only educational expenses at the facility. The parents requested a due process hearing on the matter and the hearing panel found that because the parents had acted unilaterally in placing their son at the residential facility, thereby breaching the "status quo" provision of the Education for All Handicapped Children Act (EAHCA), the school district was not liable for the cost of the placement. The parents appealed, and the California Court of Appeal held that the school district was liable under the EAHCA for the boy's educational and related expenses at the private, out-of-state residential facility. The court based its decision on the failure of the school distict to develop an IEP for the boy annually as required by the EAHCA. An IEP had been formulated in September, 1977, but as of April, 1979, a new IEP had not been developed. The court rejected the school district's contention that because the boy had been truant and was frequently involved in the juvenile court system, it would have been difficult to properly evaluate him. The boy's status in the juvenile court system was well known to school officials and their failure to update the "manifestly inappropriate" September 1977 IEP was characterized by the court as evidence of bad faith. The school district was therefore ordered to pay the cost of the private school placement. Attorney's fees were also awarded to the boy's parents. *In re John K.*, 216 Cal.Rptr. 557 (App.1st Dist.1985).

A New York case resulted in a ruling that handicapped children should be periodically reevaluated. The case arose in 1983, when the family court of Nassau County found that a young boy was handicapped within the meaning of state law and therefore ordered the county of the boy's residence to pay the cost of tuition and maintenance for the boy at a summer camp for the handicapped. The $2,450 award was payable directly to the boy's mother. One year later the mother again petitioned the family court to order the county to pay the cost of the boy's stay at the camp during the summer of 1984. She moved for summary judgment contending that since all the facts were the same as in the previous year there was no need to hold a second trial. The county, however, believed that the boy's condition had changed and that he was no longer entitled to reimbursement for summer camp expenses under New York law. The family court disagreed and held in favor of the mother. On appeal by the county to the New York Supreme Court, Appellate Division, the decision in favor of the mother was reversed. It was error to grant summary judgment in favor of the mother, said the court, because of the possible changes in her son's condition as a handicapped child. The appeals court remanded the case to the family court for a full trial, where the question of whether the boy's condition had materially changed since the preceding summer could be answered. *Schwartz v. County of Nassau*, 489 N.Y.S.2d 274 (A.D.2d Dept.1985).

In another New York case, after a family court ordered a handicapped child referred to her school district's Committee on the Handicapped (COH) for re-evaluation, to ascertain if an originally diagnosed handicapping condition continued to exist, the child's parents and the COH were unable to agree on the method by which the child was to be tested. The COH sought to test the child by using standardized tests while the parents would only consent to a home visit by the school psychologist and the school speech therapist so that they could observe and evaluate the child. A hearing was held after which the hearing officer directed the COH to designate a licensed psychologist of their choice to perform an evaluation of the child's educational needs, status and progress. The hearing officer's determination also provided that the evaluation was to take place in the home setting, where the child was then receiving home instruction.

The COH appealed this ruling to the New York Commissioner of Education, who modified the hearing officer's decision by removing the hearing officer's restrictions on the scope of the proposed examination. The parents appealed to the New York Supreme Court, which found a "reasonable foundation in fact" for the Commissioner's determination. The parents then appealed to the New York Supreme Court, Appellate Division, to decide whether there was sufficient evidence to support the Commissioner's determination.

Two related issues presented to the court were whether there were grounds for requiring the child to submit to an evaluation to determine if she had a handicapping condition and, if so, what type of evaluation was appropriate. With respect to the first issue, the court held that the fact that neither the parents nor the COH appealed the family court order requiring evaluation of the child precluded them from now presenting the issue. The unappealed family court order unequivocally required the COH to re-evaluate the child.

Regarding the second issue, the COH maintained that since the child had subsequently been enrolled in a parochial school, the parents' appeal was moot. The court held that the child's attendance at a parochial school neither obviated the family court order nor discharged the COH's duty to comply with it. Turning to the main issue of the Commissioner's determination, the court held that it was incumbent upon the Commissioner to tailor an evaluation for the child which would respond to her special needs. Thus, the Commissioner was obligated to take into consideration the mother's uncontroverted arguments that standardized testing would cause the child to regress. The failure of the Commissioner to prescribe evaluation tests having the least adverse impact on the child while enabling the COH to gather necessary information was arbitrary and capricious. The matter was therefore returned to the Commissioner for the purpose of tailoring an individualized evaluation program. *Healey v. Ambach*, 481 N.Y.S.2d 809 (A.D.3d Dept.1984).

C. Competency Testing of Handicapped Students

The right of handicapped children to a free appropriate education apparently does not include the right to receive a diploma. The inability of some handicapped children to pass minimum competency tests to qualify for graduation has not been viewed by the courts to constitute a denial of a right to the handicapped.

After the Illinois State Superintendent of Education ordered that several handicapped children be given their diplomas, an Illinois school district appealed to a U.S. district court challenging the order. The school district argued that the superintendent had allowed the issuance of the diplomas despite the fact that the children failed to pass a minimum competency test as required by the local school board. The district court held that school boards have the right to develop reasonable means to determine the effectiveness of their educational programs with respect to all individual students to whom they issue diplomas and the use of the minimum competency tests is a reasonable means of measuring that effectiveness. The court held that nothing in the EAHCA or other federal or state law stands in the way of such testing. The court further held that such competency testing need not be modified to take into account a student's disability or capacity to do well in such a test. The court did advise schools to modify tests in order to minimize the effect of physical capacity. To that end, the court suggested that a blind student not be given a competency test which was printed in a normal manner and not in Braille. However, the court stated that the test should not be modified to avoid measuring a student's mental capabilities since to do so would fail completely to measure the results of the educational process. *Brookhart v. Illinois State Board of Education*, 534 F.Supp. 725 (C.D.Ill.1982).

After the New York Commissioner of Education and a local board of education invalidated diplomas received by two handicapped students enrolled in public school, the students' guardian brought suit to enjoin the commissioner and the board of education from invalidating the diplomas. The guardian objected to the requirement of basic competency tests as a prerequisite to obtaining a high school diploma. The Court of Appeals of New York affirmed two lower court rulings in favor of the school. The court stated that the students had no reasonable expectation of receiving a high school diploma without passing the competency test. The competency testing program had been in effect for three years prior to the completion of the students' studies and, thus, the students were not denied adequate notice of the requirement. The three-year notice was not so brief as to prevent school districts from programming individualized education programs for remedially handicapped children to enable them to pass basic competency tests required for diploma graduation. *Board of Education v. Ambach*, 457 N.E.2d 775 (N.Y.1983).

III. Duty to Provide Appropriate Education

Congress was not explicit in the EAHCA as to what exactly constitutes an "appropriate" education, and in practice, parents and schools do not always agree on what is "appropriate" to the education of a particular handicapped child. The *Rowley* case has provided the standard to which courts are to look in determining whether an education is appropriate.

The parents of an Oklahoma youth brought suit in U.S. district court after their local school district refused to fund their son's placement at a residential facility. The youth, who was classified as "educable mentally handicapped" and who had serious emotional and behavioral problems, had been enrolled at the age of eighteen in his local school district's EMH program. An IEP was developed at this time with the approval of his parents, in which it was agreed that if the boy became "unmanageable" he would be suspended for three-day intervals. Although his educational program included both high school instruction and vocational instruction, he was soon expelled from the vo-tech program due to his emotional outbursts. When these outbursts continued at the high school, school officials notified his parents that an alternative to classroom placement was necessary. Homebound instruction was suggested, but the parents rejected the proposal.

For the next several months the parents considered residential placement; during this period the youth received no educational services. His parents also failed to bring him to school for testing to aid in the formulation of a new IEP, as requested by school officials. The parents then requested funding for their child's placement at an out-of-state residential facility. When their school district refused they requested a due process hearing under the EAHCA. The parents, after discovering the name of the hearing officer, believed that he would find in favor of the school district and withdrew their request for a hearing.

At the beginning of the next school year they appeared once again at the high school to enroll their son, and school officials, who had not expected the youth to enroll, requested a week to formulate an IEP. Several days later school officials attempted to arrange a meeting with the parents to discuss a new IEP for the youth, but the parents refused because a new teacher had not yet been hired to instruct him. The school officials explained that a new teacher would not be hired unless the parents approved the new IEP and assured them that they would enroll their son. This impasse caused the parents to unilaterally enroll their son in the out-of-state residential facility. A due process hearing resulted in approval of the school district's decision not to reimburse the parents for the cost of his placement, and the parents sought judicial review. The U.S. Court of Appeals, 1st Circuit, upheld the denial of tuition reimbursement and found that the district had taken all steps necessary to provide the child with a free appropriate public education. Citing the *Rowley* case, the court stated that "[a]lthough the [residential facility] undoubtedly offered . . . a superior educational program, an education which maximizes a child's potential is not required by the EAHCA." *Cain v. Yukon Public Schools, District I-27*, 775 F.2d 15 (10th Cir.1985).

The parents of a child in Virginia who suffered severe head trauma when she was injured in an automobile accident and who became mentally impaired as a result, alleged that the child was denied a "free appropriate public education" as required by the Education for All Handicapped Children Act. The parents contended that their local school district's refusal to implement an educational program proposed by the parents and its decision to implement its own program in the public school system was in violation of the EAHCA. The parents brought suit in a U.S. district court, which found the parents' plan to be unreasonable and the school's plan appropriate, saying: "The State is not required to pay all of the expenses incurred by parents in educating a child, whether the child be handicapped or non-handicapped. The State is also not required to provide a perfect education to any child . . . Rather, the Court must ascertain in the light of educational theories over which experts often disagree if the education provided plaintiff was, under the law, 'appropriate.'" The court relied on the standard for an appropriate education enunciated in *Board of Education v. Rowley,* which held that an "appropriate" education is not necessarily one that enables a child to achieve his or her full potential. The court concluded that "An appropriate education is not synonymous with the best possible education. [P]arents [do not] have the right under the law to write a prescription for an ideal education for their child and to have the prescription filled at public expense." *Bales v. Clark*, 523 F.Supp. 1366 (E.D.Va.1981).

A U.S. district court in Ohio has also held that the public school system did not fail to provide an "appropriate" education for a child where the parents alleged the school district's refusal to meet all of their requests denied their autistic and possibly mentally retarded son an "appropriate" education. Here, the court found that the public special education program developed by the school district in which the child had participated was appropriate for this child's needs. Although sympathizing with the parents' concern for their child's education, the court noted that the parents frustrated the school district's efforts at every turn and made unreasonable demands. For instance, the mother's unwavering demand that the child's teachers instruct the child to write his name cursively consumed both the teachers' and the child's time which would have been better spent teaching the child basic living skills. An "appropriate" education for this child, said the court, "was one which would give him a reasonable chance to acquire skills he needed to function outside of an institution." An appropriate education does not mean that a school system has to provide any and all services that might be beneficial, or that a school must experiment with every new teaching technique that might be suggested. It also does not mean that a school district must spend exorbitant amounts of money on one child at the expense of others. *Rettig v. Kent City School District*, 539 F.Supp. 768 (N.D.Ohio 1981).

An "appropriate" education is required only when there exists a recognized handicapping condition, as the following New York case illustrates. Here, the father of an emotionally disturbed boy failed to show that his son was "seriously and emotionally disturbed" within the meaning of the EAHCA. After the father brought suit against a New York school district for the district's alleged failure to provide an appropriate education for his son, a U.S. district court held that the father was not entitled to an injunction directing school officials to permit his son to attend a school of the father's choice (against the son's wishes). Thus, the boy was not denied a free appropriate education because, although the boy may have been socially maladjusted, this was not a recognized handicap under the EAHCA. *Johnpoll v. Elias*, 513 F.Supp. 430 (E.D.N.Y.1980).

The following two cases demonstrate that states may establish higher standards for special educations than the EAHCA's "appropriate" standard. In the first, the U.S. Court of Appeals, Third Circuit, affirmed a district court decision which held that handicapped children in New Jersey are entitled to the "best" available special education placement, as opposed to merely an appropriate one. The Court of Appeals observed that the administrative code of New Jersey's State Board of Education required that handicapped students be provided a special education "according to how the pupil can best achieve success in learning." This provision indicated that the state of New Jersey had chosen to exceed the EAHCA's minimum requirement of an "appropriate" special education. *Geis v. Board of Education of Parsippany-Troy Hills*, 774 F.2d 575 (3d Cir.1985).

In the second case, the parents of a seventeen-year-old child with Down's syndrome became dissatisfied with their child's IEP because they felt it did not adequately address his sexual misbehavior. They believed that in order to correct this misbehavior and instill in the child proper attitudes toward sex the child required a twenty-four-hour residential program. A U.S. district court found that the child was entitled to twenty-four-hour residential school placement to attempt to correct his sexual misbehavior. The court noted that under Massachusetts law a special educational program must "assure the maximum possible development of a child with special needs." Accordingly, the child was entitled to the more comprehensive behavior therapy available in a residential program, especially in light of the degree of his sexual maladjustment. The court also dismissed the school district's argument that the child should remain in the least restrictive environment, i.e., the day school program, because that alternative was clearly inappropriate here. On appeal by the school district, the U.S. Court of Appeals, First Circuit, upheld the district court's decision. The appellate court held that where state law sets a minimum educational standard for handicapped children, those standards are incorporated by reference into the federal EAHCA. *David D. v. Dartmouth School Committee*, 775 F.2d 411 (1st Cir.1985).

The following case reaches a result consistent with the U.S. Supreme Court's decision in *Board of Education v. Rowley* but uses a pre-*Rowley* standard for determining an "appropriate" education. Here, the parents of a learning disabled child in Iowa challenged their school district's proposed educational program for the child on the ground that it failed to meet the child's specific needs. The parents, convinced that a neighboring school district could provide a more adequate program for the child, sued the school district to compel it to change its district boundaries or, alternatively, to have the district pay the child's tuition in the neighboring district. The Supreme Court of Iowa ruled in favor of the school district, observing that "[o]ne district's program is not made inappropriate merely because another district has a better program." Two considerations were deemed relevant in determining the appropriateness of a handicapped child's education: 1) the limitation of funds available; and 2) the "reasonableness requirement" in Iowa's special education law, which stated that "[e]very child requiring special education shall, *if reasonably possible* receive a level of education commensurate with the level provided each child who does not receive a special education." Thus, the court concluded, although a school district "must strive to meet the needs of special education students with the same level of effort which is devoted to meeting the needs of nonhandicapped students," the "best" or "maximum" education is not required, but rather a program "appropriate" for the student's educational needs. *Buchholtz v. Iowa Department of Public Instruction*, 315 N.W.2d 789 (Iowa 1982).

A U.S. district court in Illinois found that handicapped children in Illinois were not receiving an appropriate education by reason of delays of the Illinois Superintendent of Education in resolving placement appeals. The case arose after a severely emotionally disturbed twelve-year-old child was recommended for placement by his school district in a self-contained classroom for behavior disordered students. His mother objected to the recommendation and said that she had been advised by experts that a highly structured residential program would be appropriate placement for the child. The mother appealed the decision but after five months the superintendent had made no decision. The mother claimed that the superintendent was obligated to decide within thirty days. She alleged that the long delay and inappropriate educational setting had caused the deterioration of the child's condition to the extent that the child had to be placed in a mental hospital.

The mother then brought suit against the superintendent and other school officials on behalf of her child and all handicapped school children in Illinois. The superintendent sought to dismiss the suit on the basis that the Education for All Handicapped Children Act creates no substantive rights for handicapped children. The U.S. district court disagreed saying that the EAHCA is the source of a federal statutory right to a free appropriate education in every state electing to receive financial assistance, and that is more than merely a "funding statute." The passage of time, said the court, caused the deprivation of a child's substantive right to an appropriate education. *John A. by and through Valerie A. v. Gill*, 565 F.Supp. 372 (N.D.Ill.1983).

The U.S. district court in the prior case stated that many important legal issues in that case remained unresolved. Accordingly, the plaintiff in that case, the mother of the handicapped child, once again brought suit against her school district claiming that the district's policy of disclaiming any obligation to finance "related services" that primarily serve the handicapped student's noneducational needs, even when such services are also critical to his or her ability to benefit from an education, deprived her son and other handicapped children of equal protection and a free appropriate education under the Education for All Handicapped Children Act. In a separate action the school district asked the U.S. district court which had decided the prior case to rule that the mother's action should be dismissed. The court agreed and dismissed the mother's claims.

The court held that the school district's policy of distinguishing between the educational and noneducational components of a special education with regard to related services did not deny equal protection to the handicapped child nor the class he purported to represent. It stated that the inability to look only to the school district for all needs and the occasional delay caused by the complexity of assessing noneducational needs and allocating the cost of these services to other agencies was amply justified by the state's interest in limiting the authority of local school districts to their area of expertise. The child had not proven that he or the others whom he claimed to represent were absolutely denied an education; he had merely shown that he and others like him must pursue noneducational placements from a variety of state agencies rather than obtaining financing and services from a single source, i.e., their local school district. Further, the "representative" child's claim was moot since he had moved outside the school district limits and that district, therefore, lost all prospective duties and obligations toward the child. The court noted that although state education officials still had an obligation to the child under the EAHCA, the child had not shown that he was entitled to prospective relief in his new town.

Finally, the court held that the handicapped child and his mother inappropriately brought suit on behalf of other handicapped children allegedly similarly situated. In such a suit the individual bringing suit on behalf of others must be representative of them. Here, the child's representation as to the other class members was not adequate to warrant continuation of the lawsuit as a class. The child simply had not shown that any of his class members had been denied their substantive rights to a free appropriate education under the EAHCA. *Williams y. Gill*, 591 F.Supp. 422 (N.D.Ill.1984).

A U.S. district court in Texas also found a public school education offered to a mentally handicapped child inappropriate for the child's needs. In ordering a Texas school district to provide a highly structured educational program, specifically designed to meet the child's particular and unique needs, the court analyzed its own role in assessing what an "appropriate" education is. The main factor to be taken into consideration by a district court in evaluating whether a child is receiving an appropriate education is the competing interests of the state which receives limited funding to educate handicapped children and the special and unique needs of the individual handicapped child. Nevertheless, the court found that a residential placement was warranted for the child in this case. Taking into account the limited funding provided to Texas schools, the court said that the EAHCA expressly authorizes residential placement of a handicapped child if such a program is necessary to provide an education to the child. *Stacey G. v. Pasadena Independent School District*, 547 F.Supp. 61 (S.D.Tex.1982).

A North Carolina court decided that the *Rowley* standard for an appropriate education for a handicapped child did not govern a law passed by its own legislature which provided for the education of the handicapped children. In this case the parents of a hearing impaired child requested their local school district to provide a grant to subsidize the child's education at an out-of-state residential institution. The school district maintained its own program whereby the child would receive an appropriate education by placing her in a regular 6th grade class within the public schools met the child's specific needs. The Court of Appeals of North Carolina affirmed a lower court ruling in favor of the school district. The court found the proposed public school program to be appropriate to the child's needs but reached this result using a more "restrictive" standard than that pronounced in *Rowley*. The court was apprised of the U. S. Supreme Court ruling in *Rowley* but chose, in conformity with its own state law, to adopt the standard that an appropriate education is one that gives a handicapped child an opportunity to achieve his full potential commensurate with that given other children. *Harrell v. Wilson County Schools*, 293 S.E.2d 687 (N.C.App.1982).

IV. Individualized Educational Programs

An individualized education program (IEP) under the EAHCA is a statement of a handicapped child's present education level, future educational goals for the child, future educational services to be provided, and the extent to which he or she will be able to participate in regular educational programs [section 1401(19)]. At the heart of the EAHCA's "individualized educational program" provision is the idea that each handicapped child's particular needs are unique and thus require an educational program specifically tailored to a child's particular handicap. Courts have viewed the failure to provide a program specifically designed to meet the unique needs of a child as a failure to provide a free appropriate education.

In a Georgia case, the parents of a handicapped girl challenged the appropriateness of her individualized educational program. The IEP had been developed in 1981 with the approval of the parents; however, they now contended that changes in circumstances had rendered the 1981 IEP inappropriate. After a state administrative determination that the IEP was appropriate, the parents sued the school district in U.S. district court seeking relief under the EAHCA. The court issued a ruling prior to trial which stated that in cases where parents seek to overturn a state administrative decision regarding the propriety of an IEP, the burden of proof is upon the parents. The court's ruling followed the general rule that the factual and legal conclusions reached by state administrative agencies must be afforded a proper amount of respect by reviewing courts. The case was set for trial and the parents were thus required to overcome the presumption that their daughter's IEP was appropriate. *Tracey T. v. McDaniel*, 610 F.Supp. 947 (N.D.Ga.1985).

In New Hampshire, residents of a state-run institution for the mentally retarded brought suit against the state of New Hampshire on behalf of themselves and all residents between the ages of three and twenty-one who were allegedly denied an appropriate education. Allegations against the state included the failure of the institution to formulate individualized educational programs for each of the residents who were entitled to an appropriate education under the Rehabilitation Act and the Education for All Handicapped Children Act.

The residents attacked the state's policy of making placement decisions and dispersing services based on generalized "labels" of mentally retarded individuals, for example, "profoundly retarded" or "nonambulatory," rather than on individual assessment of abilities and potentials of each resident. Further, the residents claimed that an effort should have been made to place them in the community and that their current placement was not in the "least restrictive setting" as required by the EAHCA and section 504 of the Rehabilitation Act.

A U.S. district court held that the institution was not required under the EAHCA or section 504 to provide community placements. However, the court did find other violations of the EAHCA and section 504. The court found "blanket discrimination" against the handicapped in the institution's practice of making placements and dispersing services on generalized "labels" of handicapped individuals. In addition, the fact that New Hampshire provided at least two means by which children could be placed at the institution, either through local education agencies or through the state's Division of Mental Health, violated the mandate established by the EAHCA that there be "one centralized agency" which assumes responsibility for providing a free appropriate education to handicapped children.

The state's procedures were also found lacking in that there was no requirement that an IEP be prepared for each child with the input of interested parties and no requirement charging local education agencies with financial responsibility for the children from their districts. These failings were deemed by the court to be inconsistent with the EAHCA. The court concluded that the multiple problems of the institution were "rooted" in the lack of accountability of any state agency. Thus, the court ordered state officials to revise their placement procedures to conform to the IEP requirements of the EAHCA. *Garrity v. Gallen*, 522 F.Supp. 171 (D.N.H.1981).

A U.S. district court in Texas faced the difficult task of determining the appropriate IEP for a child exhibiting maladaptive behavior, which the parents of the child contended was autistic behavior and the child's school district asserted was the result of severe mental retardation. When the child reached fifteen years of age and the parents and the school district still could not agree on the nature of the child's handicap, and consequently could not agree on an IEP for the child, the parents brought suit against the school district to compel it to formulate an IEP designed for a child suffering from autism. The federal district court declined to rule on the child's particular disability, but rather concentrated its efforts on the question, "What is the appropriate educational placement for [the child] at the present time in light of her unique needs?" Based on testimony presented by expert witnesses during the trial, the court held that the school district was required to formulate an IEP for the child which provided a highly structured educational program with input from an autistic treatment center which had conducted an evaluation of the child. The court stated that "In formulating the IEP . . ., the district and those involved with the development of the IEP should bear in mind that one of the aims of educational . . . programming is to achieve the highest level of self-sufficiency possible; the ultimate goal of education programming for [the child] is, of course, the complete avoidance of institutionalization." *Stacey G. v. Pasadena Independent School District*, 547 F.Supp. 61 (S.D.Tex.1982).

The U.S. Court of Appeals, Ninth Circuit, has held that a homebound program for a handicapped child was not an inappropriate IEP for the child. A girl in Hawaii who suffered from cystic fibrosis and tracheomalacia, which caused her windpipes to be floppy instead of rigid, wore a tracheostomey tube which allowed her to breathe and expel mucus from her lungs two or three times a day. However, her ability to attend school was contingent upon her mother's presence in the school. The child's mother, also a teacher in the private school which the child was attending, suctioned the tube when necessary during the school day.

After the child was certified by the Hawaii Department of Education as eligible for special education services under the EAHCA, the school district of the child's residence proposed a homebound program because of the unavailability in the public schools of medical services which the child required. The child's parents rejected this IEP and the child remained in the private school which she had been attending. The school district then proposed for the following year a public school program whereby it would train its staff to see to the child's medical needs which had previously been attended to by the mother. The parents also rejected this IEP, enrolled their child in the private school for the following year, and brought suit against the school district to compel it to pay for the child's private education. A U.S. district court in Hawaii held in favor of the parents, and the school district appealed.

The U.S. Court of Appeals, Ninth Circuit, held that the proposed homebound program was decidedly inappropriate for the child's needs. Because the school district was unable to offer an appropriate public school program, it was liable for the child's tuition expenses for the year the proposed IEP was to be implemented. However, the alternative program offered by the school district wherein it would train its staff to take care of the child's medical needs was appropriate. Thus, the parents were not entitled to tuition reimbursement for the following year. *Department of Education v. Katherine D.*, 727 F.2d 809 (9th Cir.1983).

In Alabama, a U.S. district court found an IEP deficient because it failed to teach a severely retarded eighteen-year-old boy functional and communicative skills which might, to an indeterminable degree, increase his independence, and because the IEP lacked specific provisions for the measurement of the child's progress in all areas. As the court said, the child's IEP ". . . does little more than to occupy [his] time with activities devoid of educational justification." The EAHCA's objective of enabling a handicapped child to become a productive member of society rather than forcing him or her to remain a burden was not met. Thus, the court held in this case where the parents of the child challenged his IEP, that the IEP should be revised to include instruction in age-appropriate and functional skills in each of four areas: 1) daily living activities, 2) vocational activities, 3) recreational activities, and 4) social and community adjustment. In addition, the school district was ordered to make specific provisions for evaluating the child's progress and to formulate a program which was to encompass the entire school year, including the summer session. *Campbell v. Talladega County Board of Education*, 518 F.Supp. 47 (N.D.Ala.1981).

A U.S. district court in California has ruled that the failure to provide a full-time private tutor for a handicapped child violated the Education for All Handicapped Children Act. In this case the parents of a sixteen-year-old autistic child sued the state of California and the county in which they resided for the failure to provide him a free, public education appropriate to his needs. The court recognized that while such demands as a private tutor will place heavy burdens on the resources of public school systems, Congress has determined that it is worth the price to develop the potential of the handicapped and has provided substantial funds to aid in this effort. The court granted the parents damages for the money spent for a private tutor over a two-year period. *Boxall v. Sequoia Union High School*, 464 F.Supp. 1104 (N.D.Cal.1979).

The U.S. Court of Appeals, Sixth Circuit, was asked to decide whether the "total" method of instruction as opposed to the "oral/aural" method was appropriate for a child suffering from a severe to profound hearing loss. The parents of a twelve-year-old hearing impaired child sought review of a Kentucky Department of Education decision regarding an appropriate educational program for the child. The state proposed to place him in a program developed in his home county wherein he would be taught by the "total" method of instruction as opposed to the "oral/aural" method under which the child had been taught in a neighboring county. The main difference between these systems is that the former uses sign language and finger spelling whereas the latter relies exclusively on residual hearing, lip reading and speech. The objection to the "total" method was that sometimes children concentrate on the sign language at the expense of speech development. A U.S. district court approved the state's plan and this determination was upheld by the Court of Appeals. The court noted that even if one were to assume the "oral/aural" method was superior this did not make the proposed program inadequate under the EAHCA. All the Act requires is an "appropriate" education. Although there was conflicting testimony here as to the appropriateness of the proposed education, a study of the evidence showed that the proposed program, was not clearly erroneous and the court therefore refused to interfere with the decision of school officials *Age v. Bullitt County Public Schools*, 673 F.2d 141 (6th Cir.1982).

When a school district wishes to conduct an evaluation of a child for the purpose of developing an individualized educational plan, under the EAHCA the district must notify the parents of the child of its intention to conduct the evaluation and the type of evaluation to be administered.

A Rhode Island case dealt with the issue of whether, once an IEP has been formulated, parental consent is required for a re-evaluation of the child. A mother of a handicapped child sought to prevent the child's school district from making a second educational assessment of her child. The school district had based the boy's IEP on an evaluation conducted by a private school formerly attended by the child. The mother maintained that the assessment sought by the school district would constitute an original evaluation and, therefore, the school was barred from conducting it without her cooperation. The school district contended that its assessment would be a re-evaluation and under the law, a parent's consent was unnecessary. It further stated that any change in placement resulting from the re-evaluation would be subject to challenge by the parent in a statutorily mandated hearing. A U.S. district court agreed with the school district's position, stating that the private school assessment on which the IEP was based did not legitimately constitute an original pre-placement evaluation. Thus, the court held in favor of the school district and the case was dismissed. *Carroll v. Capalbo*, 563 F.Supp. 1053 (D.R.I.1983).

V. Placement of Handicapped Children

A. Mainstreaming

An additional component of an "appropriate" education is the requirement that each handicapped child be educated in the "least restrictive environment." Section 1412(5)(B) of the EAHCA requires that states provide procedures to ensure that handicapped children are educated "to the maximum extent appropriate" with nonhandicapped children in regular classes. Impediments to the learning process and to the normal functioning of handicapped children in their regular school environment, where possible, are to be overcome by the provision of special aids and other support services rather than by separate schooling for the handicapped. Thus, courts prefer to uphold a "mainstreaming" decision where a child's educational needs can be met in the regular classroom.

In a New Jersey case, the parents of a hearing impaired girl with an I.Q. of 120 brought suit under the Education for All Handicapped Children Act to prevent their daughter from being assigned to a program for hearing impaired children. The girl, whose hearing loss was profound in the left ear and severe in the right, had attended her local school district's hearing impaired preschool program. Her parents, however, believed that she should be educated with her nonhandicapped peers. The superintendent of schools decided to accommodate the parents and he temporarily assigned their daughter to a regular kindergarten class. Later the school district child study team (CST) disagreed with the decision to mainstream the child. The CST formulated an individualized educational program for the child which proposed that she be placed in a hearing impaired special education class.

The girl's parents brought suit in U.S. district court and successfully blocked her removal from the regular classroom. The court noted that due to the EAHCA's "status quo" provision, the girl had remained in the regular class through kindergarten and first grade. She had made excellent progress socially and the other children in the class had helped her cope with her hearing impairment. In fact, the court felt that the girl's presence in the regular class benefited both her and her classmates. Furthermore, she "ended up making enormous progress in kindergarten, notwithstanding the dire forecasts of the CST to the contrary. . . . First grade also proved to be a success in certain respects." Also, the CST's evaluation methods were "woefully inadequate" because they had employed only one procedure: teacher evaluations. The court held that the girl should be placed in the regular classroom for homeroom, gym, art, music, lunch and free period, with part-time one-to-one instruction in a learning disabilities resource room. *Bonadonna v. Cooperman*, 619 F.Supp. 401 (D.N.J.1985).

The Hawaii case discussed in the preceding section illustrates the strong judicial preference for mainstreaming. In that case, the school district had initially proposed a "homebound" IEP for an eight-year-old girl. The school district claimed that it lacked qualified, medically trained personnel to care for the girl, who suffered from cystic fibrosis and required that her lungs be suctioned several times per day through her tracheostomy tube. The parents objected to the homebound IEP and sued in U.S. district court, which awarded them the cost of placing their daughter in a private school. On appeal, the decision was affirmed. The U.S. Court of Appeals, Ninth Circuit, held that the homebound program was not a "free appropriate education." However, the school district had in the meantime developed a satisfactory IEP that would place the child in the public school and provide medically trained staff. This plan would meet the test of "least restrictive environment;" therefore the appeals court stated that the parents would receive no future compensation if they chose to continue their daughter's education at the private school. *Department of Education v. Katherine D.*, 727 F.2d 809 (9th Cir.1983).

The parents of a severely mentally retarded girl, dissatisfied with a Missouri school district's placement of the child in a school for the severely mentally retarded, demanded reassignment to either of two public schools preferred by the parents. The reassignment was denied by the school district on the ground that the state school was found to be the most appropriate and most beneficial one for the child. The parents then withdrew the child from the state school and instituted administrative proceedings which resulted in a determination by a special hearing panel that the school district and the State Department of Education did not substantially demonstrate that the placement at the state school was the least restrictive environment. Thus, the panel decided that the child should be grouped with other children in a classroom located in a public school setting where she would have access to social interaction and modeling of less handicapped children. The school district and the Department of Education appealed from this determination. A Missouri trial court, and subsequently the Missouri Court of Appeals, agreed with the panel's decision that the placement in the state school was unacceptable. Thus, the decision to place the child in a less restrictive setting was upheld. *Mallory v. Drake*, 616 S.W.2d 124 (Mo.App.1981).

In another Missouri case, the state's Court of Appeals ruled on the questions of 1) whether a school board could assign a mentally retarded child to a regular classroom as opposed to paying tuition for the child in a special school, and 2) whether the board's decision was subject to judicial review.

The child was originally enrolled in public school and was given special help by that school pursuant to a 1973 Missouri law which required mentally retarded children to be educated in normal classroom settings in public schools as far as practicable. The parents decided, however, that more could be done for the child in a private school, so she was transferred with the parents requesting the school district to pay the bill. The district refused and introduced extensive findings showing that the district was able to give adequate service to the child. The parents appealed to the courts where a lower court found in their favor. On appeal to the Missouri Court of Appeals, however, that determination was reversed.

The appellate court found that the board could reasonably have made the determination that it did and that the services being provided the child were adequate. The court felt itself bound by the administrative determination inasmuch as a court is allowed to weigh the evidence for itself and determine the facts accordingly only where the review does not involve an exercise of administrative discretion as opposed to application by the agency of the law to the facts. *Moran v. Board of Directors, School District of Kansas City*, 584 S.W.2d 154 (Mo.App.1979).

The Appellate Court of Illinois considered the question of what is the appropriate educational placement of a trainable mentally handicapped child with Down's syndrome who is also a carrier of an infectious disease, Hepatitis Type B. The plaintiffs, local school officials, contended that because of the risk of the child transmitting the disease to other children, the appropriate placement for her was in a "homebound" setting. The defendant child maintained that the risk of transmission of the disease is remote and therefore not a sufficient reason to exclude her from classroom participation.

A hearing officer, the State Superintendent of Education and a lower court agreed with the child. So did the Appellate Court of Illinois. The main substantive matter considered on appeal was whether the child's homebound placement was mandated by the school district's health and safety obligations to its students so that she was being educated in the least restrictive environment as required by Illinois law and the Education for All Handicapped Children Act. The court held it was not. Using the *Rowley* case as its guide, the court first noted that the trial court gave due deference to the state agency's determination of educational policy under the present circumstances.

Next, the court noted that there is a strong congressional preference in favor of mainstreaming wherever possible. A major goal of the educational process is the socialization process that takes place in the regular classroom, with the resulting capacity to interact in a social way with one's peers. The Superintendent of Education recognized this and determined that the risk of transmission of the disease did not outweigh the injury to the child if she remained isolated from her peers. After a thorough examination of the testimony of expert witnesses, the court concluded that the trial court's decision was not against the manifest weight of the evidence and thus the child could be integrated into the classroom if appropriate sanitary procedures were followed. *Community High School District 155 v. Denz*, 463 N.E.2d 998 (Ill.App.1984).

A case arising in North Carolina involved a school district which placed a hearing-impaired child in a regular sixth grade class over the objections of the parents. The parents preferred an out-of-state residential institution. The disagreement reached the state's Court of Appeals after the parents unsuccessfully challenged the proposed placement in the administrative appeals process and then in a North Carolina trial court, which affirmed the final administrative decision. The Court of Appeals found that the school district had offered an appropriate educational program to the child.

The court was unpersuaded by the parents' argument that the school system had made a decision to mainstream the child and had then proceeded to develop an individualized educational program to suit mainstreaming. In effect, the parents' argument was that the placement offered to the child was not responsive and appropriate to the child's needs, but rather what the school system could most conveniently provide. The record from the administrative proceedings indicated that an extensive evaluation was performed prior to a determination of what placement was appropriate. Based on that information the school district determined that the child could be served by enrollment in a regular sixth grade class with support services. The court found this to be consistent with policies established in federal and state regulations that handicapped children be educated along with the nonhandicapped to the maximum extent possible. *Harrel v. Wilson County Schools*, 293 S.E.2d 687 (N.C.App.1982).

A severely retarded eighteen-year-old student in Alabama challenged an individualized education program which did not place him in contact with nonhandicapped students to the maximum extent consistent with an appropriate education program as required by the EAHCA. The boy had been attending a learning center which required his mother to drive him twenty-four miles to a point where a bus picked him up and took him to the learning center. When difficulties in transportation made further education there impractical, a local county board of education recommended a homebound program consisting of about an hour of instruction daily. No testing was made prior to this recommendation. The parents rejected the homebound program following which the county board tried to evaluate the child. Unable to receive any measurable response on the Stanford Binet IQ test used to evaluate the child, the county board again offered a homebound placement which was again rejected.

The parents requested an administrative hearing where a hearing officer determined that the homebound program was inappropriate and that the school be ordered to educate the child with other students. The child was then enrolled in the public school system where he met with a teacher in the rear of the classroom used by a "trainable mental retardation" class in a section curtained off for their use.

A new IEP was developed for the boy for the following year. This new plan called for his placement at a special education facility located on the campus of a local high school attended exclusively by handicapped children. The boy was attending this facility at the time his parents brought suit against the county board of education. A U.S. district court in Alabama held that the county board's actions were in clear violation of the law. There was evidence that interaction with nonhandicapped students was essential to provide the boy with role models and to increase his ability to act independently. The court found that the board effectively isolated the child from nonhandicapped students and thus denied him an "appropriate" education. *Campbell v. Talladega County Board of Education*, 518 F.Supp. 47 (N.D.Ala.1981).

The proper standard of review in examining a mainstreaming issue was the question presented to the U.S. Court of Appeals, Sixth Circuit, where the mother of a nine-year-old severely mentally retarded boy brought suit against a local school district challenging his placement under the Education for All Handicapped Children Act.

An evaluation of the child by a private facility had led to the conclusion that the child would benefit from contact with nonhandicapped children. However, the local school district determined to place the child in a county school exclusively for mentally retarded children. The parents requested a hearing and a hearing officer ordered that the child be placed in an ordinary school setting. The school appealed to the State Board of Education which ordered him placed in the county school but with provision for contact with nonhandicapped children. The mother then filed suit.

The Court of Appeals vacated and remanded the case for further action. It held that the lower court erred in reviewing the school district's placement decision under an "abuse of discretion" standard. The proper standard of review to be used is that set forth in the U.S. Supreme Court case of *Board of Education v. Rowley.*

This is a two step test, said the appeals court. First, inquiry must be made as to whether the school or the state has complied with the Act's procedural requirements. Here the requirements were clearly satisfied. The second inquiry was whether the "individualized educational program developed through the Act's procedures [is] reasonably calculated to enable the child to receive educational benefits." Because the district court employed an improper standard of review, the appellate court ordered a new trial to allow reexamination of the mainstreaming issue in light of the proper standard of review. *Roncker on Behalf of Roncker v. Walter*, 700 F.2d 1058 (6th Cir.1983).

In the following cases mainstreaming was found to be inappropriate for students whose needs could only be met in special educational settings.

A Florida high school student who was handicapped by a special learning disability brought suit against a local school district under the Education for All Handicapped Children Act and the Rehabilitation Act, alleging that her involuntary transfer from high school to an alternative learning center violated her right to a publicly financed appropriate special education. The student requested a preliminary injunction to allow her to attend high school during pendency of the proceedings.

A U.S. district court denied the student's request and she appealed to the U.S. Court of Appeals, Eleventh Circuit, arguing that 1) the hearing officer who upheld the decision to transfer her denied her the right to direct lay representation in the administrative proceedings by refusing to allow a friend of the student's, a legal and educational layman, to present her case and examine witnesses; 2) that the record of the administrative proceedings contained uncontested evidence that the school district violated her procedural right to remain in the high school during the pendency of the action as guaranteed by the EAHCA; and 3) that neither the hearing officer nor the district judge determined whether the alternative learning center was the least restrictive environment in which she could be educated.

The Court of Appeals held that the Rehabilitation Act was not the appropriate provision under which to bring suit since the EAHCA provides the exclusive avenue for asserting rights to a publicly financed special education. Further, the student had no right to direct lay representation in the administrative proceedings. The EAHCA creates no such right. The EAHCA states that a complainant has a right "to be accompanied and advised by counsel and by individuals with special knowledge or training with respect to the problems of handicapped children." The hearing officer's examination of the student's chosen representative revealed his almost complete ignorance of state administrative procedure. Thus, the hearing officer did not violate the EAHCA in limiting his role to offering advice. The uncontradicted evidence left no doubt that the student's behavior at the high school posed a threat to both students and school officials. Thus, the court found that the school district properly exercised its authority to transfer the student to the alternative learning center and the district did not violate her procedural rights to remain in the high school during the pendency of the action. Finally, the court held that because the student introduced no evidence that the proposed placement was inappropriate or that a less restrictive environment existed in which she could receive the special education she needed the proposed placement was appropriate. *Victoria L. By Carol A. v. District School Board of Lee County, Florida*, 741 F.2d 369 (11th Cir.1984).

The parents of a handicapped child in Arizona brought suit against their local school district because of the district's proposed plan to relocate the child at a school which could provide assistance from an instructor specially qualified to train her. The child suffered from cerebral palsy and physical handicaps but possessed normal intelligence. However, because of her handicaps she had difficulty in learning to read and write. For this reason the child's school believed the child could best be served in a school which had teachers certified in physical disabilities. The parents objected to the move because they feared that moving the child from her neighborhood and friends would create emotional problems and would stigmatize her as a "handicap."

The U.S. Court of Appeals, Ninth Circuit, held that the school district's decision was reasonable under the circumstances of the case. In affirming a U.S. district court decision, the Court of Appeals stated that the importance of mainstreaming a handicapped child must be balanced with the primary objective of providing handicapped children with an "appropriate education." The court found that the objective of mainstreaming would not be "thwarted" by requiring the child to be instructed for a period of time by a physical disabilities teacher at another school. At issue here, said the court, is a school district's ability, after determining that a handicapped student is not making satisfactory progress, to transfer that student to a school which can provide assistance from an instructor especially qualified to train a student with that particular disability. The court found that the school district's proposal complemented state and federal law by "providing the child with a teacher particularly suited to deal with her learning problems," and held that the transfer should be allowed. *Wilson v. Marana Unified School District No. 6 of Pima County*, 735 F.2d 1178 (9th Cir.1984).

A parents' association in Missouri brought suit against Missouri education officials on behalf of a group of handicapped children challenging the state's alleged policy of labeling certain handicapped children "severely handicapped" and automatically educating them in schools separate from nonhandicapped children. The parents claimed that this practice violated the Education for All Handicapped Children Act, the Rehabilitation Act, the Equal Protection and Due Process clauses of the U.S. Constitution and Missouri law.

The specific allegations with respect to the EAHCA were that: 1) the policy did not treat the "severely handicapped" on an individual basis; 2) the placement of handicapped children in separate settings violated the least restrictive environment concept embodied in the EAHCA and 3) the policy was inherently unable to provide appropriate educational programs to handicapped children in separate schools.

A U.S. district court in Missouri held that the policy was consistent with the EAHCA. The court found evidence of an elaborate system for formulating individualized educational programs (IEP's) and making a placement decision for each handicapped child on an individualized basis. It noted that if it were to order the wholesale transfer of all the children in separate schools to regular schools it would be committing the same wrong as the plaintiffs were alleging, which was not treating each child as a unique individual.

The court also found that the complained-of educational policy was consistent with the EAHCA's "least restrictive environment" requirement. To the plaintiffs' claim that severely handicapped children being educated in separate schools were not receiving an appropriate education, the court held that it is possible to provide an appropriate educational environment to children attending a separate educational facility. The court was not persuaded by testimony from the plaintiffs' witnesses that a separate setting was inadequate because it could not provide sufficient interaction opportunities with nonhandicapped peers and that the quality of instruction was not as high in a separate school.

The plaintiffs also asserted no valid Rehabilitation Act claim in their argument that placing the profoundly handicapped in separate schools excluded them from the benefits of regular public school placement. The court stated that the availability of organized school activities is meaningless when the evidence indicated that most, if not all, of the handicapped children in separate schools had severe problems preventing them from participating in these activities anyway. Resources are too scarce, said the court, to provide the handicapped with activities or personnel from which they cannot benefit. Finally, the court found no violations of equal protection or due process and concluded that the plaintiffs' claims were without merit. *St. Louis Developmental Disabilities Treatment Center Parents Association v. Mallory*, 591 F.Supp. 1416 (W.D.Mo.1984).

The parents of a fifteen-year-old trainable mentally retarded child with a neurological impairment brought suit against a New Jersey school district, challenging the district's determination to remove the child from a residential school and place him in his home and local schools. A hearing officer had found that the child required a structured specialized program with major assistance in the development of communication skills and that such a program could be provided in the local public schools. It had not been established, found the hearing officer, that the child required a twenty-four hour residential placement in order to learn.

A U.S. district court in New Jersey disagreed. The court found both the program offered in the public school system and the residential program to be excellent. However, it concluded that the residential program was best for this particular child. The court found that continued attendance at the residential school would enable the child to best achieve success in learning and that placing him in his home and in local schools would have an adverse effect on his ability to learn and develop to the maximum possible extent. Accordingly, the hearing officer's determination was overturned. *Geis v. Board of Education of Parsippany-Troy Hills*, 589 F.Supp. 269 (D.N.J.1984).

The Supreme Court of Kansas upheld a placement decision calling for the placement of a visually handicapped child in a state school for the visually impaired. The school district had been working with the student for ten years and had provided him with special education and counseling services. During his junior high school years he was mainstreamed into regular classes and provided with a qualified teacher to sit with him during class to lend assistance. It was determined, however, that after completing junior high school, enrollment in a regular high would not be appropriate. Among the factors listed by the district for its decision were the increased mobility problems inherent in attending high school and the diversity of subjects which would complicate the assignment of qualified teachers to provide assistance. The student was also found to be very deficient in self-help and social skills.

His parents argued that he should continue to be mainstreamed in the local public school system and presented evidence showing that he could receive some benefit from the public schools. The Supreme Court of Kansas concluded, however, that the evidence provided by the school district, particularly that which involved the student's self-help needs, was sufficient to support the district's placement decision. *Bailey v. Unified School District No. 345*, 664 P.2d 1379 (Kan.1983).

B. Placement in Public School Programs

Placements of handicapped children in special education programs provided by public schools are generally upheld if the educational program offered by the school is appropriate and responsive to the particular child's needs.

In a California case, the proposed individualized educational program for a nine-year-old boy was challenged by his parents in federal district court. The boy was severely handicapped in three major categories: he had deficiencies in cognitive abilities; he had difficulties in language and communication; and he had severe physical problems resulting in his being very small and fragile for his age and making it difficult for him to walk. As a result of these handicaps the boy functioned at the overall level of a child three to four years of age.

Previously, the child's parents and their local school district had provided for the boy's special educational and physical needs, and until 1983 the boy had been placed in the district's severe disorders of language (SDL) program. At that time all parties agreed that SDL was no longer appropriate, and a new IEP was formulated by the district which proposed to place the child in the district's program for the trainable mentally retarded (TMR). However, the parents objected to this placement on the grounds that the TMR program would not serve their child's physical or language needs. They contended that private school placement was required because the district maintained only SDL and TMR programs.

After a state hearing officer ruled that the district's proposed IEP was appropriate the parents brought suit in U.S. district court seeking review of the hearing officer's decision as provided by the Education for All Handicapped Children Act. The court found that the TMR program would be an inappropriate placement because the child would be endangered by the presence of physically larger children with Down's syndrome, and that since the program was mainly directed to children with cognitive deficiencies the child would also receive inadequate language assistance. The court reversed the hearing officer's determination that the TMR program was appropriate and ordered that the district provide a program that addressed all three of the child's areas of deficiency, or alternatively, that the district comply with the parents' request for funding of the private school placement. *Russell v. Jefferson School District*, 609 F.Supp. 605 (N.D.Cal.1985).

A learning disabled child who also suffered from emotional problems had been educated in private day schools for over nine years. The local school district, the District of Columbia Public Schools (DCPS), had found that his placement at these private day schools was appropriate and funded his education. However, when the child reached the age of fourteen, officials at the private school determined that due to his increasing emotional problems the child required a full-time residential educational placement. Accordingly, at the close of the school year the private school notified DCPS that the child had completed his program of instruction and that he needed a new educational placement. On July 15, 1982, a review session was conducted by DCPS which resulted in a revised individualized educational program for the child.

Under the new IEP, which called for placement in a public high school learning disabilities program, the child was to spend no time in regular classes but would receive twenty-five percent of his instruction in regular education. The parents rejected this proposed IEP on the grounds that their child required residential placement, and they requested a due process hearing. Prior to the hearing the parents unilaterally enrolled the child in a private residential school. On September 28, 1982, a hearing officer concluded that due to the child's status as a multihandicapped individual (i.e., emotional and learning disabilities), a change in placement from a private day school to a public high school would be detrimental to the child. The hearing officer noted that the child had never been enrolled in a public school program. He ordered DCPS to propose an appropriate placement by November 3, 1982. DCPS took no action with regard to the child's placement but instead it filed suit on January 7, 1983, to vacate the hearing officer's order. A federal court ruled against DCPS, and appeal was taken to the U.S. Court of Appeals for the District of Columbia Circuit.

The appellate court held that the hearing officer's recommendation of residential placement was correct, noting that the alternative proposal by DCPS was clearly unacceptable. The "unique needs" of the child were not adequately considered by DCPS, which had made its recommendations on preprinted forms using "boilerplate language." The court ordered that DCPS fund the child's placement at the residential school and reimburse the parents for the costs incurred in their unilateral placement decision. The lower court's award of attorney's fees to the parents was, however, reversed. *McKenzie v. Smith*, 771 F.2d 1527 (D.C.Cir.1985).

The parents of a handicapped child in Delaware challenged a local school district's decision denying tuition funding for residential placement of their child. The parents argued that a free appropriate education would not meet their child's needs unless it were a twenty-four hour residential program. A U.S. district court in Delaware disagreed with the parents and held that the educational program offered by the public school system could provide an adequate free appropriate public education within the meaning of the EAHCA.

The court found that although the child was better off emotionally because of her attendance at a private facility, the school district offered a free appropriate program which could confer educational benefits. The court also held that delays in the administrative and due process hearings did not violate the parents' rights to due process and that there was no due process violation in the school district's unilateral appointment of a hearing officer and the seating of educators as hearing officers.

In addition, the ex parte contact between the attorney for the school district and the hearing officer presiding at the hearing did not violate due process as the contact was in the nature of a letter supplying the hearing officer with requested information relevant to the hearing. Further, the school district mailed the parents a copy of the letter and the parents made no request to respond. The court held in favor of the school district. *Ahren v. Keene*, 593 F.Supp. 902 (D.Del.1984).

A U.S. district court in Tennessee addressed the issue of whether a school board recommendation to place a seriously emotionally disturbed eighteen-year-old child in a state program satisfied the requirement that a "free appropriate public education" be provided to the child within the meaning of the Education For All Handicapped Children Act. The boy's mother objected to the placement recommendation and preferred placement at a private school in Texas or alternatively a private school located in Pennsylvania. After a series of unsuccessful appeals the mother requested the district court to reverse the placement recommendation and order placement at one of the two suggested private schools. The court affirmed the school's placement recommendation saying that because the Tennessee public mental health facility provided programs which included an academic and psychiatric therapy component as well as a social interaction component, the requirements of the EAHCA were met. *Clevenger v. Oak Ridge School Board*, 573 F.Supp. 349 (E.D.Tenn.1983).

The question before a U.S. district court in Massachusetts was whether a local school district had offered a placement to a handicapped child which could be construed as an appropriate education as required by the Education for All Handicapped Children Act. The child, mentally retarded, had been enrolled in a private school at public expense. When the child's family moved into a new district it sought to continue the private school education. The new district, however, developed an individualized educational program which sought to transfer the child to the public schools with special education in speech and physical therapy, art, music, physical education and other nonacademic subjects and a special summer program.

The court held that the district carried its burden of proving that the IEP met the statutory requirement of a free appropriate education. In so doing it cited the U.S. Supreme Court case, *Board of Education v. Rowley*, which held that an appropriate education means the state provides the child with an education that is of some benefit to the child utilizing a minimally acceptable educational approach. The court upheld the public school placement. *Lang v. Braintree School Committee*, 545 F.Supp. 1221 (D.Mass.1982).

The U.S. Court of Appeals, Fourth Circuit, has held that a Maryland school district was under no duty to consider private school placement where an appropriate public education could be provided. In this case, a handicapped student and her parents brought suit seeking tuition reimbursement when the parents placed their child in a private school, which they deemed a more appropriate placement than that offered by their county board of education. They contended that the county board improperly failed to consider placing their child in a private school when formulating a special education program for her.

The court noted that, while state law permits placement of handicapped students in an appropriate nonpublic educational program, such a placement is limited to those instances in which public educational services appropriate for the handicapped child are not available. Thus, under federal regulations pertaining to the Education for All Handicapped Children Act the duty of a state to pay for nonpublic schooling does not attach "if the handicapped child has available a free appropriate public education and the parents choose to place the child in a private school or facility. . . ." Of course, parents retain the right to challenge the placement. In this case such a challenge resulted in the state board of education upholding the public school placement. *Hessler v. State Board of Education of Maryland*, 700 F.2d 134 (4th Cir.1983).

After a Virginia school district refused a handicapped child's request to be placed in a private residential academy for severely handicapped children, she and her parents brought suit against the district alleging that she was being denied a free appropriate education under the EAHCA. The issue before the U.S. district court was whether the local school district had provided and would provide an "appropriate" education for the child.

In holding that the school district offered an appropriate educational program, the court said that "an appropriate education is not synonymous with the best possible education." An appropriate education is what is required by the EAHCA, not a "perfect" education, said the court. Here, the court found that the one-on-one instruction one to two hours per day with a teacher, one-on-one language therapy several hours per week, group speech therapy two or three hours per week, physical education classes, and psychological services, constituted an impressive program for the child.

In its holding in favor of the school district the court also took into account the parents' lack of cooperation with the school district saying that from the beginning, the parents adopted an adversary relationship with the district. The court viewed the parents as creating an atmosphere of suspicion and mistrust and as having a decided emphasis on legal rights and entitlements at the forefront of their approach. The court concluded that the school district had complied with the requirement of the EAHCA to provide an appropriate education for the child. *Bales v. Clarke*, 523 F.Supp. 1366 (E.D.Va.1981).

C. Private School and Residential Placement

Private school and residential placements are made when public schools are unable or unwilling to offer a program responsive and appropriate to a handicapped child's unique needs, or where a child's ability to learn and develop is contingent upon his or her placement in a residential setting.

In Massachusetts, the parents of a seventeen-year-old child with Down's syndrome became dissatisfied with their child's individualized education program because they felt it did not adequately address his sexual misbehavior. The child, who had been receiving special educational services from his public school system in a highly structured day school program, exhibited no significant behavioral problems during the school day. However, after school he appeared preoccupied with sex, touching young girls in an inappropriate manner and attempting to sexually abuse animals. The boy's parents believed that in order to correct this misbehavior and instill in the child proper attitudes toward sex, thus enabling him to enter into private employment as an adult, the child required a twenty-four-hour residential program.

School officials rejected this proposal, stating that the child was progressing satisfactorily at school and that his sexual misbehavior after school did not mandate his placement in a residential facility. They agreed to address the parents' concerns only by adding individual therapy and family counseling to the child's IEP. After a hearing officer ruled in favor of the school district the parents brought suit in U.S. district court.

Reversing the hearing officer's decision, the court found that under the EAHCA, the child was entitled to twenty-four-hour residential school placement to attempt to correct his sexual misbehavior. The court noted that under Massachusetts law a special educational program must "assure the maximum possible development of a child with special needs." Accordingly, the child was entitled to the more comprehensive behavior therapy available in a residential program, especially in light of the degree of his sexual maladjustment. The district court also dismissed the school district's argument that the child should remain in the least restrictive environment, i.e., the day school program, because that alternative was clearly inappropriate here.

The school district appealed to the U.S. Court of Appeals, First Circuit, contending that the district court had erroneously applied the requirements of Massachusetts state law to the case. This argument was rejected by the court of appeals. Where state law sets a minimum educational standard for handicapped children, those standards are incorporated by reference into the federal EAHCA. Thus a Massachusetts child suing a school district will be able to hold it to the same educational standards regardless of whether the suit is brought in state or federal court. The Court of Appeals therefore approved the federal district court's application of Massachusetts law, and the residential placement was upheld. *David D. v. Dartmouth School Committee*, 775 F.2d 411 (1st Cir. 1985).

In a case involving placement in a residential facility, the U.S. Court of Appeals, Third Circuit, affirmed a district court decision which held that handicapped children in New Jersey are entitled to the "best available" special education placement, as opposed to merely an appropriate one. This case arose in 1981 when the child study team of a New Jersey school district decided to change a handicapped child's IEP, which had provided for his placement at a private residential school since 1974. The child study team recommended a new IEP which would remove the child from the residential school and place him in the local school district's trainable mentally retarded (TMR) program. The child's parents objected and requested a due process hearing. The hearing officer found that the school district's TMR program was one of the best in the nation and upheld the child study team's recommendation.

On appeal by the school district, the federal district court reversed the hearing officer's decision and ordered continued residential placement. The Court of Appeals agreed with the district court. The administrative code of New Jersey's State Board of Education requires that handicapped students be provided a special education "according to how the pupil can best achieve success in learning." This provision indicated that the state of New Jersey had chosen to exceed the EAHCA's minimum requirement of an "appropriate" education. As such, all handicapped children in New Jersey are entitled to the "best" special education placement suitable to their needs. The district court's determination that, although the school district's TMR program was outstanding, residential placement would be best, was therefore upheld. *Geis v. Board of Education of Parsippany-Troy Hills*, 774 F.2d 575 (3d Cir. 1985).

A school district in Delaware proposed a six-hour per day program for a profoundly retarded thirteen-year-old boy. The boy's parents requested a hearing to challenge the denial of a residential placement. Negative administrative rulings then prompted the parents to appeal to a U.S. district court in Delaware for relief. The district court held that the educational program provided by the school district was not a free appropriate public education within the meaning of the EAHCA. The district was ordered to provide the child with a full-time residential program.

State and local school officials appealed the district court ruling to the U.S. Court of Appeals, Third Circuit, which agreed with the district court that the proposed educational program was inadequate to meet the child's specific needs. The court was persuaded by testimony which indicated that every time the child faced stress he engaged in self-destructive behavior, including continuous vomiting. Apparently the only way the child would be able to benefit educationally from any instruction he received was if he were afforded a twenty-four-hour per day program which would offer consistency. Thus, the court concluded that a placement where full-time care is provided was the appropriate placement to meet the needs of the child. *Kruelle v. New Castle County School District*, 642 F.2d 687 (3d Cir. 1981).

In a later Delaware case, the parents of a handicapped child challenged a local school district's decision denying tuition funding for residential placement of their child. The parents argued that a free appropriate education would not meet their child's needs unless it were a twenty-four-hour residential program. A U.S. district court in Delaware disagreed with the parents and held that the educational program offered by the public school system could provide an adequate free appropriate public education within the meaning of the EAHCA.

The court found that although the child was better off emotionally because of her attendance at a private facility, the school district offered a free appropriate program which could confer educational benefits. The court also held that delays in the administrative and due process hearings did not violate the parents' right to due process and that there was no due process violation in the school district's unilateral appointment of a hearing officer and the seating of educators as hearing officers.

In addition, the ex parte contact between the attorney for the school district and the hearing officer presiding at the hearing did not violate due process as the contact was in the nature of a letter supplying the hearing officer with requested information relevant to the hearing. Further, the school district mailed the parents a copy of the letter and the parents made no request to respond. The court held in favor of the school district. *Ahren v. Keene*, 593 F.Supp. 902 (D.Del.1984).

In a Rhode Island case a U.S. district court found that a proposed public school placement of two learning disabled children violated the children's right to a free appropriate education under the Education for All Handicapped Children Act. The proposed placement involved pupil/teacher ratios possibly as high as ten to one and provided for some mainstreaming. The children's father brought suit against the school district which had made the placement decision seeking a permanent injunction compelling the district to fund the children's placement at a private residential school.

The district court, persuaded by evidence that the children were severely learning disabled and that both children had significant accompanying emotional problems, found that the district's proposal to educate the children in a "self-contained" classroom for learning disabled children would not serve the children's needs and that only a residential placement would provide the children with the type of education anticipated by the EAHCA. The school district appealed the case to the U.S. Court of Appeals, First Circuit, which upheld the district court ruling. *Colin K. by John K. v. Schmidt*, 715 F.2d 1 (1st Cir.1983).

A California court also found that a residential placement was necessary to serve the needs of an emotionally handicapped child. The school district charged with placing the child in a special education program disputed that the child was entitled to a special education under the EAHCA. The school asserted that the child's emotional disturbance was linked exclusively with his home environment and, therefore, did not qualify as a "handicap" under the EAHCA.

The California Court of Appeal disagreed with the district's characterization of the child's problem saying that merely because his emotional disturbance may have stemmed from his home environment, this did not preclude a finding that the child was entitled to special education services. Further, only a program calling for a residential placement was appropriate for this particular child's needs. A residential setting would remove the child from his turbulent home environment and provide consistency which would not otherwise be possible. The court found that without removal from his home situation the child would be unable to learn. The school district was ordered to fund a residential placement. *San Francisco Unified School District v. State*, 182 Cal.Rptr. 525 (Cal.App.1st Dist.1982).

In a similar case, the parents of a multiply handicapped child brought suit against a Texas school district over a dispute involving the district's proposed placement of the child. The district formulated an IEP which called for a six-hour-day program to be augmented by home support. The parents claimed this did not constitute a "free appropriate public education" as required by the EAHCA. Complicating the situation was a dispute between the child's parents and the school district as to the nature of the child's handicap. The parents maintained she suffered from organic childhood schizophrenia and the district contended that its evaluation of the child showed she suffered from severe mental retardation.

A U.S. district court held in favor of the parents. The court deemed the dispute over whether the child was schizophrenic or mentally retarded to be irrelevant. What mattered, said the court, was whether the child was receiving an education suited to her unique needs. Finding the proposed public school placement inadequate to meet the child's needs, the court said residential placement is required under the EAHCA when necessary for educational purposes. There is no obligation to provide residential placement where the placement is a response to medical, social, or emotional problems that are segregable from the learning process. Here, however, residential placement was required where the child's social, emotional, medical, and education problems were so intertwined that it was impossible to separate them. The court ordered the school district to fund a residential placement for the child. *Gladys J. v. Pearland Independent School District*, 520 F.Supp. 869 (S.D.Tex.1981).

In another District of Columbia case, a U.S. district court held that where a sixteen-year-old handicapped child's problems were so intertwined that no one single problem could be considered primary, the school district of the child's residence was responsible for providing a full-time residential educational program for him. The child, a multiply handicapped boy who was diagnosed as being epileptic, emotionally disturbed, and learning disabled, was placed in a private residential treatment facility in Pennsylvania. Approximately six months later the facility concluded it could no longer deal with the severity of the boy's emotional and other problems. The local school district offered no alternative placement. An attempt by the treatment facility to return the child to his parents proved fruitless. The parents refused to accept him. A second attempt to deliver the child to his parents was initiated, but again the parents refused to allow the child in their home. The boy was then left at the office of the Department of Human Resources which referred him to a public hospital.

Neglect proceedings were instituted against the parents. Prior to the outcome of these proceedings the parents brought suit against the school district, seeking an injunction to compel the district to place the child in a residential program with necessary psychiatric and other services. The school district responded that because the child's primary problem was that he was emotionally disturbed, all the district was required to do was provide an educational day program and that help for the child's emotional problems should come from the parents or, if they were unwilling to assist the child, the Department of Human Resources. The DHR also disclaimed responsibility for the child.

The district court found the school district liable for the child's residential care expenses for two reasons. First, the EAHCA puts the primary responsibility for a handicapped child's education on the state educational agency. Such an education includes a private residential program where necessary to provide a free and appropriate public education to a handicapped person. Second, the court was unwilling to put the child and his family through the neglect proceedings. Testimony by a doctor who had examined the child indicated that the boy's emotional problems had been significantly "exacerbated" by his perception that he had been abandoned by his parents. The stigma of having his parents adjudicated neglectful and unwilling to care for him would seriously cripple efforts to deal with his problems and to reunite his family. Thus, the only available alternative the court was willing to accept was placement and financial support for that placement by the school district.

The court declined to perform what it termed the "Solomon-like" task of separating the child's social, emotional, medical, or educational problems to determine which was dominant and to assign responsibility for placement and treatment to the agency operating in the area of that problem. Here, the child's needs were found by the court to be so intimately intertwined that realistically it was not possible for the court to determine which need was primary. Consequently, the use of federal educational laws and placement pursuant to those laws was the only legally available alternative and was clearly required. *North v. District of Columbia Board of Education*, 471 F.Supp. 136 (D.C.Civ.Div.1979).

The U.S. Court of Appeals, First Circuit, has affirmed a U.S. district court decision which upheld the right to a residential education program where an alternative public school program failed to meet a handicapped child's particular needs. The parents of a severely retarded child in Massachusetts brought suit under the EAHCA challenging the school district's placement of their child in a day school training program. The parents sought residential placement as well as a day educational program. When the parents' proposal was rejected, they appealed to the Massachusetts Bureau of Special Education Appeals which found that the day school training would provide an appropriate education and that, while the child required residential care, such needs were not "educational" in nature under the Act, and thus not the responsibility of the school board.

The Court of Appeals disagreed, saying that the only way this child would make any educational progress would be through a combined day school and residential program. The court noted that under regulations promulgated by the Secretary of the Department of Education pursuant to the act, if a public or private residential program, including nonmedical care and room and board, is necessary in order to provide services to a handicapped child, such services must be provided at no cost to the parents of the child. Here, the lower court properly concluded that not only would the child fail to make educational progress without a residential program, but would very likely regress without one. Thus, the combined day school-residential placement was upheld. *Abrahamson v. Hershman*, 701 F.2d 223 (1st Cir.1983).

The allegedly inordinate cost of residential placement, according to a U.S. district court in Illinois, did not preclude it from being the appropriate placement. This case arose after a hearing officer exonerated an Illinois school district from liability for all but "purely educational" expenses of a severely multiply handicapped child and determined that residential expenses should be borne by another agency. The mother responded to this determination by placing the child in a residential school in Kansas. She then brought suit against state educational officials seeking an injunction to prohibit the district from adhering to its policy of distinguishing between "educational" and "noneducational" components of "related services" needed to enable handicapped children to perform adequately in school. The court, finding that the child could be best served by placement in a residential facility, ordered the school district to fund in the future the child's placement at the school in Kansas. *William J. v. Gill*, 572 F.Supp. 509 (E.D.Ill. 1983).

Where a state elects to provide state-subsidized residential care for handicapped children, the U.S. Court of Appeals, Second Circuit, has held that the state may require the parents of the children to transfer temporary custody of the children to the state. The parents in this case claimed that the temporary custody transfer requirement violated their right to privacy and family integrity without sufficient justification and that it discriminated against handicapped children solely on the basis of their handicaps.

The Court of Appeals, in upholding New York's custody transfer requirement, placed great emphasis on the voluntary nature of New York's benefits program and stressed that the state, while under no constitutional obligation to provide residential treatment for handicapped children, elected to do so. Consequently when the state provided voluntary social services, it could administer the program without having to consult and satisfy the individual concerns of each of the recipients.

The court dealt with the handicap discrimination issue by saying that "*all* parents whose children need state-subsidized home substitutes must transfer custody to the state, regardless of whether the child is or is not handicapped." Therefore, New York's foster care scheme discriminated between children only as to the type of assistance needed and not solely on the basis of their handicaps. Accordingly the court upheld the constitutionality of the New York law as written. *Joyner By Lowry v. Dumpson*, 712 F.2d 770 (2d Cir.1983).

A private day school education was ordered for a child by a U.S. district court in Massachusetts after that court found a learning disabled child's individualized educational program offered by a public school system to have fallen "far short of meeting his unique needs." The parents of the child had brought suit against the school district responsible for the child's education alleging that the IEP proposed by the district was inadequate. The district court agreed. The court found that the school district, which was aware of the child's inability to work independently and also aware that the child had to be placed in an environment with few distractions, nevertheless failed to structure a program designed only to improve his basic skills.

Although it was well known in the school that the child's poor self-image and "defeatist" attitude were obstacles to his learning progress, no program was structured whereby the child might realize some success in his weaker subjects. In contrast, the program offered at the private school was specifically designed to provide children having severe learning disabilities and problems of low self-esteem with sufficient skills to return to a normalized educational program. Finding the public school program inadequate to meet the child's needs, the court ordered the school district to fund a private residential education for the child. *Norris v. Massachusetts Department of Education*, 529 F.Supp. 759 (D.Mass.1981).

Residential placement was held to be inappropriate for a profoundly handicapped child in the following Virginia case. The child's parents asked the U.S. Court of Appeals, Fourth Circuit, to reverse certain administrative decisions made by a local school district in Virginia, and to issue both a preliminary and permanent injunction requiring the state of Virginia and county school officials to provide a twenty-four-hour residential placement for their son. The child had been placed in a residential program but local school officials later recommended that the child be placed in a day education program and live at home. The parents rejected this decision and applied for tuition assistance for the residential school. Tuition assistance was denied by a country special education committee on the ground that the day program could meet the child's needs.

The parents appealed this decision to the Superintendent of Public Education of the Commonwealth of Virginia, who concurred in the committee's decision that the child would receive an appropriate education in the day program while living at home with his parents. After exhausting their administrative remedies, the parents brought suit in a U.S. district court, which released the school district from its obligation to provide twenty-four-hour residential care and education for the child.

The child and his parents appealed to the U.S. Court of Appeals, which upheld the district court ruling and found that the proposed program of day school at an elementary school for severely and profoundly retarded children and living at home constituted the free appropriate public education to which the child was entitled under the EAHCA. The court was persuaded by testimony which indicated that the child had reached the point in his education at which a continuation of the residential program would at best yield only marginal results and probably none at all. Testimony by the school district's witnesses also indicated that basic living skills, e.g., hygiene skills, could easily be taught at home by teaching the child's family the cues the child had developed for implementing such skills. *Matthews By Matthews v. Davis*, 742 F.2d 825 (4th Cir.1984).

The U.S. Department of Defense (DOD) was ordered by the U.S. District Court, District of Columbia, to place, at its expense, the children of a civilian employee of the U.S. government ("on loan" to the North Atlantic Treaty Organization) at two specific private schools in the United States. Finding that special education services appropriate to the children's needs were unavailable in the DOD's dependent schools, the parents contended that the children, clearly identified as learning disabled and their father's dependents, were entitled to be educated appropriate to their unique needs as handicapped children. The DOD, the parents said, was mandated to identify and assess their individual needs, devise an individualized education program tailored to each special situation and, if the DOD could not provide the necessary services within its own resources, it was required to make, and fund, referrals to private schools or facilities at no cost to the parents.

The court agreed with the parents and thus granted their request for an injunction to compel the DOD to immediately place and fund the children's education in two U.S. schools. The court was persuaded by testimony from a doctor who had examined the children that a "mainstreaming" approach was not in the children's best interest. The children's needs required residential placement. *Cox v. Brown*, 498 F.Supp. 823 (D.D.C.1980).

VI. "Related Services" Under the EAHCA

A. Psychological Services

Psychological services are included in the definition of "related services" in the EAHCA. However, the Act does not define psychological services, which has left to the courts the responsibility to determine what services are and are not psychological services for purposes of the EAHCA.

A federal district court has awarded $8,855 to the parents of an emotionally impaired youth as reimbursement for psychological services which their school district admittedly had failed to provide. The court's decision reverses an earlier denial of relief to the parents. The court was able to reconsider its earlier ruling because it had not yet finally disposed of the case. After the U.S. Supreme Court's ruling in *Burlington School Committee v. Department of Education*, 105 S.Ct. 1996 (1985) (see Chapter Four, § II), the parents asked the district court for a new ruling. The district court observed that its earlier ruling that the parents could not be reimbursed for their child's psychotherapy unless the school district had denied it in bad faith, was wrong in light of *Burlington*. In that case the U.S. Supreme Court stated simply that where a school district fails to provide a handicapped child with a service essential to his special education, the child's parents will be entitled to reimbursement for their efforts to provide their child with the service.

Since the parents had spent $8,850 on psychotherapy, the court ordered the school district to pay the parents this amount. The psychotherapy had been provided by a licensed psychiatrist, observed the court, and normally this meant that the amount awarded to the parents would be reduced to the level that a (non-M.D.) psychotherapist would have charged. However, since the school district failed to provide evidence that it could have supplied the psychotherapy for less than the psychiatrist selected by the parents had charged, the parents were entitled to the full $8,855. *Max M. v. Illinois State Board of Education*, 629 F.Supp. 1504 (N.D.Ill.1986).

A Tennessee child who suffered from a learning disability, impaired vision and seizures was being provided with a special education under the Education for All Handicapped Children Act by his local school district. In the fall of the 1983-84 school year, school personnel noticed that the child's behavior and performance appeared to have worsened since the previous spring. They suspected that the child had suffered several grand mal seizures during the summer and that the child had not recently been examined by a physician. After the school district's multi-disciplinary team ("M Team") made a recommendation to his parents that he be medically evaluated by a physician, the parents had the child examined by a pediatrician, a neurologist and a psychologist. Although the M Team utilized the results of these neurological and psychological evaluations, they did not result in any change in the child's individualized educational program.

A dispute later arose over whether the school district was required under the EAHCA to pay the costs of these evaluations. The parents' insurance company had paid $79 of the $265 bill for the neurological evaluation, and $99 of the $247 psychological evaluation. A hearing officer ordered the school district to pay the difference between the amount paid by the parents' insurance company and the total cost of the evaluations. The parents filed suit in U.S. district court, seeking an order that the school district reimburse them for the amount the insurer had paid to the neurologist. The parents argued that because their insurance policy provided a maximum of $30,000 lifetime coverage for psychological expenses, the $99 payment made by their insurer resulted in their coverage being reduced to $29,901. This, they alleged, was contrary to the EAHCA's requirement that "related services," i.e., psychological and neurological evaluations, be provided free of charge.

The district court agreed that the parents were entitled to reimbursement for the $99 which their insurer had paid for the psychological evaluation. However, because there was no comparable policy limit for neurological expenses, the parents had incurred no cost as a result of their insurer's payment of $79 for the neurological evaluation. The school district was thus ordered to reimburse the parents for all sums which they had paid to the neurologist and psychologist, minus the $79 paid to the neurologist pursuant to their insurance policy. The court concluded by ordering the district to pay the parents $99 to compensate for the reduction of the amount of coverage available for psychological expenses. *Seals v. Loftis*, 614 F.Supp. 302 (E.D.Tenn.1985).

The parents of an emotionally disturbed eleven-year-old boy sued a New Jersey school board seeking to have the board pay the cost of psychotherapy services allegedly provided for the boy as part of an individualized education plan developed by the board. Both the child's parents and the board agreed that the child should be placed in a therapeutic environment. Thereafter, he was placed in a special education day school for the emotionally disturbed. The school provided an integrated program of individual child psychotherapy, family therapy with the parents, a therapeutic activity group, individual and group counseling and behavior modification, as well as special education on a daily basis in self-contained and departmentalized classes.

Due to the success of the program, the child was able to return to his local school approximately two years later. The parents were informed by the school that the cost of the psychotherapy provided to the child as part of the program would be assessed to them. At the time of the child's discharge the charges had grown to a total of $25,200. The parents sought to have the school board pay the cost of the psychotherapy, which the board refused to do.

The board gave three reasons for its decision. First, it argued that psychotherapy was not part of the IEP agreed to by both the board and the parents. Second, it noted that the New Jersey Department of Education had issued a policy statement to the effect that "psychotherapy," other than that necessary for diagnostic and evaluative purposes, was not a "related service" for which a local school district would be responsible under the mandate of the Education for All Handicapped Children Act. Finally, the board took the position that nothing else in the EAHCA or its implementing regulations required it to pay for this service.

A U.S. district court in New Jersey held that psychotherapy provided to an emotionally disturbed child as an integral part of that child's special education is a "related service" within the meaning of the EAHCA. Further, the definitions contained in the EAHCA superseded inconsistent New Jersey regulations and "policy statements." Thus, while no explicit reference to psychotherapy is made in the EAHCA, the definitions of "related services" which are provided are indicative of a congressional intent to include it where appropriate among those services which are to be provided at no cost to the parents under the Act. The court concluded that the psychotherapy services should be paid for by the board of education. *T.G. v. Board of Education*, 576 F.Supp. 420 (D.N.J.1983).

An emotionally disturbed student in Connecticut sought an injunction requiring the state to pay the full cost of her attendance at a private school, including psychotherapy. The student's school district had denied such services on the ground that the psychotherapy was not a "related service" under the EAHCA because the definition of related service excludes medical services that are not diagnostic or evaluative. A. U.S. district court disagreed with the school district's characterization of related services. The plain meaning of the EAHCA distinguishes between "medical services" and other supportive services, including speech pathology and audiology, physical therapy and recreation, as well as psychological services. Only medical services are singled out as limited to services for diagnostic and evaluative purposes. Thus, the court concluded that psychological services required to assist the student to benefit from her special education were related services required to be provided by the state, without cost to the student or her parents. *Papacoda v. State of Connecticut*, 528 F.Supp. 68 (D.Conn.1981).

The Supreme Court of Montana ordered a local school district to bear the costs of a psychotherapy program for a schizophrenic child. In this case the school district had denied the parents' request for a program of psychotherapy to accompany the child's placement at a private residential school in California. The reasons given for the denial were that Montana law exluded psychotherapy as a related service and that psychotherapy was not included in the definition of "psychological services" in the Education for All Handicapped Children Act and the Act's regulations. The Act refers to "psychological services" as including "planning and managing a program of psychological services, including psychological counseling for children and parents."

The parents sued the school district arguing that psychotherapy was included in the Act as a related service. Noting that "psychological services" are not limited to diagnostic and evaluative purposes only, as are medical services, the court held that such services are included in the "planning and managing a program of psychological services" language of the Act. Thus, the federal regulations allowing for psychological services, which include psychotherapy, overrode Montana state regulations which excluded this service. *Matter of "A" Family*, 602 P.2d 157 (Mont.1979).

One case held that handicapped children are not automatically entitled to psychological services. In this case, the parents of a handicapped daughter in Virginia brought suit against a local school district alleging that their child was denied a free appropriate education. Two of the parents' numerous allegations against the district were that psychological services were not provided to their child and that the sexual composition of the child's classroom was inappropriate. A U.S. district court held that the school district was providing an excellent education for the child and that at all times psychological services were available for the child and would have been provided for her if necessary. However, the court rejected the idea that psychological counseling must be provided to all handicapped children, in the absence of serious behavioral problems. The court stated that the law does not set forth such a requirement.

There is also no requirement as to the sexual composition of a class. The court noted that it would be beneficial if both sexes were equally represented in the child's classroom and that it was unfortunate that there were no other girls in the classroom. However, a loss of that benefit does not make a classroom setting inappropriate. Accordingly, the court held in favor of the school district. *Bales v. Clarke*, 523 F.Supp. 1366 (E.D.Va.1981).

B. Medical Services

Generally, medical services are excluded from "related services" under the EAHCA unless the services are for diagnostic or evaluative purposes. However, the U.S. Supreme Court held in *Irving Independent School District v. Tatro*, 104 S.Ct. 3371 (1984) (reprinted in the Appendix of U.S. Supreme Court cases in this volume), that clean intermittent catheterization is a related service.

In the *Tatro* case, the U.S. Supreme Court ruled that clean intermittent catheterization (CIC) is a related service not subject to the "medical service" exclusion of the EAHCA. The parents of an eight-year-old daughter born with spina bifida brought suit against a local Texas school district after the district refused to provide catheterization for the child while she attended school. The parents pursued administrative and judicial avenues to force the district to train staff to perform the simple procedure.

After a U.S. district court held against the parents they appealed to the U.S. Court of Appeals, Fifth Circuit, which reversed the district court ruling. The school district then appealed to the U.S. Supreme Court.

The Supreme Court affirmed that portion of the Court of Appeals decision which held that CIC is a "supportive service," not a "medical service" excluded from the EAHCA. The court was not persuaded by the school district's argument that catheterization is a medical service because it is provided in accordance with a physician's prescription and under a physician's supervision, even though it may be administered by a nurse or trained layperson.

The court listed four criteria to determine a school's obligation to provide services that relate to both the health and education of a child.

First, to be entitled to related services, a child must be handicapped so as to require special education. Second, only those services necessary to aid a handicapped child to benefit from special education must be provided, regardless of how easily a school nurse or layperson could furnish them. Third, regulations under the EAHCA state that school nursing services must be performed by a nurse or other qualified person, not by a physician. Fourth, the child's parents in this case were seeking only the *services* of a qualified person at the school, they were not asking the school to provide *equipment*. The court reversed those portions of the Court of Appeals ruling which held the school district liable under the Rehabilitation Act and which held that the parents were entitled to attorney's fees. *Irving Independent School District v. Tatro*, 104 S.Ct. 3371 (1984).

The U.S. Court of Appeals, Third Circuit, has also found that CIC was a "related service" within the meaning of the EAHCA, where the absence of such a service would prevent the child from participating in a regular public school program. A fourth grade student in Pennsylvania who was born with spina bifida, a congenital physical condition causing paralysis from the waist down, brought suit against a Pennsylvania school district because of the district's failure to provide her with clean intermittent catheterization which would allow her to empty her bladder. The school district based its refusal to provide CIC on the ground that it was not a "related service" because it was not connected with a special education program and also because it was a medical, not an educational, service. Further, the school district insisted that under Pennsylvania law, school nurses were not required to perform catheterization. The Court of Appeals disagreed, saying the child would be effectively denied a free appropriate education without CIC provided by the school district. Her attendance in school was contingent upon receiving CIC. Thus, the school district was ordered to provide this service. *Tokarcik v. Forest Hills School District*, 665 F.2d 443 (3d Cir.1981).

Courts will generally not order a school district to pay the medical expenses of a handicapped child where the services are not diagnostic or evaluative, and are not aimed at allowing the child to benefit from his education. The following two cases illustrate.

A public school system in the District of Columbia appealed an order compelling it to pay a profoundly schizophrenic child's medical expenses during her stay at a private psychiatric hospital as a "related service" under the Education for All Handicapped Children Act. The child's mother requested special education placement at the private hospital. Treatment at the hospital involved intensive psychotherapy and a drug program. A U.S. district court held that the school system did not have to subsidize the child's medical expenses. The court reasoned that under the EAHCA, a child who is placed in a residential treatment program must have been placed there to render him educable, not for medical reasons only. Here, the placement in the residential treatment program was primarily for medical reasons and not educational reasons. The stay in the hospital was not related to the child's education but was, rather, for treatment of her condition. Therefore, the public school system, although obligated to provide the child with a "free and appropriate public education" under the EAHCA, was not obligated to finance the medical expenses. *McKenzie v. Jefferson*, 566 F.Supp. 404 (D.D.C.1983).

A U.S. district court in Illinois has ruled that state agencies were not required to pay the expenses of placing a child with severe behavioral disorders at a psychiatric hospital. In this case the parents of the child brought suit against the Illinois State Board of Education to compel it to pay the costs of their child's placement at a private residential psychiatric facility. They argued that the services were "psychological services" which are included in the definition of related services under the EAHCA. The court rejected this argument saying that the board of education properly deemed the services psychiatric rather than psychological since they were provided by licensed physicians. Further, under the EAHCA, all medical services except those provided for evaluative and diagnostic purposes are specifically excluded from "related services." *Darlene L. v. Illinois State Board of Education*, 568 F.Supp. 1340 (N.D.Ill.1983).

C. Integrated Treatment Programs

Other services, such as occupational therapy, family counseling and extracurricular activities are sometimes requested by parents or guardians of handicapped children. Whether a court will order a school district to provide such services seems to depend upon the particular facts of the case.

The U.S. Court of Appeals, Sixth Circuit, has affirmed a district court ruling that the EAHCA did not obligate school districts to provide continuous occupational therapy to a handicapped student in Ohio. The Court of Appeals also held that the inclusion of nonacademic extracurricular activities once per week was not automatically required. The court observed that the EAHCA, in and of itself, does not require that states maximize the potential of handicapped children commensurate with the opportunity provided to other children. These programs, the court found, were not necessary to permit the child to benefit from his instruction. *Punikaia v. Clark*, 720 F.2d 463 (9th Cir.1983).

Emotionally disturbed children in Illinois brought suit against a local school district challenging a rule which excluded counseling and therapeutic services from being considered special education or related services which Illinois was required to provide to handicapped children. The children contended that without therapeutic counseling they were unable to receive an appropriate education. A U.S. district court agreed with the children. The court held that the exclusion of counseling and therapeutic services deprived the children of a free appropriate education guaranteed by the Education for All Handicapped Children Act. *Gary B. v. Cronin*, 542 F.Supp. 102 (N.D.Ill.1980).

A U.S. district court in Texas ordered a local school district to provide counseling to the parents of an autistic child. The parents of the child had brought suit against the school district alleging that certain programs and services denied the child violated his right to a free appropriate education under the EAHCA. The court found that counseling to the parents in order to relieve their emotional stress was necessary to meet this child's particular and unique needs as regarded a special education. *Stacey G. v. Pasadena Independent School District*, 547 F.Supp. 61 (S.D.Tex.1982).

D. Transportation

The denial of transportation services to a handicapped child has been viewed by two courts to constitute a denial of a free appropriate education.

In the first case, a handicapped child in Hawaii claimed she was denied a free appropriate education after her school proposed a homebound program for her. A U.S. district court held that the proposed IEP did not satisfy the requirement of the EAHCA that an education be provided to a handicapped child in the "least restrictive environment." The child, the court stated, was entitled to transportation and a school-based education at public expense. *Department of Education v. Katherine D.*, 531 F.Supp. 517 (D.Hawaii 1982). In the second case, the U.S. Court of Appeals, First Circuit, upheld a $1,150 award to the parents of a Rhode Island girl for their out-of-pocket expenses incurred in driving their daughter to school. *Hurry v. Jones*, 734 F.2d 879 (1st Cir.1984).

The West Virginia Supreme Court of Appeals recently held that under state law, two handicapped children were entitled to transportation to school. In this case, two families lived on a dirt road, located in rural West Virginia, known as Dry Monday Branch. The road, which was often traversable only by four-wheel drive vehicle, was owned by a timber company which never objected to its use by the two families. The families had, respectively, a seven-year-old boy and a six-year-old girl who were both afflicted with spina bifida. Both children wore orthopedic braces from waist to feet and were unable to walk to the established school bus stop, which was located on a regular road one-half to nine-tenths of a mile from the children's homes. The county school board refused to send a school bus up Dry Monday Branch because of the road's poor condition, and the children's parents did not own a reliable vehicle in which to transport them to the established bus stop. As a result, the children were unable to attend school during the 1984-85 school year.

Throughout the summer of 1985 the children's parents attempted to persuade school officials to provide transportation for their children. Finally the superintendent sent them a letter informing them that because Dry Monday Branch was a privately owned road, was poorly maintained and was unsafe for a school bus, the parents would have to provide transportation themselves.

Because the laws of West Virginia [W.Va.Code 18-5-13(6)(a)] require that county boards of education provide "adequate" transportation to any student living more than two miles from school, the parents sought an order that the board provide their children with transportation down Dry Monday Branch. The West Virginia Supreme Court of Appeals agreed and issued a writ of mandamus directing the county school board to provide proper transportation. The court held that poor road conditions could not excuse the board from providing adequate transportation to all students. Since neither child was able to walk to the established school bus stop, the board's arrangements were inadequate as a matter of law. As further justification for its decision, the court noted that the timber company which owned Dry Monday Branch regarded it as a public road. *Kennedy v. Board of Education, McDowell County*, 337 S.E.2d 905 (W.Va.1985).

The following case deals not with the transportation expenses of handicapped children, but rather with the question of whether the family of a handicapped child is entitled to be reimbursed for expenses incurred in visiting their child who attended an out-of-state residential school.

At issue before the District Court of Appeal of Florida was whether the parents of a handicapped child were entitled to transportation expenses incurred as a result of their trips from Florida, where they lived, to Georgia to visit their son who was in a residential treatment facility in that state. The child's individualized educational program (IEP) provided for transportation and parent counseling as related services and delineated certain annual goals, including developing "satisfactory inter-personal relationships with adults and peers in the home, school and community," and, as a short term instructional objective, that the child would "[i]mprove relationships with parents and siblings through open communications and personal interaction with family members."

The parents requested reimbursement from their local school district for several therapeutic visits with their son. The expenses included airfare for the child, for his parents and for the child's two siblings, as well as hotel, food and car expenses for the entire family. The school district agreed to pay the expenses for only three of the round trips made by the child between Florida and Georgia. The parents requested and received an administrative hearing at which they argued that monthly therapeutic visits with their son were necessary to implement the goals of his treatment program. The administrative hearing officer found that by paying for three round trips per year for the handicapped student, the school district adequately met its obligation to provide funding for transportation as a service related to the child's special education. This unfavorable ruling prompted the parents to appeal to the courts.

The Court of Appeal affirmed a lower court ruling in favor of the school district. The court agreed with the hearing officer's determination stating that the child was entitled to a special education at the residential facility and that he was also entitled to transportation at public expense in order to receive education there. He was not entitled, however, to additional trips home at public expense for therapeutic purposes. The school's obligation was to educate the child, notwithstanding his severe emotional disturbance, rather than to spend money intended for the education of other students in order to provide primary treatment for the handicap itself. An improved family situation, said the court, is not an end in itself and the school district was not required to foot the bill for family gatherings. *Cohen v. School Board of Dade County*, 450 So.2d 1238 (Fla.App.3d Dist.1984).

VII. Special Education For Preschool Children and Children Over Eighteen Years of Age

The EAHCA requires that states provide a free appropriate education to children between the ages of three and twenty-one. However, section 1412(B)

of the Act states that with respect to handicapped children aged three to five and eighteen to twenty-one, the requirement to provide an education shall not apply if to do so would conflict with state law regarding public education for such age groups.

A handicapped child in Oklahoma who was about to be graduated by her school district brought suit against the school district alleging that she was in the tenth, not the twelfth, grade and was therefore entitled to two additional years of special education. The school district argued that any notations in the student's individual education program (IEP) or her report card indicating that she was in the tenth grade were a mistake and that the child was in the twelfth grade and thus eligible for graduation. The district further argued that Oklahoma state law did not obligate school districts to provide education to handicapped students from eighteen through twenty-one years of age nor did the EAHCA impose such a requirement. A U.S. district court in Oklahoma held in the child's favor and the school district appealed.

The U.S. Court of Appeals, Tenth Circuit, affirmed the district court ruling finding that since nonhandicapped children in the eighteen to twenty-one age group may be entitled to additional years of education when one or more grades are failed, handicapped children within this age group are similarly entitled to continue their education.

The court found evidence of the school district's different methods used to determine when handicapped and nonhandicapped children are in the twelfth grade and found that certain standards for the evaluation of handicapped children, as with nonhandicapped children are in the twelfth grade and found that certain standards for the evaluation of handicapped children, as with nonhandicapped children, must be met before a handicapped child can be deemed to have advanced a grade. A nonhandicapped student's performance was evaluated by standardized course content whereas a handicapped student's progress was measured by whether the goals in his or her IEP were met. The court found that the EAHCA contemplates that a handicapped child's progress in school should be measured by objective, if not standardized, criteria. It would make a farce of the clear intent of Congress to interpret the EAHCA as allowing a handicapped child to fail to meet his or her IEP objectives and yet advance a grade level. Here, the court found a failure on the part of the school district to adequately measure the child's progress. A notation in the child's IEP and in her report card indicating that she was in tenth grade prompted the court to rule that the child was entitled to two additional years of special education. *Helms v. Independent School District No. 3*, 750 F.2d 820 (10th Cir.1985).

One court has held that where, under state law, a state was not required to provide a public education for children under age six, it did not have to provide a special education for a four-year-old handicapped child. In this Oregon case, the mother of a four-year-old speech and language impaired child brought suit against an Oregon school district alleging the district had denied her child a free appropriate public education because of his age, in violation of the EAHCA and the Oregon Education Act of 1975. The Court of Appeals of Oregon held that neither the EAHCA nor an Oregon statute providing for a free appropriate education for all handicapped children under twenty-one years of age required the district to provide special education for the child.

The court found that the Oregon act did not require districts to provide special education programs for handicapped children under regular school age, where the district did not provide services to nonhandicapped children in the same age group. Under the EAHCA, if a district serves 50% or more of children in a child's age group that have the same disability, it must provide services to all such handicapped children. Here, the school district did not serve 50% or more of four-year-old speech and language impaired children. The court concluded that although a school district may choose to provide educational services for children under regular school age and to seek approval of its programs and partial reimbursement of the costs, nothing in federal or state law requires it to do. The school district's decision was affirmed. *Stewart v. Salem School District 24J*, 670 P.2d 1048 (Or.App.1983).

The U.S. Court of Appeals, Eighth Circuit, reached a different result in a case brought by the Association for Retarded Citizens of North Dakota (ARC). The ARC challenged conditions of confinement and treatment provided to mentally handicapped individuals. The ARC also wanted to know why the state of North Dakota was not providing an education for handicapped children aged three to five under the EAHCA. A U.S. district court in North Dakota failed to find a right to a preschool education for children aged three to five. North Dakota, under its public education laws was only obligatd to educate children ages six to twenty-one. However, just after this ruling North Dakota enacted a law which imposed a duty to educate preschool handicapped children. Consequently, on appeal, the Court of Appeals allowed the ARC to modify the order to provide for a right to education for children aged three to five under the EAHCA. *Walker v. Lockhart*, 713 F.2d 1378 (8th Cir.1983).

The New York Supreme Court, Appellate Division, has ruled that a local county was required to pay the tuition expenses of thirty-five handicapped preschool children. The county had been ordered to do so by a New York family court. The county argued that a family court may not order a county to pay the school tuition for preschool-age handicapped children without the school having received prior approval of the State Commissioner of Education. The appellate court rejected this contention and held that prior approval of the Commissioner of Education was not a prerequisite to a family court order requiring these tuition payments. *Matter of Jeremy G.*, 482 N.Y.S.2d 872 (A.D.2d Dept.1984).

VIII. Length of School Year for the Handicapped

The majority of cases hold that handicapped children are entitled to a summer program to prevent regression of progress made during the regular school year.

Several young handicapped children in New York were denied summer education programs to which they believed they were entitled under the Education for All Handicapped Children Act. Following the inception of a lawsuit seeking injunctive relief the children were placed in adequate summer schools. However, the lawsuit was pursued because of the plaintiff's contention that there was a reasonable expectation that the same problems were likely to occur again in the immediate future. The defendants in the case, a local school board and the state of New York, sought a dismissal of the complaint contending that because the children had been placed there was then no case or controversy to be decided. Additionally, the defendants maintained that the complaint failed to state a claim upon which relief could be granted since they had not refused to provide or arrange for special educational services for the plaintiffs on a twelve-month basis and since the statutes upon which the children relied did not require the provision of a twelve-month program for all handicapped children.

A U.S. district court in New York denied the motion to dismiss. It stated that the children were definitely suffering from severe handicaps and there was no indication in the record that the problems encountered by them would not persist. In fact, all indications were to the contrary. The court felt it had good reason to believe, therefore, that the challenged conduct would continue. In light of those circumstances, the court found that the plaintiffs had presented a justiciable controversy over which the court could exercise its jurisdiction.

The court also held that the children stated a claim under the provisions of the EAHCA. It was noted that the EAHCA provides federal funding to state and local educational agencies in order to insure provision of special education services to handicapped children. Along with the funding, however, the act also imposes an obligation upon those state and local agencies to develop for each child an "individualized education program." Here the defendants acknowledged that the children and all other members of that particular class require twelve-month schooling. However, they failed to provide for or arrange for the provision of special educational services for the summer months for these children. The motion to dismiss was denied and the case went forward for trial. *Stanton v. Board of Education of Norwich Central School District*, 581 F.Supp. 190 (N.D.N.Y.1983).

In a Pennsylvania case handicapped children, through their parents, sued the state alleging their rights to a free publicly funded education were being denied because their school year was limited to 180 days. A U.S. district court agreed with the plaintiffs and ordered education in excess of 180 days for them. The court examined the various types of students needing more than 180 days of school per year and concluded that regression was caused by interruption of educational programs for severely and profoundly impaired children and that for many of these children long periods of time were required to regain lost skills. Indeed, in many cases these children could not even achieve self-sufficiency where there was long interruption in their education. Finally, the court found that the 180-day rule violated the federal EAHCA which demands that the state supply instruction designed to meet all of the handicapped child's unique needs without limitation.

This decision was affirmed by the U.S. Court of Appeals, Third Circuit. The court noted that handicapped children seriously regress when there are long interruptions in their education and this violates the congressional policy of requiring an "appropriate" education for such children. An educational program which ignores the unique characteristics of this group of handicapped children denies them a reasonable opportunity to achieve the educational objectives intended by Congress. *Battle v. Commonwealth of Pennsylvania*, 629 F.2d 269 (3d Cir.1980).

A subsequent Georgia case presented basically the same question to the federal courts. In this case the Georgia Association of Retarded Citizens brought suit against the state of Georgia and a local school board, seeking a change in school policies and practices which refused to consider the needs of mentally retarded children for schooling beyond the traditional 180 days. The court, relying heavily on the Pennsylvania decision, decided in favor of the retarded children. It noted that federal law places the responsibility on state educational agencies to make sure that local agencies provide adequate educational services to handicapped children or directly provide such services themselves. It was pointed out that many future problems, such as financial limitations and the possibility of overburdening available school personnel, lie ahead, but those problems would have to be dealt with by a court or some other appropriate body at a future date.

This case was appealed to the U.S. Court of Appeals, Eleventh Circuit, which affirmed the district court's ruling, saying that a blanket refusal to extend the 180-day school year violated the EAHCA and the U.S. Supreme Court decision *Board of Education v. Rowley*, which imposes an obligation upon schools to consider *individual* educational needs of handicapped children. The court held that because the state of Georgia failed to follow the procedures set forth in EAHCA it also failed to develop adequate individualized educational programs for the children, which might have included an extension of the school year beyond 180 days. *Georgia Association of Retarded Citizens v. McDaniel*, 716 F.2d 1565 (11th Cir.1983).

Other cases have held that handicapped children are entitled to a year-round education.

After an Oregon school district agreed to pay for the educational expenses of a handicapped child for 180 days only, the child, a trainable mentally retarded youth, brought suit against the district to compel it to provide a year-round education. A local hearing officer determined that the child needed a residential facility for the full 365-day year. The Oregon Court of Appeals upheld this decision stating that if a local hearing officer determines that 365 days is appropriate for a particular student, then the district must pay the tuition expenses for all 365 days. *Mahoney v. Administrative School District No. 1*, 601 P.2d 826 (Or.App.1979).

The U.S. Court of Appeals, Fifth Circuit, has also held that a local school district was required to provide an education for handicapped children beyond the regular nine-month school year. The court struck down a Mississippi rule limiting the length of the school year for all school children to 180 days, saying that rigid rules such as 180-day limitations violate the EAHCA's procedural command that each child receives individual consideration, and also the substantive requirement that each child receives some benefit from his education. *Crawford v. Pittman*, 708 F.2d 1028 (5th Cir.1983).

The parents of a severely handicapped child in Missouri brought suit against a local special school district and the Missouri Department of Education alleging that the school district's refusal to provide for severely handicapped children programs extending beyond the regular nine month school year violated the Education for All Handicapped Children Act and the Rehabilitation Act. The parents claimed that such programs were provided in the summer to nonhandicapped children.

A U.S. district court issued an injunction prohibiting the Department of Education from discrimination against handicapped children. The district court found that the state's policy which did not provide for more than 180 days of education per school year for the severely handicapped denied those children "free appropriate education" in violation of the EAHCA. It quoted language from the U.S. Supreme Court case of *Board of Education v. Rowley* (see this volume's Appendix of U.S. Supreme Court cases): "access to specialized instruction and related services which are individually designed to provide educational benefit to the handicapped child" is the responsibility of the state educational agency.

The parents, dissatisfied with this ruling, appealed to the U.S. Court of Appeals, Eighth Circuit. The Court of Appeals agreed with the district court that under the EAHCA and *Rowley*, the state educational agency is exclusively responsible for providing an "appropriate" education to handicapped children. Thus, it was beyond the court's power to compel the school district to do something which was, strictly speaking, not the district's responsibility. Moreover, the special school district was not in a position to discriminate against the handicapped in the form of providing services to the nonhandicapped which it had failed to provide to the handicapped. The district's funds were used exclusively for the education of the handicapped. Since the primary responsibility to extend the school year for the severely handicapped children lay at the state level, the court affirmed the district court ruling. *Yaris v. Special School District of St. Louis County*, 728 F.2d 1055 (8th Cir.1984).

In the following two cases a year-round education was not granted.

In Ohio a handicapped student brought suit on behalf of himself and all handicapped students in Ohio who were allegedly not receiving a free appropriate education. Specifically, the plaintiffs argued that a local school district was obligated to provide a twelve-month program of special education for handicapped children. A U.S. district court held that the plaintiffs could not join themselves as a "class" on the question of length of the school year for the handicapped. The EAHCA was intended to encourage individualized treatment of school children and any action or inaction by the school district toward the plaintiffs could not be said to be based upon grounds having general application to a purported class. Thus, because the issue of length of the school year for the handicapped had application to possibly only a small number of the plaintiffs, nothing prevented those plaintiffs from bringing suit on their own. *Rettig v. Kent City School District*, 94 FRD 12 (N.D.Ohio 1980).

Year-round schooling was not mandated in a Virginia case which arose when the parents of a handicapped child brought suit against a local school district attacking the quality of the district's program which was provided to their child. Here, in ruling that the educational program afforded to the child was more than adequate to meet the child's needs, the court stated that the child was not entitled to year-round schooling without showing an irreparable loss of progress during summer months. *Bales v. Clarke*, 523 F.Supp. 1366 (E.D.Va.1981).

IX. Special Education for Incarcerated Children

Incarcerated children are entitled to a free appropriate education if otherwise eligible.

A twenty-one-year-old prison inmate in Massachusetts sued state education officials on behalf of himself and other inmates alleging that the failure to provide special education services to inmates who were under age twenty-two, and who had not already received a high school diploma, was a denial of a free appropriate education as required under state and federal law. A U.S. district court held that the incarcerated status of the plaintiffs did not preclude their entitlement to a free and appropriate special education under the EAHCA and state law. Accordingly, the court issued an injunction enjoining the education officials from failing to provide special education services to the plaintiffs. *Green v. Johnson*, 513 F.Supp. 965 (D.Mass.1981).

The procedural safeguards of the Education for All Handicapped Children Act are designed to ensure that parents and children are able to enforce their rights under the Act. The safeguards include the right to an "impartial due process hearing" when parents or guardians are dissatisfied with their child's IEP [section 1415(b)(2)]. These hearings are to be conducted by the state or local educational agency responsible for providing services. However, no employee of an agency involved in the education or care of the child may conduct the hearing; the hearing must be conducted by an impartial hearing officer. The initial due process hearing may be provided at the state or local educational agency level. If the initial hearing is held at the local level, either party may appeal "to the State educational agency which shall conduct an impartial review of such hearing" [section 1415(c)]. The decision of the initial hearing officer is final unless appealed; the decision of the state officer is likewise final unless either party brings an action in state court or federal district court [section 1415(e)(1)].

I. Role of The Hearing Officer

The role of the hearing officer at the initial hearing is to make an impartial decision on the appropriateness of a school's individualized educational program for a particular child. If the initial hearing decision is appealed, the reviewing officer "shall conduct an impartial review of such hearing" and "shall make an independent decision upon completion of such review" [section 1415(c)].

The Michigan Court of Appeals reversed on procedural grounds a state review officer's decision in favor of the parents of a handicapped child, citing a lack of impartiality on the part of the review officer. The court's opinion also indicated that it was displeased with the review officer's disregard of financial burdens on school districts. In this case a girl suffered a stroke at the age of ten which left her with a full scale I.Q. of forty-seven and a potential I.Q. of sixty-four (using the WISC-R schedule). When her parents approached their local school district requesting a free appropriate public education for their daughter, the district evaluated her and proposed placement in a classroom for the "educable mentally impaired." The parents disagreed and a due process hearing was held. The hearing officer, rejecting the parents' claim that the girl required a two-to-one student-teacher ratio, approved the school district's proposed EMI placement. The parents appealed to the state review officer, who exercised his statutory power to allow neither the school nor the parents to file written briefs or present oral arguments. After examining the evidence which had been presented to the hearing officer, the review officer ruled that the girl was entitled to a student-teacher ratio of not more than three to one, and the school district appealed.

The state court of appeals held that because the parents had written arguments attacking the hearing officer's decision on the appeal form they filed with the review officer, the review officer had, in effect, allowed the parents to file a written brief. The review officer had therefore been obligated to allow the school district to present its position as well. Since the review officer had improperly allowed only one side to file a brief, his decision was vacated and the case was remanded to the review officer with instructions that oral arguments be allowed.

Although the court cautioned that "[w]e do not pass on the merits as to which side should prevail," it went on to observe that the hearing officer had acted impartially and without bias. Further, although Michigan law requires that handicapped children be provided with a special education designed to maximize their potential, "[w]e believe that there is some limitation on what kind of program is required. When two competing educational programs which meet the child's requirements are evaluated, the needs of the handicapped child should be balanced with the needs of the state to allocate scarce funds among as many handicapped children as possible. . . . [A]ssuming in this case, that funds are available for two proposed educational programs, each suitable to enable the child to reach her maximum potential, it would appear reasonable to adopt the program requiring less expenditure." Having made these judicial comments, the appeals court remanded the case to the state review officer for reconsideration. *Nelson v. Southfield Public Schools*, 384 N.W.2d 423 (Mich.App.1986).

Two handicapped children in Alabama, dissatisfied with the educational plans that had been prescribed for them, sought and were afforded due process hearings. Prior to the hearings, the children, through their parents, filed written objections to the method used by the state for selecting due process hearing officers. In these written objections they alleged that the selection of hearing officers who are officers or employees of local school systems in which the children were enrolled or who were university personnel involved in the formulation of state policies concerning special education violated the EAHCA and its implementing regulations. Despite these objections, due process hearings were conducted and in each case a determination adverse to the children was reached. The children's claims were then evaluated by a review panel which was selected by the same method as the due process panel. Prior to the second hearing the children filed a second set of written objections to the method of selecting hearing officers. The review panel affirmed the adverse ruling of the due process panel and the children brought suit in federal court.

A U.S. district court enjoined the local school superintendent from selecting, as due process hearing officers under the EAHCA, individuals who are officers or employees of local school systems which the children attended, or university personnel who have been or are involved in the formulation of state policies on educating handicapped children.

The school district appealed to the U.S. Court of Appeals, Eleventh Circuit, which affirmed the district court ruling. The Court of Appeals found that officers and employees of local school boards in Alabama are employees of agencies "involved in the education and care of the child" with a personal or professional interest in the type of educational assistance extended to handicapped children, and thus are not eligible to serve on due process hearing panels under the EAHCA. Further, university personnel involved in the formulation of state policies for the education of the handicapped are not sufficiently impartial to serve as due process hearing officers under the EAHCA. *Mayson v. Teague*, 749 F.2d 652 (11th Cir.1984).

The father of a handicapped child in Georgia challenged Georgia's practice of treating the findings of hearing officers as "reports of special masters." Under the state procedures state and local boards of education had "veto power" over a hearing officer's findings, except that in the case of an initial hearing held at the local level the "party aggrieved" had the right of appeal to the state educational agency. The father brought suit against the Superintendent of the Georgia State Board of Education alleging that these practices were in violation of the EAHCA. A U.S. district court denied the father's motion for summary judgment and held in favor of the superintendent and the father appealed.

The U.S. Court of Appeals, Fifth Circuit, held that, at the local level, Georgia's practice of treating the finding of the hearing officer as a report of a "special master" conflicted with the federal EAHCA in theory but not in practice. Rejection of the officer's finding resulted in an automatic appeal. Acceptance of the officer's finding left his decision as final unless a party chose to appeal. Thus, at the local level, Georgia's procedures did not functionally violate the EAHCA. At the state level, however, the procedures were inconsistent with the requirements of the EAHCA and the Rehabilitation Act. In allowing the state board of education to exercise discretion in accepting a review officer's decision at the state level, Georgia's procedures violated federal law because at the state level, the decision of a hearing officer is final unless appealed to a state or federal court. *Helms v. McDaniel*, 657 F.2d 800 (5th Cir.1981).

A U.S. district court in Connecticut has dealt with the procedural problem of whether testimony of a hearing officer regarding her mental processes while making a decision can be allowed in a case involving an administrative determination that a minor's placement in a private residential facility was not necessary for educational reasons. The case arose on appeal of a state administrative determination to the district court. The defendant school board was excused from any financial obligation in excess of tuition costs by the administrative determination and the minor plaintiff, through his parents, appealed.

At the appeal stage the state defendants listed as their sole witness the hearing officer whose decision was being appealed. The plaintiffs moved to preclude her testimony at trial. Their motion was granted. The court noted that in reviewing a decision of an administrative agency, it is not the proper function of the court to probe the mental processes of the agency or its members, particularly if the agency makes a considered decision upon a full administrative record. Such probing should ordinarily be avoided and there must be a strong showing of bad faith or improper behavior before such inquiry may be made.

In this case, the state defendants based their opposition to the motion on the premise that the mental processes rule has little or no application in a case where the officer is testifying voluntarily and the purpose of the testimony is not to contradict or impeach the record which has already been established.

The court stated that this proposition was supported neither by logic nor authority. It went on to say that the objectivity and independence of the hearing officer in her role as administrative adjudicator would likely be undermined by her being offered by the state as a probative witness in support of its case. Cross examination and the court's assessment of the testimony would involve, necessarily, a review of the mental processes of the adjudicative officer. Such an examination of a judge would be destructive of judicial responsibility. Just as a judge's mind should not be subjected to scrutiny, so the integrity of the administrative process must be equally respected. The court, therefore, granted the motion to exclude the hearing officer's testimony. *Feller v. Board of Education of State of Connecticut*, 583 F.Supp. 1526 (D.Conn.1984).

A hearing officer is not charged with the responsibility of choosing between an educational program offered by a school district and counterproposals submitted by parents. To give the hearing officer such powers would be to diminish the role of the school districts in selecting the best possible educational program appropriate to the needs of handicapped children. This ruling was handed down by a federal district court in the District of Columbia in a case in which the parents of a handicapped child challenged District of Columbia hearing procedures. The court observed that the EAHCA calls for a due process hearing if the parents of a handicapped child object to the placement of their child in a program they deem inappropriate to the child's needs.

In this instance the parents were dissatisfied with the program offered by the school district. They asked the court to order the hearing officer to weigh the proposals of both the school and the parents and then to determine which of the two proposals was most appropriate for their child. The court refused to grant such powers to the hearing officer. Instead the court reiterated the duties of the hearing officer in such cases—the officer is required to hear the school district's proposal. If the parents are dissatisfied with that proposal they may offer alternative suggestions to the school district. If, after hearing the proposal and the counterproposals, the hearing officer deems the school district's proposal to be inadequate, the hearing officer must remand the district's proposal to the district with instructions to submit a new proposal within 20 days. Thus, the parents were not allowed to alter the meaning of the EAHCA. *Davis v. District of Columbia Board of Education*, 530 F.Supp. 1215 (D.D.C.1982).

A hearing officer in Rhode Island ordered a school district to fund the special education of two learning disabled children at a private school in Massachusetts. A U.S. district court upheld the hearing officer's order. The school district appealed claiming that because the hearing officer was an employee of the Department of Education, the hearing did not satisfy the requirement of the EAHCA that it not "be conducted by an employee of [the local or state educational] agency . . . involved in the education or care of the child."

The U.S. Court of Appeals, First Circuit, upheld the district court ruling saying that the school district was not within the "protected class" of handicapped children and their parents that Congress envisioned when it prohibited employees of a state educational agency from acting as review officers. Further, the district was foreclosed from challenging the procedural violation because throughout the proceedings it did not object to the fact that the review officer was a Department of Education employee. *Colin K. v. Schmidt*, 715 F.2d 1 (1st Cir.1983).

The parents of a developmentally disabled boy in California requested and received a hearing after both a county educational agency and a California health services organization had denied occupational therapy services to their child. The hearing officer ruled in favor of the child and his parents finding that he exhibited a lack of motor skills and required the related services of OT in order to benefit from his education. The hearing officer ordered the county to provide therapy.

The county appealed to a California superior court which denied its request to challenge the administrative decision. The county then sought relief from the California Court of Appeal arguing that the hearing was procedurally inadequate because it was conducted by one hearing officer instead of a panel of three officers in violation of California administrative regulations and further, that the health services organization should have been joined in the suit.

The court held that the California Education Code requirement that hearing be conducted "by a person knowledgeable in the laws governing special education" superseded the inconsistent administrative regulation requiring a panel of three persons. In addition, since the primary responsibility under the EAHCA for providing an education to a handicapped child is with the state education department, there was no reason for the health services organization to be joined as a party to the suit. *Nevada County Office of Education v. Superintendent of Public Instruction*, 197 Cal.Rptr. 152 (Cal.App.3d Dist.1983).

One court has held that a state agency does not have the right to appeal an unfavorable decision by an administrative hearing officer. In this case the Hawaii Department of Education appealed from a Hawaii trial court order dismissing its appeal of a hearing officer's decision. The appeal was prompted by the decision and order of an administrative hearing officer in favor of the parents of a handicapped student who had complained that the Department had not provided him with a free appropriate public education as required by the EAHCA.

The Supreme Court of Hawaii held that under the EAHCA the Department was not entitled to appeal from the administrative decision. Section

1415(e)(2) of the Act provides only that "any party aggrieved by the findings and decision made pursuant to the hearing process may bring a separate civil action in a state or federal district court." The court noted that the standard of review in such an action "is very different" from the standard of review in an appeal. This was discussed in the case of *Board of Education v. Rowley*, where the U.S. Supreme Court stated that in an appeal, the court's inquiry in suits brought under the EAHCA is twofold. First, how has the State complied with the procedures set forth in the Act? Second, is the individualized educational program developed through the Act's procedures reasonably calculated to enable the child to receive educational benefits? If these requirements are met, the State has complied with the obligations imposed by Congress and the courts can require no more. In a separate civil action the state court or federal district court "shall receive the records of the administrative proceedings, shall hear additional evidence at the request of a party and, basing its decision on the preponderance of the evidence, shall grant such relief as the court determines appropriate." The court concluded that the EAHCA did not confer the right of appeal upon state agencies. The district court's dismissal of the appeal was reversed, however, on the ground that a claim for relief in a separate civil action was presented, even though misdesignated on appeal. *Matter of Eric G.*, 649 P.2d 1140 (Hawaii 1982).

The California Court of Appeal was asked to decide whether a school district should have sought review of a hearing officer's decision pursuant to the federal EAHCA or by way of state administrative remedies. In this case involving a hearing officer's determination that a handicapped child should be placed in a full-time residential environment, the school district pursued the less expensive state administrative appeal procedures rather than bringing a separate civil action under the EAHCA in a state or federal court.

The school district then asked a California trial court to review the hearing officer's decision and issue an order commanding the state department of education to set it aside. The court granted the district's request but later ordered the school district to place the child at the residential school requested by the mother or in "any other appropriate twenty-four hour residential program selected by the [district]." The child refused placement in a residential school other than the one requested. Both the mother of the child and the California State Department of Education appealed arguing that the school district pursued the incorrect procedures to challenge the hearing officer's final decision.

The Court of Appeal found it unnecessary to decide which method of appeal was proper for two reasons. First, the child was not a party "aggrieved" by the administrative decision and therefore could not, under the express language of section 1415(e)(2) of the EAHCA bring a civil action. Also, he never objected to the district's use of the state administrative procedure at the trial, and thereby waived any right to complain of it on appeal. In addition, the child suffered no demonstrable prejudice from the more restrictive standard of review utilized in the state administrative procedure.

Second, the Department was neither an "aggrieved party" under the Act, nor, like the child, did it suffer prejudice from the use of that method of review. However, the court expressed a clear preference for the use of the appeal procedures set out in section 1415(e)(2) of the EAHCA, particularly where state review procedures, as in California, provide lesser protection or a more limited scope of review to the party aggrieved. Using the "substantial evidence" test as required by California state administrative procedure, rather than the "preponderance of the evidence" test as outlined in the EAHCA, the court concluded that substantial evidence warranted the child's placement in a full-time residential setting. *San Francisco Unified School District v. State*, 182 Cal.Rptr. 525 (Cal.App.1st Dist.1982).

II. Change in Placement

Recognizing that a school district's unfettered discretion to change a handicapped child's placement could result in a denial of a free appropriate education to the child, section 1415(b)(1)(C) of the EAHCA requires that prior written notice of any proposed change in the educational placement of a child be afforded to the parents or guardians of the child. A hearing must also be granted to parents wishing to contest a change in placement of their child.

A U.S. district court in Ohio issued a preliminary injunction ordering that two violently disruptive students, ages twelve and fifteen, be allowed to return to their classrooms. Both boys, wards of the state, had been evaluated as severely behaviorally handicapped (SBH) and were placed in a residential facility. The local school district conducted classes at the facility to provide the students with an appropriate education under the Education for All Handicapped Children Act. During the 1983-84 school year the boys were involved in several episodes of destructive and violent classroom behavior at the residential facility.

The school district decided that for the 1984-85 school year it would conduct the SBH classes at a regular school building. During the first week of classes the fifteen-year-old boy violently attacked another student and began throwing books and a ruler around his classroom; the twelve-year-old boy, after telling his teacher, "I'm going to kick your ass," picked up a plastic baseball bat and generally destroyed the classroom. As a result of these incidents the school district removed the students from the SBH classes and instead provided the boys with one hour per day of personalized tutoring at the residential facility. The school district then caused the boys to be prosecuted for their misbehavior and each was adjudged delinquent under Ohio law.

The boys brought suit against the school district in federal court claiming that the school district had violated the provisions of the EAHCA by changing their placement. The EAHCA provides that whenever a school district proposes to change a child's educational placement there must be a hearing before an impartial hearing officer and, most importantly, that during the pendency of these proceedings the child must remain in his then current educational placement unless the child or his guardian agrees to a change in placement. The school district argued that because of their behavior the boys presented a danger to themselves and others, and that their education could not be safely continued even in an SBH class.

The district court rejected this reasoning and granted a preliminary injunction directing that the students be allowed to return to the SBH classroom. The court was disturbed that the school district had not bothered to use its normal disciplinary procedures, which included a one to two week suspension or expulsion, before it decided to prosecute the boys and change their educational placements. Such action "is not perceived to be wholly in keeping with the spirit and purpose of the EAHCA." The court further held that although the students must be allowed to return to their classroom, and thus to their "then current" educational placements as required by the EAHCA, the school district would not be precluded from using normal disciplinary procedures to deal with any future disruptive conduct by the students. *Lamont X v. Quisenberry*, 606 F.Supp. 809 (S.D.Ohio 1984).

A U.S. district court has ruled that the party who proposes to change the placement of a handicapped child must bear the burden of proof in demonstrating the propriety of such a change. This case arose when a Georgia school district proposed to change a child's residential school placement to placement in a self-contained learning disabilities classroom in the county school district. The district had placed the boy in a residential facility under his individualized educational program and had paid all costs associated with his attendance there since 1979. However, in June 1982, the district reevaluated the boy and recommended a change from residential placement to special class placement in a regular school system. The child's parents objected to this change and two administrative hearings were held. The parents then brought suit in U.S. district court challenging the standard of proof used in the hearings. While stating that it would not address the results of the administrative hearings, the court agreed to order that the school district should bear the burden of proof in the administrative hearings. This was due to the fact that the school district was the party seeking to change the boy's placement. The residential placement, which had been previously agreed to by both the school and the boy's parents, was therefore presumed to be the child's appropriate placement under the EAHCA until the school district was able to prove otherwise. *Burger v. Murray County School District*, 612 F.Supp. 434 (N.D.Ga.1984).

The parents of a handicapped child brought a complaint against their Massachusetts school district after a privately-run after-school day care program refused to continue accepting their child. The parents alleged that the school district had deprived them of due process by failing to notify them in advance of this so-called change in placement. After the Massachusetts Bureau of Special Education Appeals ruled in favor of the parents, the school district appealed to the federal district court arguing that it had not changed the child's placement. Here, the child's IEP had included two afternoons per week at a BASS program, and three afternoons per week at a private day care center located at Driscoll Public School. Unfortunately, the following fall the day care center decided that the child was too old to attend. The parents then requested of school officials that he be allowed to attend the BASS program five days per week. The school responded by proposing that the child attend the BASS program three days per week and spend the remaining two days at an individualized public school program at the Driscoll Public School. The one-on-one aides for the child while at the Driscoll public school program would be the same persons who were involved in Driscoll's private program.

The district court ruled that such a minor alteration in the child's program (the change from two days at BASS and three days at Driscoll to three days at BASS and two days at Driscoll) was not a "change in educational placement" under section 1415(e)(2) of the EAHCA. This was especially true where the private day care group, which was composed of parents at the Driscoll school, was the entity responsible for the change in the child's schedule. Because no change in placement had occurred, the school district had been under no duty to notify the parents. The court reversed the Bureau of Special Education Appeals and ruled in the school's favor. *Brookline School Committee v. Golden*, 628 F.Supp. 113 (D.Mass.1986).

A Florida high school student who was handicapped by a special learning disability brought suit against a local school district under the Education for All Handicapped Children Act and the Rehabilitation Act alleging that her involuntary transfer from high school to an alternative learning center violated her right to a publicly financed appropriate special education. The student requested a preliminary injunction to allow her to attend high school during pendency of the proceedings. A U.S. district court denied the student's request and she appealed to the U.S. Court of Appeals, Eleventh Circuit, arguing that 1) the hearing officer who upheld the decision to transfer her denied her the right to direct lay representation in the administrative proceedings by refusing to allow the student's friend, a legal and educational layman, to present her case and examine witnesses; 2) that the record of the administrative proceedings contained uncontested evidence that the school district violated her procedural right to remain in the high school during the pendency of the action as guaranteed by the EAHCA; and 3) that neither the hearing officer nor the district judge determined whether the alternative learning center was the least restrictive environment in which she could be educated.

The Court of Appeals held that the Rehabilitation Act was not the appropriate provision under which to bring suit since the EAHCA provides the exclusive avenue for asserting rights to a publicly financed special education. Further, the student had no right to direct lay representation in the administrative proceedings. The EAHCA creates no such right. The EAHCA states that a complainant has a right "to be accompanied and advised by counsel and by individuals with special knowledge or training with respect to the problems of handicapped children." The hearing officer's examination of the student's chosen representative revealed his almost complete ignorance of state administrative procedure. Thus, the hearing officer did not violate the EAHCA in limiting his role to offering advice.

Further, the uncontradicted evidence left no doubt that the student's behavior at the high school posed a threat to both students and school officials. Thus, the court found that the school district properly exercised its authority to transfer the student to the alternative learning center and the district did not violate her procedural rights to remain in the high school during the pendency of the action. Finally, the court held that because the student introduced no evidence that the proposed placement was inappropriate or that a less restrictive environment existed in which she could receive the special education she needed, the proposed placement was deemed appropriate. *Victoria L. v. District School Board of Lee County, Florida*, 741 F.2d 369 (11th Cir.1984).

Two other cases have addressed the issue of whether changes in the individualized educational program of handicapped children constituted a "change in educational placement" triggering the procedural safeguards of the EAHCA.

In the first case the U.S. Court of Appeals, Third Circuit, held that a change in the method of transportation of a severely handicapped child to and from school did not constitute a "change in educational placement." A Pennsylvania school district changed the method of transportation from a system whereby the child's parents were reimbursed for their expenses in driving the child to school to a "combined run" involving other children and a small increase in travel time. The parents objected to the combined run on the ground that the increase in transportation time would be detrimental to the child's education. The school district denied the parents a due process hearing because it did not consider the change in transportation to be a "change in educational placement."

The Court of Appeals agreed, finding that the change in the method of transporting the child did not constitute a "change in educational placement" under the EAHCA and thus could be implemented without a prior due process hearing. It is clear, said the court, that the "stay put" provision under the EAHCA does not entitle parents to demand a hearing when minor administrative decisions alter the school day of their children. The question is whether the school district's decision is likely to affect in some significant way a child's learning experience. Here, the parents' objections were merely speculative. *DeLeon v. Susquehanna Community School District*, 747 F.2d 149 (3d Cir.1984).

In the second case, the U.S. Court of Appeals, District of Columbia Circuit, held that a change in the feeding program that a profoundly handicapped child would receive as a result of a transfer from a private hospital to a government-run institution did not constitute a "change in educational placement" within the meaning of the notice and hearing provisions of the EAHCA. The child's guardian brought suit against the District of Columbia Board of Education alleging that the change in residence from the private hospital at which the child had been placed to a government-run institution where the child would live but continue to receive a day education at the private hospital, constituted a "change in educational placement" triggering the requirement of a due process hearing. The guardian specifically alleged that differences in the feeding programs of the private hospital and the public institution constituted a sufficient change in the child's individual education program to warrant the child's retention in the private hospital until resolution of the matter.

The Court of Appeals disagreed, finding that an individual voicing objections to a handicapped child's educational program must identify, at a minimum, a fundamental change in, or the elimination of, a basic element of the education program in order for the change to qualify as a change in educational placement. Here, although the child's transfer from one facility to another was decidedly a "change in placement," it was not alone sufficient to constitute a change in educational placement requiring the board of education to keep the child at the private hospital or a comparable facility until the hearings were completed. A move from a "mainstream" program to one consisting only of handicapped students, said the court, would constitute a change in educational placement; a move from one mainstream program to another, with the elimination, for instance, of a theater arts class, would not be such a change. Here, the board of education, using the residential services of the public institution and the out-patient education program of the private hospital, had fulfilled its obligation under the EAHCA to maintain the child's educational placement pending the resolution of any complaint proceedings brought on the child's behalf. Thus, the Court of Appeals held that the child could be discharged from the private hospital prior to his guardian's consent and prior to a hearing. *Lunceford v. District of Columbia Board of Education*, 745 F.2d 1577 (D.C.Cir.1984).

In Massachusetts, parents of an eleven-year-old boy who suffered from acquired encephalopathy challenged in U.S. district court a proposed change in their son's educational placement. For seven years the child had attended a special education center for brain-injured children. This center offered special teaching techniques which would not be available to the child at the new location. The parents argued that the transfer of their child from the center to the new program would halt his progress and cause him to regress. In deciding whether the placement change was appropriate, the court relied on language set forth by the U.S. Supreme Court in *Board of Education v. Rowley*. That case held that handicapped children are to be provided a "basic floor of opportunity" and that educational services must be sufficient to confer some educational benefit upon them. Here, the court stated that the relative validity of the differing techniques used by the two institutes was a matter of dispute among special education experts. In light of the court's unwillingness to make educational policy and insufficient evidence that the child would regress at the new institute, the court refused to hold that the change of placement would be inappropriate. Judgment was rendered in favor of the school district. *Doe v. Lawson*, 579 F.Supp. 1314 (D.Mass.1984).

In a Rhode Island case, the mother of a handicapped child, enrolled in public school in accordance with an individualized education program, brought suit against the school district to prevent it from making a second educational assessment of her child. The school district had based the boy's IEP on an evaluation conducted by a private school formerly attended by the child. The mother maintained that the assessment sought by the school district would constitute an original evaluation and, therefore, the school was barred from conducting it without her cooperation. The school district contended that its assessment would be a re-evaluation and under the law, a parent's consent was unnecessary. It further stated that any such change in placement resulting from the re-evaluation would be subject to challenge by the parent in a statutorily mandated hearing. The court agreed with the school district's position, stating that the private school assessment on which the IEP was based did legitimately constitute an original pre-placement evaluation. The mother's motion for partial summary judgment was denied and the case was dismissed. *Carroll v. Capalbo*, 563 F.Supp. 1053 (D.R.I.1983).

A dispute in Missouri resulted in a U.S. district court determination that the proposed transfer of an eleven-year-old girl with cerebral palsy from a traditional elementary school to an elementary school specially designed to meet the needs of handicapped children did not violate the EAHCA. The mother brought suit against the school district which proposed the transfer alleging that her daughter was denied a free appropriate education in the least restrictive environment without due process of law. The court was persuaded that the child could not receive a satisfactory education in the traditional school, even with the use of supplementary aids and services to the maximum extent possible. Further, the mother had exhausted all of the administrative remedies available to her. Thus, the mother's due process claim was without merit because she had been afforded and had availed herself of every procedural safeguard of the EAHCA. In addition, the court held that the mother's equal protection claim asserted on behalf of her child was unfounded, because there was no showing that the child was treated any differently from other handicapped children who were being evaluated by procedures mandated by state and federal law. *Johnston v. Ann Arbor Public Schools*, 569 F.Supp. 1502 (E.D.Mich.1983).

The Supreme Judicial Court of Massachusetts held that the decision to graduate a child with special education needs is a "change in placement," triggering mandatory procedural safeguards included in the Education for All Handicapped Children Act. In this case a twenty-one-year-old male suffering from multiple cognitive and motor disabilities, emotional and behavioral difficulties, and also confined to a wheelchair, brought suit against a Massachusetts school district alleging that his graduation, which terminated his right to special education services, violated the procedural provisions of the EAHCA.

In the fall of 1980, the boy's teachers had met to formulate his individualized education plan for the 1980-81 school year. The teachers agreed that the child was to graduate at the end of the school year, although his IEP did not state this. Neither the student nor his parents were invited to the meeting at which this decision was made. The student signed the IEP but the parents did not. At no time were the parents provided formal, written notice of their right to challenge the IEP or of the procedural avenues open to them to make that challenge. Neither were they told that graduation would terminate their son's eligibility for special education services. In June, 1981, the boy was presented with a high school diploma; his eligibility for special education services was thereby terminated. In the time between the student's graduation and the commencement of this lawsuit, no special education services were afforded to the boy. Evidence showed that he failed to adapt either to sheltered workshops or independent living settings. Furthermore, at the time of the lawsuit, the boy was hospitalized in a chronic care unit.

The Massachusetts Supreme Judicial Court reversed a lower court summary judgment ruling in favor of the school district, holding that the failure to provide to the parents a formal, written notice concerning the decision to graduate the student, the failure to provide notice regarding the rights of the parents to involvement in that decision and the failure to notify them of their rights to a hearing and administrative review violated state and federal statutory law. This was true even though the parents had actual notice of the student's graduation and had participated to a limited extent in the transitional planning surrounding the graduation, and even though the student signed the IEP. *Stock v. Massachusetts Hospital School*, 467 N.E.2d 448 (Mass.1984).

Does a school closing constitute a "change in placement" for purposes of the EAHCA? This was the question before the New York Supreme Court after a local school district and concerned parents of handicapped students objected to the New York City Board of Education's refusal to renew its contract with a special school on the ground of claimed financial mismanagement. The board had conducted an audit of the school and discovered that large sums of money were being misspent and that serious educational deficiencies existed in the programs offered. Upon termination of the contract with the school, the Board of Education offered an alternative "location" for the majority of the students and was seeking placement for the balance. The school district and the parents argued that the placement of the handicapped children from one school to another involved a change in educational placement which triggered the requirement of a court order preventing the immediate closing of the school.

The court disagreed with this position, holding that a change of school is not *per se* a change in educational placement of a handicapped student. Further, for the court to order a temporary stay of the school closing, the students must show irreparable injury resulting from the closing. This could be shown by demonstrating the educational uniqueness of the school or by showing that another school would not similarly aid such students. No such potential injury was shown. Thus, although it is conceivable that the placement of a child from one school to another may involve a change in educational placement within the meaning of the EAHCA which would then trigger the requirement of an order preventing the immediate closing of a school, no sufficient proof of the required irreparable injury to the student was shown. Also, there is no right in a school district for such an order. *Cohen v. Board of Education of City of New York*, 454 N.Y.S.2d 630 (Sup.Ct.1982).

A case arising from the same school closure as in the above case was also decided in the federal courts. As in that case, the parents and guardians of several handicapped children brought suit against New York City education officials alleging that the Board of Education's transfer of their children after the closing of the special school constituted a change in educational placement. The parents claimed that the alternate school sites in which their children were placed were not meeting the children's needs. The court held that the transfers did not constitute a change in placement for purposes of the EAHCA. The court dismissed the parents' suit saying that although school boards do not possess unfettered power to close schools and transfer students, they must be permitted to make independent determinations as to the suitability of private schools to educate handicapped children and manage finances without providing a due process forum to parents. *Dima v. Macchirola*, 513 F.Supp. 565 (E.D.N.Y.1981).

III. Suspension and Expulsion of Handicapped Students

Whether suspension or expulsion of handicapped students from school constitutes a "change in placement" for purposes of the EAHCA is an issue which has been presented before the courts. Generally, definite-term suspensions (preferably ten days or less) are not viewed as creating a change in placement for purposes of the EAHCA. Indefinite suspensions, however, as

well as expulsions, do constitute a change in placement triggering the EAHCA's procedural safeguards. Furthermore, generally where a student's misbehavior is caused by his or her handicap, any attempt to expel the student from school will be turned aside by the courts.

A fourteen-year-old Virginia boy who had been identified by his school district as having a serious learning disability was suspended from school in March, 1983. The boy had acted as a middleman for two nonhandicapped girls who desired to buy "speed" from another student. He made no money doing this and took no drugs himself. The boy was suspended, but during his suspension the school district's committee on the handicapped held proceedings which culminated in the determination that the boy's handicap was not the cause of his involvement with drugs. The school board then voted to expel the boy for the remainder of the school year. One month later the parents requested and received a due process hearing pursuant to the Education for All Handicapped Children Act, at which the hearing examiner ordered the expulsion reversed because he found that the boy's misbehavior was related to his learning disability. A state reviewing officer affirmed this decision.

The school board then filed suit in U.S. district court contending that in situations like this, the EAHCA allows expulsions without review. The district court dismissed the school board's complaint and the U.S. Court of Appeals, Fourth Circuit, affirmed. The appeals court noted that it is settled law that any expulsion of a handicapped student is a "change in placement" for EAHCA purposes, triggering the Act's procedural safeguards. Also, the district court's determination that the boy's involvement in drug sales was caused by his handicap would not be overturned on appeal unless it was "clearly erroneous." The dismissal of the school board's complaint was therefore affirmed. *School Board of Prince County v. Malone*, 762 F.2d 1210 (4th Cir.1985).

In 1978, a handicapped girl obtained a preliminary injunction from a federal district court in Connecticut which prevented her school board from expelling her from high school. The board was also ordered to conduct an immediate review of her individualized educational program under the Education for All Handicapped Children Act. The girl's class action suit continued in district court for the next five years, with the girl seeking a declaratory judgment that the school board "was bound by the procedural requirements of the EAHCA if it desired to exclude a handicapped student from class attendance for longer than a ten day period." In 1984, the class action suit was dismissed because the girl graduated and was no longer a member of the class she purported to represent. She then petitioned the district court for an award of attorney's fees pursuant to section 1988 of the Civil Rights Act.

The court, while noting that attorney's fees are rarely justified in cases involving the EAHCA, ordered the school board and state department of education to pay the full amount of the girl's attorneys' fees ($57,631). Although plaintiffs in EAHCA cases often allege violations of the Civil Rights Act, the U.S. Supreme Court held in *Smith v. Robinson*, 104 S.Ct. 3457 (1984), that substantive claims made under the EAHCA will not justify the use of section 1988 as a basis for attorneys' fees. The Supreme Court held, however, that where a plaintiff is successful in proving that a school board or other state entity has deprived the plaintiff of procedural protections, attorney's fees may be awarded. In the present case, the girl proved that the board, by excluding her from class attendance for longer than a ten day period, had failed to provide her with the procedural safeguards mandated by the EAHCA. These procedural violations gave rise to an award of attorneys' fees under section 1988 of the Civil Rights Act, and the court ordered that the school board, as the primary party at fault, pay 80% of the award and that the state department of education pay 20%. *Stuart v. Nappi*, 610 F.Supp. 90 (D.Conn.1985).

In a Mississippi case, a student's sexual misconduct prevented his return to the classroom. Here a behaviorally handicapped student admitted to school officials that while in a special education class he had unbuttoned a girl's blouse and touched her breast. As a result, the school suspended him for three days and he was sent before the County Youth Court. Because this was the boy's third instance of school-related sexual misconduct, the Youth Court sent him to a state hospital for one month of treatment. After he lived at home for seven months following his hospitalization, the boy's mother sought to re-enroll him at his school under his former individualized educational program. However, school officials claimed that the old IEP was inapplicable in light of the boy's continuing sexual misconduct and proposed that he be placed in a closely supervised group home.

The boy's mother then brought suit in U.S. district court seeking a preliminary injunction to compel school officials to allow her son to attend class under his former IEP. The court ruled in favor of the school district, noting that in order to grant a preliminary injunction there must be an immediate threat of irreparable harm to the plaintiff. However, in this case the boy's mother had delayed for seven months before seeking to once again enroll her son in the school. Also, school officials had evidenced a genuine concern for the boy's welfare by offering to provide home tutoring during the time in which a new appropriate IEP could be formulated. The court held that because the boy had neither a current IEP nor a current educational placement, and because of the danger that he presented to others, there were insufficient grounds to order that he be returned to the classroom.

On appeal by the boy's mother, the U.S. Court of Appeals, Fifth Circuit, affirmed the district court, holding that when a handicapped student presents a substantial danger to himself or others, immediate removal from the classroom may be justified. The school's decision to provide the boy with home tutoring was upheld. *Jackson v. Franklin County School Board*, 765 F.2d 535 (5th Cir.1985).

In an Illinois case when a seventeen-year-old "exceptional" child told his teacher, "I'm not serving your fucking detention. Fuck you," he was promptly suspended for five days. His parents contested the suspension and he was given a hearing at which an impartial hearing officer upheld the suspension. On appeal to the Department of Education, the State Superintendent of Education overturned the suspension saying that the child's emotional outburst was evidence that the system had misplaced this child in a class setting too advanced. The school district appealed to a U.S. district court, which reversed the State Superintendent's decision. The court stated that if the seventeen-year-old had managed to complete eleven years of education and had advanced to the point where he was placed in a mainstream educational course, it was nonsense to suggest that his shameful outburst was somehow the fault of the system. The child knew, or should have known, that his behavior was unacceptable. Further, the court pointed to the U.S. Supreme Court decision *Goss v. Lopez*, 419 U.S. 565 (1975), which held that "suspension is considered not only to be a necessary tool to maintain order but a valuable educational device." The court concluded by noting that a five-day suspension should not be equated to expulsion or termination, and that federal law permits the enforcement of ordinary classroom discipline through such suspensions. *Board of Education of the City of Peoria, School District 150 v. Illinois State Board of Education*, 531 F.Supp. 148 (C.D.Ill.1982).

In a Minnesota case involving the suspension of a handicapped student, the mother of an eighth grader challenged a fifteen-day suspension of her child. The mother contended that the disciplinary procedures utilized by the school district in suspending her child were unlawful. The student had been suspended for fifteen days following an informal conference in the assistant principal's office as required by the U.S. Supreme Court case *Goss v. Lopez*. A "notice of formal suspension" was delivered to the child's mother along with a homebound readmission plan which involved homework to be completed by the child. At the time the child was suspended she was the subject of an ongoing "formal educational assessment," but she was not being treated at that time as a special education student or handicapped child by the school system.

The child's mother sued the school district arguing that because school officials, at the time of the child's suspension, perceived the girl as a handicapped student, a more formal hearing than the informal *Goss v. Lopez* conference was warranted because of the child's handicapped status. The mother also objected to the school system's practice of providing homework as the sole "alternative program" to students suspended for more than five days. Finally, the mother claimed that her child had been denied due process of the law. The mother pointed out that the informal hearing mandated by *Goss v. Lopez* was applicable only to suspensions of ten days or less and, as the suspension involved here exceeded ten days, more formal hearing procedures should have been implemented.

A U.S. district court that under the Minnesota Pupil Fair Dismissal Act, which is essentially a codification of *Goss v. Lopez*, there is no necessity for the school system to provide a formal hearing process in the suspension of a child when the suspension is for five days or less. However, when a school suspends a student for more than five days or extends a five day suspension the student is to be provided a separate informal adminstrative conference involving the parents. The court also found that the supervised homework plan provided to the child satisfied the requirement of Minnesota education law that "an alternative program" be provided suspended students.

Finally, to the mother's argument that school officials realized or should have realized that the child, in light of her emotional difficulties, was a handicapped student as that term is defined in section 1401(1) of the EAHCA, the court stated that the school system was under no obligation at the time of the suspension to treat the student as a handicapped child. To impose a duty on school districts to handle a child as handicapped on the mere suspicions of school officials would be inconsistent with federal law governing the initial classification of children as handicapped students, said the court. A school system's duty to a handicapped child formally begins only after the completion of the assessment and identification process. However, because the court found that the suspension violated the Minnesota Pupil Fair Dismissal Act, the student was granted a declaratory judgment that the fifteen-day suspension was unlawful under state law. The student was entitled to have any reference to the suspension expunged from her school records. *Mrs. A.J. v. Special School District No. 1*, 478 F.Supp. 418 (D.Minn.1979).

The following case illustrates that a suspension can constitute a "change in placement" if it is to last for an indefinite period. Here a school for the blind in New York suspended a deaf, blind and emotionally disturbed residential student who engaged in persistent self-abusive behavior. The reason for the suspension was that the school lacked the staff to supervise the fourteen-year-old girl, who needed to be watched continually. Without the proper supervisory staff the girl was a danger to herself. In fact, at one time during her enrollment at the school the girl had to be hospitalized because of self-inflicted injuries. The suspension was to last "until such time it appeared to be in the best interests of the child and the school to revoke the suspension." The student's mother brought suit against the school to compel it to reinstate her daughter as a residential student and to force it to provide a hearing in compliance with the EAHCA. Shortly after the suit was commenced the girl was reinstated in the school and the school argued that the mother's claim was then moot.

The U.S. district court disagreed with the school's claim, saying that the actions of the school were unlawful. The court observed that the time during which the child had been hospitalized as a result of self-inflicted injuries stemming from her self-abusive behavior did not constitute a "change in placement" triggering procedural safeguards. However, the indefinite suspension period which was to last until such time as "it appeared to be in the best interests of the child and the school to revoke the suspension" was unlawful within the meaning of the EAHCA. The indefinite suspension constituted a "change in placement" within the meaning of the EAHCA and thus required a hearing. *Sherry v. New York State Education Department*, 479 F.Supp. 1328 (W.D.N.Y.1979).

The following cases illustrate that expulsions are not viewed in the same light as suspensions. Expulsions trigger the procedural safeguards of the EAHCA and require a showing that the behavior leading to the expulsion was not the result of an expelled child's handicap.

A Kentucky case arose after a fifteen-year-old ninth grade student, identified and evaluated since kindergarten as a handicapped or exceptional child, defied the authority of his teacher. He refused to do assigned work, destroyed a worksheet, destroyed a coffee cup, and pushed and kicked the teacher while leaving the classroom. The following day the child was suspended. A hearing regarding the suspension was held by the school board which did not convene nor consult the Administrative Admissions and Release Committee (AARC), a multi-disciplined group which, in Kentucky, is the organization responsible for reviewing challenged placement decisions. In addition, the board did not address the relationship, if any, between the child's handicap and his disruptive behavior. Expulsion followed. The child, through his parents, then sought legal help in the federal courts.

The U.S. Court of Appeals, Sixth Circuit, affirmed a U.S. district court decision which held than an expulsion from school is a "change of placement" within the meaning of Education for All Handicapped Children Act, thus requiring certain procedural protections prior to expulsion. The Court of Appeals also determined that an expulsion must be accompanied by a determination as to whether the handicapped student's misconduct bears a relationship to his handicap. The lower court injunction requiring the expungment of expulsion records from the board minutes and school attendance records was upheld. *Kaelin v. Grubbs*, 682 F.2d 595 (6th Cir.1982).

The Nebraska Supreme Court has held that the expulsion of a disruptive handicapped student violated the EAHCA. In this case a student expelled for disruptive behavior from a school for the trainable mentally retarded was found by the court to have been denied a free appropriate education. After the expulsion the student, who suffered from autism, mental retardation and epilepsy, was placed in regional institutions by his parents. While in the institutions, many of the skills the child previously learned were lost, but the school district made no attempt to relocate the student. The Nebraska Supreme Court held that the expulsion constituted a change in placement which was subject to the procedural protections of the Education for All Handicapped Children Act. It further stated that under the Act, local school officials are prohibited from expelling students whose handicaps are the cause for their disruptive behavior. The school's only course of action in such circumstances is to transfer the disruptive student to an appropriate, more restrictive environment. The court ordered that the school district reimburse the parents for the cost incurred in the institutionalization of their child. *Adams Central School District No. 690 v. Deist*, 334 N.W.2d 775 (Neb.1983).

In a similar case arising in Indiana, the mother of a handicapped child sued a local school district challenging the child's expulsion from school. The child had been expelled for disciplinary reasons. The mother brought suit against the school district in U.S. district court which held that the school was prohibited from expelling students whose handicaps caused them to be disruptive, but was allowed to transfer the disruptive student to an appropriate, more restrictive environment.

The court noted that the EAHCA does not prohibit all expulsions of disruptive handicapped children. It only prohibits the expulsion of handicapped children who are disruptive because of their handicap. The distinction between a handicapped child and any other child is that, unlike any other disruptive child, before a disruptive handicapped child can be expelled, it must be determined whether the handicap is the cause of the child's disruptiveness. This must be determined through the change of placement procedures required by the EAHCA. In this case the school district was found to have violated the due process provisions of EAHCA when it expelled the student without first determining whether his propensity to disrupt was the result of his inappropriate placement.

The court, however, found no equal protection claim under the U.S. Constitition. To the student's argument that handicapped students are in greater need of education and thus should be considered a class of persons entitled to heightened protection under the U.S. Constitution's Equal Protection Clause, the court said that the Equal Protection Clause does not require a state to guarantee more education to students with a greater need of an education. Rather, the Equal Protection Clause requires a state to guarantee an equal educational opportunity to all students. Thus, a handicapped student can be subjected to the same disciplinary expulsions as other students, with the restriction that the behavior leading to the expulsion must not have stemmed from the child's handicap. *Doe v. Koger*, 480 F.Supp. 225 (N.D.Ind.1979).

A student in Connecticut was suspended and subsequently expelled from school following her participation in a series of school-wide disturbances. The student, who had been determined to be suffering from a learning disability as well as an emotional disturbance, had a history of defiant behavior. It was unclear as to whether a portion of the child's problem in school was attributable to the school's apparent failure to schedule the student properly or from the student's refusal to attend the special education program provided to her. The decision to expel her prompted the student to seek a preliminary injunction in a U.S. district court to prevent the school district from enforcing the expulsion.

The court granted the injunction, saying that the probable consequence of her expulsion would be irreparable injury to the student. If the student were to be expelled, she would be without any educational program from the date of her expulsion until such time as another official review of her handicap was held and an appropriate educational program developed. The court, concerned that a lengthy period of time might elapse before the student would be provided the special education to which she was entitled, was reluctant to deny the student's request for an injunction.

The second irreparable injury which the court feared the student would suffer was the exclusion from any special education programs offered in the public school system. If expelled, the student would be restricted to placement in a private school or to a homebound tutoring program, regardless of whether these two alternatives would be responsive to the student's needs. In granting the student's request for an injunction, the court noted that handicapped children are neither immune from a school's disciplinary process nor entitled to participate in programs when their behavior impairs the education of other children in a program. However, school authorities have other disciplinary measures at their disposal such as suspension. A school can also request a change in placement of handicapped children who have demonstrated that their present placement is inappropriate. *Stuart v. Nappi*, 443 F.Supp. 1235 (D.Conn.1978).

A U.S. district court in Florida granted a preliminary injunction against state and local school officials preventing them from enforcing the expulsion of nine handicapped students. The students, expelled for alleged misconduct, were all classified as "educable mentally retarded," "mildly mentally retarded," or "EMR/dull normal." The Florida school district which had expelled the students did so on the ground that the students knew right from wrong.

The students, through their parents, brought suit against the school district alleging they were denied a free appropriate education under the EAHCA as a result of their expulsions. The district court agreed with the students finding that under section 504 of the Rehabilitation Act and the EAHCA, no handicapped student could be expelled for misconduct related to the handicap. The court found that no determination was ever made of the relationship between the students' handicaps and their behavioral problems. The court also found that an expulsion is a change in educational placement. The students' request for an injunction was granted.

The school district appealed to the U.S. Court of Appeals, Fifth Circuit, which affirmed the district court ruling. The Court of Appeals held that the determination that a handicapped student knows the difference between right and wrong is not sufficient to support a determination that his misconduct was or was not a manifestation of his handicap. Neither is a determination that a handicapped student's misconduct can never be a symptom of his handicap unless he is classified as seriously emotionally disturbed. Only a trained, knowledgeable group of persons should determine whether a student's misconduct bears a relationship to his handicapping condition. Because no such determination was made in this case, the court found the expulsion of the nine students to have constituted a change in placement invoking the procedural protections of the EAHCA and section 504 of the Rehabilitation Act. *S-1 v. Turlington*, 635 F.2d 342 (5th Cir.1981).

IV. Exhaustion of Administrative Remedies

The doctrine of exhaustion of remedies provides that "no one is entitled to judicial relief for a supposed or threatened injury until the prescribed administrative remedy has been exhausted." This was pointed out by the U.S. Supreme Court in the case of *Myers v. Bethlehem Shipbuilding Corp.*, 303 U.S. 41 (1938). The reasons supporting the exhaustion of remedies doctrine were advanced in a later Supreme Court case, *McKart v. U.S.*, 395 U.S. 185(1968). Among the reasons given were the development of an accurate factual record, thus allowing more informed judicial review, encouraging "expeditious decision making," and furthering Congressional intent.

A. Operation of the Exhaustion Doctrine

Section 1415 of the EAHCA provides for an initial independent review of a contested IEP at the agency level. Section 1415(e)(2) provides that an "aggrieved party" may bring a separate civil action in state or federal court to challenge the final decision of a state educational agency. Normally the parents or guardians of a handicapped child have the duty to exhaust all administrative channels before resorting to a state or federal court. However, some courts have excused the "exhaustion" requirement under certain exceptional circumstances.

In a New York case, an eleven-year-old handicapped student who was transferred by his school district to a special school for disabled students objected to the transfer because it separated him from his former classmates and friends. The student claimed that the school district could have reasonably made his original school accessible and, through reasonable accommodation, could have permitted him to attend that school. The New York Supreme Court was requested by the student and his parents to issue an injunction compelling the school district to reverse its transfer decision and to return the child to his original school. The school district argued that the student had not exhausted his administrative remedies, a prerequisite of the Education for All Handicapped Children Act for requesting judicial relief. The court agreed, finding that the injunction requested by the student was not proper until the administrative remedies provided by the EAHCA were fully pursued.

In its ruling the court stated: "Congress intended that the complaints of . . . handicapped students should be handled expeditiously by administrative law procedure and the educational agency is to keep the student in the facility where he was when the complaint was made." Congress, found the court, obviously wanted such complaints to be resolved in a matter of weeks; otherwise, students such as the plaintiff would be in high school before the controversy was resolved by the courts. The court dismissed the student's complaint until completion of administrative proceedings. *Robideau v. South Colonie Central School District*, 487 N.Y.S. 2d 696 (Sup.Ct.1985).

In June, 1983, the parents of a twelve-year-old New York girl noticed that she seemed to be withdrawing from her friends and was spending much of her time alone in her room. Because their daughter also did not seem to be growing, the parents took her to a pediatrician, who discovered that she had not gained any weight for an entire year. When she lost weight during the summer of 1983, she was diagnosed as suffering from anorexia nervosa and put on a special diet to gain weight. Unfortunately, the diet failed and she continued to lose weight. Her parents then placed her in Rochester's Strong Medical Hospital three times in 1983 and 1984, with her third hospital stay continuing into May, 1985.

Prior to their daughter's discharge from the hospital, the parents asked their local school district's committee on the handicapped (COH) to assist them in obtaining a residential placement for her. The COH agreed that the girl's condition constituted a handicap within the meaning of the EAHCA. They prepared an IEP for her and made applications to six residential facilities in New York. All six declined to accept the girl. In March, 1985, the COH asked the State Education Department (SED) to approve a placement at the Hedges Treatment Center of the Devereux Foundation in Malvern, Pennsylvania (Hedges). The SED denied this request, explaining that a hold had been placed on new admissions, and instructed the COH to contact three other in-state residential facilities. By April 30, however, all three had denied admission to the girl. Then, on May 16, 1985, because the COH had not placed the daughter and the hospital insisted on discharging her, the girl's parents placed her at Hedges on their own initiative. They sued the New York Commissioner of Education in U.S. district court under the EAHCA, the Rehabilitation Act, and the Civil Rights Act, seeking reimbursement for their expenses in making the placement, and requesting an order that their daughter be formally placed at Hedges.

The district court denied reimbursement, holding that the parents had failed to exhaust their administrative remedies before bringing suit. Under New York law, parents may appeal a decision of a school district COH to the Board of Education, which will then appoint a hearing officer. The Board's decision may then be appealed to the Commissioner of Education. The parents argued that because they agreed with the COH that Hedges was the only appropriate placement for their daughter, they had no dispute with the COH, and thus attempting to pursue administrative remedies would have been futile. Disagreeing, the court held that the parents should have demanded placement from the COH, and if placement was not forthcoming, there would have been a dispute to adjudicate. The case would then have come before the Commissioner on an administrative appeal, and he could have personally reviewed the merits of the girl's case. It was quite possible that he would have approved placement at Hedges. As the parents had brought their claim to court prematurely, reimbursement was barred.

The district court then considered the parents' request for a preliminary injunction ordering placement at Hedges. To prevail, the court noted that they would have to show 1) irreparable harm and 2) a likelihood of success on the merits of their lawsuit. The decision on this request was deferred by the court due to an inadequate record. The court directed the parents to submit detailed information concerning their financial status, as well as affidavits from Hedges explaining what would happen to their daughter if the parents stopped making tuition payments. *Antkowiak v. Ambach*, 621 F.Supp. 975 (W.D.N.Y.1985).

In the course of locating an alternative placement for a handicapped child, the District of Columbia Public Schools (DCPS) wrote the child's mother of progress being made and stated "[w]e appreciate the effort you have extended thus far to assist us in locating an appropriate placement for your son, and we solicit your continuing efforts to secure a speedy placement for him. . . ." The following day, DCPS requested a due process hearing on the grounds that the mother had failed to cooperate with DCPS placement efforts. A hearing was held in which testimony was presented on behalf of the mother which focused on the need for residential placement. The hearing officer, believing that it was beyond her power to order residential placement, remanded the case to DCPS with the direction that it was to submit the matter to the Residential Review Committee and propose a placement. Subsequently, the mother received a letter advising her that the Committee had declined to recommend residential placement and that the child was to be placed at a day school. The mother filed suit in federal district court and unilaterally placed the child in a school.

DCPS argued before the U.S. district court that because the mother had not been "aggrieved" by a final determination of a hearing officer and because she had failed to exhaust her administrative remedies, she should be precluded from bringing suit in federal court. The court found that the mother was "aggrieved" as that term is used in the Education of the Handicapped Act and thus her claims were properly before the court. The argument that the mother had failed to exhaust her administrative remedies was also rejected. Resorting to the administrative process would have been futile in light of DCPS's blanket rejection of residential placement without setting forth the criteria upon which it based its decision. The court held that DCPS should place and fund the child at the residential school.

Further, the court rejected the argument that the Residential Review Committee had official status and that parents seeking to have their children considered for residential placement must satisfy criteria established by the

Committee. Finally, the mother's claim for compensatory and punitive damages was denied since Congress intended the EAHCA to be the exclusive avenue through which a plaintiff may assert a claim to publicly financed special education. However, the court granted the mother's claim for attorney's fees because of bad faith on the part of the school district, which had commended her for her cooperation and then the following day initiated a hostile due process hearing. *Diamond v. McKenzie*, 602 F.Supp. 632 (D.D.C.1985).

A fourteen-year-old emotionally disturbed and mentally handicapped student and his parents sued in U.S. district court in Wisconsin, arguing that the child's school district had failed to provide a free appropriate public education in violation of the EAHCA; had failed to properly evaluate and identify the severity of the child's handicap; had failed to provide special education and related services to enable the child to meaningfully benefit from his education; had failed to provide a full continuum of services, including therapy and residential placement; and had failed to consider independent educational evaluations obtained by the child's parents at their expense.

The dispute arose after the school district determined that it could provide a free appropriate public education to the child and the parents believed that only a residential treatment facility could provide the child with an appropriate education. After the school district's recommendation of public school placement, the parents unilaterally placed their child in a private treatment facility. The school district denied the parents' request for reimbursement for their expenses in sending their child to the private school. The parents requested a due process hearing. However, they later withdrew that request and brought suit in federal court.

The U.S. district court held that the failure of the parents to exhaust their state administrative remedies precluded a federal suit under the EAHCA. A federal court action can be brought only if state administrative remedies have been exhausted or if to pursue such remedies would be futile. Here, the parents had not shown that pursuing state remedies would have been futile. In addition, the parents' allegation of procedural inconsistencies between the EAHCA and Wisconsin's use of county boards to make decisions related to handicapped education conflicted with the EAHCA's requirement that local agencies make all such decisions. The court found that the parents misread the EAHCA since the Act clearly applies to both local educational agencies "or an intermediate educational unit."

The parents' argument that the Secretary of Education should withhold EAHCA funds from Wisconsin based on the alleged procedural inconsistencies was also rejected. Not only were the alleged procedural inconsistencies nonexistent, found the court, but the plaintiffs had no standing to request the enjoining of fund disbursement to the state. State funds may be withheld only if the U.S. Secretary of Education, after notice and hearing, determines that there has been no substantial compliance with the EAHCA. Thus, the Wisconsin Department of Public Instruction's motion to dismiss the parents' claims was granted. *Brandon v. Wisconsin Department of Public Instruction*, 595 F.Supp. 740 (E.D.Wis.1984).

Also in Wisconsin, two Milwaukee handicapped children, on behalf of themselves and similarly situated children, brought an action in U.S. district court against the Milwaukee Public Schools (MPS) seeking declaratory, injunctive and monetary relief. They claimed the MPS deprived them of an appropriate public education in violation of the Equal Protection Clause of the Fourteenth Amendment to the U.S. Constitution, the Rehabilitation Act of 1973, the Education for All Handicapped Children Act and the Wisconsin Constitution. The MPS moved for summary judgment. Relying on a report and recommendations made by a court-appointed special master, the court granted the motion and dismissed the action.

A number of factors were looked at by the court in making its decision. The major one involved the exhaustion of administrative remedies, something the court determined was not done. Because administrative remedies were not exhausted, and because they were not determined to be futile, the court determined it had no alternative under the law but to grant judgment for the MPS, since exhaustion of remedies is necessary before a federal court can review a school district's decisions regarding handicapped children.

The plaintiffs also contended that they had claims under the Rehabilitation Act even if they were precluded from recovering under the EAHCA. The court disagreed, stating that a plaintiff cannot proceed with a claim under the Rehabilitation Act, if the claim is cognizable under the EAHCA—whether the claim is based on a substantive or a procedural challenge to state and local agency action—without having exhausted administrative remedies available under the EAHCA. Although the plaintiffs asserted that their claim under the one statute was independent of the one under the other statute, the court disagreed stating that since both claims came from the same set of facts, they must at least be considered parallel.

A further assertion by the plaintiffs was that they had an independent right of action for violation of constitutional rights under federal civil rights statutes. This contention, too, was rejected by the court which said, "a number of courts have addressed this issue and have concluded that exhaustion of the EAHCA [administrative] procedures should be required before constitutional claims that parallel EAHCA claims can be pursued in federal court." The court concluded by granting the defendants' motion for summary judgment and dismissing both federal and state law claims. *M.R. v. Milwaukee Public Schools*, 584 F.Supp. 767 (E.D.Wis.1984).

In a third Wisconsin case, an emotionally disturbed and disabled Wisconsin fourteen-year-old student and his parents brought an action in U.S. district court, seeking to obtain relief from a decision of the Wisconsin Superintendent of Public Instruction concerning the boy's placement in a special education program. They also sought monetary damages for certain actions taken by the superintendent and other defendants which allegedly constituted bad-faith violations of the federal and state laws providing for free appropriate special education for handicapped children, constitutional deprivations of due process and other alleged wrongs. The defendants sought to dismiss the bulk of the case, and the court granted these motions.

The one count not contested by the defendants involved a review of the child's placement during the 1982-1983 school year and the effect that placement had on his education during the 1983-1984 school year. The defendants appeared to concede that the count was well-pleaded and appropriately before the court for determination.

However, several other counts were strongly objected to by the defendants. One of the counts requested declaratory relief for a number of prior years. The court dismissed the claims made under that count because the plaintiffs failed to exhaust administrative remedies. The court described the EAHCA's exhaustion requirement:

> "the philosophy of the Education for All Handicapped Children Act is that a plaintiff must first exhaust the state administrative remedies provided under the act, including the administrative appeals provisions, before bringing an action in federal court that challenges the evaluation and placement of a child. . . . Only when these state administrative remedies have been exhausted may a suit be brought in federal court. Such a philosophy protects several very important interests: the requirement respects the state interest in establishing and maintaining a comprehensive scheme of regulation for state schools. The requirement vests authority over these types of decisions in an expert supervisory body, far more familiar than a federal court with the local factors and educational needs involved in administering special education programs. The requirement insures that if the expert agency cannot resolve the problem itself, the record on which the federal court must decide will be fully and efficiently illuminated for the court's decision."

Another count upon which the plaintiffs relied heavily for relief was one claiming a deprivation of constitutional rights redressable under current federal discrimination statutes. The court rejected this claim as well by pointing out that the U.S. Supreme Court has stated that these federal statutes are not applicable in situations where the governing statute provides an exclusive remedy for violations of the act. In this case the act involved was the EAHCA. The court gave two reasons why this act provides an exclusive remedy. First, the EAHCA contains an elaborate administrative and judicial enforcement system, which includes an express right of action for a party aggrieved under the statute. Second, EAHCA makes available injunctive relief only; the monetary damages which the federal discrimination statutes provide are inconsistent with this form of remedy. It was noted that EAHCA cannot be given unimpaired effectiveness if an action under the federal discrimination statutes is available for an EAHCA violation. The defendants' motion to dismiss all counts of the complaint with one exception was granted. *Daniel B. v. Wisconsin Department of Public Instruction*, 581 F.Supp. 585 (E.D.Wis.1984).

In another Wisconsin case, a severely handicapped child, through her parents, brought suit in U.S. district court against the local school district and its special education director, alleging that her right to an appropriate special education and other constitutional rights had been violated by the school district. The child's individualized educational program called for one-to-one instruction which the parents claimed was suspended without notice to them. The school district responded that this action was an "experiment" designed to determine whether the child would benefit by a program change.

The parents appealed the child's IEP to the state superintendent of instruction.

Pending the result of the appeal the parents, dissatisfied with the child's instruction, had her independently evaluated and enrolled her at a special rehabilitation facility. When the superintendent finally ruled on the parents' claim, he concluded that the child was entitled to a full-day educational program. The case was tried and the court held that the parents' suit would be dismissed for their failure to exhaust state administrative remedies. The parents were not entitled to reimbursement for the expenses they incurred in having their child independently evaluated and for unilaterally enrolling their child in a special facility. This, said the court, was "self help" activity precluding reimbursement.

The court also found that the parents were not denied due process of law with regard to the change in the child's IEP without notification to the parents. The court stated that although it might be argued that the imposition of a change in an IEP without parental consent may deprive them of "liberty with finality," it was apparent in this case that the alleged damage as a result of the change was minimal. The parents' claim that their equal protection rights under the U.S. Constitution had been violated was without merit because the child had never been totally excluded from any program offered by the school district. The court noted that the parents' argument that exhaustion of remedies should be excused on the ground that the superintendent had failed to reach a final decision within 30 days as required by law was also without merit. This, the court said, would not excuse the parents' failure to exhaust their administrative remedies. Accordingly, the case was dismissed. *Williams v. Overturf*, 580 F.Supp. 1365 (W.D.Wis.1984).

A Virginia case illustrates the rule that the exhaustion of administrative remedies doctrine cannot be waived absent a clear showing of futility. Here the mother of an emotionally disturbed child brought suit against Virginia education officials, alleging that her son had been denied a free appropriate education. Specifically, the mother claimed that local school officials had wilfully withheld educational opportunities from her child. To support her argument the mother noted that the child, at the time suit was brought, was at home receiving no educational services whatsoever.

A U.S. district court held that the mother's claims should be dismissed because of her failure to exhaust available administrative remedies prior to bringing suit in federal court. The court arrived at this decision based on the fact that the child was receiving a homebound education and that the school district had formulated an individualized educational program. The IEP called for placement at a private residential school. The problem was that shortly after this proposal was made no openings were available in the selected school. The court stated that had the facts conclusively shown that the child was not receiving any education whatsoever and that the defendent school district had not taken any steps to provide him with an appropriate education, the school district's violation of the EAHCA would be clear. Under such circumstances, prior resort to administrative remedies would not be a prerequisite to bringing suit in federal court because "administrative remedies need not be pursued when to so would be futile." Here, however, the mother was required to exhaust the available administrative remedies prior to bringing suit. *Harris v. Campbell*, 472 F.Supp. 51 (E.D.Va.1979).

A U.S. district court in Louisiana held that the parents of handicapped and exceptional children were not entitled to bring suit in federal district court because of their failure to seek administrative review provided for in EAHCA. The parents claimed that a local school district had in effect a policy which constituted a failure to provide a meaningful, appropriate education to their handicapped children. Specifically, the parents alleged that there was no division of the students based on age or handicap. The court held that the parents must have exhausted their administrative remedies prior to bringing suit in federal court.

The court next had to determine whether to dismiss the case or "stay" the case pending exhaustion of administrative remedies. The court decided to dismiss the case, noting that courts will retain jurisdiction where not to do so would cause irreparable harm to the plaintiffs. Here, the court found no such potential irreparable harm. The court based its dismissal of the case on the general rule that where a plaintiff enters federal court prematurely, the district court is bound to dismiss the case. *Sessions v. Livingston Parish School Board*, 501 F.Supp. 251 (M.D.La.1980).

In an action brought in Puerto Rico, the U.S. Court of Appeals, First Circuit, has held that the mother of a handicapped child was required to exhaust the administrative process prior to bringing suit in federal court, despite the fact that a state agency initially failed to provide the mother with an internal remedy. The child, severely learning disabled, was placed by her parents in a residential private school in Vermont although the parents resided in Puerto Rico. They then sought funding for the child's education from the Puerto Rico Department of Education. The parents' request was denied because the Department was conducting an assessment of the child for purposes of making a placement recommendation. The parents then brought suit in a U.S. district court, which dismissed the case because of the parents' failure to exhaust administrative remedies. The parents appealed, arguing that the Department of Education had taken an excessive amount of time to make a placement recommendation. The U.S. Court of Appeals, First Circuit, affirmed the district court ruling and held that despite delays in the placement process, the parents were obligated to pursue administrative channels before bringing suit in federal court. The court noted that the doctrine of exhaustion of remedies is not to be applied inflexibly and that courts are free to use their discretion in applying the doctrine. In this case, however, the various interests served by the doctrine weighed heavily in its favor. *Ezratty v. Commonwealth of Puerto Rico*, 648 F.2d 770 (1st Cir.1981).

The exhaustion doctrine was also applied in a New York case which involved a blanket decision by the New York Commissioner of Education that learning disabled children were not eligible for residential placement unless their learning disability was accompanied by an additional problem, such as an emotional disturbance. Eighteen learning disabled children who were denied residential placement brought suit against the Commissioner in a U.S. district court without first requesting a hearing. The court enjoined the Commissioner from adhering to the policy and did not require the parents of the children to exhaust administrative remedies. The Commissioner appealed to the U.S. Court of Appeals, Second Circuit, which reversed the district court ruling.

The Court of Appeals held that the district court "acted too hastily, and should have required that the plaintiffs exhaust state administrative remedies before bringing suit in federal court." The court was not persuaded by the parents' argument that exhaustion might prove "futile." There was, according to the court, always the possiblity that, during the hearing process, the Commissioner might reverse himself in a compelling case if he were proved wrong and a residential placement was shown to be clearly necessary for a learning disabled child. The court stated that exhaustion may well have afforded relief to the children. Accordingly, the parents were not entitled to judicial relief when administrative relief might be available. *Riley v. Ambach*, 668 F.2d 635 (2d Cir.1981).

In two consolidated cases, a U.S. district court in Nebraska held that both cases should be dismissed, one for mootness and the other for failure to exhaust administrative remedies. Both cases had previously been heard by a U.S. district court but adverse rulings prompted the plaintiffs to appeal to the U.S. Court of Appeals, Eighth Circuit. The Court of Appeals remanded the cases to the district court.

The first case involved a nineteen-year-old deaf girl whose parents were dissatisfied with a proposal by the child's school district to place her in a residential school providing instruction in both the oral method and manual method of instruction for the deaf. The parents brought suit in federal court challenging the proposed IEP. However, by the time the case went to court the girl had married and moved out of the school district boundaries. Because of her change in residence and her emancipation, the court determined that the local school district no longer had responsibility for her education.

The second case involved a mentally retarded boy who also suffered from muscular dystrophy. The child, who eventually became confined to a wheelchair, was unable to continue his then current educational placement because of the school's inability to accommodate handicapped students in wheelchairs. The child's parents, dissatisfied with the alternate placement provided, also brought suit in federal court challenging the appropriateness of the placement decision. The boy and his parents never requested a due process hearing prior to bringing suit.

At the time the suit was commenced there existed inconsistencies between state and federal administrative procedures. At that time, therefore, the student was under no duty to exhaust administrative remedies. However, at the time the case went to trial the inconsistencies had been resolved. The court held that because the inconsistencies had been rectified there was no longer any justification for permitting the child to circumvent the exhaustion requirement. The court observed that a state hearing officer is in the best position to make an initial determination on a child's placement. Here, there was no reason to believe that the state could not or would not proceed in an expeditious manner if the parents opted for a due process hearing.

The two cases were once again appealed to the Court of Appeals, which affirmed the district court ruling. The Court of Appeals held that in the case involving the nineteen-year-old deaf girl, the issues were moot because the girl had married and moved out of the school district. To her argument that she planned to move back into the school district, the court said that this issue was not "ripe" for adjudication. The court also agreed with the district court ruling as to the second case. No relief could be provided by a federal court where the child's father had failed to exhaust administrative remedies. The boy and his father never invoked the impartial hearing process provided by state law. *Monahan v. State of Nebraska*, 687 F.2d 1164 (8th Cir.1982).

An epileptic child in Kansas brought suit on behalf of himself and all epileptic school-aged children in the state of Kansas contending that Kansas educational practices violated the children's rights to a free appropriate public education. The children did not object to the state's overall special education program, but claimed that the plan was insufficiently enforced against local school districts as to its identification, screening and evaluation requirements. The Kansas Commissioner of Education maintained that, at all times, the plan had been in conformity with the requirements of the EAHCA and was enforced against local school districts.

A U.S. district court denied the plaintiffs' request for an injunction on the ground that, with one exception, all the plaintiffs had failed to exhaust their administrative remedies. In fact, the court found that the available administrative review under the EAHCA had not even begun. While the exhaustion requirement is generally excused if the exhaustion would be futile, this was not established in this case. Accordingly, the plaintiffs were not entitled to relief in federal court. *Akers v. Bolton*, 531 F.Supp. 300 (D.Kan.1981).

The U.S. Court of Appeals, Fourth Circuit, has denied relief to a handicapped child and her parents in Virginia where the child and her parents had not attacked a local school district's special educational policies administratively prior to bringing suit in federal court. In this case the parents alleged that the school district had failed to provide their child with adequate educational services and procedures under the EAHCA. The Court of Appeals affirmed a U.S. district court ruling dismissing the parents' complaint. *McGovern v. Sullins*, 676 F.2d 98 (4th Cir.1982).

In a New York case the mother of a handicapped child, concerned about her son's lack of progress in his second year of kindergarten, asked that he be evaluated by a psychologist. The mother claimed that a school representative who came to her home with a parental permission form put a check mark on the form in the box indicating that she denied the district permission to conduct an evaluation of her child. The mother later brought suit in a U.S. district court claiming that as a result of being denied the special education to which he was entitled, her son suffered damages to his intellect, emotional capacity and personality, and was impeded in acquiring necessary training. In addition, she alleged that she moved to a different school district to obtain the services her child needed and that she herself had suffered emotional distress. The court held in favor of the mother and the school district appealed. The U.S. Court of Appeals, Second Circuit, held that because the mother had not availed herself of her administrative remedies under the EAHCA, she was deprived of her means of relief under the Act. However, the court did find that the mother had a claim under the Civil Rights Act. *Quakenbush v. Johnson City School District*, 716 F.2d 141 (2d Cir.1983).

Two Massachusetts cases addressed the issue of exhaustion of remedies under Massachusetts state law and the EAHCA. The first case arose after the parents of a child with special educational needs, dissatisfied with the individualized educational program proposed by a school committee, challenged the IEP before the Massachusetts Bureau of Special Education Appeals (BSEA). A hearing officer found that the education plan proposed by the school committee was "the least restrictive, adequate and appropriate education plan to meet his special needs." On a printed form notifying the parents of the BSEA's decision, the following sentence appeared: "I understand that this rejection automatically constitutes an appeal to the State Advisory Commission (SAC) without my having to separately note such an appeal." The parents returned the form with that sentence stricken and the following sentence substituted: "I will appeal directly to the U.S. District Court." The parents then filed a complaint in U.S. district court.

The school district argued that the parents should not be allowed to bring suit in federal court because of their alleged failure to exhaust their administrative remedies. Specifically, the parents had failed to appeal the decision of the BSEA to the SAC. Under Massachusetts state law, the school district argued, the decision of the BSEA did not constitute a "final decision of a state educational agency" as required by both state law and the federal EAHCA. The parents argued that any alleged failure to exhaust administrative remedies should be excused on the ground that the school failed to advise them of their due process rights.

The district court held that it lacked jurisdiction to hear the parents' complaint as to the first academic year in which the plan was to be implemented. The court found that the U.S. Department of Education was the primary "state" agency responsible for the administration of the EAHCA in Massachusetts. Because the Department had not participated in the administrative process, no final decision had been made by a state agency as required by the EAHCA.

For the years following the first year during which the plan was to be implemented, the court held that it would retain jurisdiction to hear the case after participation by the Department of Education. Under the circumstances, the court felt it particularly appropriate to seek the review of the Department as the agency primarily responsible for the EAHCA's administration and enforcement. Finding that the parties would not suffer irreparable injury due to any delay resulting from the ruling, the parties were instructed to review the matter and make changes where necessary prior to resumption of the case. *Doe v. Anrig*, 500 F.Supp. 802 (D.Mass.1980).

The second case involved a town in Massachusetts which appealed a decision of the SAC which had determined that an individualized educational program, proposed by the town for a severely handicapped child was inadequate and inappropriate. The parents of the child had rejected and appealed the proposed IEP. The BSEA sustained the town's proposed IEP and the SAC, the next review body, tentatively affirmed the IEP. However, upon review of additional material the SAC reversed and remanded the matter to the BSEA for further hearings to determine "in light of this *final decision*" what would be the least restrictive and appropriate program and placement for the child. Misled by the SAC's incorrect reference to its "final decision," the town sought judicial review of the SAC's determination without exhausting further administrative remedies. A Massachusetts trial court dismissed the suit on the ground that the town failed to exhaust its administrative remedies, and the town appealed. The Appeals Court of Massachusetts held that the trial court properly dismissed the action because the SAC's decision was not a final administrative decision, even though designated a "final decision" by the SAC. *Town of East Longmeadow v. State Advisory Committee*, 457 N.E.2d 636 (Mass.App.1983).

The Supreme Court of New Hampshire decided a case in which a fourteen-year-old girl, who suffered from a severe learning disability coupled with speech and language disorders, was placed in a private residential school in Massachusetts. The reason for this placement was the inability of the girl's New Hampshire school district to provide an appropriate educational program for her. During the summer, after the child's second year at the school in Massachusetts, the local school district in New Hampshire formulated an individualized education plan for the child which utilized public resources. The mother appealed the school district's decision to place the child in a public program, which resulted in a determination that the public program offered was both "free and appropriate," and that the school district would no longer be obliged to pay for the child's education at the school in Massachusetts or any other private facility. The determination also denied tuition reimbursement to the mother for the four month period following the proposed IEP. (The mother had enrolled the child for a third year at the private school pending the resolution of the appeals process.) The mother then petitioned the Supreme Court of New Hampshire, asking it to order the school district to pay the expenses incurred for the four months.

The court declined to rule on the matter since the child's mother had not appealed the final administrative decision to a state trial court or federal district court, as required by the EAHCA. Petitioning the supreme court of a state is not the appropriate method for seeking review of a decision of a state board of education. Although the court declined to hear the merits of the mother's complaint, it noted that if a school district can provide satisfactory assurance that its programs meet the EAHCA's standards for "free appropriate public education" of handicapped children, it will only be liable for the costs resulting from the placement of handicapped children in its own public programs and not for the cost incurred in private placements. *Petition of Darlene W.*, 469 A.2d 1307 (N.H.1983).

A profoundly mentally handicapped student in Indiana and her parents brought suit against a local school district alleging that the district failed to provide a sufficient educational program for the child under the Education for All Handicapped Children Act. The girl, since infancy, had lived in a nursing home. At age eighteen she was diagnosed as having a mental age that ranged from two to twenty-one months. She had been receiving one one-hour educational session daily but at an annual conference to develop an individualized educational program, the girl's mother requested that the child be placed in a full-day instructional program in the hope that the increased attention would lessen her persistent self-abuse. The school district refused to do this on the ground that the self-abuse would increase if the child was placed in a full-day program.

The mother filed objections to the proposed IEP and a hearing officer found that the child should be placed in a full-day instruction program. The school board appealed this finding to the State Board of Education, which remanded the case for a professional evaulation on the issue of the correlation between increased activity and self-abuse. Before a report could be made on the issue the parents filed suit in a U.S. district court which dismissed the parents' suit. The parents appealed. The U.S. Court of Appeals, Seventh Circuit, affirmed the district court's ruling, saying that not only had the parents failed to exhaust their administrative remedies, but the child was over eighteen years of age and therefore past the age at which the state was required to provide an education. The issue was therefore moot. *Timms v. Metropolitan School District of Wabash County, Indiana*, 722 F.2d 1310 (7th Cir.1983).

B. Exceptions to the Exhaustion Doctrine

The following cases illustrate that exhaustion of administrative remedies is not required when it is clear that the purpose of the administrative remedies would be futile. There are cases in which courts deem state administrative remedies inadequate and thus not subject to the exhaustion requirement. Such things as delay by an agency in making a decision, or the fact that the agency may not be empowered to grant relief, will excuse the "exhaustion" requirement. The unavailability of a state or local remedy or a predetermined result by an agency will also excuse the requirement.

A case arising in New York has held that the exhaustion doctrine did not apply to a situation involving the suspension of a multiply handicapped student from a school for the blind. In this case, the parents of the child brought suit against the New York State Education Department and the school for the blind seeking an injunction to reinstate the student at the school. The parents brought suit without first having exhausted the available administrative remedies. This was done, claimed the parents, because of a denial of procedural safeguards when the parents wished to contest their child's suspension. The parents alleged that the state had failed to provide for an impartial hearing officer and that there was no provision requiring the agency to allow the child to remain in the school pending resolution of their complaint. The school argued that it had "substantially complied" with the procedural requirements of the EAHCA. However, the court disagreed stating that a "person who claims that the state defendants have not even provided the impartial hearing as required by federal law *a fortiori* asserts a claim over which [the] court has jurisdiction." Finding the parents and the child in that position, the court denied the school's motion to dismiss the case. *Sherry v. New York State Education Department*, 479 F.Supp. 1328 (W.D.N.Y.1979).

In a second case involving the suspension and eventual expulsion of a handicapped student from an Indiana school, a federal district court held that the child and his mother were not required to exhaust administrative remedies, where the available remedies did not provide for a challenge to the procedures by which the child was expelled from school. After the child, through his mother, brought suit against the school district challenging both the child's expulsion and the procedure by which he was expelled, the school district sought to have the case dismissed on the ground that the mother and the child had failed to exhaust their administrative remedies as required by the EAHCA. The district court found that the only local and state administrative remedies available were appeals from the child's expulsion. The local and state administrative remedies did not provide for a challenge to the procedure by which the plaintiff was expelled. The court concluded that before an action may be brought in court, administrative remedies must be exhausted only if they are available. Since the available local and state administrative remedies were not designed for the claim brought by the child, the child's mother acted properly in bringing the action in federal court without exhausting the available local and state administrative remedies. *Doe v. Kroger*, 480 F.Supp. 225 (N.D.Ind.1979).

The exhaustion doctrine was also inapplicable in a case in Pennsylvania. Here, the parents of an emotionally disturbed son sought special education placement for him after he had been diagnosed as emotionally disturbed. The parents then activated the due process hearing system, but the responsible officials in the child's school district reached no decision in time to place the boy at a special school before the beginning of the following academic year. The parents then found what they believed to be an appropriate school in New York and began paying tuition. A hearing was held after the first year of the child's enrollment in the school chosen by the parents, which resulted in a determination that the placement chosen by the parents was appropriate. The parents raised the matter of tuition reimbursement but this was never resolved.

Believing they had received a favorable ruling from the hearing officer, the parents did not appeal the decision but their attempts to secure reimbursement proved unsuccessful. They claimed that there simply was no reimbursement procedure in Pennsylvania. The parents eventually brought suit in a U.S. district court against the school district, which argued that they were not entitled to do so on the ground that the reimbursement issue was never litigated at the hearing level and thus the parents had failed to exhaust their administrative remedies. The court concluded that the "exhaustion" doctrine was irrelevant where no administrative remedy had ever been available. *Hark v. School District of Philadelphia*, 505 F.Supp. 727 (E.D.Pa.1980).

Residents of a New Hampshire school for the mentally retarded brought suit against the state of New Hampshire seeking a ruling that their right to habilitation required that they be placed in the least restrictive environment. The residents claimed that no community placements were being made in violation of section 504 of Rehabilitation Act. The state argued that the residents were precluded from bringing suit because of their failure to exhaust their administrative remedies. The U.S. district court disagreed, finding that New Hampshire's administrative procedures were defective. In addition, many of the residents lacked available parents and/or guardians and the state had failed to provide them with such a guardian or a surrogate parent. Accordingly, the court found that exhaustion of administrative remedies would have been futile. *Garrity v. Gallen*, 522 F.Supp. 171 (D.N.H.1981).

The parents of a handicapped child in Illinois challenged the failure of various state agencies to assume the full cost of the child's placement at a private residential facility. The boy, seventeen years old, suffered from autism, moderate mental retardation, severe emotional disturbance, speech and language impairments and behavioral disorders. After being assessed by the state as "responsible relatives," the parents were told they must contribute $100 per month toward their son's placement. The state's reason for excluding this amount from the child's placement at the school was that it was attributable to "clothing, medical supplies and purchased services." An outstanding bill at the school in the amount of $2,154.53 resulted in the issue of a discharge notice to the child which was to become effective prior to the resolution of the parents' appeal of the decision to assess them as "responsbile relatives." The parents, without waiting for resolution of the appeal, filed suit in U.S. district court. The state sought to have the case dismissed for failure to exhaust administrative remedies.

The district court excused the exhaustion requirement because the parents had no practical opportunity to obtain the appeal decision. They had done everything possible to obtain speedy administrative review, but were unable to do so through no fault of their own. Because of the state's failure to decide the parents' administrative appeal within the time specified by federal law, the purpose of the exhaustion requirement was undermined; the parents would have been unable to obtain the decision before the time that the school intended to discharge the child. The court stated that "when the press of time makes exhaustion impractical, it is not required by the EHA." The court also found that the parents had no "real administrative remedy" in this case. It was doubtful, said the court, that administrative review could provide the parents with the relief they sought. It appeared that the agency decision had been made pursuant to state law. Thus, by adopting the responsible relatives policy, the agency had already predetermined the result it would reach in the child's case. *Parks v. Pavkovic*, 536 F.Supp. 296 (N.D.Ill.1982).

In another Illinois case, a group of emotionally disturbed children brought suit in a U.S. district court against Illinois state education officials, challenging a rule excluding counseling and therapeutic services from being considered special education or related services. The children admittedly did not exhaust their administrative remedies but argued that an exhaustion attempt would be futile. They claimed that the Illinois State Board of Education was not the "appropriate forum" to address the issues relating to the Illinois Governor's Purchased Care Review Board determinations of allowable cost for related services. Noting that none of the children had attempted to exhaust the administrative remedies prescribed by section 1415 of the EAHCA and that, ordinarily, this would require dismissal, the court excused the exhaustion requirement in this case. Based on the evidence, the court concluded that Illinois had not established a meaningful process of administrative review. *Gary B. v. Cronin*, 542 F.Supp. 102 (N.D.Ill.1980).

The U.S. Court of Appeals, Second Circuit, reversed a district court's decision to dismiss a case because of the plaintiff's failure to exhaust her administrative remedies. The controversy originally centered on whether a school district was liable, under the EAHCA, for the transportation cost of the plaintiff's son. The school district declined to provide transportation reimbursement, because the tests necessary to determine whether the child was in fact handicapped were never made due to the parent's rejection of the school district's psychologists. A final administrative decision then was rendered in favor of the school district. When the case was appealed to a U.S. district court, the judge held that the plaintiff had not exhausted her administrative remedies because the testing data had not been provided. The Court of Appeals reversed the lower court, stating that the absence of the testing data did not mean that the proper administrative route was not followed by the plaintiff. The court concluded that if a final administrative decision has been rendered, it is to be reviewed on its merits. The case was remanded for further proceedings. *Dubois v. Connecticut State Board of Education*, 727 F.2d 44 (2d Cir.1983).

V. Statute of Limitations

"Statute of limitations" refers to the time in which a person may file suit or an "aggrieved party" may appeal a decision after an alleged injury has occurred. The EAHCA does not specify a time limitation in which parties may bring suit in state or federal court after exhausting administrative remedies or appeal an adverse administrative decision. Administrative procedures are generally governed by state laws which usually specify a thirty-day limitation on appeals. However, state laws for other types of actions usually set a longer time limitation. Conflicts arise when one party files a lawsuit or appeals a decision outside what the other party perceives to be the applicable statute of limitations.

A handicapped nine-year-old New York boy who suffered from speech and motor difficulties was evaluated by his school district's committee on the handicapped (COH). The COH then made a recommendation for an educational placement of the boy which his parents believed to be inappropriate. They appealed the placement decision to the New York Commissioner of Education, who ruled in favor of the parents. However, the Commissioner declined to order that the parents be reimbursed for the boy's educational expenses incurred as a result of the parents' decision to unilaterally place their child in a private school. The private school had provided an appropriate education for the boy during the ten-month period from the time of the initial, incorrect COH evaluation to the time the Commissioner's decision was rendered.

Fifteen months after the Commissioner's decision denying reimbursement, the parents sued in U.S. district court seeking reimbursement for the private school tuition. The district court held that the suit was barred by the statute of limitations, a decision upheld by the U.S. Court of Appeals, Second Circuit. While noting that the Education for All Handicapped Children Act contains no statute of limitations, the appeals court stated that the applicable state statute of limitations will be used in lawsuits brought pursuant to the EAHCA. In this case there was a conflict between a New York statute governing educational proceedings in state courts which called for a four-month limit, and a more general New York statute providing for a three-year limit on any suit "to recover upon a liability . . . created or imposed by statute."

The district court had relied upon the law providing for a four-month limit because it was the one most closely analogous to the present cause of action had it arisen under state law. The Court of Appeals sanctioned this approach, noting that to allow the longer three-year statute of limitations to govern lawsuits seeking reimbursement for educational expenses would conflict with the EAHCA requirement that a child remain in his current educational placement during the pendency of any proceedings to review the appropriateness of a child's placement. Said the court, "this 'status quo' provision hardly contemplates a period of three years plus pendency of the proceedings. After all, it is a child's education we are talking about." The court therefore refused to allow the three-year general statute of limitations to govern the case and stated that because the parents had failed to appeal the Commissioner's decision within three months, their suit had been properly dismissed. *Adler v. Education Department of State of New York*, 760 F.2d 454 (2d Cir.1985).

Nebraska school officials sought a dismissal of a suit brought by two handicapped children who were attacking Nebraska's procedures for contesting educational placements of handicapped children. The officials claimed that Nebraska law precluded the suit brought by one of the children because of the child's failure to file suit within a thirty-day statute of limitations. The child argued that the law governing administrative procedures was not applicable in this case where the EAHCA created a federal cause of action which was not restricted by any federal statute of limitations. The court found the child's argument persuasive saying that the state judicial proceedings were not sufficiently analogous to the child's federal claim to justify the application of the state's stringent thirty-day rule. The court observed that the scope of the judicial proceedings available to a plaintiff under Nebraska law was limited. Under state law a party suing was only entitled to the limited judicial review of the administrative record. The parties in such a proceeding could not request that the court consider any evidence not contained in the administrative record.

In addition, the reviewing state court did not have the authority to make an independent factual determination based on the administrative record, but was limited to determining whether the agency decision was based on substantial evidence or was arbitrary or capricious. In contrast to the limited review available under state law, the EAHCA provides that any party involved in such a federal action is entitled to present new evidence not found in the administrative record. Moreover, the Act requires that the reviewing court make an independent decision based upon a preponderance of all the evidence. The court concluded that the thirty-day limitation period could not "best effectuate" the federal policy underlying the EAHCA. Finding that the Act's purpose would not be served if a parent was given only thirty days within which to assess the validity of a state educational agency's decision, the court held that the child's action was not barred by the state statute of limitations. *Monahan v. State of Nebraska*, 491 F.Supp. 1074 (D.Neb.1980).

Two Pennsylvania cases have held that a thirty-day Pennsylvania statute of limitations governing appeals of administrative agency decisions did not apply to actions brought by handicapped students and their parents. The first case involved a suit brought by the parents of a handicapped child against the state and a local school district. The parents sought reimbursement of expenses they incurred in placing their child in a private residential school which was eventually determined to be the appropriate school for the child. The defendants claimed that a state thirty-day statute of limitations precluded the suit. A federal district court disagreed, saying that the action was not time barred since the parents were not appealing a "decision." In fact, the parents appealed to the federal court because of the state's excessive delay in reaching a decision as to the parents' request for reimbursement. *Hark v. School District of Philadelphia*, 505 F.Supp. 727 (E.D.Penn.1980).

The second case arising in Pennsylvania relied heavily on the Nebraska case in holding that a thirty-day statute of limitations period did not bar a suit brought against the Pennsylvania Department of Education and a local school district. A handicapped student requiring clean intermittent catheterization to enable her to attend school challenged a school district policy which denied such services. The U.S. Court of Appeals, Third Circuit, affirmed a district court ruling in favor of the child. The Court of Appeals agreed with the district court's decision to apply either a two-year or a six-year statute of limitations period to the child's claim under the EAHCA. Finding that the thirty-day limitations period was incompatible with the objective of the EAHCA, the court held that it did not apply. The Court of Appeals decided that the two-year state statute of limitations which applied to actions to recover damages for injuries caused by the wrongful act or negligence of another, and controlled in medical malpractice cases, was the most analogous statute. Because the child's claim was brought within the two-year period, her action was not barred. *Tokarcik v. Forest Hills School District*, 665 F.2d 443 (3d Cir.1981).

In a Texas case, a handicapped child was placed by her school district in a public facility which was equipped to treat children with emotional disturbances and autism. She made progress during her first year there. However, during the second year she regressed significantly. The parents removed her from the facility and placed her in another institute. After tuition expenses were denied by the child's school district, the parents sought relief in a U.S. district court which held that because the parents had brought suit nine months after the denial, their claim was barred by a thirty-day statute of limitations. In addition, said the court, the parents forfeited all rights to recover tuition for the private residential facility by unilaterally withdrawing the child from the school district's program. The parents appealed this decision to the U.S. Court of Appeals, Fifth Circuit, which agreed with the district court ruling that the parents were not entitled to reimbursement, but reversed the thirty-day statute of limitations ruling, saying that the limitation was inconsistent with the EAHCA's policy of investing parents with discretion to take action regarding their children's education. *Scokin v. State of Texas*, 723 F.2d 432 (5th Cir.1984).

In Hawaii, a thirty-day statute of limitations period did apply to a suit brought outside that period by the Hawaii Department of Education. The Department had filed two suits in federal court challenging adverse hearing officer decisions on the issue of responsibility for the costs of educating two handicapped children. The U.S. Court of Appeals, Ninth Circuit, held that the Department's suit was barred by its failure to appeal the hearing officer's decision within the thirty-day limitation period set by the Hawaii Administrative Procedures Act. The court found the APA to provide a more comprehensive standard of review than the EAHCA. Further, the need to avoid delays in resolving disputes over education plans for handicapped children supported the application of a thirty-day statute of limitations period for a state agency to appeal an adverse decision. The court affirmed a U.S. district court decision to dismiss the cases. However, the court noted that it was not being asked to decide whether the same thirty-day rule would apply to parents or guardians seeking judicial review of a handicapped child's placement. The thirty-day rule may not apply in those cases. *Department of Education, State of Hawaii v. Carl D.*, 695 F.2d 1154 (9th Cir.1983).

VI. Failure To Comply With EAHCA Provisions

Due process of law is contingent upon a school district's adherence to the procedural safeguards of the EAHCA. The failure to adhere to the provisions of the EAHCA will generally result in a favorable ruling for the parents or guardians of handicapped students.

The U.S. Court of Appeals, Fourth Circuit, ruled that a school district's failure to fully advise the parents of a dyslexic child of their procedural rights under the EAHCA justified unilateral private school placement by the parents. In this North Carolina case, the child, who had been enrolled in his local public elementary school, had extreme difficulty in reading. Although he was required to repeat second grade, the child was thereafter advanced from grade to grade due to the school district's practice of making "social promotions." When the child reached the third grade, an IEP was developed which identified him as having reading deficiencies only and called for placement in a regular classroom ninety percent of the time, and placement in a learning disabilities resource room for the remainder of the time. When the child reached the fifth grade he still could not read. In desperation, his parents enrolled him in a private residential facility. At this time a private evaluation of the child was performed which finally disclosed that although he was of above average intelligence, the child suffered from dyslexia. The parents also discovered for the first time that under federal law their school district might be obligated to pay for their child's placement at the private school. The parents filed suit and a U.S. district court ruled in their favor.

On appeal, the U.S. Court of Appeals upheld the district court's ruling, ordering that the school district pay the cost of the child's placement at the private school. The child had made no educational progress while in the public schools and the IEP developed by public school officials was utterly inadequate, said the court. The school district's contention that the child had achieved educational benefits because he had advanced from grade to grade was dismissed by the appellate court, due to the school's policy of making social promotions. Furthermore, the school district's failure to fully inform the parents of their rights under the EAHCA constituted a *per se* breach of its statutory duties. The appellate court also noted that the child had finally begun to make educational progress after his placement at the private residential school. The child's parents were thus entitled to recover the costs of his placement from the school district. *Hall v. Vance County Board of Education*, 774 F.2d 629 (4th Cir.1985).

In a Rhode Island case, a federal court ruled that a school district, faced with a hostile set of parents, acted properly in attempting to provide a learning disabled boy with an appropriate special education. The parents had enrolled their child at the age of six in the Scituate, Rhode Island, public school system. He received remedial reading instruction during first grade. The following year his parents placed him in a private Catholic school, but eighteen months later they concluded that he was learning disabled and once again enrolled him in the Scituate public schools. Eighteen months after this the parents placed him at a private day school, and later at the Linden Hill School in Northfield, Massachusetts, which specializes in the education of learning disabled boys. The child never returned to the Scituate public school system.

Three years later, in April, 1981, the parents sought future financial assistance under the EAHCA for their son's placement at Linden Hill. In May, 1981, they met with Scituate's special education multi-disciplinary team (MDT) and expressed their dissatisfaction with the district's past education of their child. When the MDT said that due to flawed and dated prior tests, a new evaluation of the child would be required, the parents objected and withheld consent until June, 1981. A partial evaluation was then performed by the MDT, but due to parental resistance it was never completed. At a September, 1981, meeting with the MDT, the parents were advised that the MDT would recommend placement in a Scituate self-contained classroom. Due to delays caused by the parents, an IEP meeting was not held until October 20, 1981. They attended this meeting with their attorney and later contested the resultant IEP (which provided for Scituate placement) at a due process hearing.

The hearing officer ruled in favor of the school district, but the parents appealed and a review officer reversed. The Scituate school district appealed to a Rhode Island federal district court. The court examined the issues presented by the case, beginning with the parents' allegation that Scituate's letter notifying them of the October IEP meeting had failed to state who would be in attendance and that other individuals could attend. The court excused this failure due to the fact that the parents had attended one IEP meeting previously (in 1978) and thus were probably aware of their rights. Also, the individuals present on October 20, 1981, were the same individuals who had attended the September meeting. No one was a surprise attendee, nor was anyone absent whom the parents expected to attend. Also, there was no evidence of bad faith on the part of Scituate.

The parents' second allegation was also dismissed by the court. They had correctly pointed out that the EAHCA places great emphasis on parental involvement in the formulation of an IEP. They alleged that at the October 20 meeting, an IEP was presented to them which read "Independent Education Program," to be effective from "October 20, 1981 - October 20, 1982." The parents argued that this was an attempt to steamroll them into accepting an "immutable, unchangeable, completed plan," which was subject only to their acceptance or rejection—not their participation. The court, however, held that the parents were aware of their right to offer input and make suggestions at the IEP meeting, noting that their attorney had written a letter to school officials after the meeting which stated: "they [the parents] will then inform the school what, if anything, they feel must be added, eliminated, or changed. . . ."

Finding that Scituate was innocent of any procedural violations, the district court then proceeded to determine whether the proposed IEP was adequate. Rhode Island law requires that a school district "shall provide such type of education that will *best satisfy* the needs of a handicapped child" (emphasis added). This educational standard is incorporated into the federal EAHCA by reference. The district court, ruling on an issue of first impression, held that this standard was identical to the federal standard set forth in *Rowley v. Board of Education*. The U.S. Supreme Court held in *Rowley* that, at a minimum, an IEP must be designed to allow a handicapped child to "benefit educationally" from his or her instruction. The district court based its ruling on the fact that the Rhode Island statute using the language "best satisfy" was decades old and could not correctly be interpreted to give handicapped children the right to the best possible education. All that was required under Rhode Island law was that a child derive educational benefits under the IEP. Examining all the evidence, the court concluded that Scituate's proposed IEP was adequate.

The testimony of the parents' expert witness, Dr. Edwin M. Cole, a renowned language disability expert, was discounted by the court. It was the court's opinion that he was insufficiently familiar with the case, having met with the child for only one forty-minute period. At trial, Dr. Cole was unable to say whether the child wore glasses. These factors caused the district judge to give greater weight to the opinions of Scituate personnel, who were more familiar with the child. Finally, the court noted that the desirability of mainstreaming also supported placement in the Scituate public classroom. Reimbursement for the child's placement at Linden Hills was therefore denied to the parents. *Scituate School Committee v. Robert B.*, 620 F.Supp. 1224 (D.R.I.1985).

The parents of an emotionally handicapped, learning disabled child with severe behavioral problems brought suit against an Oregon school district alleging that an appropriate education program was not being made available to their child and that the school district violated statutes and regulations it was legally bound to follow. They requested and received a complaint hearing before the state Department of Education (DOE). The DOE found that the school district had violated applicable state and federal laws and awarded the parents partial reimbursement of tuition costs they had incurred by enrolling their son in a private school. However, it denied the parents' request for attorney's fees.

Both the parents and the school district appealed to the Court of Appeals of Oregon which defined four issues: 1) whether the allegations that the district denied the child a "free appropriate public education" and otherwise violated state and federal laws were properly before the DOE; 2) whether the DOE, after finding that such violations had occurred, had the authority to require the district to reimburse the parents, in part, for expenses they had incurred; 3) whether the DOE was empowered to award the parents attorney's fees; and 4) whether the DOE's findings of fact were supported by substantial evidence.

The court held that the DOE was the correct forum in which to bring the complaint. Had the parents' complaint alleged only that they disagreed with the district's individualized educational plan or educational placement for their child, the proper forum for resolution of that matter would have been a due process hearing. However, it alleged that an appropriate educational program was not made available to the child and also that the district violated various other federal statutes and regulations. Accordingly, the correct forum was a "complaint hearing." Such a hearing is governed by Oregon state law, which requires that local school districts comply with the Education for All Handicapped Children Act, that school districts have complaint procedures available for alleged violations and that sanctions be imposed against non-complying districts.

However, the DOE, after finding violations, did not have the authority to require the school district to reimburse the parents' expenses. The district had a duty, said the court, to provide the child with a free appropriate education and, its having failed in that duty, the DOE only had the authority to withhold funds from it. The court went on to hold that the DOE had the power to award attorney's fees even though it had not done so in this case, and that the DOE's findings of fact were supported by substantial evidence. *Laughlin v. School District No. 1*, 686 P.2d 385 (Or.App.1984).

A Missouri case involved the proposed transfer of two handicapped children from an elementary school district to a state school for the severely handicapped. The parents of the children sued the school district alleging that the children were denied due process of law in violation of the EAHCA. A federal district court agreed with the parents. The court found that the referral of the children to the State Department of Education for placement was without prior notice to the parents. In addition, the first level hearing was defective because a three-member panel failed to review the facts and make a decision as required by the EAHCA. Instead, the State Department of Education decided to withdraw the proposed assignment of the children and to conduct further proceedings before making a final determination as to an appropriate educational placement. The court found that the state was thus bound to comply with federal procedural safeguards which became effective as of the date of the hearing. The actions taken by the Department were in violation of the procedural safeguards of the EAHCA which require a determination of the facts and a decision. Finally, the court found that the state level hearing was not conducted by an impartial hearing officer. This hearing was conducted by the Missouri State Board of Education which was an "agency or unit involved in the education or care of the child" within the meaning of the EAHCA. The Act also requires that the impartial individual who conducts a due process hearing at the state level may not be an employee of the State Department of Education or "of any local or intermediate unit thereof." Here, the parents were entitled to, but did not receive, an impartial hearing officer. *Vogel v. School Board of Montrose R-14 School District*, 491 F.Supp. 989 (W.D.Mo.1980).

Another school district was found to have violated the procedural safeguards of the EAHCA by the failure to provide an impartial hearing officer. This case arose in Iowa and involved a challenge to a local school district's decision to place a child in special education classes. The child's guardian brought suit against the Iowa State Superintendent of Public Instruction alleging that the superintendent violated the "impartial hearing officer" provision of the EAHCA by presiding over the due process hearing which the child had received. A U.S. district court held that the superintendent violated the EAHCA provision barring employees of agencies involved in the education of a child from serving as hearing officers in due process hearings required by the Act. The district court remanded the case for a new hearing which was to be presided over by an outside hearing officer and the superintendent appealed to the U.S. Court of Appeals, Eighth Circuit.

The Court of Appeals was asked to decide whether the superintendent, as Superintendent of Public Instruction and an employee of the State Board of Public Instruction, was employed by a direct provider of educational services, the local school board, or whether he merely exercised supervisory authority over the direct provider. The court affirmed the district court ruling, declaring the superintendent to be statutorily disqualified from serving as a hearing officer. The EAHCA's clear language and history indicate that "no hearing may be conducted by an employee of the State or local educational agency involved in the education or care of the child." *Robert M. v. Benton*, 634 F.2d 1139 (8th Cir. 1980).

The parents of an eleven-year-old learning disabled child in the District of Columbia, dissatisfied with a local school district's placement of the child, expressed their concern to the school staff. A meeting with school staff followed in which the parents again reiterated the concerns they had expressed earlier concerning the appropriateness of the child's education. After the meeting the school sent the parents a "Notice of Continuing Special Education Services," which stated that the child was to continue in the current program at the school. The notice did not inform the parents of the need to file any form, not did it state any way by which a dissatisfied parent could challenge the school's decision. A hearing was scheduled, but it was later cancelled by the school. A letter to the parents' attorney stated that "since the [school was] 'unaware' of the [parents'] desire to change [the child's] program, no formal evaluation procedure had been initiated for the child." Accordingly, the letter continued, "the public schools will not be ready, nor are they required to participate at a hearing until they are given an opportunity to complete the formal evaluation/placement process."

The parents then brought suit against the school in federal court requesting the court to order the school to provide a due process hearing in which their objections to their child's continued placement at the school would be "fully ventilated." Without the hearing, claimed the parents, they were being denied due process guarantees mandated by the EAHCA and the Act's regulations which require that the parents or guardian of a child be afforded a hearing whenever they have a complaint about a school district's proposal to change or refusal to change a child's educational placement or any matter concerning the child's placement.

The school also argued that the parents had failed to submit a "Form 205" request which would have given the school notice of their objections. Noting that a school must be afforded reasonable notice of any parent's desire for a change of placement before the school is required to act upon the request, the court nevertheless found that the notice of placement to the parents did not inform them that filing "Form 205" was the proper procedure for objecting to their child's placement. Accordingly, the court denied the school's motion to dismiss the case and ordered that a hearing be held within five days of the court's order to address the parents' complaints about their child's IEP. *Pastel v. District of Columbia Board of Education*, 522 F.Supp. 535 (D.D.C.1981).

A handicapped child and his mother brought suit on behalf of themselves and all handicapped children not receiving an appropriate education by reason of delays of the Illinois Superintendent of Education in resolving placement appeals. A severely emotionally disturbed twelve-year-old child was recommended for placement by his school district in a self-contained classroom for behavior disorder students. His mother objected to the recommendation and said that she had been advised by experts that a highly structured residential program would be appropriate placement for the child. The mother appealed the decision but after five months the superintendent had made no decision. The mother claimed that the superintendent was obligated to decide within thirty days. She alleged that the long delay and inappropriate educational setting had caused the deterioration of the child's condition to the extent that he had to be placed in a mental hospital. The superintendent sought to dismiss the suit on the basis that the EAHCA creates no substantive rights for handicapped children.

A U.S. district court in Illinois disagreed, saying that the EAHCA is the source of a federal statutory right to a free appropriate education in every state electing to receive financial assistance, and that it is more than merely a "funding statute." The court then applied due process analysis and said that the passage of time caused the deprivation of the child's substantive right to an appropriate education and timeliness of review is an essential element of due process. The superintendent's motion to dismiss was denied. *John A. v. Gill*, 565 F.Supp. 372 (N.D.Ill.1983).

A Pennsylvania case resulted in a determination that a local school district failed to meet its legal responsibility to provide an appropriate program of education in training for an exceptional child. The court based its ruling on the fact that the district, instead of making an initial placement recommendation, merely provided the parents with a list of "approved private schools" and took twenty-one months to make an official recommendation of appropriate educational placement. *Pires v. Commonwealth of Pennsylvania, Department of Education*, 467 A.2d 79 (Pa.Cmwlth.1983).

In the following case a Rhode Island school district was not liable for its failure to follow procedural safeguards. Here the parents of a dyslexic child challenged an adverse state administrative decision concerning the child's placement. The parents alleged in federal district court that they had been deprived of due process of law because of a local school district's failure to provide them with a hearing after their local school committee decided not to fund the child's education at a private residential school. The court found that the parents' due process rights were, in fact, violated. The school committee, the court found, failed to follow procedures prescribed by state law and to provide the parents with a right to be heard at a meaningful time. However, because the parents were unable to show that had correct procedures been followed, a different result would have been reached, the parents were not entitled to a judgment against the school district. *Jaworski v. Rhode Island Board of Regents for Education*, 530 F.Supp. 60 (D.R.I.1981).

CHAPTER FOUR

REMEDIES UNDER THE EAHCA

The type of relief sought by parents or guardians of handicapped children for alleged wrongdoing on the part of local school districts or state education officials varies with the particular circumstances of the case.

I. Injunctive Relief

Injunctive relief is sought when handicapped children, through their parents or guardians, wish to compel education officials to comply with the provisions of the EAHCA. An injunction is a court order directing a person (or any legal entity) to perform a certain act, or refrain from doing an act. If the injunction is violated, the violator may be found to be in contempt of court and a fine or imprisonment may result.

Preliminary injunctions are temporary in nature and are issued prior to trial. They are issued only where (a) the plaintiff makes a showing that he or she will suffer irreparable harm if the preliminary injunction is not issued, and (b) the plaintiff is able to show there is a reasonable likelihood that he or she will succeed at trial and be awarded a permanent injunction.

A plaintiff will be awarded a permanent injunction if, after receiving all relevant evidence, the court determines that injunctive relief is necessary to protect a handicapped child's rights under the EAHCA, or to force education officials to abide by federal or state law.

Preliminary injunctive relief was granted in a case where a handicapped child was expelled from high school. In enjoining a Connecticut school district from conducting a hearing to expel the student and ordering a special education program, a U.S. district court noted that the student would possibly suffer irreparable injury if expelled. She had deficient academic skills caused by a combination of learning disabilities and limited intelligence and, if expelled, would be without any educational program from the date of expulsion until such time as another review could be held and an appropriate educational program developed for her. The student also demonstrated a likelihood of success on the merits of her claim. Thus, the student was allowed to remain in her then current educational placement until the resolution of the dispute. *Stuart v. Nappi*, 443 F.Supp. 1235 (D.Conn.1978).

A second case involving the expulsion of handicapped students from school was decided by the U.S. Court of Appeals, Fifth Circuit. The Court of Appeals affirmed a U.S. district court decision in favor of nine Florida handicapped students who had been expelled from school for disciplinary reasons. Similar reasoning was used in this case as was used in the preceding Connecticut case. Finding that expulsion may cause irreparable harm to the students, the court granted their request for an injunction. *S-1 v. Turlington*, 635 F.2d 342 (5th Cir.1981).

A U.S. district court in the District of Columbia also issued a preliminary injunction, this time on behalf of a multiply handicapped student. The student was a sixteen-year-old boy who was emotionally disturbed and learning disabled. The child's school district refused to fund for him a residential private school education including necessary psychiatric and other services on the ground that the boy was not the school district's responsibility. The court disagreed and issued a preliminary injunction restraining the District of Columbia Board of Education from further denying the child a free appropriate education in violation of the EAHCA. The court issued the injunction to prevent irreparable injury to the boy.

The district court observed that in the absence of such an injunction, the boy would be required to participate in neglect proceedings involving his parents. This, the court said, would have a devastating impact on the boy. Because he demonstrated a likelihood of success on the merits of his claim and the potential injury to him far outweighed any injury to the school district by the issuance of the injunction, the court ordered the Board of Education to place the child in a residential academic program with the necessary related services. *North v. District of Columbia Board of Education*, 471 F.Supp 136 (D.D.C.1979).

In another District of Columbia case, the parents of two handicapped children were granted a preliminary injunction requiring the Department of Defense (DOD) to place, at its expense, the children at two specific private schools in the United States. The children's father was a civilian employee of the U.S. government on loan to the North Atlantic Treaty Organization and the family lived in Europe. A U.S. district court held that if the DOD was unable to provide educational services to the children in American-run schools in Europe, it was required to fund private residential educations in the U.S. The court was persuaded by the testimony of witnesses who stated that the children could not "emotionally survive" the environment proposed by the DOD. In granting the parents' request for an injunction, the court stated that "absent extraordinary relief . . . in the nature of a preliminary injunction to prevent the defendants from interfering with the free educational rights [that the plaintiffs], and all children, enjoy and deserve, irreparable harm, of inestimable nature and span," would result. *Cox v. Brown*, 498 F.Supp. 823 (D.D.C.1980).

A group of handicapped children in Wisconsin brought suit on behalf of themselves and all similarly situated handicapped students in the state. The children, who were students placed in day treatment facilities, sought a preliminary injunction enjoining Milwaukee public school officials from terminating their current placements until the completion of a full and impartial evaluation of their educational needs and handicapping conditions. As part of their request for injunctive relief, the children also sought an order from the court requiring extended school year programs continuing into the summer months. Finally, the children requested a court order to the school officials to force them to expedite the impartial evaluation process without delay.

The U.S. district court granted the children's request for the injunction. The court held that the injury to a handicapped child who is deprived of special education facilities required to be provided under the EAHCA constituted "irreparable harm" for purposes of the preliminary injunction. The court noted that a preliminary injunction may only be granted if it is found that: (1) the plaintiffs have no adequate remedy "at law" (i.e., money damages would be inadequate) and they will be irreparably harmed if the injunction does not issue; (2) the threatened injury to the plaintiffs outweighs the threatened harm the injunction may inflict on the defendant; (3) the plaintiffs have at least a reasonable likelihood of success on the merits; and (4) the granting of a preliminary injunction will not disserve the public interests. Finding all of the tests met in this case, the court granted the injunction. *M.R. v. Milwaukee Public Schools*, 495 F.Supp. 864 (E.D.Wis.1980). See also *M.R. v. Milwaukee Public Schools*, 584 F.Supp. 767 (E.D.Wis.1984), for another Wisconsin case dealing with similar issues.

A preliminary injunction was issued by a U.S. district court in Massachusetts upon a finding that prison inmates under the age of twenty-two who were otherwise eligible for a free appropriate education were entitled to such an education. A twenty-one-year-old inmate brought suit against Massachusetts education officials seeking an injunction enjoining the officials from failing to provide special education services to inmates without high school diplomas and who were also found to be in need of special education services. The district court agreed and ordered the officials to provide educational services. *Green v. Johnson*, 513 F.Supp. 965 (D.Mass.1981).

An injunction was granted to a handicapped child in Texas who required clean intermittent catheterization which would enable her to attend school. The child's interest in attending public school outweighed the school's burden to provide this medical service to the child. *Tatro v. State of Texas*, 516 F.Supp. 968 (N.D.Tex.1981), *affirmed*, 104 S.Ct. 3371 (1984).

A seventeen-year-old handicapped boy in Illinois who suffered from autism, moderate mental retardation, severe emotional disturbances, speech and language impairments, and behavioral disorders was granted a preliminary injunction by a federal district court in Illinois. The child was about to be expelled from a private residential school he was attending for nonpayment of tuition. The child's parents sought an injunction ordering state agencies and the Illinois Superintendent of Education to pay the remaining balance of the child's tuition expenses to prevent his discharge from the school. This was requested prior to the outcome of the parents' lawsuit challenging the agencies' and the superintendent's refusal to pay the child's tuition expenses in full. The district court granted the parents' request for an injunction requiring the state and local agencies to pay the child's outstanding bill at the school or to provide the facility with sufficient assurances of payment so that he would not be discharged from the facility prior to the trial on the merits of his claim. *Parks v. Pavkovic*, 536 F.Supp. 296 (N.D.Ill.1982).

Two "school closing" cases illustrate that requests for preliminary injunctions on behalf of handicapped students are not always granted. In the first case, a handicapped student in New York challenged a decision of New York City's Board of Education to close a special education school on the ground of financial mismanagement. The New York Supreme Court held that the students were not entitled to a preliminary injunction prohibiting the school closing because there was insufficient proof of the required irreparable injury to warrant such an injunction. The children had been placed in alternate school settings and had not shown that these placements were inappropriate. *Cohen v. Board of Education of New York*, 454 N.Y.S.2d 630 (Sup.Ct. 1982).

The second case also allowed the closing of a school for handicapped children. When a treatment facility in Kentucky providing a program for emotionally handicapped children was closed for budgetary reasons by the governing school district, parents of the attending children filed suit in U.S. district court seeking a preliminary injunction to compel the school district to continue operation of the facility. The court denied the motion. The parents appealed to the U.S. Court of Appeals, Sixth Circuit, maintaining that under the EAHCA the closing of the treatment facility constituted a change of placement and that, pursuant to the Act, the state was precluded from instituting the change during the pendency of proceedings contesting the action.

The appellate court agreed that the closing of the facility constituted a change in placement, but affirmed the lower court's denial of a motion for a preliminary injunction. Stating the need for fiscal decisions to remain in the hands of school authorities, the court held that "authorities do not, by electing to receive funds under the EAHCA, abdicate their control of the fiscal decisions of their school systems." The court feared that if it granted such an injunction a school district would be compelled to finance a program it had determined to be unaffordable simply because of allegations of deficiency in substitute programs raised by one special group. The court also observed that maintaining an expensive program for some handicapped children reduced the amount of funds available for all handicapped children. *Shaffer v. Block*, 705 F.2d 805 (6th Cir.1983).

Other special education cases have also held that a preliminary injunction was not warranted.

The father of an emotionally and physically handicapped child in New York brought suit against a local school board alleging the board had denied his son a free appropriate education required by federal law. Specifically, the father requested an injunction to enjoin the board from permitting his son to attend a high school of the son's choice and ordering the board to place the child in a high school of the father's choice. The court denied the father's request for the injunction on the ground that the father had failed to prove that his son was "seriously and emotionally disturbed" within the meaning of the EAHCA. *Johnpoll v. Elias*, 513 F.Supp. 430 (E.D.N.Y.1980).

In another New York case, a child with minimal brain dysfunction sought a preliminary injunction to prevent his transfer from a school for the handicapped to a public school program for the handicapped. A U.S. district court denied the child's request for an injunction. The court found that a "preponderance of the evidence" showed that the decision to place the child in a public school program for the handicapped was well supported. *ZVI D. v. Ambach*, 520 F.Supp. 196 (E.D.N.Y.1981).

In a third New York case, a group of autistic children, their parents and a private school attended by the children sought judicial help in preventing New York officials from reducing the rate, set by the state, at which local school districts should reimburse the private school for providing the autistic children with a free appropriate public education, pursuant to the EAHCA. The reduction in the tuition rate was made following an audit of the school's financial statement. State officials determined that the rate charged to parents of autistic children was greater than it should have been in relationship to the rate charged to the parents of normal children.

A U.S. district court refused to grant the requested injunction. The court determined that there was no showing of irreparable harm, nor a showing that the school had failed to establish a serious question going to the merits. Further, there was no showing of a denial of either due process or equal protection. This decision was appealed to the U.S. Court of Appeals, Second Circuit, which affirmed. The Court of Appeals stated that Congress did not intend the EAHCA to authorize wholesale challenges to state fiscal determinations. *Fallis v. Ambach*, 710 F.2d 49 (2d Cir.1983).

II. Reimbursement For Tuition Expenses:
   "Status Quo" Requirement of the EAHCA

Section 1415(e)(3) of the Education for All Handicapped Children Act requires that "during the pendency of any proceedings conducted pursuant to this section, unless the State or local educational agency and the parents or guardian otherwise agree, the child shall remain in the then current educational placement of such child . . . until all such proceedings have been completed." This provision is designed to preserve the "status quo" pending resolution of judicial or administrative proceedings held under the Act. The primary justification for the status quo provision is to maintain stability in handicapped children's educational programs while the resolution of disputes is carried out.

Parents or guardians of handicapped children who unilaterally change the placement of their child during the pendency of any review proceedings often seek reimbursement from their school district for tuition expenses. In *Burlington School Committee v. Department of Education of Massachusetts* (reprinted in the Appendix of U.S. Supreme Court Cases in this volume), the Supreme Court ruled that parents who violate the status quo provision may nevertheless receive tuition reimbursement from the school district, if the

IEP proposed by the school is later found to be inappropriate. However, if the proposed IEP is found to be appropriate, the parents will not be entitled to reimbursement for expenses incurred in unilaterally changing their child's placement.

In the *Burlington* case, the father of a learning disabled third grade boy became dissatisfied with his son's lack of progress in the Burlington, Massachusetts, public school system. A new IEP was developed for the child which called for placement in a different public school. The father, however, followed the advice of specialists at Massachusetts General Hospital and unilaterally withdrew his son from the Burlington school system, placing him instead at the Carroll School, a state-approved private facility in Lincoln, Massachusetts. He then sought reimbursement for tuition and transportation expenses from the Burlington School Committee, contending that the IEP which proposed a public school placement was inappropriate.

The state Board of Special Education Appeals (BSEA) ruled that the proposed IEP was inappropriate and that, therefore, the father had been justified in placing his son at the Carroll School. The BSEA ordered the Burlington School Committee to reimburse the father for tuition and transportation expenses, and the School committee appealed to the federal courts. A U.S. district court held that the parents had violated the status quo provision of the EAHCA by enrolling their child in the private school without the agreement of public school officials. Thus, they were not entitled to reimbursement. The U.S. Court of Appeals, First Circuit, reversed the district court's ruling, and the Burlington School Committee appealed to the U.S. Supreme Court.

In upholding the court of appeals, the Supreme Court ruled that parents who place a handicapped child in a private educational facility are entitled to reimbursement for the child's tuition and living expenses, *if* a court later determines that the school district had proposed an inappropriate individualized educational program. The Court stated that reimbursement could not be ordered if the school district's proposed individualized educational program was later found to be appropriate. The Supreme Court observed that to bar reimbursement claims under all circumstances would be contrary to the EAHCA, which favors proper interim placements for handicapped children.

In addition, under the School Committee's reading of the EAHCA status quo provision, parents would be forced to leave their child in what might later be determined to be an inappropriate educational placement, or would obtain the appropriate placement only by sacrificing any claim for reimbursement. This result, found the Court, was not intended by Congress. However, the Court noted that "[t]his is not to say that [this provision] has no effect on parents." Parents who unilaterally change their children's placement during the pendency of proceedings do so at their own financial risk. If the courts ultimately determine that a child's proposed IEP was appropriate, the parents are barred from obtaining reimbursement for an unauthorized private school placement. *Burlington School Committee v. Dep't of Education of Massachusetts*, 105 S.Ct. 1996 (1985).

In a Virginia case, lack of state approval of a private school prevented parental reimbursement for tuition and related expenses. After being declared eligible for special education services, the fourteen-year-old boy involved in this case was placed by the Fairfax County public schools in the Lab School in Washington, D.C. Later, Fairfax County determined that the Lab School no longer met the boy's special needs and proposed a placement at the Little Keswick School, Inc., a Virginia residential school for handicapped children. This private facility is approved by the Virginia Department of Education.

Upon receiving Fairfax County's offer of placement at Little Keswick, the boy's mother wrote to Fairfax rejecting the proposal. She instead suggested that Fairfax fund her son's placement at the East Hill Farm and School in Andover, Vermont. Fairfax refused, stating that East Hill was not on the Virginia Department of Education's list of approved schools. The mother nonetheless placed her son at East Hill and requested a due process hearing to resolve the question of reimbursement for tuition and living expenses. The hearing officer provided by Fairfax County conducted a full and open evidentiary hearing, after which he concluded that Little Keswick was an appropriate placement. The boy's parents appealed; the review officer affirmed. The parents then brought an action in federal district court seeking further review.

The district court reviewed the evidence and concluded that Fairfax County was not obligated to fund the East Hill placement. Two grounds were specified for the court's decision. First, the Little Keswick School was approved by the Virginia Department of Education. The EAHCA's section 1413(a)(4)(B)(ii) allows states to establish minimum educational standards as a precondition to state approval of any school. This power of approval is expressly permitted by the EAHCA. Little Keswick was therefore an appropriate placement, said the court.

Second, East Hill was not on Virginia's list of approved schools. Indeed, it was not even on Vermont's list of schools certified for special education. Only one of East Hill's ten staff members was a certified teacher. In the court's view, lack of approval by the Virginia Department of Education precluded reimbursement. "Parents of handicapped students may not, because of personal desires, select a private institution of their choice and have the school system pay for the tuition," declared the court. "While the desires of the parents may be well motivated in that they seek the best for their child, the placement decision must be made by the school system in accordance with approved standards." The court affirmed the denial of reimbursement to the parents for the costs incurred in placing their child at the East Hill School. *Schimmel v. Spillane*, 630 F.Supp. 159 (E.D.Va.1986).

A California school district was ordered to pay the tuition and related expenses for a learning disabled boy whose parents had unilaterally placed him in an out-of-state private residential facility. In November, 1976, the boy's first individualized educational program, in which he was classified as suffering from a mild learning disability, was formulated by school district officials. The boy progressed and by June, 1977, he had successfully been partially integrated into regular classes. A new IEP was formulated at this time which provided that he continue in regular classes with minimal supplementary educational services. Three months later, in September, 1977, another IEP was developed which noted the boy's progress and recommended continued regular placement with some special education assistance. However, his performance and behavior suffered greatly during the ensuing 1977-

78 school year. School officials observed increased anger, hostility and rebelliousness during this period. The boy's parents were contacted in February, 1978, and a review session was held at which it was agreed that the September, 1977 IEP would remain in effect.

At the close of the 1977-78 school year, the boy was removed from school after slashing the tires on a teacher's car. He also ran away from home in August, 1978, and was consequently made a ward of the juvenile court. His behavior was described as "self-destructive" with "poor impulse control." In the fall of 1978 the boy was enrolled in the local high school where school officials, with the concurrence of his parents, tentatively decided that his September, 1977, IEP would remain in effect. He was thereafter truant from school on numerous occasions and ran away from home again for a week in September, 1978, at which time he committed the offenses of joyriding and marijuana possession. He spent the remainder of the school year in juvenile hall and various youth residential facilities. The school district made no effort to reevaluate the boy or develop a new IEP during this period.

Due to the school district's failure to properly evaluate their son, the parents decided to enroll him in a private residential facility in Utah in March, 1979, and asked that the school district pay the cost of his placement. The district, however, stated that it would pay only educational expenses at the facility. The parents requested a due process hearing on the matter and the hearing panel found that because the parents had acted unilaterally in placing their son at the residential facility, thereby breaching the "status quo" provision of the Education for All Handicapped Children ،_.. (EAHCA), the school district was not liable for the cost of the placement. The parents appealed and the California Court of Appeal held that the school district was liable under the EAHCA for the boy's educational and related expenses at the private, out-of-state residential facility.

The court based its decision on the failure of the school district to develop an IEP for the boy annually, as required by the EAHCA. An IEP had been formulated in September, 1977, but as of April, 1979, a new IEP had not been developed. The court rejected the school district's contention that because the boy had been truant and was frequently involved in the juvenile court system, it would have been difficult to properly evaluate him. The boy's status in the juvenile court system was well known to school officials and their failure to update the "manifestly inappropriate" September, 1977, IEP was characterized by the court as evidence of bad faith. The school district was therefore ordered to pay the cost of the private school placement. Attorney's fees were also awarded to the boy's parents. *In Re John K.*, 216 Cal.Rptr. 557 (Cal.App.1st Dist.1985).

A special education dispute of fourteen years' duration was recently settled by the U.S. Court of Appeals, Third Circuit. The court of appeals upheld a U.S. district court's ruling that the Westfield, New Jersey, board of education was not liable for the cost of nine years of private school placement. The child in this case was first identified as handicapped in 1968. At that time the Westfield Board of Education placed the child at the Midland School, a private facility. In 1972, further testing was performed by outside experts as well as Westfield's child study team. The child was thereafter labeled "mentally retarded-educable" by the child study team, and an IEP was formulated which called for placement at a different institution, the Tamaques School. Objecting to the label "mentally retarded-educable" (the parents felt their child was neurologically impaired), as well as the change in placement, the parents kept him at Midland and paid the tuition themselves.

In 1975, the parents filed a petition with the New Jersey Department of Education seeking review of Westfield's 1972 reclassification decision. The parents contended that during the pendency of all review proceedings, Westfield was obligated to pay for their child's tuition at Midland, since section 1415(e)(3) of the EAHCA requires that a child remain in his or her "then current" placement until review is completed. Due to the department's failure to comply with the procedural requirements of the EAHCA, a proper hearing on the merits of the parents' claim was not held until June 9, 1983.

During the period between the filing of the petition in 1975 and the 1983 hearing officer's decision, the child was evaluated many times by Westfield's child study team as well as the parents' outside experts. In 1976, the child study team changed its classification from mentally retarded-educable to "Multiply Handicapped: Primary—Mentally Retarded-Educable; Secondary—Neurologically Impaired." The child study team, however, did not change its recommendation of placement at the Tamaques School. Adhering to their view that the child study team's classifications were erroneous, the parents continued their child at the Midland School.

In 1980, the parents placed their child at the Maplebrook School. One year later, the Westfield child study team reclassified the child as "Neurologically or Perceptually Impaired: Perceptually Impaired" and agreed to fund the Maplebrook placement. An IEP was developed and agreed to, and pursuant to this IEP the child graduated from Maplebrook in the spring of 1982. The Westfield Board of Education granted a diploma to the child and contended that its responsibility for his education had terminated. The parents disagreed and enrolled him in the Summit Collegiate Studies Center in Jerusalem, Israel.

At the due process hearing in 1983, the parents claimed that they were entitled to tuition reimbursement for their child's education at the Midland school from 1972 to 1981, since they were entitled to leave their child at Midland during all review proceedings. They also claimed that the Westfield board of education was liable for the period their child attended school in Jerusalem. The hearing officer denied the parents' claims and they filed an action in U.S. district court, seeking review, but the court upheld the hearing officer's decision. The parents appealed their case to the U.S. Court of Appeals, Third Circuit, which similarly agreed with the hearing officer. The appeals court stated that since section 1415(e)(3) had not become effective until 1977, the Westfield Board of Education was relieved of responsibility for its 1972 decision to change the child's educational placement from Midland to Tamaques. Thus, the parents' decision to keep their child at Midland was not protected by section 1415(e)(3). The appeals court ruled that the parents should have placed the child at Tamaques in accordance with Westfield's 1972 recommendation.

The court also held that under section 1412(2)(B), the Westfield Board of Education would be responsible for the post-graduation education of the child only if the board made it a regular practice to educate children even after they had graduated. Since the board did not, and since the child had already graduated when his parents sent him to the school in Jerusalem, the board was not liable for those expenses. Noting that all the classifications and placements proposed by Westfield's child study team were appropriate under the EAHCA, the court of appeals affirmed the prior rulings against the parents. *Wexler v. Westfield Board of Education*, 784 F.2d 176 (3d Cir.1986).

Relying on the EAHCA's status quo provision, a U.S. district court ordered the New York City Board of Education to fund a handicapped child's placement at a private educational facility. The city's school system, explained the court, had been operating since 1972 under a federal court order which mandates that an offer of a public school placement must be made by the school system within sixty days of a child's identification as a handicapped individual. Under the court order, if the child is not offered such a placement within sixty days the parents have the right to place the child in a private facility at the board's expense.

The present case arose when a child was unilaterally enrolled by his parents in the Hebrew Academy for Special Children as provided by the order described above. The board agreed to pay for the placement at the academy, but at the beginning of the following school year it once again recommended public school placement. The parents, however, desired to keep their child at the academy, and he remained there during the due process hearings which ensued. The hearings culminated in an order by the state education commissioner that the board was required to fund the child's education at the academy, and the board appealed to the U.S. district court.

Ruling that the Hebrew Academy had become the child's "then current" educational placement under the EAHCA, the court upheld the commissioner's order. By initially failing to offer a placement within the required sixty days, the board had given the parents the unqualified right to place the child in a private facility at the board's expense. That placement then became the status quo, which could not be altered by the board until such time as they offered an acceptable placement. Under the EAHCA, the board then became unconditionally liable for the resulting tuition and related expenses. The court affirmed the commissioner's order of reimbursement for the parents' cost of placing the child at the Hebrew Academy. *Board of Education v. Ambach*, 628 F.Supp. 972 (E.D.N.Y.1986).

Another New York case, which also relied on New York City's sixty-day placement order, resulted in an award of tuition for private school placement. The parents of an emotionally handicapped student had sought to enroll their son in the New York City public school system in 1982. However, due to enormous delays by the Board of Education's Committee on the Handicapped (COH), the parents placed their son in a private facility. This was done pursuant to the 1982 court order, which attempted to prod New York's COH into action by granting parents of handicapped children in New York City the right to choose private school placement if the board's COH did not recommend an appropriate placement within sixty days of proposed entry of a child into the public school system. After the parents in this case enrolled their child in the private facility, the COH evaluated him and recommended public school placement. The parents disagreed with this recommendation and requested a hearing.

This hearing, which took place in March, 1983, resulted in a determination that the COH had not followed proper procedures, rendering its recommendation null and void. In May, 1983, the COH once again evaluated the child and again proposed a public school placement. The parents requested a hearing and this time an impartial hearing officer found that the COH's recommendation was proper. Appeal was taken to the state commissioner of education, who issued a decision in April, 1984, upholding the COH recommendation of public school placement. The commissioner also found that the board of education was liable for the child's private school tuition up until the date of the commissioner's decision. The board appealed to a U.S. district court, seeking a reversal of the award of tuition costs. The court stated that the Education for All Handicapped Children Act's status quo provision should govern, and hence upheld the award.

The court noted that the parents had placed their child in the private school pursuant to a court order intended to eliminate delay by New York's COH. This placement therefore became the child's "then current" educational placement, and the child was entitled to remain their until all review proceedings were completed. The fact that the COH later formulated an acceptable public school placement program for the child did not relieve the board of its duty to fund the child's private school placement until the COH's proposal was approved. The court then proceeded to award the parents the cost of the private school tuition, but only through April, 1984, the date of the commissioner's approval of the COH's public school placement recommendation. *Board of Education v. Ambach*, 612 F.Supp. 230 (E.D. N.Y.1985).

Reimbursement was denied to the parents of an Oklahoma youth, who brought suit in U.S. district court after their local school district refused to fund their son's placement at a residential facility. The youth, who was classified as "educable mentally handicapped" and who had serious emotional and behavioral problems, had been enrolled at the age of eighteen in his local school district's EMH program. An IEP was developed at this time with the approval of his parents, in which it was agreed that if the boy became "unmanageable" he would be suspended for three-day intervals. Although his educational program included both high school instruction and vocational instruction, he was soon expelled from the vo-tech program due to his emotional outbursts. When these outbursts continued at the high school, school officials notified his parents that an alternative to classroom placement was necessary. Homebound instruction was suggested, but the parents rejected the proposal. For the next several months the parents considered residential placement; during this period the youth received no educational services. His parents also failed to bring him to school for testing to aid in the formulation of a new IEP, as requested by school officials.

The parents then requested funding for their child's placement at an out-of-state residential facility. When their school district refused they requested a due process hearing under the EAHCA. The parents, after discovering the name of the hearing officer, believed that he would find in favor of the school district and withdrew their request for a hearing. At the beginning of the next school year they appeared once again at the high school to enroll their son, and school officials, who had not expected the youth to enroll, requested a week to formulate an IEP. Several days later school officials attempted to arrange a meeting with the parents to discuss a new IEP for the youth, but the parents refused because a new teacher had not yet been hired to instruct him.

The school officials explained that a new teacher would not be hired unless the parents approved the new IEP and assured them that they would enroll their son. This impasse caused the parents to unilaterally enroll their son in the out-of-state residential facility.

A due process hearing resulted in approval of the school district's decision not to reimburse the parents for the cost of his placement, and the parents sought judicial review. The U.S. Court of Appeals, First Circuit, upheld the denial of tuition reimbursement and found that the district had taken all steps necessary to provide the child with a free appropriate public education. The appeals court stated that "[a]lthough the [residential facility] undoubtedly offered . . . a superior educational program, an education which maximizes a child's potential is not required by the EAHCA." *Cain v. Yukon Public Schools, District I-27*, 775 F.2d 15 (10th Cir. 1985).

In a District of Columbia case, decided prior to *Burlington*, the parents of a handicapped student brought suit under the Education for All Handicapped Children Act, alleging that a District of Columbia public school had failed to provide their child with a free appropriate public education. The child, eleven years old, had been diagnosed as severely learning disabled with severe emotional problems. She had been attending special education classes four days a week at a learning center and regular classes one day a week at public school. Both schools were operated by the public school system. During this time the child's parents became very concerned about her schooling. They made arrangements to have the child evaluated at a private children's hospital and thereafter requested that she be placed there for the following school year. Public school officials proposed that the child continue her public school placement with increased mainstreaming. The parents then requested a due process hearing.

A hearing officer found that the child was handicapped, that she required special education and that her individualized education program failed to "address the emotional component associated with [the child's] deficiencies." The hearing officer went on to find that although mainstreaming is desirable and a "valid component in a special education program," mainstreaming attempts with the child had not proven successful and in fact had been harmful to her, perhaps even intensifying her emotional and academic difficulties. Finally, the hearing officer directed that the public school system must produce an alternative proposal with respect to mainstreaming the child. From that time on the parents claimed they were never contacted by the public school district, even though they wrote to school officials in early September of the following school year and were assured that their child would "be taken care of."

A second due process hearing was held in April of the school year in question, at which the parents stated that they had placed their child in a private school for that school year because she had no other appropriate placement, and that they were concerned that the public school district was not going to act. The hearing officer, the same individual who had presided over the first hearing, again found that the school district's proposed IEP was inappropriate to meet the child's needs but believed that the public schools could serve her educational needs.

The parents filed suit in a U.S. district court to obtain reimbursement of their expenses incurred in sending their child to the private school. The court held that the parents were entitled to reimbursement on the ground that there was a danger that the child's health would have been adversely affected but for the parents' placing her in the private school, and that the failure of the public schools to follow the determination of the hearing officer amounted to bad faith. Thus, the District of Columbia was required to reimburse the parents in the amount of the payments they were required to make to place the child in the private school. *Parker v. District of Columbia*, 588 F.Supp. 518 (D.D.C.1983).

The U.S. Court of Appeals, Fifth Circuit, reversed a district court ruling which granted a preliminary injunction to the parents of a handicapped child who had placed the child in a private school of their choice pending the outcome of the parents' action against a local Texas school district. The parents of the child had requested the district court to issue the injunction ordering the school district to pay, pending resolution of the case, the costs of the private school in which they had placed their child. The Court of Appeals held that under federal law, maintenance of the present placement of a handicapped child (or the "status quo") during the pendency of proceedings demands only that school districts and state educational agencies maintain financial commitments to continue to fund an educational placement that it already funded prior to commencement of proceedings. Nothing requires a school district to pay the costs of parent-chosen private schooling pending judicial review of placement procedures and decisions by a state agency. *Stacey G. v. Pasadena Independent School District*, 695 F.2d 949 (5th Cir.1983).

The parents of a handicapped Massachusetts child were denied reimbursement for past tuition expenses at a private school which their child attended by the choice of the parents, and the local school district was also absolved from having to pay for any future tuition. The child had attended local public schools through the third grade but the following year, at the suggestion of a learning disabilities specialist, his parents enrolled him in a remedial program at a private school. The student remained there for several years. At approximately the same time as the child began his private schooling, the public school devised an individualized education plan for him. However, the parents rejected the plan, preferring to place the child in the private school. Following an administrative determination, disputed by both the parents and the school district, a lawsuit was brought. A lower court entered judgment dismissing the parents' action for reimbursement and declaring that the school was not responsible for tuition at the private school.

On appeal to the Court of Appeals of Massachusetts, the lower court's determinations were affirmed. After resolving a number of procedural problems the court went on to say that "private placements are authorized only when the appropriate special education program . . . is not available within the public school system. . . . The private placement provisions of [the statute] only apply to a child who seeks services in the public school system and who is then identified as requiring special services which the school system either cannot, or chooses not to, provide." It was noted that parents who undertake a private placement unilaterally assume a financial risk because school authorities very possibly could recommend a different placement.

The court also commented on both federal and state laws which encourage a mainstreaming policy. It stated that the common objective of these laws is the prompt provision of needed services to learning-handicapped children through the free local public school system except where the resources of those schools cannot appropriately meet the childrens' needs. In this case, following that policy required a public school program for the child if one could be developed which would meet his special needs. Here the parents took the position that he would be better served by a private school education. This, of course, was their right but, subject to the limited exceptions, no public obligation to pay for this private education could arise unless a school authority determined that the public school system could not meet the child's special needs. Thus, the parents were obligated to pay their child's tuition costs. *School Committee of Franklin v. Commissioner of Education*, 462 N.E.2d 338 (Mass.App.1984).

An emotionally handicapped New York child and his parents sued their local school district and various state officials under the EAHCA to recover tuition and costs incurred during the year and one-half the child spent at a private school in Maine. The child had been placed in a private school in New York by his school district but was expelled. He then returned home where he received four months of home tutoring. Then, concluding that no good faith effort was being made to place the child, the parents sent him to the Maine school from which he graduated. Because the out-of-state school was not on New York's list of approved facilities the parents were denied reimbursement for expenses for this placement. Suit was then brought, but a U.S. district court in New York granted the defendants' motion to dismiss. The court said that parents are generally entitled to an impartial due process hearing if they disagree with a local placement recommendation. However, this procedure is not available to review the state Commissioner of Education's refusal to contract with an out-of-state facility. *Smrcka v. Ambach*, 555 F.Supp. 1227 (E.D.N.Y.1983).

The parents of a seventeen-year-old boy with a learning disability brought suit on behalf of their son in a U.S. district court in New York. They sought a preliminary injunction directing their local board to implement a decision of the state commissioner of education, which required the board to identify their son as handicapped and to provide special education instruction for him in a learning disability resource room. The board declined to implement the order even after a hearing officer concurred in the commissioner's decision. Suit was brought after the board stated that it would not implement the commissioner's order until all proceedings had been completed, a process which would take months.

At trial, the school board maintained that the finding of the commissioner and the hearing officer had placed too much emphasis on individual testing and had ignored the assessment of teachers who had worked with the student for several years. The board also pointed to the fact that the boy was passing his subjects and advancing through the grades at a normal pace. The court stated that a child should remain in his current educational placement until proceedings are completed unless an agreement is reached between the state or local education agency and the parents regarding an alternative program. The fact that the commissioner and the parents both wanted the boy to be placed in a special education program constituted such an agreement. The court also relied on the U.S. Supreme Court decision of *Board of Education v. Rowley,* which held that the court should maintain a hands-off rule in cases where a commissioner has chosen an appropriate educational program for a student. The preliminary injunction was granted. *Blazejewski v. Board of Education of Allegany Central School District,* 560 F.Supp. 701 (W.D. N.Y.1983).

In a District of Columbia case, a seventeen-year-old learning disabled boy had spent one year in a private special education boarding school. His parents were notified by the school board that it would not continue financial support of their son's placement at that school during the next year. The school board also informed the parents that it had decided on an alternative school for their boy's placement. The parents became very confused when, a few days after receiving the first notification, a second notice arrived recommending that their son attend yet another school. Letters written by the parents seeking an explanation for the conflicting recommendation went unanswered. When the next school year started, the parents reenrolled their son in the private boarding school. They then sued in the U.S. District Court for the District of Columbia, where they sought to have the school board held financially responsible for the boarding school placement.

The parents contended that since the school board had approved the boarding school during the previous year the provisions of the EAHCA dictated that the boy must remain at that school pending all administrative or judicial proceedings and until another appropriate placement was finally determined. The school board maintained that the boy's parents had purposefully delayed the proceedings and frustrated its attempts to find a new placement. The court held that while it was true that the parents had delayed the due process hearing, they did so out of confusion over the conflicting placement recommendations. Further, the notifications sent by the school board did not comply with the requirements set forth in the EAHCA. The court agreed with the parents' contention that the boarding school was the boy's current placement, and due to the procedural failures of the school board he must remain there pending further appeals. Summary judgment was granted in favor of the parents. *Jacobsen v. District of Columbia Board of Education,* 564 F.Supp. 166 (D.D.C.1983).

In an Illinois case, the mother of an emotionally handicapped child brought an action on behalf of her child. The mother, because of dissatisfaction with her school district's recommendation for educational placement of the child, unilaterally transferred him to a private school of her choosing. Thereafter, the Illinois Office of Education determined the local school district could provide an appropriate education of the child. The mother appealed this decision to the Illinois courts which reversed and ordered reimbursement for educational expenses. Employing a pre-*Burlington* legal standard, the Appellate Court of Illinois held that there generally are two circumstances where a parent should be able to be reimbursed for expenses relating to unilateral placement in a private school without undergoing lengthy administrative processes. One is where a child's physical health is endangered. The other is where a school has acted in bad faith in refusing to assign a child to a special school. Here the court stated that both circumstances could arguably have existed. Therefore, the placement of the child at the special school was proper and the mother was entitled to reimbursement from the child's district of residence. *Walker v. Cronin*, 438 N.E.2d 582 (Ill.App.1982).

A Massachusetts case involved a Down's syndrome child who, almost since birth, had been living at a private special education school at his parents' expense. When the parents sought an IEP the initial response was to place the child in a nonresidential public school. The parents objected and a long series of hearings and appeals ensued. Pursuant to the provisions of the EAHCA the boy remained at the private school at his parents' expense pending the outcome of the proceedings. The district court finally settled the placement question by ruling that the private school was indeed the proper IEP for the child. The district court, however, declined to reimburse the parents for their private school expenditures while the proceedings were taking place.

When the reimbursement question was appealed to the U.S. Court of Appeals, First Circuit, it held that the EAHCA made provisions for reimbursement only under circumstances not met by this case (a pre-*Burlington* decision). It noted, however, that Massachusetts law did provide for reimbursement in some situations and remanded the case to the district court to decide this question. The district court held that the parents were entitled to reimbursement under Massachusetts law. *Doe v. Anrig*, 561 F.Supp. 121 (D.Mass.1983).

In a case which was consolidated with the above opinion, parents enrolled their son in a private school contrary to the IEP that had been prepared for him. On three occasions hearings concerning the IEP either excluded the parents or were held when school officials knew that they would not be in attendance. The parents sought to have the IEP overturned and to obtain reimbursement for tuition paid to the private school. School officials moved for summary judgment, arguing that even if the court reversed the IEP the parents would still not be entitled to reimbursement. The court, in denying the motion for summary judgment, referred to a provision in the Code of Federal Regulations (34 CFR sec. 300.345) which states that "each public agency shall take steps to insure that one or both of the parents of the handicapped child are present at each meeting. . . ." The code goes on to state that these steps include early notification of the hearing and scheduling of the mutually agreed upon time and place. The school officials repeatedly violated these provisions, thus nullifying their IEP decision. The court held that tuition reimbursement would be appropriate if the parents' placement were to be ruled to be the correct one. *Doe v. Anrig*, 561 F.Supp. 121 (D.Mass.1983).

Schools also have a duty not to unilaterally change the placement of a handicapped child during pending proceedings. Two U.S. district court cases held, respectively, that a school for the blind located in New York and a Connecticut school district would not be allowed to expel handicapped students pending proceedings to determine an appropriate placement for the children. *Sherry v. New York State Department of Education*, 479 F.Supp. 1328 (W.D.N.Y.1979) and *Stuart v. Nappi*, 443 F.Supp. 1235 (D.Conn. 1978).

III. Reimbursement for Other Expenses

In addition to tuition reimbursement expenses, parents sometimes request reimbursement for other related expenses.

A Tennessee child who suffered from a learning disability, impaired vision and seizures was being provided with a special education under the Education for All Handicapped Children Act by his local school district. In the fall of the 1983-84 school year, school personnel noticed that the child's behavior and performance appeared to have worsened since the previous spring. They suspected that the child had suffered several grand mal seizures during the summer and that the child had not recently been examined by a physician. After the school district's multi-disciplinary team ("M Team") made a recommendation to his parents that he be medically evaluated by a physician, the parents had the child examined by a pediatrician, a neurologist and a psychologist. Although the M Team utilized the results of these neurological and psychological evaluations, they did not result in any change in the child's individualized educational program. A dispute arose over whether the school district was required under the EAHCA to pay the costs of these evaluations. The parents' insurance company had paid $79 of the $265 bill for the neurological evaluation, and $99 of the $247 psychological evaluation. A hearing officer ordered the school district to pay the difference between the amount paid by the parents' insurance company and the total cost of the evaluations.

The parents filed suit in U.S. district court seeking an order that the school district reimburse them for the amount the insurer had paid to the neurologist. The parents argued that because their insurance policy provided a maximum of $30,000 lifetime coverage for psychological expenses, the $99 payment made by their insurer resulted in their coverage being reduced to $29,901. This, they said, was contrary to the EAHCA's requirement that "related services," i.e., psychological and neurological evaluations, be provided free of charge. The district court agreed that the parents were entitled to reimbursement for the $99 which their insurer had paid for the psychological evaluation. However, because there was no comparable policy limit for neurological expenses, the parents had incurred no cost as a result of their insurer's payment of $79 for the neurological evaluation. The school district was thus ordered to reimburse the parents for all sums which they had paid to the neurologist and psychologist, minus the $79 paid to the neurologist pursuant to their insurance policy. The court concluded by ordering the district to pay the parents $99 to compensate for the reduction of the amount of coverage available for psychological expenses. *Seals v. Loftis*, 614 F.Supp. 302 (E.D.Tenn.1985).

In a Virginia case, a handicapped child brought suit against a school district alleging that the district failed to provide her with an appropriate education. The child, through her parents, requested reimbursement for the cost of summer programs which the child had attended as well as placement at a private school of the parents' choice. In addition, the child's parents requested reimbursement for their travel expenses incurred while the child was a patient and student at a home for crippled children in Pennsylvania. The U.S. district court held that neither state law nor the EAHCA required the state to pay all of the expenses incurred by parents in educating a child, whether the child is handicapped or nonhandicapped. Thus, the parents were not entitled to reimbursement for their travel expenses. *Bales v. Clarke*, 523 F.Supp. 1366 (E.D.Va.1981). See also *Helms v. Independent School District No. 3*, 750 F.2d 820 (10th Cir.1984), a similar Florida case in which the parents of a handicapped child enrolled in a Georgia residential school were denied reimbursement for their travel expenses incurred as a result of visits to their son in Georgia.

Private tutor fees for an autistic child were held by a federal district court to be a reasonable expense and one which the local school board should pay since it was appropriate to the needs of the child. *Boxall v. Sequoia Union High School District*, 464 F.Supp. 1104 (N.D.Cal.1979).

IV. Statutory Ceilings on Reimbursement

A statutory ceiling on reimbursement for tuition expenses is not allowed.

Florida statutory law imposed a limit on the amount of tuition a school district in that state could spend on private school education of the handicapped. The Florida Supreme Court, however, struck down the application of the statutory ceiling where the ceiling itself imposed a denial of a handicapped child's right to a free public education appropriate to his needs. *Scavella v. School Board of Dade County*, 363 So.2d 1095 (Fla.1978).

V. Monetary Damages

Suits wherein parents have sought money damages for what they believe has been improper placement of their children are generally unsuccessful because the EAHCA does not provide for payment of money damages. (See § VII for discussion of money damages under federal civil rights laws.)

In one such unsuccessful case, the parents of a Missouri child brought suit in U.S. district court under the Education for All Handicapped Children Act and section 1983 of the Civil Rights Act, alleging that their local school district had failed to provide their daughter with a free appropriate public education. The parents claimed over $1.5 million in damages as a result of this failure. After a series of motions and appeals the district court dismissed the parents' claims under the EAHCA, stating that damage awards were inappropriate under the Act. The parents' section 1983 claim was also dismissed because no discriminatory intent was proven, nor were procedural violations alleged which were not compensable through the EAHCA. The court granted the parents' motion to amend their complaint to include a claim under the Rehabilitation Act. This resulted in the present decision, in which the court dismissed the parents' amended complaint, stating that the Rehabilitation Act is inapplicable to cases where the relief sought can be obtained under the EAHCA. All the parents claimed in this lawsuit was that their child had been denied an appropriate education under the Act. Therefore a lawsuit could be maintained only under the EAHCA and the parents' claims were dismissed. *Miener v. Special School District*, 607 F.Supp. 1425 (E.D.Mo.1985).

Another case involved a fifteen-year-old learning disabled student in Connecticut who sued his school board pursuant to provisions of the EAHCA seeking a court order requiring board members to implement an individualized course of instruction designed to meet this student's educational needs. In addition, the complaint sought $1,000,000 in monetary damages for the alleged negligence of the board members in failing to implement an appropriate educational program earlier in the student's school career. Subsequent to the filing of the lawsuit the parties agreed to an appropriate educational program for this student. Thus, the question remaining was whether damages could be recovered for alleged negligence in failing to provide proper special education under federal law. A U.S. district court held that there was no implied private remedy for damages under the Act. The legislative history is devoid, said the court, of even the slightest suggestion that Congress intended it to serve as a vehicle through which to initiate a private cause of action for damages. The court dismissed the lawsuit against the board members. *Loughran v. Flanders*, 470 F.Supp. 110 (D.Conn.1979).

A U.S. district court in New York also held that money damages were not intended by Congress as a remedy for failure of a school board to place a handicapped child in an appropriate educational program. The question arose when parents of an emotionally handicapped student sued their school board seeking money damages as punishment for the board's failure to properly place their child in an appropriate educational program. The court noted that Congress passed the EAHCA in order to assist states in educating their handicapped. The legislation provides procedural safeguards to ensure appropriate placement while recognizing that diagnosis of special education problems is difficult and that errors can be made. The court also noted that the field of special education was new and undeveloped, and in need of flexibility for testing of new methods of educating handicapped children. Thus, if school officials were held to monetary liability for incorrect placement of a handicapped child, they would hesitate to implement innovative programs, which in turn would cause the education of handicapped children to suffer. For these reasons, the court held that money damages were not appropriate within the meaning of the EAHCA. *Davis v. Maine Endwell Central School District*, 542 F.Supp. 1257 (N.D.N.Y.1982).

A Wisconsin child was also not allowed to recover compensatory damages for an alleged inappropriate educational placement. In this case the U.S. Court of Appeals, Seventh Circuit, held that Congress, although including within the EAHCA a private right to action which authorizes district courts to award appropriate relief, did not intend to provide an award of money damages in the absence of exceptional circumstances. Such exceptional circumstances would include a situation where a child's health was endangered by the inappropriate placement or where school officials act in bad faith. Since no exceptional circumstances existed in this case, money damages were denied. *Anderson v. Thompson*, 658 F.2d 1205 (7th Cir.1981).

In a Georgia case, a young child, through his parents, brought an action against his school district, board of education and certain of its administrators seeking declaratory, injunctive and monetary relief for alleged violations of the EAHCA. When the child started school he was tested and it was determined by school authorities that he should be assigned to a self-contained learning disability classroom. The parents agreed to this placement. Approximately one year later the child's progress was reviewed and placement was changed to "research learning disability" which gave him part-time assistance. Again, the parents approved. Shortly thereafter, the parents insisted that their child be placed in a regular first grade class without resource assistance. This request was denied by the school board.

A hearing was later held at which the hearing officer determined that assistance was unnecessary, thus clearing the way for regular classroom placement. The school rejected this decision, prompting an automatic appeal to the state board of education. That board determined that the current school board placement was appropriate. Suit was then filed in federal court by the child and his parents. During pendency of the suit, the child was placed in a regular classroom setting. The trial court entered summary judgment for the local school board, a decision appealed to the U.S. Court of Appeals, Eleventh Circuit. The primary issue before the appellate court was whether the parents' monetary claims under the EAHCA were "moot" due to the child's removal from all special education during pendency of the action. The court said yes. The parents were entitled to no damages because, as a general rule, compensatory damages are not available under the EAHCA. *Powell v. Defore*, 699 F.2d 1078 (11th Cir.1983).

The parents of a high school freshman in Illinois sued a local school district seeking relief for their child who had been placed in a special education program. The child was referred to the district's Department of Special Education which recommended outside intensive psychotherapy. An individualized educational program, which did not include psychotherapy, was developed without participation by the child's parents. The child's condition worsened; nonetheless, the school district later issued the child a diploma. The parents brought suit seeking a revocation of the diploma, a court order directing remedial education for their child in a private residential facility, reimbursement for costs expended in providing services to their child under his independently prepared IEP, and $1,000,000 in general damages for alleged violations of the EAHCA.

In ruling against the parents, a U.S. district court cited Illinois law which requires that the state provide tuition-free education, but held that that did not require the state to provide psychotherapy. Further, general money damages are not available under the EAHCA. The attempt to have the diploma revoked was likewise dismissed since it would make no sense to revoke the diploma if the state was not required to provide the educational placement the parents sought. *Max M. v. Thompson*, 566 F.Supp. 1330 (N.D.Ill.1983). The case was appealed to the U.S. Court of Appeals, Seventh Circuit, which affirmed the district court ruling. The district court, however, was asked to reconsider its prior holding dismissing the child's claim for a compensatory education, and the case was remanded.

The Court of Appeals pointed out to the district court that shortly after it had rendered its opinion dismissing the child's claim for compensatory services, *Timms v. Metropolitan School District of Wabash County*, 722 F.2d 1310 (7th Cir.1983), was decided. That case denied a handicapped student's claim for a compensatory education on the ground that her parents failed to exhaust their administrative remedies prior to bringing suit. However, the court of appeals in *Timms* stated that an obligation placed upon the state to correct the effects of past educational shortcomings would not "fall afoul" of the Eleventh Amendment, which serves to bar lawsuits against public officials (see Chapter 6, § II). Further, because compensatory services in *Timms* were recharacterized as prospective, they were allowable under the EAHCA. The district court, hearing the case for a second time, held that the *Timms* decision was controlling and reinstated the student's claim for compensatory services. *Max M. v. Thompson*, 585 F.Supp. 317 (N.D.Ill.1984).

The mother of a handicapped student in Pennsylvania brought suit claiming money damages for the alleged mental and emotional suffering and loss of earnings which she and her son had experienced as a result of a local school district's failure to follow the provisions of the Pennsylvania Public School Code. Specifically, the mother claimed that her son suffered from a learning disability which was not identified by school officials, who had a statutory duty to identify exceptional children and provide them with a proper education. The Commonwealth Court of Pennsylvania held that the Pennsylvania Code reflected the intent of Congress in enacting the EAHCA, i.e., to improve the educational opportunity of exceptional children. Since the EAHCA afforded no private cause of action for money damages, no such remedy could be inferred from Pennsylvania law. *Lindsay v. Thomas*, 465 A.2d 122 (Pa.Cmwlth.1983).

Money damages were allowed in a case in New York. The parents of a seventeen-year-old deaf child brought suit in a U.S. district court, seeking to compel their local school district and the New York State Commissioner of Education to pay for their child's education since 1973-1974 at a special school for the deaf in Massachusetts. The suit was brought under the EAHCA with the parents claiming that the defendants' failure to bear such costs deprived their child of a free appropriate public education in violation of the Act. Up to the time of the suit the parents paid the expenses of sending the child to the school. The defendants claimed that adequate schools existed in New York, that the Massachusetts school was not approved by the Commissioner and that money damages may not be awarded in an action under the Act.

The court disagreed and held that money damages may be awarded in an action under the Act, "at least to the extent of reimbursement for tuition and expenses related to providing an appropriate educational placement for the handicapped child. The statute's language authorizing the court to fashion such relief as it determines to be 'appropriate' grants a substantial amount of discretion to the court." However, the court did state that such damages could be awarded against the school district only and not against the Commissioner. The mere fact that the school was not approved by the commissioner did not necessarily preclude the plaintiffs from maintaining the present action but they were told by the court that they could not maintain an action for school years for which they had not made prior request that the school district pay. The net result of the lawsuit was that a motion by the defendants to dismiss was denied but the parents were required to undergo additional administrative proceedings to further clarify the issues involved. In the meantime, court action was stayed. *Matthews v. Ambach*, 552 F.Supp. 1273 (W.D.N.Y.1982).

VI. Compensatory Education

A compensatory education, like monetary damages, is not usually awarded under the EAHCA.

A twenty-five-year-old California man with Down's syndrome brought suit against the California education commissioner on the grounds that he had been excluded from the educational system prior to 1973. The lawsuit alleged that for several years his mother had unsuccessfully tried to enroll him in a San Francisco public school special education class. In 1973, at the age of twelve, he was finally allowed to enroll in the special education program. When he reached the age of twenty-one, his school district sought to terminate his placement in the special education program as provided by section 1415(b)(2) of the EAHCA. He claimed, however, that he should be allowed to stay in the program to compensate for the seven years he was wrongfully denied a special education prior to 1973. A federal district court denied his request, and he appealed to the U.S. Court of Appeals, Ninth Circuit, which affirmed the district court's decision.

The appeals court ruled that even though the man had been denied access to a special education prior to the enactment of the EAHCA in 1975, he was barred from bringing suit under any other statute, including the Rehabilitation Act. The court cited the U.S. Supreme Court's 1984 decision of *Smith v. Robinson*, 104 S.Ct. 3457 (1984), which stated that all special education lawsuits must be brought under the EAHCA. In *Smith* the Supreme Court held that Congress, having passed the EAHCA, had removed all other Acts as possible bases for special education lawsuits. Extending this doctrine to lawsuits which arose even before 1975, the court of appeals held that the man could make no claim under any Act but the EAHCA. Since the EAHCA contains no provision authorizing "compensatory educations" for pre-1975 denials of special educational services, and explicitly states that persons over the age of twenty-one are not entitled to such services, the man's lawsuit was dismissed. *Alexopulos v. Riles*, 784 F.2d 1408 (9th Cir.1986).

The parents of a profoundly mentally handicapped twenty-year-old girl in Indiana who had received one and one-half hours of educational instruction from 1976 to 1980 requested, in 1979, that their daughter be placed in a full-day instructional program in the hope that she would respond to increased attention. The school district denied the request because of a belief that there was a correlation between the girl's self-abusive behavior and increased attention. After exhausting their administrative remedies the parents brought suit in a U.S. district court, which held in favor of the school district. On appeal to the U.S. Court of Appeals, Seventh Circuit, the parents sought an injunction to prohibit the school district from excluding their daughter from a full school day and, in addition, asking for one full year of day-long instruction to compensate for the 1979-80 school year during which she received one and one-half hours of instruction. The Court of Appeals held that the request for an injunction was moot because the girl was past the age at which the school district was required to provide educational services. The court also denied a compensatory education on the ground that since neither the EAHCA nor the Rehabilitation Act provide for general money damages for an alleged inadequate IEP, except in cases of bad faith refusal to abide by the procedures set out in those acts, the remedy of a compensatory education also could not be implied. *Timms v. Metropolitan School District of Wabash County*, 718 F.2d 212 (7th Cir. 1983).

The parents of a handicapped student in Georgia sought in federal court a compensatory education for their son, whom they claimed was inappropriately placed. The child had been attending a special education program which had been recommended by his school district. The parents insisted that he be placed in a regular classroom. A series of administrative appeals resulted in a determination that a special education environment would be best for the boy. However, the parents disagreed and filed suit in a U.S. district court, which entered summary judgment for the local school board. The parents appealed to the U.S. Court of Appeals, Eleventh Circuit, arguing that their son was entitled to a compensatory education so he could catch up to his age group, having fallen behind his nonhandicapped peers because of a year spent in the special education program. The court ruled against the parents, stating that there is nothing in the EAHCA requiring a school board to remediate a previously handicapped child. *Powell v. Defore*, 699 F.2d 1078 (11th Cir. 1983).

The governor of Illinois and state education officials appealed a court order reinstating the parents' claim for a compensatory education for their child. The officials alleged that the order should be amended on four grounds: 1) the parents' failure to assert the compensatory educational claim at the state level administrative hearing; 2) the requested relief was moot because the child had turned twenty-one and was no longer eligible for special education services; 3) the parents failed to allege sufficient wrongdoing on the part of the school district, i.e., that the school district had acted in bad faith; and 4) state educational officials should not be held legally responsible for the acts of a local educational agency.

A U.S. district court held that the record of the administrative proceedings revealed that the parents did raise the compensatory education issue at the state level hearing. Second, the issue was not moot because Congress did not intend to prevent compensatory educational relief in cases where a child may have passed the age where he is legally entitled to special education services. A contrary holding, said the court, could result in school districts intentionally delaying services until the districts are no longer responsible for the child's education. Third, the state's argument that the plaintiffs had failed to allege sufficient wrongdoing on the part of the state was invalid. The court held that the pre-*Burlington* "exceptional circumstances" test, where parents are entitled to reimbursement only when a school district has acted in bad faith or somehow endangered or threatened the health and safety of the child, did not apply. Here, the parents were asking for prospective relief, and the exceptional circumstances test applied only when retroactive relief is requested.

Finally, the court did not absolve the state defendants from liability for the local school district's actions. The court noted that Congress intended that responsibility for the implementation of all services under the EAHCA be at the state level. However, the plaintiffs could only sue the state defendants in their official, not individual, capacity. The court held that there was no basis for holding the governor liable. The state's motion to amend the previous order was thus granted in part and denied in part. *Max M. v. Thompson*, 592 F.Supp. 1450 (N.D.Ill.1984). See also *Max M. v. Thompson*, 592 F.Supp. 1437 (N.D.Ill.1984), a case involving the same child and included in the material in this volume addressing related services [Chapter 2, § VI(A)].

VII. Availability Of Civil Rights Remedies

Section 1983 of the federal Civil Rights Act and the Rehabilitation Act of 1973 are sometimes invoked by plaintiffs as a remedy where the EAHCA fails to provide one. Both Acts prohibit unfair discrimination against handicapped individuals. Unlike the EAHCA, the Rehabilitation Act does not necessarily mandate that action be taken, but rather forbids action detrimental to the handicapped. The 1984 U.S. Supreme Court case *Smith v. Robinson* (see § VIII) has barred recourse to the Rehabilitation Act in cases where the relief sought is available under the EAHCA. Additionally, *Smith v. Robinson* held that the Civil Rights Act may not be resorted to in special education cases, unless the child has been denied the benefits of the procedures outlined in the EAHCA.

The U.S. Court of Appeals, Eleventh Circuit, held that where a school district deprives a handicapped child of a due process hearing under the Education for All Handicapped Children Act, a lawsuit may be brought under section 1983 of the Civil Rights Act. This case involved an emotionally and physically impaired high school girl in Florida who was placed in a county special education school pursuant to her individualized educational program. Although the girl made excellent progress at school she fought incessantly with her family. As a result her mother decided that placement at an out-of-state residential facility was warranted, and she requested a due process hearing on this matter. The school district special education director forwarded the mother's request for a due process hearing to the school district attorney, but no hearing was provided within the Act's forty-five day limit.

The child's parents then unilaterally placed the girl in the private facility and filed suit against the school district seeking to recover their tuition costs and attorney's fees. The parents' lawsuit was based upon the EAHCA, the Rehabilitation Act and section 1983. A U.S. district court held that 1) the EAHCA cannot provide the basis for an award of compensatory damages; 2) the Rehabilitation Act provides no private cause of action for money damages; and 3) section 1983 is inapplicable to special education cases because Congress intended that the EAHCA be the exclusive remedy.

The parents appealed to the U.S. Court of Appeals, Eleventh Circuit, which reversed in part and affirmed in part. The court held that section 1983 may provide the basis for a lawsuit in special education cases where, as here, the plaintiff has been denied the procedural protections of the EAHCA. This was significant because of the relative ease of obtaining money damages and attorney's fees under section 1983. The appeals court affirmed the district court ruling with regard to the claim under the Rehabilitation Act and remanded the case to the district court for a determination of money damages. *Manecke v. School Board of Pinellas County, Florida*, 762 F.2d 912 (11th Cir.1985).

The U.S. Court of Appeals, Sixth Circuit, affirmed a U.S. district court decision which dismissed claims under the Rehabilitation Act and Civil Rights Act. The Court of Appeals based its decision on *Smith v. Robinson*, which held that the Rehabilitation Act is inapplicable when relief is available under the EAHCA to remedy a denial of education services, and which also disposed of the issue of whether a plaintiff can base a claim under the Civil Rights Act when a handicapped child has been denied equal protection of the law due to the failure of school authorities to provide a free appropriate public education. *Smith* concluded that Congress intended the EAHCA to be the "exclusive avenue through which a plaintiff may assert an equal protection claim to a publicly financed special education," observed the court of appeals.

The court of appeals also denied the parents' contention that the alleged mistreatment of their child by school authorities constituted an independent constitutional claim. The parents asserted that allegations of mistreatment, e.g., isolation, corporal punishment, withholding of the child's coat, and exclusion from a school field trip were violations actionable under the Civil Rights Act, independent of their claim that the child was not provided a free and appropriate public education in accordance with the EAHCA. The court of appeals found that the parents' civil rights claim did not identify an independent claim, but rather alleged that education officials violated the Civil Rights Act by failing to obey commands of the EAHCA. The parents could not circumvent the procedural requirements of the EAHCA by basing their claim upon the Civil Rights Act. *Austin v. Brown Local School District*, 746 F.2d 1161 (6th Cir.1984).

A young Missouri girl, suffering from behavioral, emotional and learning handicaps, brought an action in U.S. district court in 1979 against a number of school defendants, including the St. Louis School District. She sought to remedy denial of appropriate educational opportunities for herself through declaratory and injunctive relief as well as damages. The district court dismissed the complaint. An appeal to the U.S. Court of Appeals, Eighth Circuit, followed with that court affirming in part and reversing in part. Affirmed were dismissals of all claims against the state and all EAHCA damage claims. However, dismissal of the Rehabilitation Act damage claims was reversed, as were the plaintiff's claims under the federal Civil Rights Act. The case was then remanded to the district court with instructions to consider the civil rights claims.

On remand, the district court held that the plaintiff could not seek damages under the Civil Rights Act. It said that the damages sought under the act are coextensive with damages sought under the EAHCA and the Rehabilitation Act. Regarding the EAHCA the court noted that "the remedial devices in the act are sufficiently comprehensive to demonstrate congressional intent to preclude a suit under section 1983 [of the Civil Rights Act]. This Court is cognizant of the fact that the overwhelming weight of authority is in accord with this opinion. . . . In sum, the availability of a private right of action under the EAHCA, the detailed statutory administrative and judicial scheme, the fact that Congress intended the EAHCA to create new rights, and the absence of a traditional damage remedy, together compel our conclusion that the judicial remedy provided in the EAHCA was intended to be exclusive."

Regarding the Rehabilitation Act, the court held that "a section 1983 action is not available for violations of the Rehabilitation Act. The existence of a damage remedy in a private Rehabilitation Act action renders section 1983 remedies less inconsistent with the act's remedies, but this does not necessarily negate the possibility of such inconsistency. . . . It is possible that . . . damages . . . may not be recoverable under a Rehabilitation Act action to the extent that they are under section 1983. Any such restriction would, like the private action itself, be implied from Congress' intent as expressed in the act. This possibility of inconsistency is but one reason for this Court's conclusion that the relief available under the Rehabilitation Act, whether express or implied, is exclusive and precludes a section 1983 action." In short, the court determined that the EAHCA and the Rehabilitation Act provide remedial devices sufficiently comprehensive to indicate congressional intent to preclude suit under section 1983 of the federal Civil Rights Act. An order in accordance with this determination was issued. *Miener v. Special School District of St. Louis*, 580 F.Supp. 562 (E.D.Mo.1984).

A U.S. district court in Wisconsin rejected the claims of two handicapped children who contended that they had valid claims under the Rehabilitation Act even if they were precluded from recovering under the EAHCA. The court stated that a plaintiff cannot proceed with a claim under the latter statute—whether it is based on a substantive or a procedural challenge to state and local agency action—without having exhausted administrative remedies under the EAHCA. Although the plaintiffs asserted that their claim under the one statute was independent of the one under the other statute, the court disagreed, stating that since both claims came from the same set of facts, they must at least be considered parallel. A further assertion by the plaintiffs was that they had an independent right of action for violation of constitutional rights under federal civil rights statutes. This contention was also rejected by the court, which noted that "a number of courts have addressed this issue and have concluded that exhaustion of the EAHCA's [administrative] procedures should be required before constitutional claims that parallel EAHCA claims can be pursued in federal court." The court concluded by granting the defendants' motion for summary judgment and dismissing both federal and state law claims. *M.R. v. Milwaukee Public Schools*, 584 F.Supp. 767 (E.D.Wis.1984).

The mother of a handicapped child in New York claimed that she and her son suffered damages as a result of a local school district's failure to evaluate the child and provide him the special education to which he was entitled. The child allegedly suffered damages to his intellect, emotional capacity and personality, and was impeded in acquiring necessary training. In addition, the mother alleged that she moved to a different school district to obtain the services her child needed and that she herself suffered emotional distress. A U.S. district court held in favor of the mother and child, and the school district appealed.

The U.S. Court of Appeals, Second Circuit, held that because the mother had not availed herself of her administrative remedies under the EAHCA, she was deprived of her means of relief under that Act. However, the court found it unthinkable that Congress would have intended that a parent in this situation, where the district had refused to evaluate the child, should be left without any remedy. Accordingly, the court permitted the Civil Rights Act to supply the remedy for the mother who had been denied procedural safeguards under the EAHCA. The court viewed the absence of any prescribed remedy in the EAHCA as a "gap" to be filled by section 1983 of the Civil Rights Act. The case was remanded to determine the amount of damages. *Quakenbush v. Johnson City School District*, 716 F.2d 141 (2d Cir.1983).

The New Mexico Association for Retarded Citizens and others commenced a class action against the state of New Mexico, seeking declaratory and injunctive relief on behalf of handicapped children allegedly denied certain federally guaranteed special education services. The case, decided by the U.S. Court of Appeals, Tenth Circuit, involved the interpretation of section 504 of the Rehabilitation Act. Section 504 provides that "no otherwise qualified handicapped individual in the United States . . . shall, solely by reason of his handicap, be excluded from participation in, be denied the benefits of, or be subjected to discrimination under any program or activity receiving federal financial assistance." Under the regulations to this act schools are required to provide "free appropriate public education" to all handicapped students within their territorial jurisdiction.

The court of appeals observed that the U.S. Supreme Court has held, in interpreting section 504, that its purpose is to prohibit discrimination against the handicapped rather than mandate affirmative relief for them. This is distinguished from the affirmative duties required under the EAHCA, which makes the receipt of federal money contingent on a state's performing affirmative duties with respect to the education of the handicapped. The state of New Mexico had chosen not to participate in the EAHCA program. Against this legislative and regulatory backdrop, citizens in New Mexico contended that the state's entire program in dealing with the special needs of handicapped children was deficient. The court, while recognizing that discrimination against handicapped children could require the fashioning of a judicial remedy, remanded the case to a lower court, stating that section 504 violations must be evaluated in light of the Supreme Court's decision that the statute and its regulations are designed to prohibit discrimination rather than to require action. *New Mexico Association for Retarded Citizens v. State of New Mexico*, 678 F.2d 847 (10th Cir.1982).

A fifteen-year-old New York girl, three and one-half feet tall with a partially amputated right arm, a functionally impaired left arm and hand, and legs of approximately one foot in length, asked for and received from her school district a special van to transport her to school and the help of an aide during the school day. The school sponsored a Spanish class trip to Spain for which this student was academically qualified. The trip involved tours of historical sites which required the students to walk many miles. The school denied this student permission to go on the trip on the ground that she would endanger herself by attending. She sued the school seeking to enjoin it from enforcing its ban on her attendance. She argued that because the school was receiving federal funding for this trip she could not be barred from going simply on the ground that she was handicapped.

A U.S. district court in New York noted that the Rehabilitation Act of 1973 specifically states that a handicapped student may not be excluded from participation in a program receiving federal funding solely on the basis of his or her handicap if that student is otherwise qualified. However, in this case, after the court itself witnessed the difficulty this child had even climbing onto the witness stand, it held that she was not otherwise qualified since she could not fulfill the physical requirements of the trip. Her complaint against the school district was dismissed. *Wolff v. South Colonie School District*, 534 F.Supp. 758 (N.D.N.Y.1982).

In ruling that Rhode Island school officials failed to provide two learning disabled children an appropriate education, the U.S. Court of Appeals, First Circuit, nevertheless ruled that the children were not entitled to damages under the Rehabilitation Act for their alleged time, expense, inconvenience and suffering resulting from a local school district's failure to provide the children the appropriate education. The court said that because the EAHCA provided no remedy for damages, recourse to the more general provisions of the Rehabilitation Act could not be taken. *Colin K. v. Schmidt*, 715 F.2d 1 (1st Cir.1983).

The mother of an eleven-year-old girl with cerebral palsy, who challenged the proposed transfer of her child from a traditional elementary school to an elementary school specially designed to meet the needs of handicapped children, was denied relief under the EAHCA and the Rehabilitation Act. In holding that the child could not receive a satisfactory education in a traditional school, even with the use of supplementary aids and services to the maximum extent possible, a U.S. District Court in Michigan stated that there was no valid claim under the Rehabilitation Act because, under this Act, there must be an intentional, bad faith denial of education resources, or a grossly negligent placement decision. This was not the case here. Thus, the transfer decision was upheld. *Johnston v. Ann Arbor Public Schools*, 569 F.Supp. 1502 (E.D.Mich.1983).

VIII. Attorney's Fees

There is no provision in the EAHCA for attorney's fees. Accordingly, the U.S. Supreme Court held in *Smith v. Robinson* (reprinted in the Appendix of U.S. Supreme Court cases in this volume) that attorney's fees are not recoverable for special education claims made under the EAHCA.

In *Smith* the U.S. Supreme Court ruled that attorney's fees are not available under the EAHCA, the Civil Rights Act, or the Rehabilitation Act. This case involved a child in Rhode Island who suffered from cerebral palsy and other physical and emotional handicaps. The child's parents had prevailed in their claim against their local school district and the district was obligated to maintain the child in his then current residential school placement while a dispute involving who was to pay for the placement was resolved. After the parents collected their child's tuition costs from the school district, they sought attorney's fees. The federal district court granted them under the Civil Rights Act and the Rehabilitation Act, both of which contained provisions authorizing an award of attorney's fees to a successful plaintiff. The U.S. Court of Appeals, First Circuit, reversed and denied attorney's fees, and the U.S. Supreme Court upheld the reversal.

The Supreme Court undertook a three-step analysis. First, under the common law, attorney's fees are not available unless a specific statutory provision authorizes them. Second, the EAHCA contains no attorney's fees provision. Third, by enacting the EAHCA, Congress intended to make it the exclusive remedy for handicapped public school students, thereby preventing them from relying on either the Civil Rights Act or the Rehabilitation Act. The comprehensiveness of the EAHCA's "carefully tailored scheme," assuring that school districts will educate handicapped children, convinced the Supreme Court that when Congress gave handicapped children the rights contained in the EAHCA, it removed any other Act as a basis for special education lawsuits. Hence, a special education plaintiff could not use the Civil Rights Act or the Rehabilitation Act as the basis for an award of attorney's fees.

An exception was made, however, for cases in which a school district deprives a handicapped student of his or her procedural rights under the EAHCA. If a student proves that a school district denied him or her the procedural rights to which every handicapped child is entitled, then an attorney's fees award under the Civil Rights Act would be justified. This is because the EAHCA places great emphasis on following certain procedures. If the district denies a student due process of law, then a due process challenge under the Civil Rights Act is a legitimate remedy. In the present case, however, there was no evidence that the school district had violated the EAHCA's procedural safeguards, and attorney's fees were denied. *Smith v. Robinson*, 104 S.Ct. 3457 (1984).

A U.S. district court in Texas awarded attorney's fees to the mother of a handicapped child who successfully challenged denial of a free appropriate education under the EAHCA, the Equal Protection Clause and the Civil Rights Act. The defendant school district in that case appealed the award of attorney's fees to the U.S. Court of Appeals, Fifth Circuit, which deferred its decision until the U.S. Supreme Court case *Smith v. Robinson* was decided. The Court of Appeals held that under *Smith*, that portion of the award of attorney's fees compensating the attorneys for their efforts in securing relief which alternatively could have been provided by resort to the administrative avenues of the EAHCA was erroneous and should be reversed. In addition, any portion of the award of attorney's fees for Rehabilitation Act claims cognizable under either the EAHCA or on the equal protection theory must be reversed. Since the EAHCA itself can be employed to require the school district to grant appropriate relief from this violation, resort to the Rehabilitation Act or an equal protection theory was unnecessary, and a grant of fees inappropriate.

The court observed that *Smith* made it clear that where the Rehabilitation Act gives no more to a plaintiff's substantive claim than does the EAHCA, a plaintiff may not employ the Rehabilitation Act to circumvent the EAHCA's administrative procedures as a means to collect attorney's fees. The mother's due process claim based on the district's failure to involve her in the development of individualized education plans, found the court, precluded an award of attorney's fees because these fees may be appropriate in EAHCA cases where procedural due process claims are involved. Because the mother's right to privacy claim did not overlap or interfere with the EAHCA, it was also not precluded by the *Smith* case. Other constitutional challenges in the mother's claim which did not rest on the EAHCA also did not preclude attorney's fees. Finally, the court held that the district court, on remand, must, pursuant to *Smith*, only award attorney's fees to the extent that the plaintiffs actually prevailed on their constitutional claims. Any additional fees based on mere allegations of constitutional violations should be vacated. Accordingly, the case was remanded to the district court for a redetermination of attorney's fees. *Teresa Diane P. v. Alief Independent School District*, 744 F.2d 484 (5th Cir. 1984).

After a U.S. district court in New Hampshire declared a state institution providing educational services to the mentally retarded an "educational wasteland" and awarded the residents of the institution attorney's fees in their lawsuit against state officials, both parties appealed. The residents claimed that the award was too low and that they should have been awarded fees against nine local school districts whose attempt to intervene in the lawsuit was aborted. The residents also claimed that they were entitled to interest on the award due to alleged delays in the district court's decision. The state officials challenged on appeal the inclusion of several items in the award to the plaintiffs and the fact that an award was made to the plaintiffs' at all when some of the plaintiffs' claims had been unsuccessful.

The U.S. Court of Appeals, First Circuit, held that the plaintiffs' overall success in "overhauling" the practices of the institution entitled them to a general award of attorney's fees without regard to whether some of the claims had been unsuccessful. However, the appellate court agreed with the defendants' arguments that no grounds to support attorney's fees connected with EAHCA claims. The U.S. Supreme Court made it clear in *Smith v. Robinson* that the EAHCA is the "exclusive avenue through which a [handicapped] plaintiff may assert an equal protection claim to a publicly financed special education." The Supreme Court similarly ruled out reliance upon the fees provision of the Rehabilitation Act, on the ground that the Rehabilitation Act does "not require affirmative action on behalf of handicapped persons, but only the absence of discrimination against those persons." In light of the *Smith* case, the Court of Appeals reversed that portion of the attorney's fees award allocable to EAHCA claims.

The court upheld the portion of the award attributable to post-judgment monitoring fees, which were incurred in the process of making certain that the district court's orders were carried out, finding that such services necessary for reasonable monitoring of a court order are compensable. The court also upheld a twenty percent "bonus" awarded to two of the plaintiffs' counsel. The rule governing such bonuses requires that the legal representation rendered by the recipients of the bonuses be "unusually good and exceptional results obtained." The court, noting that such bonuses are only awarded on rare occasions, observed that exceptional results were indeed obtained in this case. Turning, then, to the residents' claim for interest on the fee award, the court held that because the district court, in its discretion, chose not to award interest on the award, the appellate court would not disturb the district court's ruling on this issue. Likewise, the appellate court rejected the residents' claim against the nine would-be intervenors, i.e., the school districts, on the ground that the only claims against the districts were EAHCA claims. *Garrity v. Sununu*, 752 F.2d 727 (1st Cir.1984).

In January, 1980, the New York State Education Department notified its County Boards of Cooperative Education Services (BOCES) that under current law, state funding for the education of learning disabled children by BOCES would no longer be available. The education department stated that funding would henceforth be available only for school district-run learning disabled programs. BOCES therefore notified its school districts that it would discontinue its learning disabled programs. On April 3, 1980, the state legislature amended its education code to allow continued funding of the BOCES programs. Despite this action on the part of the state to guarantee the ongoing provision of special educational services to children in BOCES-run programs, several parents of children in these programs brought a class action suit in U.S. district court against the commissioner of education. The lawsuit sought an injunction against the termination of learning disabled programs, to which the children were entitled under the Education for All Handicapped Children Act (EAHCA), and asked for an award of attorney's fees under the Civil Rights Act. The parents claimed that attorney's fees were justified in this case because, due to the former proposal that BOCES funding would be discontinued, their children had been in danger of being deprived of an appropriate education without benefit of a hearing. The district court awarded attorney's fees in the amount of $8,818 and the commissioner of education appealed.

The U.S. Court of Appeals, Second Circuit, reversed the award, holding that the children had never been in any danger of being deprived of appropriate educations. At the time the lawsuit was commenced, the legislature had already acted to assure continued funding for the BOCES programs. Thus the parents could hardly claim to have been successful in their lawsuit. In order for the Civil Rights Act to provide a basis for attorney's fees in EAHCA cases, the plaintiffs must be successful in their claims, and they must prove a violation of the EAHCA's procedural safeguards. As neither of these factors were present in this case, the court of appeals reversed the award of attorney's fees. Furthermore, in light of the parents' decision to bring suit after the state had already acted to assure the continued education of their children, the appeals court remanded the case to the district court for a determination of whether the commissioner of education was entitled to attorney's fees from the parents. *Bonar v. Ambach*, 771 F.2d 14 (2d Cir.1985).

In 1978, a handicapped girl obtained a preliminary injunction from a U.S. district court in Connecticut which prevented her school board from expelling her from high school. The board was also ordered to conduct an immediate review of her individualized educational program under the Education for All Handicapped Children Act. The girl's class action suit continued in district court for the next five years with the girl seeking a declaratory judgment that the school board "was bound by the procedural requirements of the EAHCA if it desired to exclude a handicapped student from class attendance for longer than a 10 day period." In 1984, the class action suit was dismissed because the girl had graduated and was no longer a member of the class she purported to represent. She then petitioned the district court for an award of attorney's fees pursuant to section 1988 of the Civil Rights Act. The court, while noting that attorney's fees are rarely justified in cases involving the EAHCA, ordered the school board and state department of education to pay the full amount of the girl's attorney's fees ($57,631).

Although plaintiffs in EAHCA cases often allege violations of the Civil Rights Act, the district court noted that *Smith v. Robinson* held that substantive claims made under the EAHCA will not justify the use of section 1988 as a basis for attorney's fees. The court observed, however, that where a plaintiff is successful in proving that a school board or other state entity has deprived the plaintiff of procedural protections, attorney's fees may be awarded. In the present case, the girl proved that the board, by excluding her from class attendance for longer than a ten day period, had failed to provide her with the procedural safeguards mandated by the EAHCA. These procedural violations gave rise to an award of attorney's fees under section 1988 of the Civil Rights Act, and the court ordered that the school board, as the primary party at fault, pay eighty percent of the award and that the state department of education pay twenty percent. *Stuart v. Nappi*, 610 F.Supp. 90 (D.Conn.1985).

The U.S. Court of Appeals, Eleventh Circuit, was asked by the U.S. Supreme Court to revise one of its prior holdings in light of *Smith v. Robinson*. In the original case, the Court of Appeals affirmed the judgment of a trial court granting an injunction against a Georgia school district's continuing policy of not considering or providing more than 180 days of education for profoundly mentally retarded children. The subsequent U.S. Supreme Court decision caused the court of appeals to reconsider its earlier opinion. Although the issue of attorney's fees was not presented in the earlier court of appeals case, the court of appeals did expressly state that recovery could be had under the Rehabilitation Act. The court of appeals, in light of the *Smith* decision, now found this to be incorrect. The court therefore modified its previous opinion by deleting certain references in its original opinion to the Rehabilitation Act. The court affirmed a U.S. district court ruling in favor of the plaintiffs in the prior case to the extent that it granted relief under the Education for All Handicapped Children Act, and reversed those portions of the ruling which held that the plaintiffs were entitled to relief under the Rehabilitation Act. *Georgia Association of Retarded Citizens v. McDaniel*, 740 F.2d 902 (11th Cir.1984). See also *Hayward v. Thompson*, 593 F.Supp. 57 (N.D.Ill.1984), an Illinois case wherein relief under the Rehabilitation Act was denied on similar grounds.

The U.S. Court of Appeals, Seventh Circuit, was asked to decide whether the prevailing party in a lower court action was entitled to attorneys fees in an action brought under the EAHCA. The parents of a handicapped girl brought suit against state and local education and health officials in Indiana, alleging that their daughter had been denied the free, appropriate public education to which she was entitled under the EAHCA. A U.S. district court held that 1) the EAHCA did not provide a private cause of action for damages; 2) the parents had failed to comply with the EAHCA's statutory requirements by removing their daughter from her current educational placement before completing the administrative remedies available under the Act; 3) the parents had not exhausted available administrative procedures; and 4) the parents' claim was barred by a prior controlling court decision which had disposed of this issue. The school and health officials then filed a motion in U.S. district court for attorney's fees arguing that because the parents' claim for damages was brought in bad faith, the court should award fees. The district court held that the parents had litigated in bad faith, but denied attorney's fees to the school officials on the ground that the case of *Anderson v. Thompson*, 658 F.2d 1205 (7th Cir.1981), barred attorney's fees to a prevailing defendant even when the plaintiff litigated in bad faith.

The U.S. Court of Appeals affirmed the holding of the district court, but on different grounds. It disagreed with the district court that *Anderson* barred an award of attorney's fees. *Anderson* (decided prior to the Supreme Court's ruling in *Burlington School Committee v. Department of Education of Massachusetts*) held that, absent special circumstances, damages were not an appropriate remedy under the EAHCA. Two special circumstances may exist: 1) if the child's physical health was endangered by the current placement, or 2) if the defendant acted in bad faith. *Anderson*, therefore, did not present a complete bar to the parents' claim, as there was evidence that the school officials acted in bad faith in their dealings with the parents. Thus, the district court's conclusion that the parents litigated in bad faith was erroneous, but its ruling was upheld. Attorney's fees were denied. *Benner v. Negley*, 725 F.2d 446 (7th Cir.1984).

At issue before the Court of Appeal of California was whether a handicapped child, who had prevailed in a court action against a local school district for the district's failure to provide an appropriate special education for him, was entitled to have his attorney's fees paid by the school district. The Court of Appeal affirmed a California trial court decision which held that the student was not entitled to attorney's fees. The court noted that section 1988 of the federal Civil Rights Act provides for an award of attorney's fees to the prevailing part in an action to enforce a provision of the Civil Rights Act. However, the court held that the student, in an action under the EAHCA, could not invoke this provision to recover attorney's fees. The court relied upon other cases which have held that, although the violation of a federal statute can be the basis of a civil rights action, violation of the EAHCA may not be the basis of such an action. The EAHCA already provides for a comprehensive scheme of state administrative proceedings, and an action under section 1983 would, therefore, serve "no purpose other than that of a conduit for attorney's fees."

The court also held that there was no valid claim under the Rehabilitation Act for attorney's fees. The court stated that the student would be required to allege something more than mere failure to provide a "free appropriate education" required by the EAHCA. The severely language-handicapped student failed to allege a substantial claim under the Rehabilitation Act and thus was not entitled to attorney's fees under that Act. Finally, Government Code section 800 could not be relied upon to provide attorney's fees. To recover under this provision the plaintiff must show that the hearing officer at the administrative level acted arbitrarily and capriciously, and no such showing was made. Attorney's fees were denied. *Byrnes v. Capistrano Unified School District*, 204 Cal.Rptr. 100 (Cal.App.4th Dist.1984).

The parents of a handicapped child in Oregon brought a complaint before the Oregon Department of Education (DOE) alleging that the school district had violated various state and federal statutes and administrative rules concerning the education of their child. The DOE agreed and awarded the parents partial reimbursement of tuition and costs, but denied their request for attorney's fees. The Oregon Court of Appeals, in a prior holding, had reversed the DOE's ruling, stating that the department had the power to award attorney's fees. The school district sought reconsideration of this holding in light of the intervening U.S. Supreme Court decision of *Smith v. Robinson.*

The Court of Appeals held that because *Smith* does not specifically address situations where the EAHCA is not available, or situations where the right claimed is not provided by the EAHCA with more clarity and precision than the right provided by the Rehabilitation Act, the prior holding would not be disturbed. It was not apparent from the record of the prior proceedings that the parents relied solely on the Rehabilitation Act for an award of attorney's fees, or that the rights the parents claimed under the Rehabilitation Act were more clearly and precisely guaranteed by the EAHCA. The court concluded that the case should be remanded to the DOE for specific consideration of the parents' Rehabilitation Act claims before *Smith* could effectively bar the parents' claim for attorney's fees. *Laughlin v. School District No. 1*, 689 P.2d 334 (Or.App.1984).

The U.S. Court of Appeals, Seventh Circuit, was asked to decide whether attorney's fees were available to an Indiana parent who had challenged the practice and policy of school officials in expelling special education students for disciplinary reasons. The parents sought reimbursement for attorney's fees under the Rehabilitation Act, as the EAHCA contains no provisions for attorney's fees. The general rule is that attorney's fees are not recoverable unless a specific statute provides for such a recovery. The court held that since the EAHCA provided all the necessary avenues for relief, the parent could not look to the Rehabilitation Act for additional relief. Attorney's fees were denied. *Doe v. Kroger*, 710 F.2d 1209 (7th Cir.1983).

Parents of a learning disabled child sought state financing of a private residential education, plus attorney's fees. The case had been partially settled before the trial to the extent that the school district agreed to pay private school expenses until the resolution of the dispute. The parents claimed that they were entitled to fees under the Rehabilitation Act, which allows a grant of attorney's fees under section 504 whenever a party presents a "substantial section 504 claim, even if settlement takes place prior to adjudication."

A U.S. district court in Delaware was asked to determine whether the parents had a "substantial claim" to justify the award of attorney's fees. The court held that since the child had available to him a public school education, state and local officials were not required to finance a private education placement. The court found no legal basis to justify the award of fees as the parents sought no more than the EAHCA grants, rather than something which could be granted under the Rehabilitation Act. Thus, the generalized remedies of the Rehabilitation Act, which includes attorney's fees, could not be utilized to circumvent the specifically enumerated administrative procedures of the EAHCA, if the EAHCA was applicable. *Rollison v. Biggs*, 567 F.Supp. 964 (D.Del.1983).

The rationale behind the general rule against attorney's fees was set forth by the U.S. Court of Appeals, First Circuit, in its opinion in the *Smith v. Robinson* case. In this case the Cumberland, Rhode Island, school district successfully appealed an award of attorney's fees to a child handicapped by cerebral palsy. The child had been enrolled in a private program which all parties agreed provided him with an appropriate education. The school district paid tuition for a period of time, then discontinued such payments under the belief that the Rhode Island Department of Mental Health, Retardation and Hospitals was the responsible agency. Following a lawsuit by the student and his parents, judgment was rendered in their favor. The plaintiffs then sought attorney's fees, which were awarded by a U.S. district court. The U.S. Court of Appeals, First Circuit, reversed. The court stated that "under what is labeled the American Rule, attorney's fees are only available as a general matter when statutory authority so provides." Here the action fell within the parameter of the EAHCA, a federal law which contains no provisions for attorney's fees. The court said no right to attorney's fees could be created when it appeared that Congress, perhaps recognizing the shortness of school funds, made no effort to include such a provision in the law. *Smith v. Cumberland School Committee*, 703 F.2d 4 (1st Cir.1983); affirmed, 104 S.Ct. 3457 (1984).

The "prevailing" plaintiffs in a civil rights class action suit, which challenged the conditions and practices at a center for retarded children, brought suit in U.S. district court against the state of New York for an award of attorney's fees incurred in the prior litigation. The court held that the plaintiffs were entitled to an award of attorney's fees even though the court had not yet finally disposed of the case. The computation of the amount of fees was determined by the number of hours reasonably expended by the prevailing party's counsel, and that number was then multiplied by a reasonable hourly rate. The court also considered facts such as the risk of compensation to the sole practitioner who had handled the very complex and time-consuming case, the high quality of representation the lawyer gave the case and the excellent result obtained. The court declined, however, to award the plaintiffs the full amount of travel time spent by a consulting lawyer who practiced in Washington, D. C., nor fees for communications with newspapers and television stations and for press conferences, as these were not hours "expended on litigation."

This decision was reversed by the U.S. Court of Appeals, Second Circuit. The court of appeals reasoned that since it had previously vacated and remanded the case on appeal, *Society For Good Will To Retarded Children v. Cuomo*, 572 F.Supp. 1300 (E.D.N.Y.1983), and *Society For Good Will To Retarded Children v. Cuomo*, 737 F.2d 1239 (2d Cir.1984), the plaintiffs had not yet prevailed on the merits of the case. An award of attorney's fees is available under section 1988 "only to a party who has established his entitlement to some relief on the merits on his claims." The court found that while its earlier opinion rendered on appeal may have made it seem likely that the plaintiff would be entitled to some relief, it was impossible to be certain how much—if any—would eventually be granted. Therefore, an award of attorney's fees at this point, said the court, would be premature. The court further held that the defendant state of New York was not entitled to attorney's fees as the plaintiff's action was not groundless. *Society For Good Will To Retarded Children v. Cuomo*, 737 F.2d 1243 (2d Cir.1984).

CHAPTER FIVE

STUDENTS

I. Injuries

Courts have generally held schools and their agents liable for injuries received by handicapped children during the course of the regular school day which resulted from the schools' or their agents' failure to provide a reasonably safe environment, failure to warn participants of known hazards or to remove known dangers where possible, failure to properly instruct participants in an activity, or failure to provide supervision adequate for the type of activity, the ages of the participants involved and their physical and mental capabilities. However, the doctrine of governmental immunity, which has been eliminated in many states by legislation or judicial decision, may provide an absolute shield against liability for schools and their agents in the states where the doctrine still exists.

In a case arising in the state of Washington, a mentally handicapped high school junior was seriously burned during metal shop class. The eighteen-year-old boy's shirt had ignited while he stood with his back to the forge. He sued the school district and shop instructor for his injuries, claiming negligent supervision. At trial, the evidence established that the boy had a tested mental age of eleven. He therefore sought a jury instruction that he should only be held to the standard of care of a child. The trial judge instead instructed the jury that the boy should be held to the standard of care of any reasonable person. The jury reached a verdict in favor of the boy, awarding him $50,000 in damages for his injuries. However, based upon the "reasonable person" standard of care, the jury also found that the boy had been seventy percent contributorily negligent, which reduced his damages to $15,000. The boy appealed, seeking a new trial on the issue of damages.

The Washington Court of Appeals ruled against the boy, stating that the trial judge's instruction to the jury was correct and hence the reduction of the damage award was proper. Although the boy had a mental age of eleven, holding him to the reduced standard of care of a child would have been improper in light of the following Washington statute: "Except as otherwise provided by law, all persons should be deemed and taken to be of full age for all purposes at the age of eighteen years." Because the boy had already reached the chronological age of eighteen, he was not entitled to a jury instruction imposing only the standard of care of a child. Interestingly, the court pointed out that a "diminished capacity" jury instruction, under which the boy would have been expected to exercise only the degree of care for his own safety which was naturally possible for him, would have been appropriate in this case. However, the boy's attorney had not asked for such an instruction and the court of appeals held that it was too late to ask for one now. The reduction of the damage award to $15,000 due to the boy's contributory negligence was affirmed. *Higgins v. East Valley School District*, 704 P.2d 630 (Wash.App.1985).

A quadriplegic student at the Southwest Louisiana State School brought a negligence lawsuit against the school after suffering a spiral-type fracture of his right femur. On the morning of the injury the boy's mother bathed him, fed him and strapped him into his wheelchair. She then gave him his usual dosage of phenobarbital. The school bus arrived and he was wheeled out to meet it without apparent incident. The bus driver testified that the boy was in his usual good spirits as he transported him to the State School. He said that he strapped the boy's wheelchair down securely that morning. Upon his arrival at the State School, the boy, who weighed only thirty-two pounds, was wheeled into class where two of his instructors noticed that he was "crying and fussing." They sought to alleviate his discomfort by placing him on a mat. When this proved unsuccessful, one instructor lifted him off the mat and placed him on a table. She testified that as she did so, she heard a loud "pop." The boy was immediately taken to a doctor, and the spiral fracture was diagnosed. He was hospitalized for three weeks and he recovered completely. Believing that the State School and its employees had somehow been negligent, causing their son's injury, the child's parents brought a lawsuit in state district court. They pointed to a statement one of the teachers had made immediately after taking their son to the doctor. She had said that she did not understand how the child's leg could have broken unless she had accidently knelt on it.

However, evidence was also presented of an incident which occurred one year after the original fracture. The child, while strapped in his wheelchair at home, became excited and pushed his leg until it became caught in the chair, then twisted it, causing the same type of spiral fracture as had occurred the previous year. He was using the same wheelchair at the time of this later incident. In light of this evidence, the district court ruled in favor of the State School and its employees, stating that a number of other explanations existed for the boy's injury besides negligence on the part of a State School employee. On appeal by the parents, the Louisiana Court of Appeal upheld this ruling. Stated the court: "The mere fact that an accident occurred does not necessarily mean that someone was negligent." The court held that the parents had failed to meet their burden of proving by a preponderance of the evidence that a State School employee had caused their son's injury. *Henry v. State*, 482 So.2d 962 (La.App.3d Cir.1986).

In a Maryland case, as part of a handicapped female student's new individualized educational program, she was placed in a regular eighth grade physical education class, with no restrictions placed upon her participation. Her parents failed to express any dissatisfaction or challenge this new IEP. Midway through the school year, the girl was seriously injured while maneuvering on a "Swedish Box." Her parents filed suit in state court against the school board and the physical education teacher, claiming that they had been negligent in placing their daughter in a regular physical education class without adequate safeguards. The parent's complaint did not allege negligent supervision, but negligent placement in the class.

The circuit court ruled that the parents could not base their lawsuit on negligent placement. The parents had not contested the revised IEP when it was initially implemented, and thus they were barred from contesting it now in a civil lawsuit. The court's ruling was based on the elaborate state procedural system through which disputes over special education placements could be contested. The parents had not availed themselves of this system and the circuit court refused to allow the parents to do in a civil lawsuit what they should have done through established procedures. This ruling effectively destroyed the parents' case since they would now have to prove that the teacher failed to use "reasonable care" in supervising their daughter. The circuit court therefore rendered a decision in favor of the school board and teacher.

The parents then appealed to the Maryland Court of Special Appeals, which affirmed the decision of the circuit court. When the parents failed to contest the IEP which placed their daughter in the regular physical education class, they placed her in the same legal position as any other student in the class and no suit for "negligent placement" would be possible. Because the parents were unable to prove that the teacher had failed to exercise reasonable care in the supervision of their daughter, the appeals court upheld the lower court's ruling against the parents. *Alban v. Board of Education of Harford County*, 494 A.2d 745 (Md.App.1985).

In a New York case, a severely disabled individual sustained serious injuries after being placed in a residential facility. Suit was brought on his behalf, alleging negligence on the part of the facility's employees. The suit alleged that employees at the Kings Park Developmental Center had allowed the plaintiff to participate in a normalization program designed to allow familiarization with tasks of daily living. During the program he accidently overturned a covered pot of hot water used to demonstrate the preparation of tea and coffee, causing him to be severely burned.

Reversing a lower court, the New York Court of Appeals dismissed the claim that employees had negligently placed him in the therapy program, stating that the decision to place him in the program involved medical judgement for which no liability could be imposed. The lower court's ruling that the use of a covered pot of hot water to instruct severely disabled persons was so negligent that a trial was not even necessary was reversed by the Court of Appeals, which stated that while a residential facility owes a duty of reasonable care to severely disabled persons, it is not required to maintain constant surveillance of each individual. After noting that "there are certain risks inherent in any therapeutic program, especially, as in this case, one which is designed to provide a normal homelike setting," the Court of Appeals remanded the case to the lower court for reconsideration of whether the lawsuit should be allowed to proceed. *Killen v. State*, 498 N.Y.S.2d 358 (1985).

The Supreme Court of Montana has affirmed the dismissal of a lawsuit for wrongful placement in a special education program. The suit was brought in 1980 by a minor girl and her foster mother against their school board and various state and local officials, alleging that the girl had suffered irreparable emotional harm as a result of her placement in 1973 in a special education program. The evidence showed that she was required to repeat a year of school, was called a "retard" and was taunted about flunking. When the trial court dismissed the case, the girl and her mother appealed. The Supreme Court of Montana upheld the trial court's decision, stating that insufficient evidence had been presented to prove that the girl had suffered compensable emotional damage. The court held that in a suit for wrongful placement, expert testimony was necessary to prove that emotional harm had occurred. Because the only evidence offered to the trial court was the testimony of the girl and her mother, the suit was properly dismissed. *Berger v. State*, 698 P.2d 399 (Mont.1985).

A twelve-year-old student enrolled in a school for trainable mentally re-tarded children was discovered during recess lying face down at the foot of a set of steps leading back into the school's classrooms. As a result of his prob-able fall, the child suffered extensive head injuries. Through his guardian, he brought suit against the board of education of New York and his teacher, whom he alleged negligently failed to supervise the children in her care. The teacher testified before the trial court that she was aware of the child's per-ceptual motor difficulties and poor eye-hand coordination. She also testified that the child and another boy with whom he had been running on the day of the accident often played a chasing game called "monster" during recess. The child called an expert witness, trained in the field of special education and familiar with the teaching policies of various school districts, who testified that purposeless, "freestyle" running during school hours was dangerous and should never be permitted for any child, and was especially hazardous where mentally retarded children were concerned. She further testified that the proper procedure for a teacher to follow under the circumstances would have been to stop the children either by word or physical act. The trial court held, on the basis of the testimony, that the school board was liable for damages for personal injuries the child suffered. The school board appealed to the New York Supreme Court, Appellate Division, which held that the child had established a *prima facie* case of negligence on the part of the teacher for failing to supervise her students. The trial court ruling was affirmed. *Rodri-guez v. Board of Education, City of New York*, 480 N.Y.S.2d 901 (A.D.2d Dept.1984).

In the following two cases, courts absolved schools of liability for inju-ries to handicapped students. In the first case, the mother of a blind, deaf and mute student in the District of Columbia, who had been sexually as-saulted by the coordinator of a program for blind and deaf students, brought suit against the coordinator and the District of Columbia. She contended that the district was liable for damages arising from the assault on her daughter due to the district's negligence in hiring or failing to supervise the coordina-tor. The District of Columbia Court of Appeals affirmed a trial court ruling in favor of the school district. The court found that although an employer may be held liable for the acts of employees committed within the scope of their employment, there was no showing that the coordinator's assault of the child was within that scope.

In this regard, the court rejected the mother's argument that the assault was a direct result of the coordinator's job assignment since his employment necessarily included some physical contact with the child. The mother argued that a deaf, blind and mute child can be taught only through the sense of touch and, therefore, the fact that physical touching was necessarily a part of the teacher-student relationship made it foreseeable that sexual assaults would occur. The court found that a sexual assault cannot be deemed a direct result of a school official's authorization to take a student by the hand or arm in guiding her past obstacles in the building. Further, the court stated that in this case the attack was "unprovoked," had not arisen from the coordinator's instructions or job assignment and was not an integral part of the school's activities, interests or objectives. The coordinator's acts could not be viewed as being within the scope of his employment, and thus the school district was not liable. *Boykin v. District of Columbia*, 484 A.2d 560 (D.C.App.1984).

The Court of Appeals of Georgia was asked to decide whether a local board of education, a school district, a bus driver for the school district and the school district's insurer were liable for injuries resulting from the assault of a handicapped student on a school bus. A finding that the insurance policy applied, contended the injured child, would result in the school district waiving its governmental immunity, thus rendering it susceptible to a lawsuit. The school district's insurance policy covering its vehicles provided that the insurer "will pay all sums the Insured legally must pay as damages because of bodily injury or property damage to which this insurance applies, caused by the accident and resulting from the ownership, maintenance or use of a covered auto." The injured child argued that the school bus was a motor vehicle being used to transport handicapped children to and from their homes and school, and alleged that he was injured when two fellow passengers ganged up and attacked him while they were riding the bus, kicking and beating him for the entire length of the forty minute bus ride. Thus, claimed the child, his injuries arose out of the use or maintenance of a motor vehicle, triggering the school district's insurance policy.

The Georgia appellate court did not agree, finding that the alleged assault upon the student was not covered by the policy, and thus the school district's governmental immunity was not waived. Further, the school board was not a "political subdivision" under a statute providing for waiver of governmental immunity to the extent of the amount of motor vehicle liability insurance purchased by a political subdivision. In addition, the bus driver, who was acting in her official capacity at the time of the alleged assault and who was not guilty of wilful or malicious conduct in connection with the alleged assault, was entitled to governmental immunity. The appellate court affirmed a trial court ruling in favor of the defendants. *Hicks v. Walker County School District*, 323 S.E.2d 231 (Ga.App.1984).

II. Handicapped Students in School Athletics

Handicapped students are not presumptively excluded from school athletics.

A New York junior high school girl was prohibited from participating in contact sports by her school district by reason of her visual impairment, which resulted from a congenital cataract. New York law provides that upon a school district's determination that a student shall not be permitted to participate in an athletic program by reason of physical impairment, the student may commence a special proceeding to enjoin the school district from prohibiting such participation. Further, if the court finds that it is in the best interests of the student to participate in the athletic program and that it is reasonably safe to do so, the court shall grant permission to participate. The law further protects a school district from liability for any injury sustained by a student participating pursuant to such a court determination.

In this case, the lower court determined that with protective eyewear it would be reasonably safe for this student to participate in the athletic program, but denied her application on the grounds that it would not be in her best interests to so participate, because of the immunity from liability granted to the school district should an injury occur. The New York Supreme Court, Appellate Division, rejected this lower court finding and granted the student permission to participate. The court said that whatever immunity from liability is enjoyed by a school district is not to be weighed by the court in considering the best interests of the student. Here, ample evidence suggested that with protective eyewear it would be in the best interests of this student to permit participation in the athletic program. *Kampmeier v. Harris*, 411 N.Y.S.2d 744 (A.D.4th Dept.1978).

A high school athletic regulatory agency in Texas barred a high school student from participating in high school football because he had moved to another district to live with his grandparents. The boy had suffered emotional problems and as a result was handicapped within the meaning of federal law which provided that a handicapped individual could not, by reason of his handicap, be excluded from participation in, be denied the benefits of, or be subjected to discrimination under any program or activity receiving federal assistance. The boy, through his mother, alleged that there were compelling medical reasons why the boy should be permitted to participate in the football program. The U.S. district court issued a preliminary injunction restraining the athletic regulatory agency from enforcing its rule. The court said that the purpose of the rule was to prevent recruiting abuses and to prevent an athlete from irresponsibly shopping around for a school or coach. These evils were not present here. It was the court's view that to deny this boy the opportunity to play football would violate his rights as a handicapped individual. *Doe v. Marshall*, 459 F.Supp. 1190 (S.D.Tex.1978).

A student in New Jersey who was born with one kidney brought suit against a local board of education seeking compensatory damages for the board's denial of his right to participate in his high school's interscholastic athletic program due to his handicap. In holding that the student could not be denied the right to participate in the program, the U.S. district court, stated that the federal Rehabilitation Act prohibits such discrimination against otherwise qualified handicapped individuals in federally funded programs solely on the basis of their handicap. The court noted that the school board was aware that the student's parents knew of the dangers involved, but had encouraged their son's participation in the program despite his handicap. Summary judgment was granted in favor of the student. *Poole v. South Plainfield Board of Education*, 490 F.Supp. 948 (D.N.J.1980).

A nineteen-year-old neurologically impaired high school senior challenged a New York Department of Education regulation prohibiting students over eighteen years of age from participating in interscholastic athletics. The boy had entered the public school system at the ninth grade level after leaving a private school, where he had failed the ninth grade. He was diagnosed as being developmentally behind, having a lack of motivation and having a poor self image. His participation in wrestling from the ninth grade until his senior year appeared to have significantly improved his self image. The boy brought suit in U.S. district court, alleging he had been discriminated against on the basis of his handicap and had been unlawfully denied the opportunity to participate in interscholastic wrestling in violation of the equal protection provisions of the U.S. Constitution and the Rehabilitation Act. The court held that because the student had reached the age of nineteen and had not been treated any differently than any other nonphysically handicapped nineteen-year-old student, there was no violation of equal protection, nor was there unfair discrimination. *Cavallaro v. Ambach*, 575 F.Supp. 171 (W.D.N.Y.1983).

III. Student Records

Generally, access to handicapped students' records will not be allowed when the privacy interest of the students outweighs the asserted need for inspection of the records.

A human rights advocacy committee in Florida petitioned for access to confidential school records which it considered pertinent to its investigation of the alleged abuse of four developmentally disabled students by public school personnel. A Florida trial court denied the committee's request and appeal was taken to the District Court of Appeal of Florida. The appeals court affirmed the trial court rulings, saying that the committee was not entitled to access to the confidential school records of the students because a state statute limited the committee's area of jurisdiction, for the purpose of obtaining client records, to matters occurring solely within a program or facility operated, funded or regulated by the Department of Health and Rehabilitative Services. The court also based its decision on a school code provision protecting the privacy interests of every student with regard to his or her educational records. *Human Rights Advocacy Committee For Developmental Services For District VIII v. Lee County School Board*, 457 So.2d 522 (Fla.App.2d Dist.1984).

The Human Rights Authority of the State of Illinois Guardianship and Advocacy Commission appealed an order of an Illinois district court denying the enforcement of a subpoena issued by the Commission. Acting on a complaint which alleged that a local school district was not providing occupational and physical therapy for its students, the Commission began an investigation and asked the district superintendent to produce the students' educational program records. The records were to be masked so as to delete any information by which students could be identified. When the school district failed to turn over the information, the Commission issued a subpoena for the masked records. Again, the school district refused to comply. The Commission then sought judicial enforcement of the subpoena.

The district court ruled that the Commission had no right to examine the records because it did not satisfy the access requirements of Illinois state law regarding student records. After the Commission appealed to the Appellate

Court of Illinois, the school district argued that, along with the access provisions of the Student Records Act, the Commission had no authority to investigate or review special education programs, and that the Commission's right to investigate did not apply to all of the handicapped students in a school district, but was limited to individual cases. The thrust of the school district's first argument was that the Commission was somehow usurping the role of the State Board of Education by investigating the special education program of the school district. According to the school district, the Commission's inquiry was "tantamount to the control and direction of special education which makes local school authorities accountable to the [Commission] rather than the State Board of Education as required by the School Code."

The Appellate Court disagreed. The court held that the statutory authority of the Commission to investigate complaints concerning violations of the rights of handicapped persons, including the right to special education programs, was not subordinate to that of the State Board of Education. Further, the Commission's investigation of the school district's overall special education program, and not merely individual students, was within the bounds of the Commission's statutory authority. Finally, the Student Records Act did not bar enforcement of the subpoena issued by the Commission. *Human Rights Authority of the State of Illinois Guardianship Commission v. Miller*, 464 N.E.2d 833 (Ill.App.3d Dist.1984).

CHAPTER SIX

SCHOOLS AND SCHOOL DISTRICTS

Many of the problems public and private schools encounter in connection with operating special education programs are typical of problems encountered in other facets of school operations. Some problems, such as a private school's eligibility to educate handicapped children, a private school's contract to perform special educational services, or a public school's training of personnel employed in the special education area or the parents of handicapped children, are unique to the field of special education.

I. Employees

The following cases address issues involving special education employees. Employee misconduct, discrimination, teachers' constitutional privacy rights, hiring practices, salary, termination, seniority, tenure, and unemployment compensation benefits represent the range of special education employee-related concerns which have been before the courts.

A. Dismissals for Cause

The following cases involve dismissals of special education employees "for cause," i.e., due to misconduct or incompetence.

The Orange County, Florida, school board operates the Woodlands School for learning disabled, physically handicapped and multi-handicapped children. The school is located on the campus of the Sunland State Hospital and is a tenant of the hospital. Due to the Woodland School's location on the grounds of the State Hospital, work-release prisoners sometimes are present at Woodlands. Hospital rules expressly prohibit any fraternization by employees with work-release prisoners.

Beginning in 1979, a woman was employed by the school board as a non-certified special education teacher's aide at Woodlands on a series of ten-month contracts. In March, 1982, her principal recommended that her contract for the following year not be renewed due to numerous minor problems: excessive absenteeism, reading magazines on the job, wearing inappropriate shoes, failure to require her guests to check in when visiting her, and inability to get along with other teacher's aides. The superintendent and the school board concurred. After the teacher's aide was informed of the decision not to renew, she was reprimanded for fraternizing on the job with work-release prisoners. She began harassing the teacher who reported her infractions of the no-fraternization rule, and on one occasion chased the teacher to her home in her car. The board immediately relieved the teacher's aide of duty, with pay, for the remaining two weeks of her contract. She then brought suit alleging that a number of her constitutional rights had been violated, but a federal district court ruled against her on all counts.

First, the court rejected her due process claim because she had not achieved tenure; she had been employed under a fixed-term contract. Also, the board had not deprived her of her right to a good reputation because she had admitted to fraternizing with the prisoners while at work. Second, her First Amendment right to freedom of association did not include a right to engage in social contact with prisoners while on the job in violation of official written policy. The court's decision was made easier by the fact that the teacher's aide admitted that her contact with prisoners was purely social in nature, because political association is more vigorously protected by the First Amendment. In any event, she had failed to prove that the board's decision not to renew her teacher's aide contract was based upon her fraternization with prisoners. Finding no constitutional violation, the federal judge dismissed the suit. *Brew v. School Board of Orange County*, 626 F.Supp. 709 (M.D.Fla.1985).

In an Arkansas case, the state's supreme court refused to set aside a tenured special education teacher's dismissal, where her attorney did not adequately prove the case in the lower court. Here a special education teacher had been employed in a school district for thirteen years. She had never received an unsatisfactory evaluation and in the past had been used as a model for new teachers. However, soon after a new principal arrived at her school he informed her that her performance was inadequate. He recommended dismissal, and her employment was terminated by the school board shortly thereafter. The teacher sued in county court seeking reinstatement to her position on the ground that her dismissal had been politically motivated. Evidence was presented that the teacher's husband had been a former school employee and had twice engaged in disputes with the superintendent. Also, her husband had twice (unsuccessfully) run for the school board, and a board member had once stated that he wanted to "get a shot" at the teacher. The county court, however, found that the school board had acted out of dissatisfaction with the special education teacher's classroom performance, and she appealed.

The Arkansas Supreme Court upheld the county court. Although admitting that the teacher's attorney had presented strong evidence of political reasons for her dismissal, he had not sufficiently explored during trial the bases for her principal's unsatisfactory evaluations. Without proof that the principal had possessed political motives, the school board was entitled to rely upon his recommendation of dismissal. The Supreme Court declined to intervene. *Kirtley v. Dardanelle Public Schools*, 702 S.W.2d 25 (Ark.1986).

A Pennsylvania school board's decision to dismiss a school psychologist because of incompetency has been upheld by the Commonwealth Court of Pennsylvania. The psychologist argued that her dismissal should have been based on provisions contained in the Public School Code which states that, in evaluating school personnel, due consideration shall be given to "personality, preparation, technique and pupil reaction." She maintained that her dismissal did not relate to these concerns. The court, in rejecting that argument, stated that the fact that consideration should be given to the qualities mentioned in the statute does not mean that other matters, such as lack of judgment or simple ability, may not also be considered. The school board's dismissal order was affirmed. *Grant v. Board of School Directors of the Centennial School District*, 471 A.2d 1292 (Pa.Cmwlth.1984).

In a Maryland case, reinstatement was ordered for a teacher who was also a Catholic priest. The teacher, who had taught in Japan for over twenty years, took employment teaching groundskeeping and home maintenance to severely retarded males of secondary school age at a center for the mentally handicapped. His teaching objective was to train students to enter the employment market as handymen or custodial workers. The teaching program consisted of working with a small group of students in the classroom for several days a week, and at various outdoor worksites on the remaining school days.

One day, without authorization, the teacher left four of his six students under a teaching aide's supervision at a recreational center, where they were to clean the building and the adjacent grounds. He took the two remaining students with him to work on other groundskeeping projects. When it began to snow the teacher took the boys to a work shed located behind his home and directed them to work on a project at this site. One of the boys became disruptive and began throwing glass bottles and mishandling the saw he was using. The teacher ordered him to stop his disruptive behavior but to no avail. At this point, the teacher decided that the boy needed to be "timed out," a behavior modification technique used by some special education teachers whereby a misbehaving student is isolated and kept still, in order to calm him and to cause him to reflect on his misbehavior. The teacher ordered the boy to leave the shed and kneel outside on two wooden blocks under a plastic-covered picnic table for an extended period in below-freezing snowy weather. Throughout the incident, the other boy remained inside the shed shivering and shaking from the cold. A neighbor who witnessed the episode called the police, who found the boy sobbing and crying.

The County Board of Education terminated the teacher's employment and the teacher appealed to the State Board of Education, which modified the disciplinary sanction from dismissal to suspension. The County Board appealed and the case finally reached the Court of Appeals of Maryland, which held that the dismissal was not warranted and that the State Board did not exceed its statutory power in imposing a lengthy suspension instead of dismissal. The court took note of the teacher's excellent teaching record and stated that the teacher's action, although improper, was motivated by and intended to modify the behavior of a student whom he could not reach by verbal direction. *Board of Education of Prince George's County v. Waeldner*, 470 A.2d 332 (Md.1984).

B. Racial, Sexual, and Handicap Discrimination

Under Title VII of the Civil Rights Act of 1964 (42 U.S.C. § 2000e *et seq.*), a plaintiff has the initial burden to establish that he or she was not hired or promoted due to racial or sexual discrimination by the employer. The plaintiff must show that he or she 1) is a member of a protected minority class; 2) applied and was qualified for the position sought; 3) was not hired or promoted; and 4) that a non-minority was hired or promoted to the position the plaintiff was seeking.

Once the plaintiff makes this initial showing, the burden shifts to the employer to articulate a legitimate, nondiscriminatory reason for not hiring the plaintiff. If the employer is able to do so, then the courts will rule in favor of the employer.

An Alabama sex and race discrimination case concluded with a federal judge's dismissal of the case. The plaintiff, a black female teacher at a school for handicapped children, applied for the position of principal. The selection committee interviewed a total of twenty individuals for the principal position, including sixteen white males, one black female, one oriental female and two white females. The committee selected a white male for the job, citing his superior academic credentials, his experience in securing government grants, his extensive managerial experience and his experience with multi-handicapped children. The black female applicant brought suit in U.S. district court under Title VII of the Civil Rights Act, claiming sex and race discrimination. The court disagreed with her contentions. Although the selection committee was dominated by white males, the two black females on the committee had ranked the white male applicant higher than the plaintiff. The evidence established that he was clearly better qualified for the position than the plaintiff. The court also took notice of evidence that the plaintiff's attitudes were "too rigid." This put her at a disadvantage in seeking promotion to a position where she would be required to deal continuously with handicapped children and "their justifiably distressed parents." The case was dismissed due to the lack of evidence of any discrimination in the principal selection process. *Love v. Alabama Institute for the Deaf and Blind*, 613 F.Supp. 436 (N.D.Ala.1984).

A Lutheran school for the deaf in New York hired a female art teacher in March, 1979. She possessed permanent certification as an art teacher, but was not certified as a teacher for the deaf as required by state law. At the time she was hired, she was told that in order to waive the certification requirement she would have to pursue courses toward deaf education certification. At the close of the 1980-81 academic year, however, the teacher had taken only two courses toward certification. In November, 1981, she left to have a baby and began her child-rearing leave in January, 1982. In March, 1982, school officials wrote to the woman and again informed her that in order to waive certification she must pursue at least six semester hours of study per year. She then met with the school superintendent, assuring him that she would continue to work toward certification. She was also granted an additional year of child-rearing leave.

In March, 1983, the superintendent asked the woman if she intended to return to her position in the fall. He refused to extend her child-rearing leave but told her that if she became pregnant again she would have "no trouble" in receiving additional pregnancy leave. At this time the woman told the superintendent that she had taken only three semester hours of courses toward certification in the past year. One month later she told the principal that she was pregnant. This prompted him to offer her a woodworking teacher position instead of art because when she would be forced to leave again in the fall a woodworking teacher's sudden absence would be less disruptive to the learning process. The woman refused this offer and one month later she was dismissed.

She sued in U.S. district court, alleging unlawful discrimination due to pregnancy. The court disagreed with her claims, holding that the school had proven that the decision to terminate her employment was based upon her lack of deaf education certification. It was entirely proper for school officials to show concern for the continuity and quality of instruction at the school in the face of the woman's lack of certification and lengthy child-rearing leaves. The court noted that while pregnancy leaves are protected by the Civil Rights Act, child-rearing leaves are not. Because no unlawful discrimination was proven, the court dismissed the woman's complaint. *Record v. Mill Neck Manor Lutheran School for the Deaf*, 611 F.Supp. 905 (E.D.N.Y.1985).

A black woman who was employed by a Missouri school board as an assistant special education teacher sued the board in U.S. district court alleging that the board had failed to promote her to the position of teacher because of her race. The court ruled in favor of the school board holding that the board had articulated legitimate, nondiscriminatory reasons for not hiring the woman as a full teacher. Her superiors, including one other black woman, had conducted periodic evaluations of her abilities and had interviewed her. The evaluations revealed that she was unable to speak clearly and correctly and that her writing style was ungrammatical. The court agreed that these alone were grave deficiencies in an applicant for the position of special education teacher. Furthermore, the woman's interviews revealed that she had never given any diagnostic tests while she was employed as an assistant teacher, and she could not tell the interviewers how any of these tests were used. The court held that these deficiencies constituted sufficient grounds for the school board to refuse to promote her to the position of teacher. Judgment was rendered for the school board in all respects. *Love v. Special School District of St. Louis County*, 606 F.Supp. 1320 (E.D.Mo.1985).

Since 1975, a Louisiana school board had employed a woman as special education supervisor. In 1982, after becoming dissatisfied with her performance, the board obtained an opinion from the Louisiana Attorney General which stated that because the supervisor was not certified for the position, she was not tenured under the state's tenure laws. The board then notified her that her contract would not be renewed for the following year. No dismissal hearing was held. She sued the board in state court, contending that she was tenured, and the court ordered that the board hold a dismissal hearing. When this was done the board once again voted to dismiss, but failed to follow proper procedures. Once again the supervisor successfully sued the board, winning reinstatement and back pay. She then commenced the present lawsuit in federal court, claiming that her federal civil rights had been violated by the board's failure to adhere to state notice and hearing requirements. In essence, she claimed that this failure had deprived her of her federal due process rights.

The U.S. Court of Appeals, Fifth Circuit, disagreed with her claims. The fact that the state courts had forced the board to hold a dismissal hearing completely satisfied all federal due process requirements. Under the U.S. Constitution, due process requires only compliance with minimal notice and hearing requirements; the fact that state law provided greater protection was irrelevant. The court stated: "There is not a violation of due process every time a . . . government entity violates its own rules. Such action may constitute a breach of contract or violation of state law, but unless the conduct trespasses on federal constitutional safeguards, there is no constitutional deprivation." The dismissal of the special education supervisor's federal claims was thus affirmed. *Franceski v. Plaquemines Parish School Board*, 772 F.2d 197 (5th Cir.1985).

An applicant for a special education teaching position in Iowa sued a local education agency under the federal Rehabilitation Act and Iowa law alleging that the agency refused to hire him due to his physical disability. The teacher, a resident of Vermont, suffered from several severe handicaps but was able to walk without assistance and to lift children and drive. The teacher applied to the Iowa agency for a job, and was scheduled for an interview in Iowa at his own expense, with possible reimbursement if he were hired.

After arranging the interview, the teacher became concerned that he had not disclosed his handicaps. Because of limited financial resources, he did not wish to fly to Iowa only to be rejected because of his handicaps. He called the Iowa school, explained his handicaps and was told that the job involved transporting children which, in turn, required a bus driver's permit that the teacher probably could not get because of his handicaps. The agency suggested a trip to Iowa would probably be futile.

The teacher then sued in a U.S. district court, which found in his favor. The test of proof for a discrimination claim under the Rehabilitation Act is: 1) that the plaintiff is a handicapped individual under the terms of the Act; 2) that the plaintiff is otherwise qualified to participate in the program or activity at issue; 3) that the plaintiff was excluded from the program or activity solely by reason of her or his handicap; and 4) that the program or activity receives federal financial assistance.

Here, there was no dispute that the plaintiff was a handicapped individual within the meaning of the Rehabilitation Act. The court also had little difficulty in finding that the plaintiff was otherwise qualified for the position, because of his superior credentials. The court also found that the plaintiff had satisfied the third and fourth prongs of the test, in that the defendant agency was a recipient of federal financial assistance, including funds received pursuant to the EAHCA and that, with a minimum of accommodation, the school district could have arranged an alternative situation whereby the teacher would not have had to transport children. The court awarded the teacher $1,000 damages for mental anguish, and $5,150 for loss of earnings.

Fitzgerald v. Green Valley Education Agency, 589 F.Supp. 1130 (S.D.Iowa 1984).

C. Right to Privacy

Special education teachers, like most other government employees, possess a right to privacy guaranteed by the U.S. Constitution. The government, as an employer, may not infringe upon this right absent a compelling reason.

A U.S. district court in Washington, D.C., has declared that school bus attendants may not be subjected to mandatory urine testing unless there is probable cause to suspect that the attendant has engaged in drug use. In this case, a school bus attendant for handicapped children was forced to give a urine sample as part of a program instituted by the Washington school district to ferret out drug use by its transportation employees. When the bus attendant's urine tested positive, her employment was terminated. She sued in U.S. district court, contending that the school district's urinalysis program violated her Fourth Amendment rights.

The court first ruled that the test results were flawed. Although the manufacturers of the urinalysis test used, the EMIT Cannabinoid Assay Test, recommended that the test results be verified through an alternate testing method, the school district had not obtained such verification. After the bus attendant's first urinalysis test, effected by computer, showed that THC metabolites (indicative of marijuana use) were present in her urine, the school district ran the same test manually to verify that result. No alternative test was performed. Having disregarded the instructions of the manufacturers of the EMIT test, the school district could not use the results as a ground for termination.

Next, the court held that urinalysis testing could not be required without probable cause to suspect the bus attendant of drug use. Unlike school bus drivers or mechanics, who expect that their privacy rights will be limited by public safety considerations, school bus attendants legitimately expect a zone of personal privacy. Urine testing imposes upon this expectation of privacy. Therefore, the court stated, urine testing of school bus attendants is a "search" under the Fourth Amendment to the U.S. Constitution and requires probable cause. Since the school district had no probable cause to suspect that the bus attendant had ever used drugs, the board's decision to terminate her employment was reversed. Full back pay and reinstatement were ordered. *Jones v. McKenzie*, 628 F.Supp. 1500 (D.D.C.1986).

A Massachusetts public school teacher was suspended for two days and involuntarily transferred from her teaching position after being found guilty of insubordination and conduct unbecoming a teacher. The teacher had disagreed with her principal regarding the treatment of a handicapped boy. She wrote a case study paper for a night class that she was taking, which described the boy's situation and which was highly critical of the principal. Shortly thereafter, at a meeting held to evaluate the boy's progress, the teacher gave her paper to the special education supervisor at her school. She did not tell him that her case study paper contained confidential material. The supervisor never read her paper and returned it to the teacher the same day.

On the following day the principal requested that the teacher turn over a copy of the paper, claiming that it was part of the boy's official file which the principal had a duty to examine. The teacher refused and the principal informed her that she was being insubordinate. Two weeks later she turned over a copy of the paper, but the principal left the question of disciplinary action open until a later date. Several months later, on Parent's Night, the teacher posted copies of her correspondence with the principal concerning the allegedly insubordinate refusal to immediately turn over her case study paper. A parent later complained to school officials regarding the teacher's public display of this correspondence. The teacher was then suspended for two days and involuntarily transferred from her teaching post as a result of her insubordination in refusing to promptly furnish the principal with a copy of her paper, and for engaging in conduct unbecoming a teacher by posting the letters on Parents' Night.

Concluding that her constitutional rights had been violated, the teacher sued her school district in U.S. district court. The court held in favor of the school district and the U.S. Court of Appeals, First Circuit, affirmed. The appeals court held that the teacher had no Fourth Amendment privacy interest in her paper because she had given it to the special education supervisor. Therefore, when the principal demanded the paper she could not assert her right to privacy. The court further held that her act of posting the principal's letters to her concerning the paper were unprotected as well since the matter was primarily an employment dispute, and not a matter of public interest. The disciplinary sanctions against the teacher were, therefore, held not to violate the teacher's constitutional rights. *Alinovi v. Worcester School Committee*, 777 F.2d 776 (1st Cir.1985).

D. Collective Bargaining

In 1978, the Leonard Kirtz Mahoning County School for the Retarded hired a woman as a special education teacher. She was assigned to Developmental Classroom I, which consisted of students who were the least fortunate in terms of educational potential. After three years she discovered that three teachers for students with the most potential were leaving the school. She made a request to both the superintendent and the principal that she be transferred to one of the vacant positions. However, the county board denied her request and immediately transferred two other teachers, neither of whom had requested reassignment, and hired one new teacher, in order to fill the three vacancies.

The Ohio Supreme Court rebuked the county board for its blatant disregard of its own collective bargaining agreement. Reversing an errant lower court, the Supreme Court reinstated an arbitrator's ruling that because the agreement required the county board to respect a teacher's transfer requests, the board was bound to transfer her. Held the court: "The board argues, and the court of appeals decided, that collective bargaining agreements are not as binding upon public employers as they are upon private employers. It is time to put an end to that notion and categorically reject the argument. Today's decision gives notices that negotiated collective bargaining agreements are just as binding upon public employers as they are upon private employers." The county board was ordered to honor its contractual obligation to the teacher. *Mahoning County Board of Mental Retardation and Developmental*

Disabilities v. Mahoning County TMR Education Association, 488 N.E.2d 872 (Ohio 1986).

The Supreme Judicial Court of Massachusetts recently vacated a preliminary injunction entered by a three-judge panel of the Superior Court, which had enjoined a strike by bus drivers for special needs children. The case arose when several bus companies, with whom the Boston School Committee had contracted, and their bus drivers, failed to negotiate a mutually acceptable collective bargaining agreement. The bus drivers, who are affiliated with the AFL-CIO, declined to work without a contract. Parents of handicapped children were left to make their own arrangements for their children's transportation to and from school. As a result, the parents commenced a class action suit and asked the Superior Court for an injunction ordering the striking school bus drivers back to work, which was granted. On appeal by the school bus drivers' union, the Supreme Judicial Court reversed and held that under Massachusetts law [M.G.L.A. ch. 150E, sec. 9A(b)] the parents could not sue to enjoin the strike because the bus drivers, although ostensibly employed by private bus companies, were public employees. As such, only the public employer could petition the court to enjoin the strike. The court also noted that although state law clearly outlaws any strike by public employees, it just as clearly forbids anyone but the relevant public employer from seeking a back-to-work order. The Superior Court's injunction was therefore vacated. *Allen v. School Committee of Boston*, 487 N.E.2d 529 (Mass.1986).

The Board of Trustees of the Florida School for the Deaf and the Blind entered into a three-year collective bargaining agreement with its teachers' union, effective July 1, 1983, to June 30, 1986. The agreement contained annual reopeners on salary, insurance benefits and any other two articles chosen by each. Less than one year after the contract had been in effect, the Board of Trustees and the teachers' union reached an impasse over the number of hours teachers were to work each day. A special master was consulted in an attempt to work out a solution, but the board rejected his report. Under Florida law, the board was required to submit the dispute to its legislative body for resolution [F.S.A. sec. 447.403(4)]. The term "legislative body" is defined as the state legislature, any county board of commissioners, any district school board, or the governing body of any municipality. The term also includes any body having authority to make appropriations of public funds [447.203(10)]. The Board of Trustees informed the teachers' union that in its opinion the board itself was a legislative body. The board claimed that since it transferred monies between categories of appropriations, it was a body that appropriates public funds. Therefore the Board of Trustees unilaterally changed the working hours of its special education teachers from seven to seven and one-half hours per day.

The teachers' union filed a complaint with the Public Employees' Relations Commission and received a ruling that the board had committed an unfair labor practice by unilaterally increasing the working hours of its special education teachers. On appeal, this ruling was affirmed. The court stated that just because the Board of Trustees transferred monies into different categories did not mean it was a legislative body. The board only acted pursuant to statutory authority; it was the legislature itself which did the actual appropriating. Since it was not a "legislative body," the Board of Trustees was without authority to unilaterally modify the collective bargaining agreement with the special education teachers' union. The court upheld the Commission's award of penalties and attorney's fees against the board. *Florida School for the Deaf and the Blind v. Florida School for the Deaf and the Blind, Teachers United, FTP-NEA*, 483 So.2d 58 (Fla.App.1st Dist.1986).

E. Tenure, Seniority, Salary and Benefits

In the following case, state tenure laws were deemed inapplicable to special education teachers. Here an eighteen-year veteran at the Arizona State School for the Deaf and the Blind (ASDB) was suspended, with pay, pending investigation of reports of his actions with regard to certain students. Ten days later he was dismissed from employment at the school, effective immediately without further pay. He commenced a special legal action in superior court to contest his dismissal, arguing that the ASDB had not followed its own policies concerning suspension and dismissal from employment and that he had been denied due process of law. He contended that he should have been paid full salary until such time as a dismissal hearing was held. The superior court ruled in favor of the ASDB, and the teacher appealed to the Arizona Court of Appeals.

In upholding the lower court's decision, the Court of Appeals first disposed of the teacher's contention that the school had failed to follow proper procedures. An Arizona statute provided that any teacher at the ASDB may be discharged for cause. Under this statute, held the court, the superintendent of the ASDB had no choice but to discontinue the dismissed teacher's salary. If the teacher had been employed by a public school district, then the tenure statutes would apply, but this was not the case. Under the statutes regulating the ASDB, the teacher could not be paid any salary after dismissal even if the school had purported to adopt a policy to the contrary, because school policies cannot supersede state law.

The appellate court also rejected the teacher's argument that by dismissing him and then discontinuing his salary prior to a termination hearing, the school had deprived him of due process of law. The court stated that due process would be satisfied by a post-termination hearing. If the hearing resulted in a determination that the teacher had been improperly dismissed, then full back pay could be awarded. If on the other hand after the hearing an opposite conclusion was reached, the teacher would not be entitled to receive any pay. Stated the court: "Why should public funds be paid to an employee who has been discharged for cause and is no longer working, and who can recover the lost wages if vindicated? . . . Not only is wage continuation not mandated by due process, it might constitute wasteful expenditure of public funds." The superior court's rejection of the teacher's claims was thus upheld. *Bower v. Arizona State School for the Deaf and the Blind*, 704 P.2d 809 (Ariz.App.1984).

Special education employees in New York challenged the infringement of their seniority rights in the following two cases. In the first, two tenured teachers employed by the New York Board of Cooperative Educational Services (BOCES) in the special education area brought suit alleging that after two school districts for which BOCES provided special education services established their own special education programs, no longer utilizing the

BOCES program, BOCES improperly dismissed them. The teachers were hired as of the date of their dismissal by the respective school districts as teachers in their programs. The teachers sought to have themselves reinstated to their former positions as tenured BOCES teachers. The court held that because BOCES retained teachers in the special education tenure area having less seniority that the dismissed teachers, the abolition of the teachers' positions may have violated teacher tenure law. The New York Supreme Court, Appellate Division, reversed a lower court ruling dismissing the teachers' complaint and remanded the case to the lower court, which was to reinstate the teachers if it found that teachers with less seniority than the dismissed teachers were retained by BOCES, in violation of New York tenure law. BOCES would then be directed to follow an appropriate procedure for correctly determining the teachers with less seniority to be made eligible for hiring by the school districts which had established their own special education program. *Koch v. Putnam-Northern Westchester Board of Cooperative Educational Services*, 470 N.Y.S.2d 651 (A.D.2d Dept.1984).

In a later case, a dispute arose after a school district and four other component districts took over part of a learning achievement program which had formerly been operated by BOCES. Two special education teachers who had been employed by BOCES sought to fill the new positions created but their applications were rejected. They brought suit against the school district claiming that they had a right, at their option, to claim such positions under a statute defining teachers' rights as a result of a school district taking over a program formerly operated by BOCES. The New York Supreme Court, Appellate Division, disagreed, saying that absent a showing that the teachers had been "excessed," the school district was not required by statute to hire them. *Buenzow v. Lewiston-Porter Central School District*, 474 N.Y.S.2d 161 (A.D.4th Dept.1984).

The first two cases which follow involved allegations by special education employees that their positions were wrongfully terminated. In the first case, the Director of Special Education Services for a local school district in South Dakota alleged that the board of education acted illegally in not finding him another position in the district after his position was eliminated due to economic necessity. The director argued before the state Supreme Court that the board was obligated to follow the state's staff reduction policy. Under the statute, he argued, he was classified as a "teacher" and thus was protected from termination under the circumstances. The board insisted that despite the fact that the director held a teaching certificate and was employed under a "Teaching Contract," only certain provisions of the statute were applicable to him because his employment was administrative in nature. The director, continued the board, was an "other administrative employee" under the statute. The director's other certifications, claimed the board, were not taken into account. The court held in the director's favor. The board was found to have acted illegally in not following the staff reduction procedures applicable to continuing contract teachers. Though the director may have been classed as an "other administrative employee" under the statute, the statute also provided that such persons were "teachers" for purposes of tenure. *Burke v. Lead-Deadwood School District No. 40-1*, 347 N.W.2d 343 (S.D.1984).

A different result was reached by the Supreme Court of Iowa in a case involving a teacher who had filled a special education teaching vacancy for one year. The teacher was not special education-certified but was given special permission by the State Department of Public Instruction to teach a special education class, because of the school district's inability to find a replacement for a special education teacher who had resigned. At the close of the school year, the "substitute" teacher expressed an interest in returning the following year either in the same capacity or as a regular classroom teacher. He also offered to receive special education training over the summer months. However, he was not reemployed. The state Supreme Court affirmed a lower court ruling in the district's favor, finding that the teacher was a "temporary substitute" and therefore did not have probationary teaching status. The statutory tenure provisions thus did not apply to the teacher and his termination was upheld. *Fitzgerald v. Saydel Consolidated School District*, 345 N.W.2d 101 (Iowa 1984).

The following case illustrates that, for purposes of tenure, a transfer from a position not related to special education to one involving special education responsibilities is not a lateral transfer. After an "excessed" elementary school principal in New York was assigned to a position as assistant to the director of special education he filed suit against the school district claiming that his tenure rights had been violated. Following dismissal of his case by a lower court, he appealed to the Supreme Court, Appellate Division. The major issue before the appellate court was whether the new assignment, which would have required the principal to serve a 3-year probationary term, was outside the area in which he was granted tenure. The school district argued that the two positions were essentially the same because both included implementation of the curriculum and supervision of the teachers. The court rejected this argument, pointing to the unique responsibilities in special education and the need to focus on the remedial needs of certain groups of students in accordance with federal and state law. The court ordered the plaintiff appointed to a suitable position. *Cowan v. Board of Education of Brentwood Union*, 472 N.Y.S.2d 429 (A.D.2d Dept.1984).

Salary errors were alleged in a Louisiana case, where two special education teachers brought suit against their school board alleging that the board had wrongly calculated their salary supplements. Under a former statute, special education teachers were to be paid ten percent of their base salary. That statute was later amended, making the ten percent supplement discretionary, but mandating that no teacher currently receiving the supplement shall suffer a loss in pay. The lower court granted summary judgment to the board, stating that after passage of the amendment the plaintiffs had suffered no loss in pay. The Louisiana Court of Appeal overturned the lower court's judgment, stating that the amendment had no bearing on the factual issue of whether the plaintiffs' salaries were miscalculated. The case was remanded for further factual development. *Wattigney v. Jefferson Parish School Board*, 445 So.2d 1318 (La.App.5th Cir.1984).

In a case arising in the state of Washington, unemployment compensation benefits were claimed by employees of a state school for the deaf and blind. The noninstructional employees appealed a decision of the Washington

Commissioner of the Department of Employment Security who denied them unemployment benefits during the summer closure of the schools. Washington Unemployment Compensation law prescribes that to deny unemployment benefits to an employee off work during the summer months, written notices to the employee must state that he or she will perform services at the end of the summer months. The civil service employees claimed that written notices they received advising them of the summer closure of the schools, informing them that they were being placed on "leave without pay," and stating that they would be expected to resume their positions at a time to be specified later, were ineffective when applied to civil service employees to exempt them from the unemployment compensation statute. The schools argued that the employees were noninstructional employees rendering services for an educational institution, thus making them ineligible for unemployment benefits while not working during summer recess. The Court of Appeals of Washington was persuaded by the schools' argument and found that the employees were not entitled to unemployment benefits. The written notices the employees received satisfied the unemployment compensation statute's exemption requirement by being "reasonable assurances" of reemployment and were consistent with civil service law. *Alexander v. Employment Security Department of the State of Washington*, 688 P.2d 516 (Wash.App.1984).

II. Governmental Immunity

Broadly speaking, governmental immunity is a doctrine which prohibits a lawsuit against any governmental entity or its officials. The doctrine, which has its roots deep in Anglo-American common law, has suffered a great decline in the last century. While some states retain the doctrine in full force, others have partially or completely eliminated it by legislative or judicial decision. Congress has at least partially authorized lawsuits against the U.S. Government through passage of the Federal Tort Claims Act.

Where a lawsuit is brought against state education officials in state court, the type of relief available depends upon that state's view of governmental immunity. In some states, while a state agency such as an education department may not be sued by a private citizen, a lawsuit can usually be brought against a local political subdivision such as a city or school district. Nearly all states permit local political subdivisions to be sued by private citizens.

Where a lawsuit is brought against state officials in *federal* court, the Eleventh Amendment to the U.S. Constitution comes into play. Generally, a private citizen is barred by the Eleventh Amendment from seeking in federal court an award of money damages against a state or against state officials in their official capacities. However, the federal courts may issue injunctions ordering states and state officials to conform their future conduct to the dictates of federal law; this is known as "prospective relief" and is not barred by the Eleventh Amendment.

Local political subdivisions, unlike states and official state departments, are fully subject to lawsuits brought by private citizens in federal court be-

cause they are not considered "states" under the Eleventh Amendment. Further, the Eleventh Amendment is inapplicable to suits brought by the federal government against a state, and is inapplicable to any lawsuit brought in state court.

In a New Hampshire case, the parents of a handicapped child brought suit in federal court under the Education for All Handicapped Children Act seeking reimbursement for the cost of maintaining their child in a private residential facility. The federal judge certified two questions to the Supreme Court of New Hampshire: first, has that state waived its defense of sovereign immunity in cases involving tuition reimbursement for handicapped children, and second, has the state waived its privileges under the Eleventh Amendment to the U.S. Constitution, thus consenting to be sued in federal court? A unanimous supreme court answered both questions in the negative. As to the first question, the state of New Hampshire had implemented a program under the EAHCA by which its local school districts shouldered financial responsibility for the education of handicapped children. Thus, although a lawsuit against a school district could be brought in state or federal court, the state itself could not be named as a defendant.

As to the second question, the supreme court held that the state also could not be sued under the EAHCA in federal court. Parents could bring a proceeding in federal court to review a state agency or court decision, however. The court explained that while New Hampshire had received federal funds under the EAHCA, the state had left the actual provision of special educational services to the local school districts. Therefore, the supreme court held that the state of New Hampshire had not become involved in the provision of special educational services to such an extent as to waive its immunity from suit in federal court. The case was sent back to the U.S. district court with both certified questions answered in the negative. *John H. v. Brunelle*, 500 A.2d 350 (N.H.1985).

After the mother of a fourteen-year-old handicapped child brought suit against the Board of Education of the District of Columbia, the board sought to dismiss the case on several grounds. First, claimed the board, the mother improperly brought suit in her own name to enforce her rights and the rights of her child under the EAHCA. Second, the Board of Education may not be sued. Third, as government officers, the individual defendants were not properly included in the lawsuit. Fourth, the mother failed to state a claim for which relief could be granted under the Rehabilitation Act and the Civil Rights Act.

The U.S. district court held that the child's mother could maintain an action in her own name to enforce her rights and the rights of her child under the EAHCA. The court found that the EAHCA gives parents of handicapped children certain limited rights and that parents may sue to enforce those rights consistent with the purposes of the EAHCA. The court further held that the District of Columbia Board of Education was not subject to a lawsuit. Thus, the court dismissed the action against the Board of Education.

However, the individual defendants who were named in the mother's complaint, found the district court, were properly included since she sought injunctive relief against the individual defendants in their official, as opposed to their individual, capacities. Thus, the board's motion to dismiss the individual defendants was denied. Finally, the court held that the mother's claims under the Rehabilitation Act and Civil Rights Act were not properly before the court in light of the U.S. Supreme Court's ruling in *Smith v. Robinson*, which held that the EAHCA is the exclusive avenue of relief for claims involving the right to a special education. The mother's Rehabilitation Act and Civil Rights Act claims were therefore dismissed. *Tschanneral v. District of Columbia Board of Education*, 594 F.Supp. 407 (D.D.C.1984).

A group of handicapped children and their parents brought suit against Oregon state and local education officials to enjoin their school district from discontinuing an educational program provided to handicapped children. A U.S. district court held in favor of the children and their parents, ruling that 1) the state defendants and, in particular, the Oregon Department of Education, were in violation of the Education for All Handicapped Children Act for failure to ensure that the plaintiffs would receive free appropriate public educations, and 2) the defendant school districts were not in violation of the EAHCA because they had no legal responsibility under Oregon law to provide the plaintiffs with free appropriate public educations under the EAHCA. The court also stated that in deference to the Oregon legislature, which has the responsibility and the expertise to resolve the problem, it would decline at that time to consider the remedy of injunctive relief, but it did enter a temporary, ninety-day injunction pursuant to the consent of all parties. The court further stated that during that ninety-day period the parties should meet and attempt to agree upon a plan to resolve the dispute. It then said that at the end of ninety days, if the matter had not been resolved, it would make a further determination as to what steps and procedures should then be taken.

Because no agreement was reached between the parties at the end of ninety days, a supplemental opinion was then issued by the court, which addressed the Eleventh Amendment issue and forced action upon the parties. The Eleventh Amendment issue was raised by the state of Oregon, which claimed absolute immunity from suit under that amendment. However, the court observed that the EAHCA had been enacted pursuant to section 5 of the Fourteenth Amendment, and thus constituted a congressional abrogation of Oregon's immunity from suit in federal court. Since the Eleventh Amendment did not bar suit and in light of the court's earlier ruling, the court held that the state of Oregon's receipt of federal funds for assistance in educating the plaintiffs required the state to comply with its part of the bargain—namely, to provide sufficient funds to cover the full cost of their educations. Budgetary constraints could not excuse the state from the obligations arising from the acceptance of federal funds. In other words, the Oregon legislature could not refuse or neglect to enact a legislative program—in whatever manner it should deem to be appropriate—to provide funding for the full cost of the plaintiffs' educations. The court ordered the parties to act in accordance with its decision. *Kerr Center Parents Association v. Charles*, 581 F.Supp. 166 (D.Or.1983).

In an Illinois case, a handicapped student and his parents brought suit against the governor of Illinois and state and local educational officials, charging violations of the officials' legal duties created by the child's condition as a handicapped child. The officials moved for partial dismissal of the parents' complaint on four grounds. First, argued the officials, there was no basis for joining the governor as a defendant. Nothing the governor does, continued the argument, is asserted to have caused the alleged harm suffered by the parents and the child. Second, the parents should not be allowed to assert a Rehabilitation Act claim, as this Act was not a predicate for the relief sought. Third, the parents should not be allowed to assert their state law claim under an Illinois statute governing identification, evaluation and placement of handicapped children in special education in light of the U.S. Supreme Court's recent decision interpreting the Eleventh Amendment, *Pennhurst State School & Hospital v. Halderman*, 104 S.Ct. 900 (1984). Fourth, the officials claimed that once the Rehabilitation Act claim was gone, their request for attorney's fees should vanish with it because the EAHCA does not embody such relief. A U.S. district court in Illinois agreed with the officials' arguments and granted all four of their requests. Thus, the parents were allowed to proceed with their complaint only as narrowed. *Hayward v. Thompson*, 593 F.Supp, 57 (N.D.Ill.1984).

A U.S. district court in Wisconsin applied the doctrine of Eleventh Amendment governmental immunity in a claim against the Milwaukee public school system. A handicapped child brought suit in federal court against the school system on behalf of himself and all other similarly situated children in Milwaukee who were placed in day treatment facilities. After the state proposed termination of the day service placements, the parents of the children alleged that their children were being denied educational facilities in violation of the EAHCA. The court held that the parents' claim for damages against the Wisconsin state superintendent of public instruction was essentially a claim against state funds, and that no congressional authorization existed to abrogate the state's Eleventh Amendment immunity from retroactive monetary claims payable from the state treasury. However, the court did grant an injunction to the children against the superintendent of public instruction in her official capacity. The injunction restrained the Milwaukee public schools from terminating the current placement of the children and removing the children from those schools until completion of a full and impartial evaluation of their education needs. The injunction, said the court, was prospective in nature and thus was not barred by governmental immunity. *M.R. v. Milwaukee Public Schools*, 495 F.Supp. 864 (E.D.Wis.1980).

Georgia hearing procedures were successfully attacked by a handicapped child who, through her father, sued the Georgia Superintendent of the Georgia State Board of Education alleging that the procedures were in violation of the EAHCA. Specifically, the child alleged that in Georgia, the decision of a state educational agency, which should have been treated as final, was subject to "veto" by the state board of education. The U.S. Court of Appeals, Fifth Circuit, held that Eleventh Amendment immunity does not bar a federal court from enjoining state officials to conform their future conduct to the requirements of federal law. Accordingly, the state of Georgia was ordered to alter its procedures to conform to the provisions of the EAHCA, which provide that the decision of a state education agency is final. *Helms v. McDaniel*, 657 F.2d 800 (5th Cir.1981).

In a Michigan case, the parents of a handicapped child brought suit against a local school district alleging that the district had misdiagnosed their child's language impairment. The school district's motion for summary judgment was granted by the court on the ground that the school, in its operation of a speech therapy program, was involved in a government program and thus entitled to governmental immunity. In handing down its decision, the court outlined the guidelines it used in deciding whether a particular function is entitled to immunity. The court stated that it examines the precise activity giving rise to the plaintiff's claim, rather than the overall department operations. In this situation the examination and diagnosis of students in a public school was "intended to promote the general public health and [is] exercised for the common good of all." The court held, therefore, that the school district was immune from liability in performing the function. *Brosnan v. Livonia Public Schools*, 333 N.W.2d 288 (Mich.App.1983).

A federal district court held that the Commonwealth of Pennsylvania was immune from suit in a case where a handicapped child and his parents alleged that a Pennsylvania school district improperly excluded the child from a high school, failed to formulate an individual educational program for him, and failed to assure that he was receiving a free appropriate education. The court observed that Pennsylvania state agencies are immune from suit, unless the state has specifically waived its Eleventh Amendment immunity. The Pennsylvania legislature explicitly preserved Eleventh Amendment immunity in a law which stated: "Nothing contained in this act shall be construed to waive the Commonwealth's immunity from suit in Federal courts guaranteed by the Eleventh Amendment to the United States Constitution." Accordingly, the court held that since Pennsylvania had not waived its Eleventh Amendment immunity, that portion of the complaint against state education officials acting in their official capacities was dismissed. However, the question remained as to whether the handicapped children could sue the officials in their individual capacities. Noting that the Eleventh Amendment is no impediment to a damage suit against state officials in their individual capacities, the court held that since good faith is an affirmative defense against such a suit, that issue had yet to be determined in another proceeding. *Stubbs v. Kline*, 463 F.Supp, 110 (W.D.Pa.1978).

III. Private Schools

States receiving federal funding under the EAHCA are required to maintain a list of approved private schools to educate handicapped children where no public school program is available or appropriate.

A. Eligibility to Educate Handicapped Children

Disputes sometimes arise between states and private schools or states and students when a private school is excluded, for a particular reason or reasons, from the state's list of approved private schools.

The U.S. Supreme Court ruled unanimously on the issue of state aid to handicapped students at private religious schools. The Court held that the First Amendment to the U.S. Constitution does not prevent a state from providing financial assistance to a handicapped individual attending a Christian college. The plaintiff in this case, a blind person, sought vocational rehabilitative services from the state of Washington's Commission for the Blind pursuant to state law [Wash.Rev.Code sec. 74.16.181 (1981)]. The law provided that visually handicapped persons were eligible for educational assistance to enable them to "overcome vocational handicaps and to obtain the maximum degree of self-support and self-care." However, because the plaintiff was a private school student intending to pursue a career of service in the church, the Commission for the Blind denied him assistance. The Washington Supreme Court upheld this decision on the ground that the First Amendment to the U.S. Constitution prohibited state funding of a student's education at a religious college.

The U.S. Supreme Court took a different, much less restrictive view of the First Amendment and reversed the Washington court. The operation of Washington's program was such that the commission paid money directly to the student, who would then attend the school of his or her choice. The fact that the student in this case chose to attend a religious college did not constitute state support of religion, because "the decision to support religious education is made by the individual, not the state." The First Amendment was therefore not offended. *Witters v. Washington Department of Services for the Blind*, 106 S.Ct. 748 (1986).

New Jersey's department of education recently issued detailed regulations governing private schools which educate handicapped children. The regulations apply only to private schools to which local school boards have sent handicapped children in order to satisfy the local board's educational obligations. These private schools are required to submit detailed budgets, establish strict bookkeeping and accounting procedures, submit to annual audits by the state, and most objectionably, a school's profit is limited to 2.5% of its per pupil costs. Several private school associations sued the department seeking to have the regulations declared invalid. They claimed that the regulations were "confiscatory" and had been enacted without proper authority.

The New Jersey Superior Court, Appellate Division, upheld the regulations as within the scope of the department's powers. Especially persuasive to the court was the argument that private schools, by choosing to accept handicapped students on referral from local school boards, should expect to relinquish a degree of privacy and autonomy over their affairs. The 2.5% profit ceiling is a reasonable exercise of department authority over private schools which, said the court, have voluntarily submitted to department control. However, the court left open the possibility that in the future, if a private school were able to show that due to its financial condition the regulations were unreasonable as applied to it, then a waiver of the regulations might be justified. *Council of Private Schools for Children with Special Needs, Inc. v. Cooperman*, 501 A.2d 575 (N.J.Super.A.D.1985).

A private school in Pennsylvania alleged it was denied due process of law after the Pennsylvania Secretary of Education denied the school's application for status as an approved private school for socially and emotionally disturbed children. A hearing examiner determined that three State Board of Education standards were not met: first, the student interns used in the school classrooms did not provide full-time supportive assistance to the classroom teachers; second, the school lacked an immediately available supervisor or other competent and trained person to handle a student in a period of crisis and to remove that student, if necessary from the classroom; third, the school's behavior management systems did not permit its classroom teachers to control classroom conduct adequately. The school appealed to the Commonwealth Court of Pennsylvania, which affirmed the hearing examiner's decision. The school then appealed to the Supreme Court of Pennsylvania, which found that the evidence was sufficient to support a finding that the school failed to provide adequate staff assistance to classroom teachers. The court concluded that the hearing examiner's findings went to the heart of the Pennsylvania regulatory scheme of insuring that approved private schools were able to provide adequate and necessary training and education to handicapped children. *Wiley House v. Scanlon*, 465 A.2d 995 (Pa.1983).

A U.S. district court in New York held that the removal by the New York Commissioner of Education of all residential schools treating learning disabled children from a list of schools approved for the treatment of handicapped children, thereby eliminating such schools as options for the placement of learning disabled children, conflicted with the EAHCA. The court observed that only a small number of learning disabled children require residential placement and that some local programs were inadequate to serve learning disabled children. Thus, the policy was declared invalid. *Riley v. Ambach*, 508 F.Supp. 1222 (E.D.N.Y.1980). However, this case was reversed by the U.S. Court of Appeals, Second Circuit, on the ground that the plaintiffs had failed to exhaust their administrative remedies prior to bringing suit in federal court. *Riley v. Ambach*, 668 F.2d 635 (2d Cir.1981).

Another case arising in New York upheld a school district's right not to contract for placement with a private school. In this case, the parents of handicapped children brought suit against the state of New York, alleging that the transfer of their children from a special education school violated the EAHCA. The children were transferred to alternate sites after the Board of Education of the City of New York decided not to renew its contract with the school on the ground of financial mismanagement. A U.S. district court held that "while a school board and a state do not have unfettered power in all cases to close schools and transfer students, they must be permitted to make independent determinations regarding the suitability of private institutions to fulfill the educational and fiscal needs of a school system without first according parents and guardians a due process forum." *Dima v. Macchiarola*, 513 F.Supp. 565 (E.D.N.Y.1981).

The U.S. Court of Appeals, Second Circuit, has ruled on the proper educational placement of an emotionally disturbed twenty-year-old. The child had been maintained by the state of New York at an approved institution for handicapped children. The institution later was removed from the state list of certified facilities on the grounds it was a hospital, not a school, and was therefore not appropriate for placement. Although the child continued to reside there for some time following decertification, the state ultimately determined that it was not obligated to pay the costs of maintenance (approximately $185 per day). The parents sued for the maintenance costs and to have the child remain at the institution during the interim necessary to determine an alternative placement that satisfied the requirements of the EAHCA.

The Court of Appeals, basically upholding a federal district court decision, held that the state was obligated to pay for maintenance at the institution. Both sides in the case had relied on the "status quo" provisions of the Act, with the parents stating that status quo meant the child should be maintained at no cost to them, and the state claiming status quo meant a continuation of residence at the parents' expense. The court ruled that the state could not disclaim its statutory responsibility by decertifying an institution. A free appropriate public education in a suitable institution remains the responsibility of the state, held the court. *Vander Malle v. Ambach*, 673 F.2d 49 (2d Cir.1982).

B. Facilities and Programs

The appropriateness of private school facilities and programs to the particular needs of handicapped students has been a source of dispute between schools and students, schools and parents, and schools and states.

Students at a school for the blind in California brought suit against state education officials under the EAHCA and the Rehabilitation Act, challenging a move of the school to a new site. Among the objections to the move were allegations that the new site was an earthquake-prone, dangerous area. The school had been granted permission to open over the protest of the students because some parents objected to the possibility that, if the move was blocked, no special school for the blind would be available. The students sought a preliminary injunction to stop the move and made the seismic safety claims a major focus of their lawsuit. A U.S. district court ordered seismic studies of the site and, finding California's pre-construction seismic safety investigation inadequate, the court granted the students' request for a preliminary injunction.

The state appealed this ruling to the U.S. Court of Appeals, Ninth Circuit, which held that under the prohibition of the Rehabilitation Act against discriminating against the handicapped, California was required to make its school for the blind as safe as other schools and to make such reasonable adjustments as were necessary to make the school as safe as schools for non-handicapped students. To the state's argument that the general anti-discrimination provisions of the Rehabilitation Act cannot be used to make an "end run" around the more specific provisions of the EAHCA, the court said that while the EAHCA is more specific than the Rehabilitation Act as to educational programs, the Rehabilitation Act is more specific as to physical facilities. The court found no conflict between the two Acts.

Finally, because a strong argument could be made that a seismically unsafe school denied the students a "free appropriate education" under the EAHCA, the Court of Appeals held that the district court properly granted the students' request for a preliminary injunction. The district court ruling was affirmed and the superintendent of Public Instruction of California appealed to the U.S. Supreme Court, which held that the question of whether the district court erred in issuing the preliminary injunction was moot; subsequent to the time of the district court's order, and prior to the Supreme

Court's ruling, the tests had been completed. *Honig v. Students of California School for the Blind*, 105 S.Ct. 1820 (1985).

The mother of a seriously emotionally disturbed nineteen-year-old brought suit against a Tennessee school district alleging that her son had not been placed in an appropriate facility. A hearing officer had determined that a Tennessee residential school providing psychiatric treatment was the appropriate placement for the boy. The mother, however, wanted him placed in a special school in Texas. She appealed the hearing officer's decision to a federal district court, which held for the school district. The mother then appealed to the U.S. Court of Appeals, Sixth Circuit, which reversed the district court ruling. The Court of Appeals was persuaded by psychiatric testimony which established that the Texas school, which offered long-term treatment and had locked wards, was a better school for the boy. The court rejected the school district's argument that because the Texas school cost $88,000 per year as compared to $55,000 per year for the school chosen by the board, placement at the Tennessee school was warranted. It stated that cost considerations, when devising programs for individual handicapped students, are only relevant when choosing between several options, all of which offer an "appropriate" education. *Clevenger v. Oak Ridge School Board*, 744 F.2d 514 (6th Cir.1984).

The following case involved a dispute between a school for the handicapped and the state of Illinois over the nature of a program offered by the school. The school alleged in federal district court that the Illinois Guardianship and Advocacy Commission (GAC) violated the school's First Amendment right to freedom of speech and its constitutional right to due process of law. The school contended that the GAC's prevailing philosophy with respect to the proper way to handle the education of multiply handicapped and developmentally disabled children conflicted with the school's philosophy, and that the GAC sought to punish the school for the school's nonconformist philosophy and for criticisms of the GAC's philosophy. The school argued that the GAC instituted an harassment campaign under the guise of an investigation of charges the GAC knew were false.

Allegations by the school included the GAC's numerous visits to the school's campus to question students and employees and burdensome document requests, all of which disrupted the school's operation. Further, argued the school, the GAC held a public "hearing" at which it released a number of false charges against the school and its executive director, including charges of understaffing, improper distribution of medication and permitting sexual abuse of its residents. The school claimed that the GAC refused its several requests for advance notice of the nature of the charges, that the school was not given the opportunity to object or respond at the hearing, and that without the school's input, the GAC released its findings and recommendations to the press.

The GAC subsequently recommended that other Illinois agencies and the Illinois legislature take action against the school, including cutting off the school's funding, removing the executive director and revoking the school's licenses. The school claimed that as a result of the GAC's actions and the adverse publicity, it suffered disruption in providing its services, frustration in accomplishing its educational goals and a loss of reputation, enrollment and revenues. The school sought compensatory and punitive damages against the GAC.

The district court held that the school stated a valid First Amendment claim but that its due process claim was not supported by the evidence. The school had failed to prove that merely threatening the revocation of its licenses, which had not actually been revoked, deprived it of its alleged "prospective business advantage" or that the alleged loss of funding from two sources was attributable to the GAC's actions. Thus, the school was allowed to proceed with its First Amendment claims but the due process claims were dismissed. *Grove School v. Guardianship and Advocacy Commission*, 596 F.Supp. 1361 (N.D.Ill.1984).

In the following case, which involved insurance coverage for a disabled child's placement at a residential facility, the U.S. Court of Appeals ordered an insurer to pay for the costs. Here, a child who suffered from a functional nervous disorder was admitted to the Clear Water Ranch Children's House, a residential treatment facility in California which specializes in the treatment of such disorders. The staff at the facility consisted of one registered nurse, who worked days only, child care workers who were present twenty-four hours per day, and licensed clinical social workers. A psychiatrist supervised this staff. The child's stepfather, who was issued a group medical insurance policy by his employer, submitted a claim to his insurer for the cost of the child's treatment at the facility. The insurer denied the claim and stated that the facility did not quality as a "hospital," which was defined in the policy as "an institution . . . primarily engaged in providing on an in-patient basis for the medical care and treatment of sick and injured persons through medical, diagnostic and major surgical facilities, all of which facilities must be provided on its premises under the supervision of a staff of Physicians with 24-hour a day nursing service." The U.S. Court of Appeals, Ninth Circuit, awarded coverage. The term "nursing service" was not defined in the policy. The insurer's argument that coverage could be provided only for facilities with twenty-four hour a day registered nurses was rejected by the court, which found that the child care workers who were on duty twenty-four hours a day satisfied the policy requirements. Furthermore, the court held that the fact that the treatment facility possessed no major surgical facilities presented no bar to coverage, since it was the insurer's admitted practice to disregard this policy requirement for facilities which treat mental illnesses. *Hanson v. Prudential Insurance Co. of America*, 772 F.2d 580 (9th Cir.1985).

C. Contracts

Most cases concerning contract disputes involve private schools, which enjoy the unfettered ability to enter into contractual agreements with the parents of handicapped children, or school districts, to provide special education services.

The parents of a handicapped child in Illinois brought suit against a Massachusetts private school, alleging that the school violated the terms of an agreement between the parents and the school. The parents claimed the agreement provided that the school would apply for increased funding from the state of Illinois for their handicapped daughter's placement at the Massachusetts school. As a result of Massachusetts and Illinois using different criteria in setting tuition rates, and dramatic increases in tuition rates at the school, the amounts the parents received in assistance from the state of Illinois proved to be insufficient to cover the costs of the child's attendance at the school. The parents also claimed that a school official called the child's mother requesting that the child not return to school for the summer session preceding the 1979-80 school year, as well as the following school year, because of the tuition reimbursement problem, and that if the parents sent their daughter to the school on a plane, there would be no one to meet her at the airport.

The child's father negotiated an arrangement with the school whereby the child would be allowed to return for summer session, with the parents paying the full cost of her attendance and the school applying for the funds due from Illinois. When summer session ended, the school received a contract from Illinois for the child's placement for the 1980-81 school year. The school refused to sign the contract, knowing it was not going to get the tuition reimbursement it was due. Further, the school had never received a formal letter from the child's father saying he would pay the child's tuition in full.

The father then wrote a letter to the school requesting that his daughter be allowed to remain there, while the school investigated the possibility of receiving funding from Illinois. The school's investigation revealed that it was not even on the Illinois State Board of Education's (ISBE) list of approved schools; thus, even if the school had singed the contract it would not have been paid. Further, new Illinois law would not allow Massachusetts to assess parents the difference between what Illinois would pay and what the Massachusetts school charged. The school then informed the parents that the child would be allowed to remain as a private student only; otherwise she would be requested to leave and not return after Christmas vacation of the 1980-81 school year. The child stayed at the school during Christmas because of a family disruption. Shortly thereafter, the father visited the director of the school, who signed an agreement to apply to Illinois for ISBE eligibility. Eligibility was denied by Illinois. The child remained at the school until March, with no money from any source being offered for the child's placement.

In April, with approximately $30,000 owing for the child's placement, the school threatened to return the child to Illinois. The father went to Massachusetts once again and obtained a temporary restraining order preventing the school from discharging the child. The child returned to Illinois in June and entered another school. The father sued the Massachusetts school for failing to apply for Illinois funds, and the school sued the father for tuition, room and board owed. In the parents' lawsuit, a jury awarded the parents $4,000 in compensatory damages, $30,000 for fraud and $50,000 to the wife on her claim of intentional infliction of emotional distress resulting from the phone call she received from the school. The school appealed and both lawsuits were consolidated in a U.S. district court in Illinois, which upheld the compensatory damage award but set aside the jury's awards for fraud and emotional distress.

The parents appealed to the U.S. Court of Appeals, Seventh Circuit, which held that the parents were not entitled to damages. The child's father, a medical doctor, had not shown that on the days of his trips to Massachusetts to resolve the problems with the school, that he would otherwise have been in consultation with patients. Thus, the $4,000 damage award, consisting of travel and lodging costs, lost consulting fees and attorney expenses was denied. The court also found that there was no implied contract wherein the parents agreed to pay the complete tuition for the 1979-80 school year. Thus, the parents were not liable for tuition for that year. However, the parents re-enrolled their child in the school the following year with the full knowledge that the school was having tuition reimbursement problems with Illinois. Thus, there was an implied contract for the 1980-81 school year for the parents to bear the tuition expenses.

Further the telephone call to the child's mother regarding the school's request that the child not return to school was not intentional infliction of emotional distress. Under Massachusetts law, only "extreme and outrageous" conduct can give rise to such a claim. Such conduct does not qualify as extreme and outrageous unless it is "beyond all bounds of decency and utterly intolerable in a civilized community." Finally, the court found no evidence of fraud as the school merely made a promise to apply for additional funding and, although not always gracious about the circumstances, intended to carry out that promise. In fact, said the court, whenever the possibility arose that the child would be requested to withdraw, the school accommodated the parents' request to reconsider its position. It did so, observed the court, because of its respect for the family situation in light of the son's illness. *Dr. Franklin Perkins School v. Freeman*, 741 F.2d 1503 (7th Cir.1984).

The breach of contract claim in the case below resulted from a New York private school's alleged misrepresentations with regard to its specialized faculty and capabilities. After the school brought an action to recover tuition expenses from the mother of a student, the mother counterclaimed against the school for breach of contract, fraudulent/negligent misrepresentation and negligent infliction of emotional distress. The school moved to dismiss the mother's counterclaim for failure to state a claim for which relief could be granted. The mother's counterclaim alleged that the school's agents represented to her that they possessed a specialized faculty that could identify and individually treat children with learning disabilities. She claimed that these representations were fraudulently and/or negligently made, and that, to her detriment, she relied on the representations in entering into her agreement with the school. She also claimed that the school did not provide the stated services and therefore breached their contract. Finally, the mother alleged that psychiatric intervention was necessary because her son received services which proved to be inappropriate and harmful when the school failed to diagnose (or misdiagnosed) his learning disability. This, she claimed, constituted negligent infliction of emotional distress.

The Civil Court of the City of New York granted a portion of the private school's motion and denied part of the motion. The court held that the mother's breach of contract claim, alleging that the school agreed to detect her child's learning deficiencies and to provide the necessary tutorial and guidance services but failed to do so, was permissible. However, the mother could make a claim for fraudulent misrepresentation only if she could show that the school knowingly made the misrepresentations to her. Thus, she could only maintain an action based on intentional misrepresentation, not negligent misrepresentation. Finally, the mother could not recover under her claim for negligent infliction of emotional distress. The court noted that it is well established that physical contact or injury is no longer necessary for such a claim. However, the courts have unanimously held that monetary damages for educational malpractice based on a negligence theory are not recoverable. Therefore, the mother could not sue for alleged mental distress caused by negligence in educational practices. *Village Community School v. Adler*, 478 N.Y.S.2d 546 (N.Y.City Civ.Ct.1984).

In a breach of contract case, a private residential facility for the treatment of mentally handicapped adolescent boys located in Milwaukee, Wisconsin, brought suit in Illinois against the Chicago Board of Education and another local suburban school district to recover the value of services rendered to students from the defendant school districts. The dispute arose from the placement with the facility of six high school students. The facility, unfamiliar with Illinois procedures for the payment of tuition to private facilities for handicapped students, accepted the Illinois students into its program before it had received approval from Illinois for its rate structure. Without such approval, the facility was ineligible under Illinois law to receive tuition payments from Illinois school boards. The facility ultimately received the necessary approval and then sought payment of tuition for the entire time the children were at the facility. The school districts, however, refused to pay for any treatment provided prior to the facility's approval for Illinois funds. The facility then filed suit, seeking recovery for breach of contract.

A lower court held that the facts were not sufficient to prove the existence of an express or implied contract since the districts had not agreed to assume responsibility for the tuition for services provided prior to Illinois approval of the facility, nor did the districts have authority to enter into such agreements. The case was appealed to the Appellate Court of Illinois, which affirmed the lower court.

The Appellate Court rejected an argument made by the facility that a statute involved here was not applicable. Said the court, "the statute on its face clearly prohibits the placement of Illinois students in a nonapproved institution," such as the one involved here. The facility also argued that, under federal law, the school districts had a duty to provide handicapped children with a free education and that, therefore, the Illinois School Code could not be construed to prohibit the school districts from contracting with the facility. The court dismissed this argument by stating that a private education facility, such as the one involved here, lacks standing to assert the rights of handicapped children to a free education. The facility, therefore, could not rely on the students' rights under federal law to advance its contract claim.

Also rejected was a contention by the facility that the evidence supported a finding that it should be permitted to recover in quasi-contract. The law will not imply an agreement which would be illegal if it were express. Because the court held that Illinois law prohibited the placement of students in nonapproved private facilities such as the one here, the law cannot imply a contract for the placement of the students prior to the facility's approval in Illinois. The lower court decision was affirmed. *Juneau Academy v. Chicago Board of Education*, 461 N.E.2d 597 (Ill.App.1st Dist.1984).

IV. Training Personnel Under the EAHCA

Section 1431 of the EAHCA provides grants to colleges and state agencies to facilitate training of personnel for the education of handicapped. Whether this "training" provision also applies to parents is an issue which has been presented before the courts.

The parents of a handicapped student in Ohio attacked the quality of education their son was receiving. The parents asserted that the Education for All Handicapped Children Act obligated school districts to provide in-service training to parents of handicapped students. The parents also claimed that the Act required the school district to include summer classes and continuous occupational therapy in their child's curriculum. They requested and received a hearing but were unsuccessful in reversing the district's denial of the services. The Ohio State Board of Education affirmed the hearing officer's determination and the parents appealed to a U.S. district court, which affirmed the hearing officer's decision but directed the school district to provide the student with one hour of extracurricular activities each week. Both the parents and the school board appealed. The U.S. Court of Appeals, Sixth Circuit, affirmed the district court ruling, saying that the EAHCA did not obligate school districts to provide in-service training to parents of handicapped students. The court also affirmed the district court's denial of summer classes and continuous occupational therapy. These programs, the court found, were not necessary to permit the child to benefit from his instruction. Finally, the court reversed the district court decision to include a nonacademic extracurricular activity once per week, saying that the EAHCA did not require that states maximize the potential of handicapped children commensurate with the opportunity provided to other children. Accordingly, the district court holding was affirmed in part and reversed in part. *Rettig v. Kent City School District*, 720 F.2d 463 (6th Cir.1983).

A U.S. district court in Texas, however, held that the parents of a handicapped child were entitled to training in behavioral techniques to handle their autistic and possibly mentally retarded daughter. *Stacey G. v. Pasadena School District*, 547 F.Supp. 61 (S.D.Tex.1982).

V. Gifted Programs

A "placement lottery" was recently upheld by a New York appeals court. In this case a school district established a talented and gifted (TAG) program for its elementary school students. Although it identified 109 children as being gifted, it established a full-time TAG program with space available for only 27 students. The school district then used the lottery method to determine which of the 109 children would be admitted to the full-time TAG program. Consequently, the parents of a gifted child (one of the original 109) whose name was not chosen sued the school district, contending that the lottery was an arbitrary and capricious method of selection. The New York Supreme Court, Appellate Division, rejected this contention due to the fact that there is no constitutional right to a "gifted or talented" education. The parents' attempt to analogize their case to one in which a lottery was employed to select children for a handicapped student program was rejected by the court. The lottery method was upheld as a valid, reasonable way for the school district to solve its space limitation problem. *Bennett v. City School District*, 497 N.Y.S.2d 72 (A.D.2d Dept.1985).

A student in Pennsylvania sought an injunction from a U.S. district court in Pennsylvania to compel a local school district to admit her to a special communications class for gifted students. The student charged that the minimum cutoff score on a standardized aptitude test to qualify students for special classes was arbitrary. This, claimed the student, violated her constitutional rights to equal protection and due process of law. The court held that the testing procedure did not violate equal protection since the use of the minimum cutoff score was rationally related to the objective of identifying gifted students. Further, although the student was entitled to due process of law before being deprived of the right to public education created by Pennsylvania law, the student had failed to exhaust her administrative remedies provided by the state and thus could not claim that she was denied procedural due process. The court dismissed the student's complaint. *Student Doe v. Commonwealth of Pennsylvania*, 593 F.Supp. 54 (E.D.Pa.1984).

CHAPTER SEVEN

HANDICAP DISCRIMINATION

The **Rehabilitation Act of 1973** prohibits discrimination against the handicapped in programs receiving federal financial assistance. Under the Act, no otherwise qualified handicapped individual is to be excluded from employment, programs or services to which he or she is entitled. Additionally, claims for alleged discrimination are sometimes brought under the Equal Protection Clause of the U.S. Constitution, which also prohibits discrimination by guaranteeing that laws will be applied equally to all citizens. The availability of the Rehabilitation Act as the basis for a lawsuit was, however, greatly diminished for handicapped students by the Supreme Court in *Smith v. Robinson* (see Chapter 4, § VIII).

I. Duty Not to Discriminate Against the Handicapped

The duty not to discriminate against handicapped individuals may arise by statute, and/or may be concomitant with the receipt of federal funding. Where a state's asserted interest in discriminating against the handicapped is outweighed by the liberty interests of the handicapped, the state must affirmatively act to eliminate the source of discrimination, or, in other cases, must refrain from acting when doing so would promote unfair discrimination.

A. Students, Patients and Other Individuals

The U.S. Supreme Court ruled recently that mental retardation is not a "suspect classification" calling for heightened protection under the U.S. Constitution. This case arose when the operator of a proposed group home for mentally handicapped individuals was denied a building-use permit by the city council of Cleburne, Texas. The city council determined that the group home would be classified as a "hospital for the feebleminded" under the zoning laws and proceeded to deny a permit to the group home. The operator sued the city in federal court, claiming that the council's action unlawfully discriminated against mentally retarded citizens in violation of the Equal Protection Clause of the U.S. Constitution.

The Supreme Court, while ordering that the group home be granted a permit, held that government regulations regarding mentally retarded individuals are not to be subjected to rigorous judicial analysis as are classifications based on race, alienage or sex. The Equal Protection Clause, held the

Court, does not afford the same protection to handicapped citizens as it does to minorities. Although in this case the group home won its building-use permit, the Supreme Court's holding limited the scope of the Equal Protection Clause to cases involving irrational, unfounded or arbitrary action against the handicapped. *City of Cleburne, Texas v. Cleburne Living Center*, 105 S.Ct. 3249 (1985).

Six years after a handicapped individual was denied admission to a California nursing school, a federal appeals court ruled that she was entitled to damages for unlawful discrimination. The prospective student suffered from Crohn's Disease, an inflammatory bowel disorder which causes loss of weight, nausea, vomiting and other complications. She had been accepted to the Los Angeles County Medical Center School of Nursing in April, 1979, and had attended an orientation session. Two days before classes were to begin she was told that due to an unacceptable physical examination, she was being denied admission to the school. She filed suit in federal district court under the Rehabilitation Act, seeking an order that the school be compelled to accept her.

After twice being denied relief by the district court, the case came before the U.S. Court of Appeals, Ninth Circuit. The appeals court found that the woman was a handicapped individual within the meaning of the Rehabilitation Act, and noted that the school's physician had recommended that her application for admission be rejected because, in his opinion, it would be "too stressful" for her to study at the school. The court stated that "[i]t is precisely this type of general assumption about a handicapped person's ability that [the Act] was designed to avoid." Finding that the woman had been denied admission solely on the basis of her handicap, the court remanded the case to the district court with instructions to award her monetary damages and attorney's fees. *Kling v. County of Los Angeles*, 769 F.2d 532 (9th Cir.1985).

An Illinois case resulted in a ruling that a handicapped student may not sue the U.S. Secretary of Education. Here, a graduate student pursuing an MBA at Chicago's Roosevelt University failed to inform university officials that he was handicapped, and did not tell them that he was learning disabled. Instead, the university thought that he was recovering from a serious illness. In view of the student's "illness," the university allowed him to continue in its MBA program even though he had received his third "C," which usually results in academic dismissal. Eventually, the student was unable to meet the MBA program's requirements. He attempted to bring suit under the Rehabilitation Act directly against the U.S. Secretary of Education, seeking damages due to the secretary's refusal to review his claim that the university had discriminated against him on the basis of his handicap.

The federal district court observed that the student had never informed the university that he was handicapped by a learning disability (the latter stemmed from his past history of cryptococcal meningitis and hydrocephalus with a posterior right shunt). Unquestionably, he had no claim against the university since the Rehabilitation Act imposes no duty upon institutions which are unaware of a person's handicap, said the court, and this no doubt explained why he had attempted to sue the secretary instead. The student's lawsuit was thus dismissed by the court, which stated: "There is no doubt that a recipient or applicant of federal funds has a cause of action against the Secretary under Section 603 [of the Rehabilitation Act]. There is also no doubt that a beneficiary in [the handicapped student's] position has a private right of action against the recipient institution. But no private cause of action exists under Section 504 [of the Act] for a beneficiary against the Secretary." Accordingly, the student's complaint against the secretary was dismissed. *Salvador v. Bell*, 622 F.Supp. 438 (N.D.Ill.1985).

As a result of reports of patient abuse at the Pennhurst State Hospital, a Pennsylvania institution for the severely mentally retarded, a state police officer was assigned to become an undercover aide at the hospital. Several hospital employees were later indicted by a federal grand jury, and a male aide was convicted of violating the right of severely retarded persons to personal security, a federal crime. The evidence showed that the aide frequently "punched, kicked, kneed, or shoved" patients for no reason and that he frequently flicked cigarette butts on the floor where he hoped that more severely retarded patients would ingest them. The U.S. Court of Appeals, Third Circuit, upheld his conviction. The aide had knowingly deprived the patients of their federally protected right to personal security while acting under the authority of state law. *United States v. Dise*, 763 F.2d 586 (3d Cir.1985).

In a Texas case, a migrant worker brought suit on behalf of his children against state education officials alleging that the officials had violated the Education Consolidation and Improvement Act of 1981 and his children's rights to equal protection. The Act provides in part that federal funds received by state educational agencies "will be used for programs and projects . . . which are designed to meet the special educational needs of migratory children of migratory agricultural workers. . . ." The funding obtained from the Texas Education Agency was used to operate a migrant education program called "Extended Day," which provided tutorial services to migrant children for one hour each day after regular school hours. The purpose of Extended Day was to compensate for the instruction migrant children miss because of their late return to school necessitated by the seasonal nature of migratory work.

A prerequisite to earning a diploma under the Extended Day program was that enrollment in the program be completed by October 17. This cut-off date was the half-way point of the fall semester and reflected the board of education's belief that a valid educational experience could not be realized unless a student attended class for at least fifty percent of the operational days of the district. The family objected to this condition. In the school year giving rise to the dispute the family had returned to their home on October 21, 1983. Although the children were permitted to enroll and attend classes, they were not allowed to attend Extended Day or receive credit for any work completed during the fall semester. The U.S. district court held that the cut-off date had been adopted without regard to the special educational needs of migrant children and, therefore, the students were entitled to a preliminary injunction to permit all eligible migrant children to be given the opportunity to make up work and earn credit for the full semester. *Zavala v. Contreras*, 581 F.Supp. 701 (S.D.Tex.1984).

In another Texas case, the parents of a mentally handicapped child, who was enrolled in a private school, contacted a public school district regarding a possible public school placement for their child. A meeting was held a year later at which the parents were not present and of which they had no knowledge. At the meeting, it was decided that the child should be placed in an EMR class in the public schools. When the parents were finally contacted they rejected the recommendation, saying that their son was not mentally retarded. The parents continued private school placement for their child.

Approximately two years later the school district started a public awareness "blitz" to reach handicapped children not then receiving a free appropriate public education. A year after they became aware of this "child find" program, the parents once again contacted the school district for a possible public school placement. The child was eventually enrolled in a public school program, and the parents sought reimbursement for their private school tuition expenses in a U.S. district court.

The court held that the school district had been under an affirmative duty to determine what special services would be needed for the child and then to provide those services. In failing to do so, the school district had discriminated against the child in violation of section 504 of the Rehabilitation Act. The parents were not entitled to damages under the Education for All Handicapped Children Act, but were entitled to private school tuition reimbursement under the Rehabilitation Act. However, the court found that the parents were not entitled to tuition reimbursement subsequent to the time they became aware of the "child find" program. *David H. v. Spring Branch Independent School District*, 569 F.Supp. 1324 (S.D.Tex.1983).

A group of mentally retarded children in Virginia brought suit against the Virginia Commissioner of the Department of Welfare, and other state officials, seeking injunctive relief enjoining the defendants from maintaining them in an institution or state hospital. The children claimed that these placements were made in lieu of providing them with an appropriate education, treatment, care, and services in a foster home or other community-based facility in their home communities. A U.S. district court held that the children had a valid claim under the Developmentally Disabled Assistance and Bill of Rights Act, the Education for All Handicapped Children Act and the Rehabilitation Act. These statutes afford personal civil rights to beneficiaries under the statutes, which were intended to promote equal treatment of and equal opportunity to the beneficiaries. Further, the also applicable Community Mental Health Center Act is a Congressional commitment to the principle that rehabilitation of the handicapped should be facilitated in the least restrictive setting. Thus, the defendants' motion for summary judgment on the ground that the children had failed to state a valid claim was denied. *Medley v. Ginsberg*, 492 F.Supp. 1294 (S.D.W.Va.1980).

A group of mentally retarded children brought suit against the Board of Education of the City of New York challenging a proposed plan to segregate within the public schools those retarded children who were carriers of hepatitis B virus. The board argued that the plan was valid because it was formulated pursuant to New York City health department guidelines. A U.S. district court held in favor of the children, saying that the health department guidelines, which were adopted without public hearings, without notices of proposed rule making, and with only limited opportunity for input by interested persons were more "akin to general statements of policy than mandatory prescriptions." Thus, the guidelines would not be afforded "presumptive validity." The plan was also flawed because it violated the Rehabilitation Act and the EAHCA. The New York Board of Education had not shown that the hepatitis B carriers had actually engaged in unhygienic contacts. The board was unable to demonstrate that even one instance of disease transmission had occurred in the classroom setting.

Further, the court noted that the segregation plan would violate the EAHCA in that the children would not be educated in the "least restrictive environment." Finally, despite the fact that there were over one million school children in New York City's public school system, no group other than the mentally retarded students was tested for hepatitis B. This, the district court said, violated the children's equal protection rights under the U.S. Constitution. This decision was affirmed by the U.S. Court of Appeals, Second Circuit, which reiterated the district court's observation that the board of education had failed to show that the alleged hazard was anything more than a remote possibility. The potential detrimental effects of isolating the children outweighed the state's relatively weak interest in segregating hepatitis B carriers. *New York State Association for Retarded Children v. Carey*, 612 F.2d 644 (2d Cir.1979).

In New Hampshire an unsuccessful discrimination claim was brought by the mother of a disabled child in U.S. district court, alleging discrimination under the federal Rehabilitation Act. She alleged that the New Hampshire Medical Assistance Program (NHMAP) unlawfully discriminated against her son solely on the basis of his handicap. The NHMAP provides medical assistance under the medical needs program only to persons under eighteen years of age who are blind, she pointed out, while denying benefits to persons under eighteen years of age who are handicapped by any other disability. The state moved to dismiss the action for failure to state a claim upon which relief could be granted and the motion was granted.

The court stated that the state's refusal to expand the eligibility requirements for medical assistance to include the plaintiff in this case was not so unreasonable and arbitrary as to constitute unlawful discrimination. It was noted that the plaintiffs did not allege that New Hampshire's exclusion of sight-disabled children from medical assistance was motivated by an animus against handicapped individuals. In fact, the statutory history revealed that the exclusion was based on congressional authorization designed to encourage continued state participation in the Medicaid program, through limitation of the state's financial commitment. In the absence of any statutory or regulatory requirement identifying as discriminatory the refusal to undertake affirmative action by extending additional services to the handicapped, the court held that it was not at liberty to fashion its own affirmative action requirements. Thus, in spite of the plaintiff's obvious need for medical assistance and the compelling nature of his request for medical assistance equal to that afforded other disabled persons under the NHMAP, the court determined it should not overrule the judgment of state of New Hampshire and Congress on this matter of social policy. *Duquette v. Dupuis*, 582 F.Supp. 1365 (D.N.H.1984).

In a case involving access for physically handicapped persons to buildings used by the public, the Court of Appeal of California held that a restaurant with all of its public facilities on the second floor of a building must make the primary entrance accessible to the handicapped. The restaurant, located on the ocean waterfront, was forced to construct a multi-storied building to comply with an easement for pedestrian access along the waterfront. Consequently, the lower portion of the building was used by restaurant personnel as a service area. Access to the building and bar areas for able-bodied patrons was provided through a glass and wood door into an attractive foyer decorated with plants and skylights. Physically handicapped persons were restricted to entering through the service entrance, which was neither designated nor decorated for patron access and was locked during business hours.

After several complaints from handicapped patrons of the restaurant, the California Department of Rehabilitation brought suit to force the restaurant to comply with California Health and Safety Code requirements regarding "primary entrances." The Court of Appeals reversed a trial court ruling in favor of the restaurant, saying that where a second primary entrance to a building is necessary to satisfy the primary entrance requirements it need not be identical in character to the first. However, it must be free from difficulties or obstacles and potential hazards which would endanger even the most cautious physically handicapped person. Further, "primary entrance" means a principal entrance, one which has a substantial flow of pedestrian traffic to any specific major function of the facility. In this case, in order to comply with the code requirements, the only viable option was for the restaurant to install an elevator in the main entrance. *People v. Che Inc.*, 197 Cal.Rptr. 484 (Cal.App.4th Dist.1983).

A group of students and would-be students at the University of Texas at Austin sought declaratory and injunctive relief in federal district court requiring the university to make its shuttle buses accessible to wheelchairs. The plaintiffs were all confined to wheelchairs and, therefore, handicapped individuals under the Rehabilitation Act of 1973. They were required to pay a mandatory student services fee each semester, which was used in part to pay for the operation of the shuttle bus system. However, they could not use the system because the buses were not accessible to wheelchairs. They contended that the university's failure to provide them with accessible shuttle service limited their ability to fully participate in academic and extracurricular programs, and that this failure was in violation of federal law. They also contended that the failure to accommodate wheelchairs was a breach of their contract with the university to provide them with bus transportation in exchange for student service fees.

The district court disagreed with these contentions. It held that the shuttle bus system was not a program receiving federal financial assistance for purposes of the Rehabilitation Act and therefore was not subject to the requirements of the Act, that the university had no obligation under the Equal Protection Clause of the Fourteenth Amendment to make major expenditures of funds required to make the shuttle bus system accessible to wheelchairs, and that the university had not "contracted" to provide shuttle bus service to mobility-impaired students on the basis of statements made in the university general information booklet. The students' request for declaratory and injunctive relief was therefore denied. *Ferris v. University of Texas at Austin*, 558 F.Supp. 536 (W.D.Tex.1983).

B. Teachers

Teachers and other school employees are also protected by the Rehabilitation Act against discrimination on the basis of handicap.

An applicant for a special education teaching position in Iowa sued a local school district under both the federal Rehabilitation Act and Iowa law, alleging that the district refused to hire him due to his physical disability. The teacher, a resident of Vermont, suffered from several severe handicaps, but was able to walk without assistance and to lift children and drive. The teacher applied to the Iowa school district for a job and was scheduled for an interview in Iowa, at his own expense, with possible reimbursement if he were hired. After arranging the interview, the teacher became concerned that he had not disclosed his handicaps. Because of his limited financial resources, he did not wish to fly to Iowa, only to be rejected because of his handicaps. He called the school district and explained his handicaps. He was told that the job involved transporting children which, in turn, required a bus driver's permit that the teacher probably could not get because of his handicaps. The district suggested that a trip to Iowa would probably be futile. The teacher then sued in U.S. district court, which found in his favor.

The court stated that the test of proof for a discrimination claim under the Rehabilitation Act is: 1) that the plaintiff is a handicapped individual under the terms of the statute; 2) that the plaintiff is otherwise qualified to participate in the program or activity at issue; 3) that the plaintiff was excluded from the program or activity solely by reason of her or his handicap; and 4) that the program or activity receives federal financial assistance. There was no dispute that the plaintiff was a "handicapped individual" within the meaning of the Rehabilitation Act, the court had little difficulty in finding that the plaintiff was "otherwise qualified" for the position because of his superior credentials. The court also found that the plaintiff had satisfied the third and fourth prongs of the test in that the district was a recipient of federal financial assistance, including funds received pursuant to the EAHCA and that, with a minimum of accommodation, the school district could have arranged an alternative situation whereby the teacher would not have had to transport children. The court awarded the teacher $1,000 damages for mental anguish, and $5,150 for loss of earnings. *Fitzgerald v. Green Valley Education Agency*, 589 F.Supp. 1130 (S.D.Iowa 1984).

In 1979, the Council for the Hearing Impaired of Long Island and others brought suit in U.S. district court against the Commissioner of Education of the State of New York, and several federal officials, alleging that the offering of lower salaries at educational institutions for handicapped students was unlawful. Specifically, the plaintiffs contended that because teaching salaries at these institutions were lower than those found in other schools, there existed a relatively high staff turnover rate which had an adverse impact on handicapped students' educations. The plaintiffs charged that this violated the Education for All Handicapped Children Act, section 504 of the Rehabilitation Act, section 1983 of the Civil Rights Act, and the First and Ninth Amendments to the U.S. Constitution.

On a motion for summary judgment, the district court dismissed the claim that a high staff turnover rate was violative of the EAHCA, noting that nothing in the EAHCA requires that the education of handicapped children be "equal" to that of other children. All that is required is that handicapped children be provided with an "educational benefit." Also dismissed were the plaintiff's claims under the First and Ninth Amendments, since education is not guaranteed by the U.S. Constitution. However, the plaintiffs were allowed to proceed with their claims under the Rehabilitation Act and the Civil Rights Act, insofar as they alleged that the state of New York had unlawfully discriminated between handicapped and nonhandicapped children in the provision of educational services. The district court then proceeded to admonish the plaintiffs for failing to diligently prosecute their case, stating that they "have been content to file repetitive motions with this Court without developing the factual bases necessary to support their claims." The court stated that unless the plaintiffs brought new evidence establishing their claims, the case would be dismissed for lack of prosecution. *Council for the Hearing Impaired v. Ambach*, 610 F.Supp. 1051 (E.D.N.Y.1985).

II. Racial Discrimination In Placement Programs

The de facto overrepresentation of minority students in special education programs, or underrepresentation of such students in gifted programs is insufficient to prove racial discrimination in placement programs. A plaintiff must prove that the alleged overrepresentation or underrepresentation is the result of purposeful discriminatory intention.

The Georgia chapter of the NAACP commenced a class action lawsuit in U.S. district court on behalf of all black children in the state, claiming that the Georgia State Board of Education and a number of local school districts were assigning black students to programs for the educable mentally retarded in a racially discriminatory manner. The NAACP produced uncontroverted statistical evidence that a disproportionately high number of black students had been taken out of regular classrooms and placed in EMR programs. Depending on the school district, this was done on the basis of state I.Q. tests, the Metropolitan Achievement Test, the Development Indicators for the Assessment of Learning Tests, the MacMillan Placement Test, as well as other familiar evaluation devices and procedures. The NAACP made two basic allegations: 1) the use of these placement methods was intended to produce intraschool racial segregation, and 2) black children were assigned to the EMR programs in a discriminatory manner. Thus, the essence of the plaintiff's lawsuit was that since a disproportionately large number of black children were assigned to EMR programs, racial segregation had been the inevitable result. The methods of assignment to the programs, as well as the programs themselves, were alleged to be in violation of the U.S. Constitution, the Civil Rights Act and the Rehabilitation Act. The district court ruled against the plaintiffs on all counts and an appeal was taken to the U.S. Court of Appeals, Eleventh Circuit.

The appellate court held that ability grouping *per se*, and placement of black students in special education programs, did not violate federal law "even when it results in racial disparity in a school district's classrooms." The problem, said the court of appeals, stemmed from past racial segregation. Georgia's black children had previously been confined to grossly inferior "black" schools, receiving substandard public educations. When integration took place, "lack of [prior] educational quality would predictably cause [black] students from the inferior system to immediately be resegregated" within special education classes. The court of appeals had previously struck down this practice, holding that a newly-integrated school district may not use ability groupings if the result is racial segregation.

However, in the present case none of the black children had ever attended racially segregated public schools; all of Georgia's public schools had been integrated since the early 1970's. Therefore, the black children in this case could not claim that they had been placed in special education classes due to their past attendance at substandard schools. Past segregation had not caused them to be assigned to special education classes. Indeed, the court found that "'family background' and 'hard work,' rather than race, had the most powerful and consistent relationship to scholastic success." Accordingly, the court declared that the grouping of students on the basis of ability or achievement was permissible, even if the impact of such ability grouping was not racially neutral, as long as the school district had operated a nonsegregated school system "for a period of at least several years."

The NAACP also argued that "ability grouping exacerbates, rather than relieves, the problem of disproportionately lower achievement by black students." This argument was dismissed by the court, which found that ability grouping was educationally sound and "permits more resources to be routed to lower achieving students in the form of lower pupil-teacher ratios and additional instructional materials." Although nearly all of the district court's rulings against the NAACP were affirmed, the court of appeals remanded the case to the district court for a hearing on whether the NAACP was entitled to relief under the Rehabilitation Act for the school district's misinterpretation of state I.Q. regulations. *Georgia State Conference of Branches of NAACP v. State of Georgia*, 775 F.2d 1403 (11th Cir.1985).

A group of Mexican-American children and their parents brought a class action suit against their local Texas school board, claiming that the Raymondville Independent School District was discriminating against them on the basis of race. Among other things, the plaintiffs challenged the school district's practice of using English language achievement tests to determine whether children needed special help and which children were suited for regular or gifted classrooms. A high concentration of Mexican-American students in remedial and "lower" classrooms proved, said the plaintiffs, that the district's ability grouping was causing unconstitutional racial segregation.

The U.S. Court of Appeals, Fifth Circuit, affirmed a district court ruling and held that the method of ability grouping used by the school district was constitutionally sound. Admittedly, a large proportion of students placed in special education classes were Mexican-Americans, but Mexican-Americans constituted eighty-eight percent of the student population in the Raymondville district. The court also stated that since English achievement test scores were only one of the many factors used in determining a child's placement, the possibility that placement would be determined solely by a child's racial or ethnic background was remote. Because English achievement tests were not the "decisive factor" in determining placement, the Raymondville ability grouping system was upheld. *Castaneda v. Pickard*, 781 F.2d 456 (5th Cir.1986).

Black parents in Maryland sought to reopen a school desegregation case which had been decided in 1972. The parents, who had been plaintiffs in the earlier case, now alleged that the school district was not in compliance with the 1972 desegregation order. The parents claimed that the district was intentionally discriminating on racial grounds in the area of special education. They claimed that statistical evidence showed that racial imbalances existed in the district's special education and talented and gifted education programs.

The same U.S. district court held that despite the statistical overrepresentation of blacks in special education programs, the procedures followed by the school system in placing children in special education programs did not discriminate against black children. The district utilized a checklist which included physical, emotional and academic evaluations and from which, once a handicapping condition was verified, it formulated an individualized education program. If parents objected to the proposed IEP or any part of the process of identification, diagnosis or formulation of an IEP, they were afforded administrative hearings as required by the Education for All Handicapped Children Act. The court also upheld the district's use of the California Achievement Test and the Cognitive Abilities Test for admission into the district's gifted student program. It also found that there had been a constant effort on the part of the district's staff to include greater numbers of black children in the gifted program. Accordingly, it concluded that the district had not intentionally discriminated against black children in the area of special education.

The case was appealed to the U.S. Court of Appeals, Fourth Circuit, which partially upheld the district court. The lower court had properly noted that usually, where numerical racial disparities exist in special programs, it is presumed that such disparities are the result of "chance" and not illegal racial discrimination. However, the rule is different in school districts that have a past history of racial segregation. The appeals court held that in such districts, the burden of proof is on the district to show that the disparities in the number of minority youths assigned to special and gifted programs is not the result of racial discrimination. Because the Maryland school district in this case had, in the past, operated a racially segregated school system, the Court of Appeals remanded the case to the lower court with instructions to force the school district to meet its higher standard of proof in determining whether the placement of students in special programs was discriminatory. *Vaughs v. Board of Education of Prince George's County*, 758 F.2d 983 (4th Cir.1985).

APPENDIX A

THE EDUCATION FOR ALL HANDICAPPED CHILDREN ACT OF 1975

AS AMENDED THROUGH APRIL, 1986

[The EAHCA is reproduced here in its entirety, fully compiled, as amended by Congress through April, 1986. No separate section on amendments is included in this volume because all amendments have been placed in the appropriate location in the statutory text, and any repealed sections have been deleted from the text (saving a brief explanation of what the deleted material involved). The statutory text provided here is completely updated and allows for handy, one-stop referencing of the EAHCA—eds.]

CHAPTER 33—EDUCATION OF THE HANDICAPPED

SUBCHAPTER I—GENERAL PROVISIONS

SUBCHAPTER II—ASSISTANCE FOR EDUCATION OF ALL HANDICAPPED CHILDREN

SUBCHAPTER III—CENTERS AND SERVICES TO MEET SPECIAL NEEDS OF THE HANDICAPPED

SUBCHAPTER IV—TRAINING PERSONNEL FOR THE EDUCATION OF THE HANDICAPPED

SUBCHAPTER VII—SPECIAL PROGRAMS FOR CHILDREN WITH SPECIFIC LEARNING DISABILITIES

Sec.
1461.   Repealed.

CHAPTER REFERRED TO IN OTHER SECTIONS

This chapter is referred to in sections 2323, 2372, 2421, 3441 of this title; title 29 sections 721, 1577; title 42 section 6024.

SUBCHAPTER I—GENERAL PROVISIONS

§ 1400. Congressional statements and declarations

(a) Short title

This chapter may be cited as the "Education of the Handicapped Act".

(b) Findings

The Congress finds that—

(1) there are more than eight million handicapped children in the United States today;

(2) the special educational needs of such children are not being fully met;

(3) more than half of the handicapped children in the United States do not receive appropriate educational services which would enable them to have full equality of opportunity;

(4) one million of the handicapped children in the United States are excluded entirely from the public school system and will not go through the educational process with their peers;

(5) there are many handicapped children throughout the United States participating in regular school programs whose handicaps prevent them from having a successful educational experience because their handicaps are undetected;

(6) because of the lack of adequate services within the public school system, families are often forced to find services outside the public school system, often at great distance from their residence and at their own expense;

(7) developments in the training of teachers and in diagnostic and instructional procedures and methods have advanced to the point that, given appropriate funding, State and local educational agencies can and will provide effective special education and related services to meet the needs of handicapped children;

(8) State and local educational agencies have a responsibility to provide education for all handicapped children, but present financial resources are inadequate to meet the special educational needs of handicapped children; and

(9) it is in the national interest that the Federal Government assist State and local efforts to provide programs to meet the educational needs of handicapped children in order to assure equal protection of the law.

(c) Purpose

It is the purpose of this chapter to assure that all handicapped children have available to them, within the time periods specified in section 1412(2)(B) of this title, a free appropriate public education which emphasizes special education and related services designed to meet their unique needs, to assure that the rights of handicapped children and their parents or guardians are protected, to assist States and localities to provide for the education of all handicapped children, and to assess and assure the effectiveness of efforts to educate handicapped children.

(Pub. L. 91-230, title VI, § 601, Apr. 13, 1970, 84 Stat. 175; Pub. L. 94-142, § 3(a), Nov. 29, 1975, 89 Stat. 774.)

CODIFICATION

This section was formerly classified as a note under section 1401 of this title.

AMENDMENTS

1975—Pub. L. 94-142 designated existing provisions as subsec. (a) and added subsecs. (b) and (c).

SHORT TITLE OF 1983 AMENDMENT

Pub. L. 98-199, § 1, Dec. 2, 1983, 97 Stat. 1357, provided: "That this Act [enacting sections 1407 and 1427 of this title, amending sections 1401 to 1404, 1406, 1411 to 1414, 1416 to 1426, 1431 to 1435, 1441 to 1444, 1452, 1454, and 1461 of this title, repealing section 1461 of this title, omitting section 1436 of this title, enacting a provision set out as a note under section 1401 of this title, and amending provisions set out as notes under sections 101, 681, and 1411 of this title] may be cited as the 'Education of the Handicapped Act Amendments of 1983'."

EFFECTIVE DATE OF 1975 AMENDMENT

Amendment by Pub. L. 94-142 effective Nov. 29, 1975, see section 8(b) of Pub. L. 94-142, set out as an Effective Date of 1975 Amendment note under section 1411 of this title.

SHORT TITLE OF 1977 AMENDMENT

Pub. L. 95-49, § 1, June 17, 1977, 91 Stat. 230, provided: "That this Act [amending sections 1426, 1436, 1441, 1444 and 1454 of this title, and enacting provisions set out as a note under section 1426 of this title] may be cited as the 'Education of the Handicapped Amendments of 1977'."

SHORT TITLE OF 1975 AMENDMENT

Section 1 of Pub. L. 94-142 provided: "That this Act [enacting sections 1405, 1406, 1415, 1416, 1417, 1418, 1419, and 1420 of this title, amending sections 1232, 1400, 1401, 1411, 1411 notes, 1412, 1412 note, 1413, 1413 note, 1414 and 1453 of this title, and enacting provisions set out as a note under section 1411 of this title] may be cited as the 'Education for All Handicapped Children Act of 1975'."

SHORT TITLE OF 1974 AMENDMENT

Pub. L. 93-380, title VI, § 611, Aug. 21, 1974, 88 Stat. 579, provided that: "This title [enacting section 1424a of this title amending sections 1402, 1403, 1411 to 1413, 1426, 1436, 1444, 1452, 1454, and 1461 of this title, and enacting provisions set out as notes under sections 1402 and 1411 to 1413 of this title] may be cited as the 'Education of the Handicapped Amendments of 1974'."

SECTION REFERRED TO IN OTHER SECTIONS

This section is referred to in section 1411 of this title.

§ 1401. Definitions

(a) As used in this chapter—

(1) The term "handicapped children" means mentally retarded, hard of hearing, deaf, speech or language impaired, visually handicapped, seriously emotionally disturbed, orthopedically impaired, or other health impaired children, or children with specific learning disabilities, who by reason thereof require special education and related services.

(2) Repealed. Pub. L. 98-199, § 2(2), Dec. 2, 1983, 97 Stat. 1357.

(3) The term "Advisory Committee" means the National Advisory Committee on the Education of Handicapped Children.

(4) The term "construction", except where otherwise specified, means (A) erection of new or expansion of existing structures, and the acquisition and installation of equipment therefor; or (B) acquisition of existing structures not owned by any agency or institution making application for assistance under this chapter; or (C) remodeling or alteration (including the acquisition, installation, modernization, or replacement of equipment) of existing structures; or (D) acquisition of land in connection with activities in clauses (A), (B), and (C); or (E) a combination of any two or more of the foregoing.

(5) The term "equipment" includes machinery, utilities, and built-in equipment and any necessary enclosures or structures to house them, and includes all other items necessary for the functioning of a particular facility as a facility for the provision of educational services, including items such as instructional equipment and necessary furniture, printed, published, and audio-visual instructional materials, telecommunications, sensory, and other technological aids and devices, and books, periodicals, documents, and other related materials.

(6) The term "State" means any of the several States, the District of Columbia, the Commonwealth of Puerto Rico, the Virgin Islands, Guam, American Samoa, the Northern Mariana Islands, or the Trust Territory of the Pacific Islands.

(7) The term "State educational agency" means the State board of education or other agency or officer primarily responsible for the State supervision of public elementary and secondary schools, or, if there is no such officer or agency, an officer or agency designated by the Governor or by State law.

(8) The term "local educational agency" means a public board of education or other public authority legally constituted within a State for either administrative control or direction of, or to perform a service function for, public elementary or secondary schools in a city, county, township, school district, or other political subdivision of a State, or such combination of school districts or counties as are recognized in a State as an administrative agency for its public elementary or secondary schools. Such term also includes any other public institution or agency having administrative control and direction of a public elementary or secondary school.

(9) The term "elementary school" means a day or residential school which provides elementary education, as determined under State law.

(10) The term "secondary school" means a day or residential school which provides secondary education, as determined under State law, except that it does not include any education provided beyond grade 12.

(11) The term "institution of higher education" means an educational institution in any State which—

(A) admits as regular students only individuals having a certificate of graduation from a high school, or the recognized equivalent of such a certificate;

(B) is legally authorized within such State to provide a program of education beyond high school;

(C) provides an educational program for which it awards a bachelor's degree, or provides not less than a two-year program which is acceptable for full credit toward such a degree, or offers a two-year program in engineering, mathematics, or the physical or biological sciences which is designed to prepare the student to work as a technician and at a semiprofessional level in engineering, scientific, or other technological fields which require the understanding and application of basic engineering, scientific, or mathematical principles or knowledge;

(D) is a public or other nonprofit institution; and

(E) is accredited by a nationally recognized accrediting agency or association listed by the Secretary pursuant to this paragraph or, if not so accredited, is an institution whose credits are accepted, on transfer, by not less than three institutions which are so accredited, for credit on the same basis as if transferred from an institution so accredited: *Provided, however,* That in the case of an institution offering a two-year program in engineering, mathematics, or the physical or biological sciences which is designed to prepare the student to work as a technician and at a semiprofessional level in engineering, scientific, or technological fields which require the understanding and application of basic engineering, scientific, or mathematical principles or knowledge, if the Secretary determines that there is no nationally recognized accrediting agency or association qualified to accredit such institutions, he shall appoint an advisory committee, composed of persons specially qualified to evaluate training provided by such institutions, which shall prescribe the standards of content, scope, and quality which must be met in order to qualify such institutions to participate under this Act and shall also determine whether particular institutions meet such standards. For the purposes of this paragraph the Secretary shall publish a list of nationally recognized accrediting agencies or associations which he determines to be reliable authority as to the quality of education or training offered.

(12) The term "nonprofit" as applied to a school, agency, organization, or institution means a school, agency, organization, or institution owned and operated by one or more non-profit corporations or associations no part of the net earnings of which inures, or may lawfully inure, to the benefit of any private shareholder or individual.

(13) The term "research and related purposes" means research, research training (including the payment of stipends and allowances), surveys, or demonstrations in the field of education of handicapped children, or the dissemination of information derived therefrom, including (but without limitation) experimental schools.

(14) The term "Secretary" means the Secretary of Education.

(15) The term "children with specific learning disabilities" means those children who have a disorder in one or more of the basic psychological proc-

esses involved in understanding or in using language, spoken or written, which disorder may manifest itself in imperfect ability to listen, think, speak, read, write, spell, or do mathematical calculations. Such disorders include such conditions as perceptual handicaps, brain injury, minimal brain dysfunction, dyslexia, and developmental aphasia. Such term does not include children who have learning problems which are primarily the result of visual, hearing, or motor handicaps, of mental retardation, of emotional disturbance, or of environmental, cultural, or economic disadvantage.

(16) The term "special education" means specially designed instruction, at no cost to parents or guardians, to meet the unique needs of a handicapped child, including classroom instruction, instruction in physical education, home instruction, and instruction in hospitals and institutions.

(17) The term "related services" means transportation, and such developmental, corrective, and other supportive services (including speech pathology and audiology, psychological services, physical and occupational therapy, recreation, and medical and counseling services, except that such medical services shall be for diagnostic and evaluation purposes only) as may be required to assist a handicapped child to benefit from special education, and includes the early identification and assessment of handicapping conditions in children.

(18) The term "free appropriate public education" means special education and related services which (A) have been provided at public expense, under public supervision and direction, and without charge, (B) meet the standards of the State educational agency, (C) include an appropriate preschool, elementary, or secondary school education in the State involved, and (D) are provided in conformity with the individualized education program required under section 1414(a)(5) of this title.

(19) The term "individualized education program" means a written statement for each handicapped child developed in any meeting by a representative of the local educational agency or an intermediate educational unit who shall be qualified to provide, or supervise the provision of, specially designed instruction to meet the unique needs of handicapped children, the teacher, the parents or guardian of such child, and, whenever appropriate, such child, which statement shall include (A) a statement of the present levels of educational performance of such child, (B) a statement of annual goals, including short-term instructional objectives, (C) a statement of the specific educational services to be provided to such child, and the extent to which such child will be able to participate in regular educational programs, (D) the projected date for initiation and anticipated duration of such services, and (E) appropriate objective criteria and evaluation procedures and schedules for determining, on at least an annual basis, whether instructional objectives are being achieved.

(20) The term "excess costs" means those costs which are in excess of the average annual per student expenditure in a local educational agency during the preceding school year for an elementary or secondary school student, as may be appropriate, and which shall be computed after deducting (A) amounts received under this subchapter or under title I [20 U.S.C. 2701 et seq.] or title VII [20 U.S.C. 3221 et seq.] of the Elementary and Secondary Education Act of 1965, and (B) any State or local funds expended for programs which would qualify for assistance under this subchapter or under such titles.

(21) The term "native language" has the meaning given that term by section 703(a)(2) of the Bilingual Education Act [20 U.S.C. 3223(a)(2)].

(22) The term "intermediate educational unit" means any public authority, other than a local educational agency, which is under the general supervision of a State educational agency, which is established by State law for the purpose of providing free public education on a regional basis, and which provides special education and related services to handicapped children within that State.

(b) For purposes of subchapter III of this chapter, "handicapped youth" means any handicapped child (as defined in subsection (a) (1) of this section) who

(1) is twelve years of age or older; or

(2) is enrolled in the seventh or higher grade in school.

(Pub. L. 91-230, title VI, § 602, Apr. 13, 1970, 84 Stat. 175; Pub. L. 94-142, § 4(a), Nov. 29, 1975, 89 Stat. 775; Pub. L. 98-199, §§ 2, 3(b), Dec. 2, 1983, 97 Stat. 1357, 1358.)

REFERENCES IN TEXT

This Act, referred to in par. (11)(E), is Pub. L. 91-230, Apr. 13, 1970, 84 Stat. 121, as amended, which is popularly known as the Elementary and Secondary Education Amendments of 1970. For complete classification of this Act to the Code, see Short title of 1970 Amendment note set out under section 2701 of this title and Tables.

The Elementary and Secondary Education Act of 1965, referred to in par. (20), is Pub. L. 89-10, Apr. 11, 1965, 79 Stat. 27, as amended generally by Pub. L. 95-561, Nov. 1, 1978, 92 Stat. 2152. Title I of the 1965 Act, which was formerly classified to subchapter II (§ 241a et seq.) of chapter 13 of this title, is classified generally to subchapter I (§ 2701 et seq.) of chapter 47 of this title. Title VII of that Act, known as the Bilingual Education Act, was formerly classified to subchapter IV-A (§ 880b et seq.) of chapter 24 of this title, and is classified generally to subchapter VII (§ 3221 et seq.) of chapter 47 of this title. For complete classification of this Act to the Code, see Short Title note set out under section 2701 of this title and Tables.

CODIFICATION

Par. (2), which in the original read "The term 'Commissioner' means the Commissioner of Education", has been omitted in view of the transfer of all functions of the Commissioner of Education to the Secretary of Education pursuant to sections 301(a)(1) and 507 of Pub. L. 96-88, which are classified to sections 3441(a)(1) and 3507 of this title. This transfer would result in the definition in par. (2) being identical to the definition in par. (14).

AMENDMENTS

1983—Subsec. (a). Pub. L. 98-199, § 2(6), designated existing provisions as subsec. (a).

Subsec. (a)(1). Pub. L. 98-199, § 2(1), included language impaired children within term "handicapped children".

Subsec. (a)(2). Pub. L. 98-199, § 2(2), struck out definition of "Commissioner" as meaning the Commissioner of Education.

Subsec. (a)(3). Pub. L. 98-199, § 2(3), inserted "the Education of" after "Committee on".

Subsec. (a)(6). Pub. L. 98-199, § 2(4), included the Northern Mariana Islands within the term "State".

Subsec. (a)(11)(E). Pub. L. 98-199, § 3(b), substituted "Secretary" for "Commissioner" wherever appearing.

Subsec. (a)(14). Pub. L. 98-199, § 2(5), substituted "Secretary of Education" for "Secretary of Health, Education, and Welfare".

Subsec. (b). Pub. L. 98-199, § 2(7), added subsec. (b).

1975—Par. (1). Pub. L. 94-142, § 4(a)(1), substituted "orthopedically impaired" for "crippled" and inserted reference to children with specific learning disabilities.

Par. (5). Pub. L. 94-142, § 4(a)(2), inserted reference to telecommunications, sensory, and other technological aids and devices.

Par. (15). Pub. L. 94-142, § 4(a)(3), added children with learning problems which are primarily the result of cultural or economic disadvantage to the enumeration of children not to be included within the term "children with specific learning disabilities".

Pars. (16) to (22). Pub. L. 94-142, § 4(a)(4), added pars. (16) to (22).

EFFECTIVE DATE OF 1983 AMENDMENT

Section 18 of Pub. L. 98-199 provided that:

"(a) Except as provided in subsection (b), the provisions of this Act [enacting sections 1407 and 1427 of this title; amending sections 1401 to 1404, 1406, 1411 to 1414, 1416 to 1426, 1431 to 1435, 1441 to 1444, 1452, 1454, and 1461 of this title; repealing section 1461 of this title; omitting section 1436 of this title; enacting a provision set out as a note under section 1400 of this title; and amending provisions set out as notes under sections 101, 681, and 1411 of this title] shall take effect on the date of enactment of this Act [Dec. 2, 1983].

"(b)(1) To the extent that the amendments made by this Act to parts C, D, E, and G of the Education of the Handicapped Act [subchapters III, IV, V and VII of this chapter] prohibit or limit the use of funds, such amendments shall apply only to funds obligated after the date of enactment of this Act [Dec. 2, 1983].

"(2) As determined necessary by the Secretary of Education for purposes of providing services under the Education of the Handicapped Act [this chapter] pending the issuance of regulations implementing the amendments made by this Act, the Secretary shall provide financial assistance under parts C, D, E, and G of the Act as in effect on the day before the date of enactment of this Act until issuance of such regulations or March 1, 1984, whichever is earlier."

EFFECTIVE DATE OF 1975 AMENDMENT

Amendment by Pub. L. 94-142 effective Oct. 1, 1977, see section 8(c) of Pub. L. 94-142, set out as an Effective Date of 1975 Amendment note under section 1411 of this title.

TRANSFER OF FUNCTIONS

"Secretary", meaning the Secretary of Education, was substituted for "Commissioner" in par. (11)(E), and "Secretary of Health, Education, and Welfare" in par. (14), pursuant to sections 301(a)(1), (2)(H) and 507 of Pub. L. 96-88, which are classified to sections 3441(a)(1), (2)(H) and 3507 of this title and which transferred all functions of the Commissioner of Education and all functions of the Secretary of Health, Education, and Welfare under this chapter to the Secretary of Education.

TERMINATION OF ADVISORY COMMITTEE

The National Advisory Committee on Handicapped Children terminated Oct. 1, 1977 pursuant to section 1403 of this title.

SECTION REFERRED TO IN OTHER SECTIONS

This section is referred to in sections 238, 244, 1087ee, 1119b-4, 2771, 3112 of this title; title 42 section 9835.

§ 1402. Office of Special Education Programs

(a) Establishment; purposes

There shall be, within the Office of Special Education and Rehabilitative Services in the Department of Education, an Office of Special Education Programs which shall be the principal agency in the Department for administering and carrying out this chapter and other programs and activities concerning the education and training of the handicapped.

(b) Deputy Assistant Secretary: selection and supervision, compensation; Associate Deputy Assistant Secretary and minimum number of assistants: establishment, compensation

(1) The office established under subsection (a) of this section shall be headed by a Deputy Assistant Secretary who shall be selected by the Secretary and shall report directly to the Assistant Secretary for Special Education and Rehabilitative Services. The position of Deputy Assistant Secretary shall be in grade GS-18 of the General Schedule under section 5104 of title 5, and shall be a Senior Executive Service position for the purposes of section 3132(a)(2) of such title.

(2) In addition to such Deputy Assistant Secretary, there shall be established in such office not less than six positions for persons to assist the Deputy Assistant Secretary, including the position of the Associate Deputy Assistant Secretary. Each such position shall be in grade GS-15 of the General Schedule under section 5104 of title 5.

(Pub. L. 91-230, title VI, § 603, Apr. 13, 1970, 84 Stat. 177; Pub. L. 93-380, title VI, § 612(a), Aug. 21, 1974, 88 Stat. 579; Pub. L. 98-199, § 3(a), Dec. 2, 1983, 97 Stat. 1357.)

REFERENCES IN TEXT

The General Schedule, referred to in subsec. (b), is set out under section 5332 of Title 5, Government Organization and Employees.

AMENDMENTS

1983—Pub. L. 98-199 substituted provisions respecting establishment of Office of Special Education Programs within the Office of Special Education and Rehabilitative Services in the Department of Education, including executive personnel thereof for provisions designating a bureau for education and training of handicapped within the Office of Education, including executive personnel consisting of a Deputy Commissioner of Education, appointed and supervised by the Commissioner, and an Associate Deputy Commissioner and four assistantships, and providing for compensation of such personnel under the General Schedule.

1974—Pub. L. 93-380 designated existing provisions as subsec. (a) and added subsec. (b).

EFFECTIVE DATE OF 1983 AMENDMENT

Amendment by Pub. L. 98-199 effective Dec. 2, 1983, see section 18 of Pub. L. 98-199, set out as a note under section 1401 of this title.

EFFECTIVE DATE OF 1974 AMENDMENT

Section 612(b)(2) of Pub. L. 93-380 provided that: "The amendments made by subsection (a) [amending this section] shall become effective upon the enactment of this Act [Aug. 21, 1974]."

TRANSFER OF FUNCTIONS

"Department of Education" and "Secretary", meaning the Secretary of Education, were substituted for "Office of Education" and "Commissioner", respectively, in subsecs. (a) and (b)(1) pursuant to sections 301(a)(1), (b)(2) and 507 of Pub. L. 96-88, which are classified to sections 3441(a)(1), (b)(2) and 3507 of this title and which transferred the Office of Education to the Department of Education and transferred the functions of the Commissioner of Education to the Secretary of Education.

For authority of Secretary of Education to consolidate, alter, or discontinue the bureau for education and training of the handicapped, or to reallocate any functions vested by statute in the bureau, see section 413 of Pub. L. 96-88, which is classified to section 3473 of this title.

DEPUTY COMMISSIONER AND ASSOCIATE DEPUTY COMMISSIONER OF EDUCATION AND OTHER ASSISTANTS; ADDITIONAL POSITIONS

Section 612(b)(1) of Pub. L. 93-380, as amended by Pub. L. 94-482, title V, § 501(a)(11), Oct. 12, 1976, 90 Stat. 2235, provided that: "The positions created by subsection (b) of section 603 of the Education of the Handicapped Act [subsec. (b) of this section] shall be in addition to the number of positions placed in the appropriate grades under section 5108 of title 5, United States Code and such positions shall be in addition to, and without prejudice against, the number of positions otherwise placed in the Office of Education [now Department of Education] under such section 5108 or under other law. Nothing in this section shall be deemed as limiting the Commissioner [now Secretary of Education] from assigning additional General Schedule positions in grades 16, 17, and 18 to the Bureau should he determine such additions to be necessary to operate programs for educating handicapped children authorized by this Act [see Short Title note for Pub. L. 93-380, set out under section 2701 of this title]."

Provision effective on and after sixtieth day after Aug. 21, 1974, see section 2(c) of Pub. L. 93-380, set out as an Effective Date of 1974 Amendment note under section 244 of this title.

§ 1403. National Advisory Committee on the Education of Handicapped Children and Youth

(a) Establishment; membership

The Secretary shall establish in the Department of Education a National Advisory Committee on the Education of Handicapped Children and Youth, consisting of fifteen members, appointed by the Secretary. Not less than five such members shall be parents of handicapped children and the remainder shall be handicapped persons (including students), persons affiliated with education, training, or research programs for the handicapped, and those having demonstrated a commitment to the education of handicapped children.

(b) Functions; recommendations; report to Congress

The Advisory Committee shall review the administration and operation of the programs authorized by this chapter and other provisions of law administered by the Secretary with respect to handicapped children (including the effect of such programs in improving the educational attainment of such children) and make recommendations for the improvement of such programs. Such recommendations shall take into consideration experience gained under this and other Federal programs for handicapped children and, to the extent appropriate, experience gained under other public and private programs for handicapped children. The Advisory Committee may make such recommendations to the Secretary as the Committee considers appropriate and shall make an annual report of its findings and recommendations to the Secretary not later than June 30 of each year. The Secretary shall transmit each such report, together with comments and recommendations, to the Congress.

(c) Authorization of appropriations

There are authorized to be appropriated for the purposes of this section $200,000 for fiscal year 1984, and for each of the two succeeding fiscal years.

(Pub. L. 91-230, title VI, § 604, Apr. 13, 1970, 84 Stat. 177; Pub. L. 93-380, title VI, § 613, Aug. 21, 1974, 88 Stat. 580; Pub. L. 94-273, §§ 3(14), 13(2), Apr. 21, 1976, 90 Stat. 376, 378; Pub. L. 98-199, § 4, Dec. 2, 1983, 97 Stat. 1358.)

AMENDMENTS

1983—Pub. L. 98-199 amended section generally, substituting provisions establishing the National Advisory Committee on the Education of Handicapped Children and Youth for provisions establishing the National Advisory Committee on Handicapped Children and providing for the termination of the Committee on Oct. 1, 1977.

1976—Subsec. (b). Pub. L. 94-273 substituted "October" for "July" and "June 30" for "March 31".

1974—Subsec. (b). Pub. L. 93-380, § 613(a), continued existence of National Committee until July 1, 1977.

Subsec. (c). Pub. L. 93-380, § 613(b), added subsec. (c).

EFFECTIVE DATE OF 1983 AMENDMENT

Amendment by Pub. L. 98-199 effective Dec. 2, 1983, see section 18 of Pub. L. 98-199, set out as a note under section 1401 of this title.

EFFECTIVE DATE OF 1974 AMENDMENT

Amendment by Pub. L. 93-380 effective on and after sixtieth day after Aug. 21, 1974, see section 2(c) of Pub. L. 93-380, set out as a note under section 241b of this title.

TERMINATION OF ADVISORY COMMITTEES

Advisory committees established after Jan. 5, 1973, to terminate not later than the expiration of the two-year period beginning on the date of their establishment, unless, in the case of a committee established by the President or an officer of the Federal Government, such committee is renewed by appropriate action prior to the expiration of such two-year period, or in the case of a committee established by the Congress, its duration is otherwise provided by law. See section 14 of Pub. L. 92-463, Oct. 6, 1972, 86 Stat. 776, set out in the Appendix to Title 5, Government Organization and Employees.

§ 1404. Acquisition of equipment and construction of necessary facilities

(a) Authorization for use of funds

In the case of any program authorized by this chapter, if the Secretary determines that such program will be improved by permitting the funds authorized for such program to be used for the acquisition of equipment and the construction of necessary facilities, he may authorize the use of such funds for such purposes.

(b) Recovery of payments under certain conditions

If within twenty years after the completion of any construction (except minor remodeling or alteration) for which funds have been paid pursuant to a grant or contract under this chapter the facility constructed ceases to be used for the purposes for which it was constructed, the United States, unless the Secretary determines that there is good cause for releasing the recipient of the funds from its obligation, shall be entitled to recover from the applicant or other owner of the facility an amount which bears the same ratio to the then value of the facility as the amount of such Federal funds bore to the cost of the portion of the facility financed with such funds. Such value shall be determined by agreement of the parties or by action brought in the United States district court for the district in which the facility is situated.

(Pub. L. 91-230, title VI, § 605, Apr. 13, 1970, 84 Stat. 177; Pub. L. 98-199, § 3(b), Dec. 2, 1983, 97 Stat. 1358.)

AMENDMENTS

1983—Subsec. (a). Pub. L. 98-199 substituted "Secretary" for "Commissioner".

EFFECTIVE DATE OF 1983 AMENDMENT

Amendment by Pub. L. 98-199 effective Dec. 2, 1983, see section 18 of Pub. L. 98-199, set out as a note under section 1401 of this title.

TRANSFER OF FUNCTIONS

"Secretary", meaning the Secretary of Education, was substituted for "Commissioner" in subsec. (a) pursuant to sections 301(a)(1) and 507 of Pub. L. 96-88, which are classified to sections 3441(a)(1) and 3507 of this title and which transferred all functions of the Commissioner of Education to the Secretary of Education.

§ 1405. Employment of handicapped individuals

The Secretary shall assure that each recipient of assistance under this chapter shall make positive efforts to employ and advance in employment qualified handicapped individuals in programs assisted under this chapter.

(Pub. L. 91-230, title VI, § 606, as added Pub. L. 94-142, § 6(a), Nov. 29, 1975, 89 Stat. 795.)

EFFECTIVE DATE

Section effective Nov. 29, 1975, see section 8(b) of Pub. L. 94-142, set out as an Effective Date of 1975 Amendment note under section 1411 of this title.

§ 1406. Grants for removal of architectural barriers; authorization of appropriations

(a) The Secretary is authorized to make grants and to enter into cooperative agreements with State educational agencies to assist such agencies in making grants to local educational agencies or intermediate educational units to pay part or all of the cost of altering existing buildings and equipment in accordance with standards promulgated under the Act approved August 12, 1968 (Public Law 90-480) [42 U.S.C. 4151 et seq.], relating to architectural barriers.

(b) For the purposes of carrying out the provisions of this section, there are authorized to be appropriated such sums as may be necessary.

(Pub. L. 91-230, title VI, § 607, as added Pub. L. 94-142, § 6(a), Nov. 29, 1975, 89 Stat. 795, and amended Pub. L. 98-199, §§ 3(b), 5, Dec. 2, 1983, 97 Stat. 1358.)

AMENDMENTS

1983—Subsec. (a). Pub. L. 98-199, § 5, amended subsec. (a) generally, substituting provisions authorizing the Secretary to make grants and to enter into cooperative agreements with State educational agencies to assist such agencies in making grants to local educational agencies or intermediate educational units in accordance with standards promulgated under Pub. L. 90-480 for provisions authorizing the Secretary to make grants, upon application by any State or local educational agency or intermediate educational unit, in the same manner and same extent as authorized by Pub. L. 90-480.

Pub. L. 98-199, § 3(b), substituted "Secretary" for 'Commissioner".

Subsec. (b). Pub. L. 98-199, § 5, reenacted subsec. (b) without charge.

EFFECTIVE DATE OF 1983 AMENDMENT

Amendment by Pub. L. 98-199 effective Dec. 2, 1983, see section 18 of Pub. L. 98-199, set out as a note under section 1401 of this title.

REFERENCES IN TEXT

The Act approved August 12, 1968 (Public Law 90-480), referred to in subsec. (a), is Pub. L. 90-480, Aug. 12, 1968, 82 Stat. 718, as amended, which is popularly known as the Architectural Barriers Act of 1968. The Act is classified generally to chapter 51 (§ 4151 et seq.) of Title 42, The Public Health and Welfare. For complete classification of this Act to the Code, see Short Title note set out under section 4151 of Title 42 and Tables.

EFFECTIVE DATE

Section effective Nov. 29, 1975, see section 8(b) of Pub. L. 94-142, set out as an Effective Date of 1975 Amendment note under section 1411 of this title.

TRANSFER OF FUNCTIONS

"Secretary", meaning the Secretary of Education, was substituted for "Commissioner" in subsec. (a) pursuant to sections 301(a)(1) and 507 of Pub. L. 96-88, which are classified to sections 3441(a)(1) and 3507 of this title and which transferred all functions of the Commissioner of Education to the Secretary of Education.

§ 1407. Regulation requirements

(a) Minimum period for comment before effective date

For purposes of complying with section 1232(b) of this title with respect to regulations promulgated under subchapter II of this chapter, the thirty-day period under such section shall be ninety days.

(b) Lessening of procedural or substantive protections as in effect on July 20, 1983, prohibited

The Secretary may not implement, or publish in final form, any regulation prescribed pursuant to this chapter which would procedurally or substantively lessen the protections provided to handicapped children under this chapter, as embodied in regulations in effect on July 20, 1983 (particularly as such protections relate to parental consent to initial evaluation or initial placement in special education, least restrictive environment, related services, timelines,[1] attendance of evaluation personnel at IEP meetings, or qualifications of personnel), except to the extent that such regulation reflects the clear and unequivocal intent of the Congress in legislation.

(c) Transmission to Advisory Committee

The Secretary shall transmit a copy of any regulations promulgated under this chapter to the National Advisory Committee on the Education of the Handicapped[2] concurrently with publication in the Federal Register.

(Pub. L. 91-230, title VI, § 608, as added Pub. L. 98-199, § 6, Dec. 2, 1983, 97 Stat. 1359.)

EFFECTIVE DATE

Section effective Dec. 2, 1983, see section 18 of Pub. L. 98-199, set out as an Effective Date of 1983 Amendment note under section 1401 of this title.

---

[1]Reproduced as in original. Probably should be "timeliness."

[2]Reproduced as in original. Probably should be "of Handicapped Children and Youth."

SUBCHAPTER II—ASSISTANCE FOR EDUCATION OF ALL HANDICAPPED CHILDREN

SUBCHAPTER REFERRED TO IN OTHER SECTIONS

This subchapter is referred to in sections 1407, 1422, 1431 of this title.

§ 1411. Entitlements and allocations

(a) Formula for determining maximum State entitlement

(1) Except as provided in paragraph (3) and in section 1419 of this title, the maximum amount of the grant to which a State is entitled under this subchapter for any fiscal year shall be equal to—

(A) the number of handicapped children aged three to twenty-one, inclusive, in such State who are receiving special education and related services:

multiplied by—

(B)(i) 5 per centum, for the fiscal year ending September 30, 1978, of the average per pupil expenditure in public elementary and secondary schools in the United States;

(ii) 10 per centum, for the fiscal year ending September 30, 1979, of the average per pupil expenditure in public elementary and secondary schools in the United States;

(iii) 20 per centum, for the fiscal year ending September 30, 1980, of the average per pupil expenditure in public elementary and secondary schools in the United States;

(iv) 30 per centum, for the fiscal year ending September 30, 1981, of the average per pupil expenditure in public elementary and secondary schools in the United States; and

(v) 40 per centum, for the fiscal year ending September 30, 1982, and for each fiscal year thereafter, of the average per pupil expenditure in public elementary and secondary schools in the United States:

except that no State shall receive an amount which is less than the amount which such State received under this subchapter for the fiscal year ending September 30, 1977.

(2) For the purpose of this subsection and subsection (b) through subsection (e) of this section, the term "State" does not include Guam, American Samoa, the Virgin Islands, the Northern Mariana Islands, and the Trust Territory of the Pacific Islands.

(3) The number of handicapped children receiving special education and related services in any fiscal year shall be equal to number of such children receiving special education and related services on December 1 of the fiscal year preceding the fiscal year for which the determination is made.

(4) For purposes of paragraph (1)(B), the term "average per pupil expenditure" in the United States, means the aggregate current expenditures, during the second fiscal year preceding the fiscal year for which the computation is made (or, if satisfactory data for such year are not available at the time of computation, then during the most recent preceding fiscal year for which

satisfactory data are available) of all local educational agencies in the United States (which, for purposes of this subsection, means the fifty States and the District of Columbia), as the case may be, plus any direct expenditures by the State for operation of such agencies (without regard to the source of funds from which either of such expenditures are made), divided by the aggregate number of children in average daily attendance to whom such agencies provided free public education during such preceding year.

(5)(A) In determining the allotment of each State under paragraph (1), the Secretary may not count—

(i) handicapped children in such State under paragraph (1)(A) to the extent the number of such children is greater than 12 per centum of the number of all children aged five to seventeen, inclusive, in such State; and

(ii) handicapped children who are counted under section 241c-1 of this title.

(B) For purposes of subparagraph (A), the number of children aged five to seventeen, inclusive, in any State shall be determined by the Secretary on the basis of the most recent satisfactory data available to him.

(b) Distribution and use of grant funds by States for fiscal year ending September 30, 1978

(1) Of the funds received under subsection (a) of this section by any State for the fiscal year ending September 30, 1978—

(A) 50 per centum of such funds may be used by such State in accordance with the provisions of paragraph (2); and

(B) 50 per centum of such funds shall be distributed by such State pursuant to subsection (d) of this section to local educational agencies and intermediate educational units in such State, for use in accordance with the priorities established under section 1412(3) of this title.

(2) Of the funds which any State may use under paragraph (1)(A)—

(A) an amount which is equal to the greater of—

(i) 5 per centum of the total amount of funds received under this subchapter by such State; or

(ii) $200,000;

may be used by such State for administrative costs related to carrying out sections 1412 and 1413 of this title;

(B) the remainder shall be used by such State to provide support services and direct services, in accordance with the priorities established under section 1412(3) of this title.

(c) Distribution and use of grant funds by States for fiscal years ending September 30, 1979, and thereafter

(1) Of the funds received under subsection (a) of this section by any State for the fiscal year ending September 30, 1979, and for each fiscal year thereafter—

(A) 25 per centum of such funds may be used by such State in accordance with the provisions of paragraph (2); and

(B) except as provided in paragraph (4), 75 per centum of such funds shall be distributed by such State pursuant to subsection (d) of this section to local educational agencies and intermediate educational units in such State, for use in accordance with priorities established under section 1412(3) of this title.

(2)(A) Subject to the provisions of subparagraph (B), of the funds which any State may use under paragraph (1)(A)—

(i) an amount which is equal to the greater of—

(I) 5 per centum of the total amount of funds received under this subchapter by such State; or

(II) $350,000;

may be used by such State for administrative costs related to carrying out the provisions of sections 1412 and 1413 of this title; and

(ii) the remainder shall be used by such State to provide support services and direct services, in accordance with the priorities established under section 1412(3) of this title.

(B) The amount expended by any State from the funds available to such State under paragraph (1)(A) in any fiscal year for the provisions of support services or for the provision of direct services shall be matched on a program basis by such State, from funds other than Federal funds, for the provision of support services or for the provision of direct services for the fiscal year involved.

(3) The provisions of section 1413(a)(9) of this title shall not apply with respect to amounts available for use by any State under paragraph (2).

(4)(A) No funds shall be distributed by any State under this subsection in any fiscal year to any local educational agency or intermediate educational unit in such State if—

(i) such local educational agency or intermediate educational unit is entitled, under subsection (d) of this section, to less than $7,500 for such fiscal year; or

(ii) such local educational agency or intermediate educational unit has not submitted an application for such funds which meets the requirements of section 1414 of this title.

(B) Whenever the provisions of subparagraph (A) apply, the State involved shall use such funds to assure the provision of a free appropriate education to handicapped children residing in the area served by such local educational agency or such intermediate educational unit. The provisions of paragraph (2)(B) shall not apply to the use of such funds.

(d) Allocation of funds within States to local educational agencies and intermediate educational units

From the total amount of funds available to local educational agencies and intermediate educational units in any State under subsection (b)(1)(B) or subsection (c)(1)(B) of this section, as the case may be, each local educational agency or intermediate educational unit shall be entitled to an amount which bears the same ratio to the total amount available under subsection (b)(1)(B) or subsection (c)(1)(B) of this section, as the case may be, as the number of handicapped children aged three to twenty-one, inclusive, receiving special education and related services in such local educational agency or intermediate educational unit bears to the aggregate number of handicapped children aged three to twenty-one, inclusive, receiving special education and related services in all local educational agencies and intermediate educational units which apply to the State educational agency involved for funds under this subchapter.

(e) Territories and possessions

(1) The jurisdictions to which this subsection applies are Guam, American Samoa, the Virgin Islands, the Northern Mariana Islands, and the Trust Territory of the Pacific Islands.

(2) Each jurisdiction to which this subsection applies shall be entitled to a grant for the purposes set forth in section 1400(c) of this title in an amount equal to an amount determined by the Secretary in accordance with criteria based on respective needs, except that the aggregate of the amount to which such jurisdictions are so entitled for any fiscal year shall not exceed an amount equal to 1 per centum of the aggregate of the amounts available to all States under this subchapter for that fiscal year. If the aggregate of the amounts, determined by the Secretary pursuant to the preceding sentence, to be so needed for any fiscal year exceeds an amount equal to such 1 per centum limitation, the entitlement of each such jurisdiction shall be reduced proportionately until such aggregate does not exceed such 1 per centum limitation.

(3) The amount expended for administration by each jurisdiction under this subsection shall not exceed 5 per centum of the amount allotted to such jurisdiction for any fiscal year, or $35,000, whichever is greater.

(f) Indian reservations

(1) The Secretary is authorized to make payments to the Secretary of the Interior according to the need for such assistance for the education of handicapped children on reservations serviced by elementary and secondary schools operated for Indian children by the Department of the Interior. The amount of such payment for any fiscal year shall not exceed 1 per centum of the aggregate amounts available to all States under this subchapter for that fiscal year.

(2) The Secretary of the Interior may receive an allotment under this subsection only after submitting to the Secretary an application which meets the applicable requirements of section 1414(a) of this title and which is approved by the Secretary. The provisions of section 1416 of this title shall apply to any such application.

(g) Reductions or increases

(1) If the sums appropriated for any fiscal year for making payments to States under this subchapter are not sufficient to pay in full the total amounts which all States are entitled to receive under this subchapter for such fiscal year, the maximum amounts which all States are entitled to receive under this

subchapter for such fiscal year shall be ratably reduced. In case additional funds become available for making such payments for any fiscal year during which the preceding sentence is applicable, such reduced amounts shall be increased on the same basis as they were reduced.

(2) In the case of any fiscal year in which the maximum amounts for which States are eligible have been reduced under the first sentence of paragraph (1), and in which additional funds have not been made available to pay in full the total of such maximum amounts under the last sentence of such paragraph, the State educational agency shall fix dates before which each local educational agency or intermediate educational unit shall report to the State educational agency on the amount of funds available to the local educational agency or intermediate educational unit, under the provisions of subsection (d) of this section, which it estimates that it will expend in accordance with the provisions of this subchapter. The amounts so available to any local educational agency or intermediate educational unit, or any amount which would be available to any other local educational agency or intermediate educational unit if it were to submit a program meeting the requirements of this subchapter, which the State educational agency determines will not be used for the period of its availability, shall be available for allocation to those local educational agencies or intermediate educational units, in the manner provided by this section, which the State educational agency determines will need and be able to use additional funds to carry out approved programs.

(Pub. L. 91-230, title VI, § 611, Apr. 13, 1970, 84 Stat. 178; Pub. L. 93-380, title VI, § 614(a), (e)(1), (2), Aug. 21, 1974, 88 Stat. 580, 582; Pub. L. 94-142, §§ 2(a)(1)-(3), 5(a), (c), Nov. 29, 1975, 89 Stat. 773, 776, 794; Pub. L. 95-561, title XIII, § 1341(a), Nov. 1, 1978, 92 Stat. 2364; Pub. L. 96-270, § 13, June 14, 1980, 94 Stat. 498; Pub. L. 98-199, §§ 3(b), 15, Dec. 2, 1983, 97 Stat. 1358, 1374.)

REFERENCES IN TEXT

Section 241c-1 of this title, referred to in subsec. (a)(5)(A)(ii), was in the original "section 121 of the Elementary and Secondary Education Act of 1965" and was repealed by Pub. L. 95-561, title I, § 101(c), Nov. 1, 1978, 92 Stat. 2200. See section 2771 et seq. of this title.

AMENDMENTS

1985—Subsec. (c)(1)(B) and subsec. (c)(2)(B)(i)(II) were amended by Act Nov. 22, 1985 § 601(b) and § 601(a).

1983—Subsec. (a)(2). Pub. L. 98-199, § 15, excluded from the term "State" the Northern Mariana Islands.

Subsec. (a)(5). Pub. L. 98-199, § 3(b), substituted "Secretary" for "Commissioner".

Subsec. (e)(1). Pub. L. 98-199, § 15, extended applicability of subsec. (e) to the Northern Mariana Islands.

Subsecs. (e)(2), (f). Pub. L. 98-199, § 3(b), substituted "Secretary" for "Commissioner".

1980—Subsec. (c)(2)(A)(i)(II). Pub. L. 96-270 substituted "$300,000" for "$200,000".

1978—Subsec. (a)(3). Pub. L. 95-561 substituted "equal to the number of such children" for "equal to the average of the number of such children" and "December 1 of the fiscal year" for "October 1 and February 1 of the fiscal year".

1975—Pub. L. 94-142, § 5(a), effective Oct. 1, 1977, completely revised the section so as to incorporate within its provisions the authority for the basic entitlement and allocation of funds, the formula for determining State entitlement, the distribution of grant funds within the State, coverage for territories and possessions, coverage for Indian reservations, and reductions or increases in funds and allocations. Pending the effective date of that revision, Pub. L. 94-142 amended this section as it applies through the end of the fiscal year ending Sept. 30, 1977, as described hereunder.

Subsec. (a)(5)(A). Pub. L. 94-142, § 5(c), effective on the date upon which final regulations prescribed by the Commissioner under section 5(b) of Pub. L. 94-142 take effect, struck out provision in section as effective Oct. 1, 1977, that, in determining the allotment of each State, the Commissioner may not count, as part of the figure of 12 per centum of the number of all children aged five to seventeen in the State, any children with specific learning disabilities to the extent that the number of those children is greater than one-sixth of that percentage.

Subsec. (b)(2). Pub. L. 94-142, § 2(a)(1)(A), effective for the period from July 1, 1975, through the end of the fiscal year ending Sept. 30, 1977, deleted the Commonwealth of Puerto Rico from the definition of "State".

Subsec. (c)(1). Pub. L. 94-142, § 2(a)(1)(B), effective for the period from July 1, 1975, through the end of the fiscal year ending Sept. 30, 1977, deleted the Commonwealth of Puerto Rico from the enumeration of territories and possessions to which subsec. (c) applies.

Subsec. (c)(2). Pub. L. 94-142, § 2(a)(2), effective for the period from July 1, 1975, through the end of the fiscal year ending Sept. 30, 1977, substituted "years ending June 30, 1975, and 1976, and for the fiscal year ending September 30, 1977" for "year ending June 30, 1975" and "1 per centum" for "2 per centum".

Subsec. (d). Pub. L. 94-142, § 2(a)(3), effective for the period from July 1, 1975, through the end of the fiscal year ending Sept. 30, 1977, substituted "years ending June 30, 1975, and 1976, and for the fiscal year ending September 30, 1977" for "year ending June 30, 1975".

1974—Pub. L. 93-380, § 614(a), amended provisions as follows:

"Section 614(a) of Pub. L. 93-380 enacted provisions for grants to States and Territories and assistance for Indian Reservation schools for education of handicapped children, effective for fiscal years ending June 30, 1975, and 1976, for the period beginning July 1, 1976, and ending Sept. 30, 1976, and for the fiscal year ending Sept. 30, 1977."

Subsec. (a). Pub. L. 93-380, § 614(e)(1), inserted provision for grants "in order to provide full educational opportunity to all handicapped children", effective July 1, 1975.

Subsec. (b). Pub. L. 93-380, § 614(e)(2), substituted appropriations authorization of $100,000,000 and $110,000,000 for fiscal years ending June 30, 1976 and 1977, for prior authorization of $200,000,000; $210,000,000; and $220,000,000 for fiscal years ending June 30, 1971 through 1973, effective July 1, 1975.

EFFECTIVE DATE OF 1985 AMENDMENT

Act of Nov. 22, 1985 § 601(a) effective 7/1/85 as provided by § 602 of such Act.

EFFECTIVE DATE OF 1983 AMENDMENT

Amendment by Pub. L. 98-199 effective Dec. 2, 1983, see section 18 of Pub. L. 98-199, set out as a note under section 1401 of this title.

EFFECTIVE DATE OF 1978 AMENDMENT

Section 1341(b) of Pub. L. 95-561 provided that: "The amendments made by subsection (a) of this section [amending this section] shall take effect with respect to determinations made in fiscal year 1979 and thereafter."

EFFECTIVE DATE OF 1975 AMENDMENT

Section 5(c) of Pub. L. 94-142 provided in part that the amendment of subsec. (a)(5)(A) by section 5(c) of Pub. L. 94-142 is effective on the date upon which final regulations prescribed by the Commissioner of Education under section 5(b) of Pub. L. 94-142, set out as a note below, take effect.

Section 8 of Pub. L. 94-142 provided that:

"(a) Notwithstanding any other provision of law, the amendments made by sections 2(a), 2(b), and 2(c) [amending subsecs. (b)(2), (c)(1), (c)(2), and (d) of this section and section 1412(a) of this title as in effect through Sept. 30, 1977, and amending provisions set out as notes under this section and sections 1412 and 1413 of this title] shall take effect on July 1, 1975.

"(b) The amendments made by sections 2(d), 2(e), 3, 6, and 7 [enacting sections 1405, 1406, and 1412(d) of this title, amending sections 1232 and 1453 of this title, enacting provisions set out as a note under this section, and amending provisions set out as a note under section 1401 of this title] shall take effect on the date of the enactment of this Act [Nov. 29, 1975].

"(c) The amendments made by sections 4 and 5(a) [enacting sections 1415 to 1420 of this title and amending sections 1401, 1411, 1412, 1413, and 1414 of this title] shall take effect on October 1, 1977, except that the provisions of clauses (A), (C), (D), and (E) of paragraph (2) of section 612 of the Act [section 1412 of this title], as amended by this Act, section 617(a)(1)(D), of the Act [section 1417(a)(1)(D) of this title], as amended by this Act, section 617(b) of the Act [section 1417(b) of this title], as amended by this Act, and section 618(a) of the Act [section 1418(a) of this title], as amended by this Act, shall take effect on the date of the enactment of this Act [Nov. 29, 1975].

"(d) The provisions of section 5(b) [amending this section and enacting provisions set out as notes under this section] shall take effect on the date of the enactment of this Act [Nov. 29, 1975]."

EFFECTIVE DATE OF 1974 AMENDMENT

Pub. L. 93-380, § 614(a), which, as originally enacted, provided that the 1974 amendment of this section by section 614(a) of Pub. L. 93-380 was effective for fiscal year 1975 only, was amended by section 2(b)(1) of Pub. L. 94-142 to extend the life of the amendment of this section by section 614(a) of Pub. L. 93-380 by making it effective for the fiscal years ending June 30, 1975, and 1976, the period beginning July 1, 1976 and ending Sept. 30, 1976, and the fiscal year ending Sept. 30, 1977.

Section 614(e)(3) of Pub. L. 93-380 provided that: "The amendments made by subsection (e) [amending subsecs. (a) and (b) of this section] shall become effective and shall be deemed to have been enacted on July 1, 1975."

TRANSFER OF FUNCTIONS

"Secretary", meaning the Secretary of Education, was substituted for "Commissioner" in subsecs. (a)(5), (e)(2), and (f) pursuant to sections 301(a)(1) and 507 of Pub. L. 96-88, which are classified to sections 3441(a)(1) and 3507 of this title and which transferred all functions of the Commissioner of Education to the Secretary of Education.

LIMITATION ON AUTHORIZATION OF APPROPRIATIONS FOR FISCAL YEAR 1982, 1983, AND 1984

Pub. L. 97-35, title VI, § 602(a)(1), Aug. 13, 1981, 95 Stat. 483, as amended by

Pub. L. 98-199, § 16(a), Dec. 2, 1983, 97 Stat. 1374, provided that: "There is authorized to be appropriated to carry out part B of the Education of the Handicapped Act [this subchapter], other than sections 618 and 619 [sections 1418 and 1419 of this title], $969,850,000 for fiscal year 1982, and $1,017,900,000 for the fiscal year 1983, and $1,071,850,000 for the fiscal year 1984."

AUTHORIZATION OF APPROPRIATIONS

Section 2(e) of Pub. L. 94-142 provided that: "Notwithstanding the provision of section 611 of the Act [this section] as in effect during the fiscal years 1976 and 1977, there are authorized to be appropriated $100,000,000 for the fiscal year 1976, such sums as may be necessary for the period beginning July 1, 1976, and ending September 30, 1976, and $200,000,000 for the fiscal year 1977, to carry out the provisions of part B of the Act [this subchapter], as in effect during such fiscal years."

RULES AND REGULATIONS FOR DETERMING SPECIFIC LEARNING DISABILITIES, DIAGNOSTIC PROCEDURES, AND MONITORING PROCEDURES; PROMULGATION BY COMMISSIONER OF EDUCATION; REVIEW OF REGULATIONS BY CONGRESSIONAL COMMITTEES

Section 5(b) of Pub. L. 94-142 provided that:

"(1) The Commissioner of Education shall, no later than one year after the effective date of this subsection [Nov. 29, 1975], prescribe—

"(A) regulations which establish specific criteria for determining whether a particular disorder or condition may be considered a specific learning disability for purposes of designating children with specific learning disabilities;

"(B) regulations which establish and describe diagnostic procedures which shall be used in determining whether a particular child has a disorder or condition which places such child in the category of children with specific learning disabilities; and

"(C) regulations which establish monitoring procedures which will be used to determine if State educational agencies, local educational agencies, and intermediate educational units are complying with the criteria established under clause (A) and clause (B).

"(2) The Commissioner shall submit any proposed regulation written under paragraph (1) to the Committee on Education and Labor of the House of Representtives and the Committee on Labor and Public Welfare of the Senate, for review and comment by each such committee, at least fifteen days before such regulation is published in the Federal Register.

"(3) If the Commissioner determines, as a result of the promulgation of regulations under paragraph (1), that changes are necessary in the definition of the term 'children with specific learning disabilities', as such term is defined by section 602(15) of the Act [section 1401(15) of this title], he shall submit recommendations for legislation with respect to such changes to each House of the Congress.

"(4) For purposes of this subsection:

"(A) The term 'children with specific learning disabilities' means those children who have a disorder in one or more of the basic psychological processes involved in understanding or in using language, spoken or written, which disorder may manifest itself in imperfect ability to listen, think, speak, read, write, spell, or do mathematical calculations. Such disorders include such conditions as perceptual handicaps, brain injury, minimal brain dysfunction, dyslexia, and developmental aphasia. Such term does not include children who have learning problems which are primarily the result of visual, hearing, or motor handicaps, of mental retardation, of emotional disturbance, or environmental, cultural, or economic disadvantage.

"(B) The term 'Commissioner' means the Commissioner of Education."

DUTIES AND RESPONSIBILITIES OF SECRETARY OF THE INTERIOR
RESPECTING FUNDS

Pub. L. 92-318, title IV, § 421(b)(2), June 23, 1972, 86 Stat. 341, provided that:
"For the purposes of titles II and III of the Elementary and Secondary Education Act
of 1965 [sections 1411 to 1414 of this title], the Secretary of the Interior shall have the
same duties and responsibilities with respect to funds paid to him under such titles, as
he would have if the Department of the Interior were a State educational agency
having responsibility for the administration of a State plan under such titles."

SECTION REFERRED TO IN OTHER SECTIONS

This section is referred to in sections 1413, 1414, 1419 of this title.

§ 1412. Eligibility requirements

In order to qualify for assistance under this subchapter in any fiscal year,
a State shall demonstrate to the Secretary that the following conditions are
met:

(1) The State has in effect a policy that assures all handicapped children
the right to a free appropriate public education.

(2) The State has developed a plan pursuant to section 1413(b) of this
title in effect prior to November 29, 1975, and submitted not later than August 21, 1975, which will be amended so as to comply with the provisions of
this paragraph. Each such amended plan shall set forth in detail the policies
and procedures which the State will undertake or has undertaken in order to
assure that—

(A) there is established (i) a goal of providing full educational opportunity to all handicapped children, (ii) a detailed timetable for accomplishing such a goal, and (iii) a description of the kind and number of facilities,
personnel, and services necessary throughout the State to meet such a
goal;

(B) a free appropriate public education will be available for all handicapped children between the ages of three and eighteen within the State
not later than September 1, 1978, and for all handicapped children between the ages of three and twenty-one within the State not later than
September 1, 1980, except that, with respect to handicapped children aged
three to five and aged eighteen to twenty-one, inclusive, the requirements
of this clause shall not be applied in any State if the application of such
requirements would be inconsistent with State law or practice, or the order
of any court, respecting public education within such age groups in the
State;

(C) all children residing in the State who are handicapped, regardless
of the severity of their handicap, and who are in need of special education
and related services are identified, located, and evaluated, and that a practical method is developed and implemented to determine which children
are currently receiving needed special education and related services and
which children are not currently receiving needed special education and
related services;

(D) policies and procedures are established in accordance with detailed criteria prescribed under section 417(c) of this title; and

(E) the amendment to the plan submitted by the State required by this section shall be available to parents, guardians, and other members of the general public at least thirty days prior to the date of submission of the amendment to the Secretary.

(3) The State has established priorities for providing a free appropriate public education to all handicapped children, which priorities shall meet the timetables set forth in clause (B) of paragraph (2) of this section, first with respect to handicapped children who are not receiving an education, and second with respect to handicapped children, within each disability, with the most severe handicaps who are receiving an inadequate education, and has made adequate progress in meeting the timetables set forth in clause (B) of paragraph (2) of this section.

(4) Each local educational agency in the State will maintain records of the individualized education program for each handicapped child, and such program shall be established, reviewed, and revised as provided in section 1414(a)(5) of this title.

(5) The State has established (A) procedural safeguards as required by section 1415 of this title, (B) procedures to assure that, to the maximum extent appropriate, handicapped children, including children in public or private institutions or other care facilities, are educated with children who are not handicapped, and that special classes, separate schooling, or other removal of handicapped children from the regular educational environment occurs only when the nature or severity of the handicap is such that education in regular classes with the use of supplementary aids and services cannot be achieved satisfactorily, and (C) procedures to assure that testing and evaluation materials and procedures utilized for the purposes of evaluation and placement of handicapped children will be selected and administered so as not to be racially or culturally discriminatory. Such materials or procedures shall be provided and administered in the child's native language or mode of communication, unless it clearly is not feasible to do so, and no single procedure shall be the sole criterion for determining an appropriate educational program for a child.

(6) The State educational agency shall be responsible for assuring that the requirements of this subchapter are carried out and that all educational programs for handicapped children within the State, including all such programs administered by any other State or local agency, will be under the general supervision of the persons responsible for educational programs for handicapped children in the State educational agency and shall meet education standards of the State educational agency.

(7) The State shall assure that (A) in carrying out the requirements of this section procedures are established for consultation with individuals involved in or concerned with the education of handicapped children, including handicapped individuals and parents or guardians of handicapped children, and (B) there are public hearings, adequate notice of such hearings, and an opportunity for comment available to the general public prior to adoption of the policies, programs, and procedures required pursuant to the provisions of this section and section 1413 of this title.

(Pub. L. 91-230, title VI, § 612, Apr. 13, 1970, 84 Stat. 178: Pub. L. 92-318, title IV, § 421(b)(1)(C), June 23, 1972, 86 Stat. 341; Pub. L. 93-380, title VI, §§ 614(b), (f)(1), 615(a), title VIII, § 843(b), Aug. 21, 1974, 88 Stat. 581, 582,

611; Pub. L. 94-142, §§ 2(a)(4), (c), (d), 5(a), Nov. 29, 1975, 89 Stat. 773, 774, 780; Pub. L. 98-199, § 3(b), Dec. 2, 1983, 97 Stat. 1358.)

AMENDMENTS

1983—Pub. L. 98-199 substituted in provision preceding par. (1) and in par. (2)(E) "Secretary" for "Commissioner".

1975—Pub. L. 94-142, § 5(a), effective Oct. 1, 1977, completely revised the section so as to incorporate within its provisions seven conditions which must be met by States in order to qualify for assistance. Pending the effective date of that revision, Pub. L. 94-142 amended this section as it applies through the end of the fiscal year ending Sept. 30, 1977, as described hereunder.

Subsec. (a). Pub. L. 94-142, § 2(a)(4), (c), effective for the period from July 1, 1975, through the end of the fiscal year ending Sept. 30, 1977, substituted "years ending June 30, 1975, and 1976, for the period beginning July 1, 1976, and ending September 30, 1976, and for the fiscal year ending September 30, 1977" for "year ending June 30, 1975" and "preceding fiscal year" for "fiscal year 1974" and added "or $300,000, whichever is greater" following "preceding fiscal year".

Subsec. (d). Pub. L. 94-142, § 2(d), effective for the period from Nov. 29, 1975, through the end of the fiscal year ending Sept. 30, 1977, added subsec. (d)

1974—Pub. L. 93-380, § 614(b), amended provisions as follows:

"Section 614(b) of Pub. L. 93-380 enacted provisions for allocations of appropriations to States, basis for such allocations, and reductions or increments thereof, effective for fiscal years ending June 30, 1975, and 1976, for the period beginning July 1, 1976, and ending Sept. 30, 1976, and for fiscal year ending Sept. 30, 1977."

Subsec. (a)(1). Pub. L. 93-380, § 843(b)(3), reduced rate from "3" to "1" per centum, effective after June 30, 1975.

Subsec. (a)(1)(A). Pub. L. 93-380, § 843(b)(1), struck "Puerto Rico," preceding "Guam," effective after June 30, 1975.

Subsec. (a)(1)(B). Pub. L. 93-380, § 614(f)(1), substituted "1977" for "1973", effective on and after July 1, 1973.

Subsec. (a)(2). Pub. L. 93-380, §§ 615(a)(1), 843(b)(2), substituted $300,000 for $200,000, effective on and after July 1, 1975; and struck out "the Commonwealth of Puerto Rico," preceding "Guam," effective after June 30, 1975.

Subsec. (a)(3). Pub. L. 93-380, § 615(a)(2), added par. (3), effective on and after July 1, 1975.

1972—Subsec. (a)(1)(B). Pub. L. 92-318 substituted "July 1, 1973" for "July 1, 1972".

EFFECTIVE DATE OF 1983 AMENDMENT

Amendment by Pub. L. 98-199 effective Dec. 2, 1983, see section 18 of Pub. L. 98-199, set out as a note under section 1401 of this title.

EFFECTIVE DATE OF 1975 AMENDMENT

Amendment of subsec. (a) as in effect through Sept. 30, 1977, by section 2(a)(4) and (c) of Pub. L. 94-142 effective July 1, 1975, see section 8(a) of Pub. L. 94-142, set out as an Effective Date of 1975 Amendment note under section 1411 of this title.

Enactment of subsec. (d) as in effect through Sept. 30, 1977, by section 2(d) of Pub. L. 94-142 effective Nov. 29, 1975, see section 8(b) of Pub. L. 94-142, set out as an Effective Date of 1975 Amendment note under section 1411 of this title.

Complete revision of this section by section 5(a) of Pub. L. 94-142 effective Oct. 1, 1977, except for clauses (A), (C), (D), and (E) of par. (2) of this section as so revised which are effective Nov. 29, 1975, see section 8(c) of Pub. L. 94-142, set out as an Effective Date of 1975 Amendment note under section 1411 of this title.

EFFECTIVE DATE OF 1974 AMENDMENT

Section 614(b) of Pub. L. 93-380 which, as originally enacted, provided that the 1974 amendment of this section by section 614(b) of Pub. L. 93-380 was effective for fiscal year 1975 only, was amended by section 2(b)(2) of Pub. L. 94-142 to extend the life of the amendment of this section by section 614(b) of Pub. L. 93-380 by making it effective for the fiscal years ending June 30, 1975, and 1976, the period beginning July 1, 1976, and ending Sept. 30, 1976, and the fiscal year ending Sept. 30, 1977.

Section 843(b) of Pub. L. 93-380 provided that amendment of subsec. (a)(1), (1)(A), and (2) of this section and section 1413(a)(1) of this title by Pub. L. 93-380 shall be effective after June 30, 1975.

Section 614(f)(2) of Pub. L. 93-380 provided that: "The amendment made by this subsection [amending subsec. (a)(1)(B) of this section] shall be effective on and after July 1, 1973."

Section 615(a) of Pub. L. 93-380 provided that amendment of subsec. (a)(2) and enactment of subsec. (a)(3) by section 615(a) shall be effective on and after July 1, 1975.

Section 615(d) of Pub. L. 93-380 provided that: "The amendment made by subsections (a)(1) and (b) of this section [amending subsec. (a)(2) of this section and section 1413(a)(1) of this title] shall be effective in any fiscal year for which the aggregate of the amounts allotted to the States for that fiscal year for carrying out part B of the Education of the Handicapped Act [this subchapter] is $45,000,000 or more."

TRANSFER OF FUNCTIONS

"Secretary", meaning the Secretary of Education, was substituted for "Commissioner" in text pursuant to sections 301(a)(1) and 507 of Pub. L. 96-88, which are classified to sections 3441(a)(1) and 3507 of this title and which transferred all functions of the Commissioner of Education to the Secretary of Education.

FISCAL YEAR TRANSITION PERIOD OF JULY 1, 1976, THROUGH SEPTEMBER 30, 1976, DEEMED PART OF FISCAL YEAR BEGINNING OCTOBER 1, 1976

Fiscal year transition period of July 1, 1976, through Sept. 30, 1976, deemed part of fiscal year beginning Oct. 1, 1976, for purposes of this section, see Pub. L. 94-274, title II, § 205(8), Apr. 21, 1976, 90 Stat. 393, set out as a note under section 5532 of Title 5, Government Organization and Employees.

SECTION REFERRED TO IN OTHER SECTIONS

This section is referred to in sections 1400, 1411, 1413, 1414, 1416, 1418, 1419, 1423, 2334 of this title; title 29 section 796d.

§ 1413. State plans

(a) Requisite features

Any State meeting the eligibility requirements set forth in section 1412 of this title and desiring to participate in the program under this subchapter shall submit to the Secretary, through its State educational agency, a State plan at such time, in such manner, and containing or accompanied by such information, as he deems necessary. Each such plan shall—

(1) set forth policies and procedures designed to assure that funds paid to the State under this subchapter will be expended in accordance with the

provisions of this subchapter, with particular attention given to the provisions of sections 1411(b), 1411(c), 1411(d), 1412(2), and 1412(3) of this title;

(2) provide that programs and procedures will be established to assure that funds received by the State or any of its political subdivisions under any other Federal program, including section 241c-1 of this title, section 844a(b)(8) of this title or its successor authority, and section 1262(a)(4)(B) of this title, under which there is specific authority for the provision of assistance for the education of handicapped children, will be utilized by the State, or any of its political subdivisions, only in a manner consistent with the goal of providing a free appropriate public education for all handicapped children, except that nothing in this clause shall be construed to limit the specific requirements of the laws governing such Federal programs;

(3) set forth, consistent with the purposes of this chapter, a description of programs and procedures for (A) the development and implementation of a comprehensive system of personnel development which shall include the inservice training of general and special educational instructional and support personnel, detailed procedures to assure that all personnel necessary to carry out the purposes of this chapter are appropriately and adequately prepared and trained, and effective procedures for acquiring and disseminating to teachers and administrators of programs for handicapped children significant information derived from educational research, demonstration, and similar projects, and (B) adopting, where appropriate, promising educational practices and materials development through such projects;

(4) set forth policies and procedures to assure—

(A) that, to the extent consistent with the number and location of handicapped children in the State who are enrolled in private elementary and secondary schools, provision is made for the participation of such children in the program assisted or carried out under this subchapter by providing for such children special education and related services; and

(B) that (i) handicapped children in private schools and facilities will be provided special education and related services (in conformance with an individualized educational program as required by this subchapter) at no cost to their parents or guardian, if such children are placed in or referred to such schools or facilities by the State or appropriate local educational agency as the means of carrying out the requirements of this subchapter or any other applicable law requiring the provision of special education and related services to all handicapped children within such State, and (ii) in all such instances the State educational agency shall determine whether such schools and facilities meet standards that apply to State and local educational agencies and that children so served have all the rights they would have if served by such agencies;

(5) set forth policies and procedures which assure that the State shall seek to recover any funds made available under this subchapter for services to any child who is determined to be erroneously classified as eligible to be counted under section 1411(a) or 1411(d) of this title;

(6) provide satisfactory assurance that the control of funds provided under this subchapter, and title to property derived therefrom, shall be in a public agency for the uses and purposes provided in this subchapter, and that a public agency will administer such funds and property;

(7) provide for (A) making such reports in such form and containing such information as the Secretary may require to carry out his functions

under this subchapter, and (B) keeping such records and affording such access thereto as the Secretary may find necessary to assure the correctness and verification of such reports and proper disbursement of Federal funds under this subchapter;

(8) provide procedures to assure that final action with respect to any application submitted by a local educational agency or an intermediate educational unit shall not be taken without first affording the local educational agency or intermediate educational unit involved reasonable notice and opportunity for a hearing;

(9) provide satisfactory assurance that Federal funds made available under this subchapter (A) will not be comingled with State funds, and (B) will be so used as to supplement and increase the level of State and local funds expended for the education of handicapped children and in no case to supplant such State and local funds, except that, where the State provides clear and convincing evidence that all handicapped children have available to them a free appropriate public education, the Secretary may waive in part the requirement of this clause if he concurs with the evidence provided by the State;

(10) provide, consistent with procedures prescribed pursuant to section 1417(a)(2) of this title, satisfactory assurance that such fiscal control and fund accounting procedures will be adopted as may be necessary to assure proper disbursement of, and accounting for, Federal funds paid under this subchapter to the State, including any such funds paid by the State to local educational agencies and intermediate educational units;

(11) provide for procedures for evaluation at least annually of the effectiveness of programs in meeting the educational needs of handicapped children (including evaluation of individualized education programs), in accordance with such criteria that the Secretary shall prescribe pursuant to section 1417 of this title; and

(12) provide that the State has an advisory panel, appointed by the Governor or any other official authorized under State law to make such appointments, composed of individuals involved in or concerned with the education of handicapped children, including handicapped individuals, teachers, parents or guardians of handicapped children, State and local education officials, and administrators of programs for handicapped children, which (A) advises the State educational agency of unmet needs within the State in the education of handicapped children, (B) comments publicly on any rules or regulations proposed for issuance by the State regarding the education of handicapped children and the procedures for distribution of funds under this subchapter, and (C) assists the State in developing and reporting such data and evaluations as may assist the Secretary in the performance of his responsibilities under section 1418 of this title.

(b) Additional assurances

Whenever a State educational agency provides free appropriate public education for handicapped children, or provides direct services to such children, such State educational agency shall include, as part of the State plan required by subsection (a) of this section, such additional assurances not specified in such subsection (a) of this section as are contained in section 1414(a) of this title, except that funds available for the provision of such education or services may be expended without regard to the provisions relating to excess costs in section 1414(a) of this title.

(c) Notice and hearing prior to disapproval of plan

The Secretary shall approve any State plan and any modification thereof which—
(1) is submitted by a State eligible in accordance with section 1412 of this title; and
(2) meets the requirements of subsection (a) and subsection (b) of this section.

The Secretary shall disapprove any State plan which does not meet the requirements of the preceding sentence, but shall not finally disapprove a State plan except after reasonable notice and opportunity for a hearing to the State.

(d) Participation of handicapped children in private schools; payment of Federal amount; determinations of Secretary: notice and hearing; judicial review: jurisdiction of court of appeals, petition, record, conclusiveness of findings, remand, review by Supreme Court

(1) If, on December 2, 1983, a State educational agency is prohibited by law from providing for the participation in special programs of handicapped children enrolled in private elementary and secondary schools as required by subsection (a)(4) of this section, the Secretary shall waive such requirement, and shall arrange for the provision of services to such children through arrangements which shall be subject to the requirements of subsection (a)(4) of this section.
(2)(A) When the Secretary arranges for services pursuant to this subsection, the Secretary, after consultation with the appropriate public and private school officials, shall pay to the provider of such services an amount per child which may not exceed the Federal amount provided per child under this subchapter to all handicapped children enrolled in the State for services for the fiscal year preceding the fiscal year for which the determination is made.
(B) Pending final resolution of any investigation or complaint that could result in a determination under this subsection, the Secretary may withhold from the allocation of the affected State educational agency the amount the Secretary estimates would be necessary to pay the cost of such services.
(C) Any determination by the Secretary under this section shall continue in effect until the Secretary determines that there will no longer be any failure or inability on the part of the State educational agency to meet the requirements of subsection (a)(4) of this section.
(3)(A) The Secretary shall not take any final action under this subsection until the State educational agency affected by such action has had an opportunity, for at least 45 days after receiving written notice thereof, to submit written objections and to appear before the Secretary or his designee to show cause why such action should not be taken.
(B) If a State educational agency is dissatisfied with the Secretary's final action after a proceeding under subparagraph (A) of this paragraph, it may, within 60 days after notice of such action, file with the United States court of

appeals for the circuit in which such state is located a petition for review of that action. A copy of the petition shall be forthwith transmitted by the clerk of the court to the Secretary. The Secretary thereupon shall file in the court the record of the proceedings on which he based his action, as provided in section 2112 of title 28.

(C) The findings of fact by the Secretary, if supported by substantial evidence, shall be conclusive; but the court, for good cause shown, may remand the case to the Secretary to take further evidence, and the Secretary may thereupon make new or modified findings of fact and may modify his previous action, and shall file in the court the record of the further proceedings. Such new or modified findings of fact shall likewise be conclusive if supported by substantial evidence.

(D) Upon the filing of a petition under subparagraph (B), the court shall have jurisdiction to affirm the action of the Secretary or to set it aside, in whole or in part. The judgment of the court shall be subject to review by the Supreme Court of the United States upon certiorari or certification as provided in section 1254 of title 28.

(Pub. L. 91-230, title VI, § 613, Apr. 13, 1970, 84 Stat. 179; Pub. L. 93-380, title VI, §§ 614(c), (d), 615(b), (c), title VIII, § 843(b)(2), Aug. 21, 1974, 88 Stat. 581, 583, 611; Pub. L. 94-142, § 5(a), Nov. 29, 1975, 89 Stat. 782; Pub. L. 98-199, §§ 3(b), 7, Dec. 2, 1983, 97 Stat. 1358, 1359.)

REFERENCES IN TEXT

Section 241c-1 of this title, referred to in subsec. (a)(2), was in the original "section 121 of the Elementary and Secondary Education Act of 1965" and was repealed by Pub. L. 95-561, title I, § 101(c), Nov. 1, 1978, 92 Stat. 2200. See section 2771 et seq. of this title.

Section 844a(b)(8) of this title, referred to in subsec. (a)(2), was in the original "section 305(b)(8) of such Act (20 U.S.C. 844a(b)(8)" meaning section 305 of title III of the Elementary and Secondary Education Act of 1965, Pub. L. 89-10, title III, § 305, as added Pub. L. 90-247, title I, § 131, Jan. 2, 1968, 91 Stat. 792, which was omitted in the general revision of title III of the Elementary and Secondary Education Act of 1965 by Pub. L. 95-561, title III, § 301, Nov. 1, 1978, 92 Stat. 2210.

Section 1262 of this title, referred to in subsec. (a)(2), has been omitted. See section 2330(b) of this title.

AMENDMENTS

1983—Subsecs. (a),(c), Pub. L. 98-199, § 3(b), substituted "Secretary" for "Commissioner" wherever appearing.

Subsec. (d). Pub. L. 98-199, § 7, added subsec. (d).

1975—Pub. L. 94-142, § 5(a), effective Oct. 1, 1977, completely revised the section so as to incorporate within its provisions updated features which any State plan must have when submitted to the Commissioner through its State educational agency and so as to strike out provisions covering the administrative proceedings and judicial review attendant upon the submission of a State plan. See sections 1414 et seq. of this title.

1974—Subsec. (a). Pub. L. 93-380, § 614(c), substituted in first sentence "is entitled to receive payments" for "desires to receive grants", effective for fiscal years ending June 30, 1975, and 1976, for the period beginning July 1, 1976, and ending Sept. 30, 1976, and for the fiscal year ending Sept. 30, 1977.

Subsec. (a)(1). Pub. L. 93-380, §§ 65(b), 843(b)(2), substituted $200,000 for $100,000 and struck out "the Commonwealth of Puerto Rico," preceding "Guam".

Subsec. (a)(12), (13). Pub. L. 93-380, § 614(d), added pars. (12) and (13).

Subsec. (b). Pub. L. 93-380, § 615(c)(1), added subsec. (b). Former subsec. (b) redesignated (c).

Subsecs. (c), (d). Pub. L. 93-380, § 615(c)(1), redesignated former subsec. (b) and (c) as (c) and (d). Former subsec. (d) redesignated (e).

Subsec. (e). Pub. L. 93-380, § 615(c)(1), (2), redesignated former subsec. (d) as (e) and substituted in par. (1) reference to subsection "(d)" for "(c)" of this section.

EFFECTIVE DATE OF 1983 AMENDMENT

Amendment by Pub. L. 98-199 effective Dec. 2, 1983, see section 18 of Pub. L. 98-199, set out as a note under section 1401 of this title.

EFFECTIVE DATE OF 1975 AMENDMENT

Complete revision of this section by section 5(a) of Pub. L. 94-142 effective Oct. 1, 1977, see section 8(c) of Pub. L. 94-142, set out as an Effective Date of 1975 Amendment note under section 1411 of this title.

EFFECTIVE DATE OF 1974 AMENDMENT

Section 614(c) of Pub. L. 93-380 which, as originally enacted, provided that the amendment of subsec. (a) by section 614(c) of Pub. L. 93-380 was effective for fiscal year 1975 only, was amended by section 2(b)(3) of Pub. L. 94-142 to extend the life of the amendment by section 614(c) of Pub. L. 93-380 by making it effective for the fiscal years ending June 30, 1975, and 1976, the period beginning July 1, 1976, and ending Sept. 30, 1976, and the fiscal year ending Sept. 30, 1977.

Amendment of subsec. (a)(1) by Pub. L. 93-380 effective after June 30, 1975, see section 843(b) of Pub. L. 93-380, set out as an Effective Date of 1974 Amendment note under section 1412 of this title.

Enactment of subsec. (a)(12), (13) by section 614(d) of Pub. L. 93-380 effective on and after sixtieth day after Aug. 21, 1974, see section 2(c) of Pub. L. 93-380, set out as an Effective Date of 1974 Amendment note under section 244 of this title.

TRANSFER OF FUNCTIONS

"Secretary", meaning the Secretary of Education, was substituted for "Commissioner" in subsecs. (a) and (c) pursuant to sections 301(a)(1) and 507 of Pub. L. 96-88, which are classified to sections 3441(a)(1) and 3507 of this title and which transferred all functions of the Commissioner of Education to the Secretary of Education.

SECTION REFERRED TO IN OTHER SECTIONS

This section is referred to in sections 1411, 1412, 1414 to 1416, 1419 of this title.

§ 1414. Application

(a) Requisite features

A local educational agency or an intermediate educational unit which desires to receive payments under section 1411(d) of this title for any fiscal year shall submit an application to the appropriate State educational agency. Such application shall—

(1) provide satisfactory assurance that payments under this subchapter will be used for excess costs directly attributable to programs which—

(A) provide that all children residing within the jurisdiction of the local educational agency or the intermediate educational unit who are handicapped, regardless of the severity of their handicap, and are in need of special education and related services will be identified, located, and evaluated, and provide for the inclusion of a practical method of determining which children are currently receiving needed special education and related services and which children are not currently receiving such education and services;

(B) establish policies and procedures in accordance with detailed criteria prescribed under section 1417(c) of this title;

(C) establish a goal of providing full educational opportunities to all handicapped children, including—

(i) procedures for the implementation and use of the comprehensive system of personnel development established by the State educational agency under section 1413(a)(3) of this title;

(ii) the provision of, and the establishment of priorities for providing, a free appropriate public education to all handicapped children, first with respect to handicapped children who are not receiving an education, and second with respect to handicapped children, within each disability, with the most severe handicaps who are receiving an inadequate education;

(iii) the participation and consultation of the parents or guardian of such children; and

(iv) to the maximum extent practicable and consistent with the provisions of section 1412(5)(B) of this title, the provision of special services to enable such children to participate in regular educational programs;

(D) establish a detailed timetable for accomplishing the goal described in subclause (C); and

(E) provide a description of the kind and number of facilities, personnel, and services necessary to meet the goal described in subclause (C);

(2) provide satisfactory assurance that (A) the control of funds provided under this subchapter, and title to property derived from such funds, shall be in a public agency for the uses and purposes provided in this subchapter, and that a public agency will administer such funds and property, (B) Federal funds expended by local educational agencies and intermediate educational units for programs under this subchapter (i) shall be used to pay only the excess costs directly attributable to the education of handicapped children, and (ii) shall be used to supplement and, to the extent practicable, increase the level of State and local funds expended for the education of handicapped children, and in no case to supplant such State and local funds, and (C) State and local funds will be used in the jurisdiction of the local educational agency or intermediate educational unit to provide services in program areas which, taken as a whole, are at least comparable to services being provided in areas of such jurisdiction which are not receiving funds under this subchapter;

(3)(A) provide for furnishing such information (which, in the case of reports relating to performance, is in accordance with specific performance criteria related to program objectives), as may be necessary to enable the State educational agency to perform its duties under this subchapter, including information relating to the educational achievement of handicapped children participating in programs carried out under this subchapter; and

(B) provide for keeping such records, and provide for affording such access to such records, as the State educational agency may find necessary to assure the correctness and verification of such information furnished under subclause (A);

(4) provide for making the application and all pertinent documents related to such application available to parents, guardians, and other members of the general public, and provide that all evaluations and reports required under clause (3) shall be public information;

(5) provide assurances that the local educational agency or intermediate educational unit will establish, or revise, whichever is appropriate, an individualized education program for each handicapped child at the beginning of each school year and will then review and, if appropriate revise, its provisions periodically, but not less than annually;

(6) provide satisfactory assurance that policies and programs established and administered by the local educational agency or intermediate educational unit shall be consistent with the provisions of paragraph (1) through paragraph (7) of section 1412 and section 1413(a) of this title; and

(7) provide satisfactory assurance that the local educational agency or intermediate educational unit will establish and maintain procedural safeguards in accordance with the provisions of sections 1412(5)(B), 1412(5)(C), and 1415 of this title.

(b) Approval by State educational agencies of applications submitted by local educational agencies or intermediate educational units; notice and hearing

(1) A State educational agency shall approve any application submitted by a local educational agency or an intermediate educational unit under subsection (a) of this section if the State educational agency determines that such application meets the requirements of subsection (a) of this section, except that no such application may be approved until the State plan submitted by such State educational agency under subsection (a) of this section is approved by the Secretary under section 1413(c) of this title. A State educational agency shall disapprove any application submitted by a local educational agency or an intermediate educational unit under subsection (a) of this section if the State educational agency determines that such application does not meet the requirements of subsection (a) of this section.

(2)(A) Whenever a State educational agency, after reasonable notice and opportunity for a hearing, finds that a local educational agency or an intermediate educational unit, in the administration of an application approved by the State educational agency under paragraph (1), has failed to comply with any requirement set forth in such application, the State educational agency, after giving appropriate notice to the local educational agency or the intermediate educational unit, shall—

(i) make no further payments to such local educational agency or such intermediate educational unit under section 1420 of this title until the State educational agency is satisfied that there is no longer any failure to comply with the requirement involved; or

(ii) take such finding into account in its review of any application made by such local educational agency or such intermediate educational unit under subsection (a) of this section.

(B) The provisions of the last sentence of section 1416(a) of this title shall apply to any local educational agency or any intermediate educational unit receiving any notification from a State educational agency under this paragraph.

(3) In carrying out its functions under paragraph (1), each State educational agency shall consider any decision made pursuant to a hearing held under section 1415 of this title which is adverse to the local educational agency or intermediate educational unit involved in such decision.

(c) Consolidated applications

(1) A State educational agency may, for purposes of the consideration and approval of applications under this section, require local educational agencies to submit a consolidated application for payments if such State educational agency determines that any individual application submitted by any such local educational agency will be disapproved because such local educational agency is ineligible to receive payments because of the application of section 1411(c)(4)(A)(i) of this title or such local educational agency would be unable to establish and maintain programs of sufficient size and scope to effectively meet the educational needs of handicapped children.

(2)(A) In any case in which a consolidated application of local educational agencies is approved by a State educational agency under paragraph (1), the payments which such local educational agencies may receive shall be equal to the sum of payments to which each such local educational agency would be entitled under section 1411(d) of this title if an individual application of any such local educational agency had been approved.

(B) The State educational agency shall prescribe rules and regulations with respect to consolidated applications submitted under this subsection which are consistent with the provisions of paragraph (1) through paragraph (7) of section 1412 and section 1413(a) of this title and which provide participating local educational agencies with joint responsibilities for implementing programs receiving payments under this subchapter.

(C) In any case in which an intermediate educational unit is required pursuant to State law to carry out the provisions of this subchapter, the joint responsibilities given to local educational agencies under subparagraph (B) shall not apply to the administration and disbursement of any payments received by such intermediate educational unit. Such responsibilities shall be carried out exclusively by such intermediate educational unit.

(d) Special education and related services provided directly by State educational agencies: regional or State centers

Whenever a State educational agency determines that a local educational agency—

(1) is unable or unwilling to establish and maintain programs of free appropriate public education which meet the requirements established in subsection (a) of this section;

(2) is unable or unwilling to be consolidated with other local educa-

tional agencies in order to establish and maintain such programs; or
    (3) has one or more handicapped children who can best be served by a
regional or State center designed to meet the needs of such children;

the State educational agency shall use the payments which would have
been available to such local educational agency to provide special education
and related services directly to handicapped children residing in the area
served by such local educational agency. The State educational agency may
provide such education and services in such manner, and at such locations
(including regional or State centers), as it considers appropriate, except that
the manner in which such education and services are provided shall be consistent with the requirements of this subchapter.

(e) Reallocation of funds

Whenever a State educational agency determines that a local educational
agency is adequately providing a free appropriate public education to all
handicapped children residing in the area served by such agency with State
and local funds otherwise available to such agency, the State educational
agency may reallocate funds (or such portion of those funds as may not be
required to provide such education and services) made available to such
agency, pursuant to section 1411(d) of this title, to such other local educational agencies within the State as are not adequately providing special education and related services to all handicapped children residing in the areas
served by such other local educational agencies.

(f) Programs using State or local funds

Notwithstanding the provisions of subsection (a)(2)(B)(ii) of this section,
any local educational agency which is required to carry out any program for
the education of handicapped children pursuant to a State law shall be entitled to receive payments under section 1411(d) of this title for use in carrying
out such program, except that such payments may not be used to reduce the
level of expenditures for such program made by such local educational
agency from State or local funds below the level of such expenditures for the
fiscal year prior to the fiscal year for which such local educational agency
seeks such payments.

(Pub. L. 91-230, title VI, § 614, Apr. 13, 1970, 84 Stat. 181; Pub. L. 94-
142, § 5(a), Nov. 29, 1975, 89 Stat. 784; Pub. L. 98-199, § 3(b), Dec. 2, 1983,
97 Stat. 1358.)

AMENDMENTS

1983—Subsec. (b)(1). Pub. L. 98-199 substituted "Secretary" for
"Commissioner".
    1975—Pub. L. 94-142, effective Oct. 1, 1977, completely revised the
section so as to incorporate within its provisions the process through which
local educational agencies and intermediate educational units desiring to receive payments submit applications to the appropriate State educational

agency and so as to eliminate former provisions covering State matching funds.

EFFECTIVE DATE OF 1983 AMENDMENT

Amendment by Pub. L. 98-199 effective Dec. 2, 1983, see section 18 of Pub. L. 98-199, set out as a note under section 1401 of this title.

EFFECTIVE DATE OF 1975 AMENDMENT

Complete revision of this section by section 5(a) of Pub. L. 94-142 effective Oct. 1, 1977, see section 8(c) of Pub. L. 94-142, set out as an Effective Date of 1975 Amendment note under section 1411 of this title.

TRANSFER OF FUNCTIONS

"Secretary", meaning the Secretary of Education, was substituted for "Commissioner" in subsec. (b)(1) pursuant to sections 301(a)(1) and 507 of Pub. L. 96-88, which are classified to sections 3441(a)(1) and 3507 of this title and which transferred all functions of the Commissioner of Education to the Secretary of Education.

SECTION REFERRED TO IN OTHER SECTIONS

This section is referred to in sections 1401, 1411, 1412, 1413, 1418, 1420, 2334 of this title; title 29 section 796d.

§ 1415. Procedural safeguards

(a) Establishment and maintenance

Any State educational agency, any local educational agency, and any intermediate educational unit which receives assistance under this subchapter shall establish and maintain procedures in accordance with subsection (b) through subsection (e) of this section to assure that handicapped children and their parents or guardians are guaranteed procedural safeguards with respect to the provision of free appropriate public education by such agencies and units.

(b) Required procedures; hearing

(1) The procedures required by this section shall include, but shall not be limited to—
(A) an opportunity for the parents or guardian of a handicapped child to examine all relevant records with respect to the identification, evaluation, and educational placement of the child, and the provision of a free appropriate public education to such child, and to obtain an independent educational evaluation of the child;
(B) procedures to protect the rights of the child whenever the parents or guardian of the child are not known, unavailable, or the child is a ward of the State, including the assignment of an individual (who shall not be an employee of the State educational agency, local educational agency, or in-

termediate educational unit involved in the education or care of the child) to act as a surrogate for the parents or guardian;

(C) written prior notice to the parents or guardian of the child whenever such agency or unit—

(i) proposes to initiate or change, or

(ii) refuses to initiate or change,

the identification, evaluation, or educational placement of the child or the provision of a free appropriate public education to the child;

(D) procedures designed to assure that the notice required by clause (C) fully inform the parents or guardian, in the parents' or guardian's native language, unless it clearly is not feasible to do so, of all procedures available pursuant to this section; and

(E) an opportunity to present complaints with respect to any matter relating to the identification, evaluation, or educational placement of the child, or the provision of a free appropriate public education to such child.

(2) Whenever a complaint has been received under paragraph (1) of this subsection, the parents or guardian shall have an opportunity for an impartial due process hearing which shall be conducted by the State educational agency or by the local educational agency or intermediate educational unit, as determined by State law or by the State educational agency. No hearing conducted pursuant to the requirements of this paragraph shall be conducted by an employee of such agency or unit involved in the education or care of the child.

(c) Review of local decision by State education agency

If the hearing required in paragraph (2) of subsection (b) of this section is conducted by a local educational agency or an intermediate educational unit, any party aggrieved by the findings and decision rendered in such a hearing may appeal to the State educational agency which shall conduct an impartial review of such hearing. The officer conducting such review shall make an independent decision upon completion of such review.

(d) Enumeration of rights accorded parties to hearings

Any party to any hearing conducted pursuant to subsections (b) and (c) of this section shall be accorded (1) the right to be accompanied and advised by counsel and by individuals with special knowledge or training with respect to the problems of handicapped children, (2) the right to present evidence and confront, cross-examine, and compel the attendance of witnesses, (3) the right to a written or electronic verbatim record of such hearing, and (4) the right to written findings of fact and decisions (which findings and decisions shall also be transmitted to the advisory panel established pursuant to section 1413(a)(12) of this title).

(e) Civil action; jurisdiction

(1) A decision made in a hearing conducted pursuant to paragraph (2) of subsection (b) of this section shall be final, except that any party involved in such hearing may appeal such decision under the provisions of subsection (c) and paragraph (2) of this subsection. A decision made under subsection (c) of

this section shall be final, except that any party may bring an action under paragraph (2) of this subsection.

(2) Any party aggrieved by the findings and decision made under subsection (b) of this section who does not have the right to an appeal under subsection (c) of this section, and any party aggrieved by the findings and decision under subsection (c) of this section, shall have the right to bring a civil action with respect to the complaint presented pursuant to this section, which action may be brought in any State court of competent jurisdiction or in a district court of the United States without regard to the amount in controversy. In any action brought under this paragraph the court shall receive the records of the administrative proceedings, shall hear additional evidence at the request of a party, and, basing its decision of the preponderance of the evidence, shall grant such relief as the court determines is appropriate.

(3) During the pendency of any proceedings conducted pursuant to this section, unless the State or local educational agency and the parents or guardian otherwise agree, the child shall remain in the then current educational placement of such child, or, if applying for initial admission to a public school, shall, with the consent of the parents or guardian, be placed in the public school program until all such proceedings have been completed.

(4) The district courts of the United States shall have jurisdiction of actions brought under this subsection without regard to the amount in controversy.

(Pub. L. 91-230, title VI, § 615, as added Pub. L. 94-142, § 5(a), Nov. 29, 1975, 89 Stat. 788.)

EFFECTIVE DATE

Section effective Oct. 1, 1977, see section 8 of Pub. L. 94-142, set out as an Effective Date of 1975 Amendment note under section 1411 of this title.

SECTION REFERRED TO IN OTHER SECTIONS

This section is referred to in sections 1412, 1414 of this title.

§ 1416. Withholding of payments

(a) Failure to comply with this subchapter; limitations; public notice

Whenever the Secretary, after reasonable notice and opportunity for hearing to the State educational agency involved (and to any local educational agency or intermediate educational unit affected by any failure described in clause (2)), finds—

(1) that there has been a failure to comply substantially with any provision of section 1412 or section 1413 of this title, or

(2) that in the administration of the State plan there is a failure to comply with any provision of this subchapter or with any requirements set forth in the application of a local educational agency or intermediate educational unit approved by the State educational agency pursuant to the State plan,

the Secretary (A) shall, after notifying the State educational agency, withhold any further payments to the State under this subchapter, and (B) may, after notifying the State educational agency, withhold further payments to the State under the Federal programs specified in section 1413(a)(2) of this title within his jurisdiction, to the extent that funds under such programs are available for the provision of assistance for the education of handicapped children. If the Secretary withholds further payments under clause (A) or clause (B) he may determine that such withholding will be limited to programs or projects under the State plan, or portions thereof, affected by the failure, or that the State educational agency shall not make further payments under this subchapter to specified local educational agencies or intermediate educational units affected by the failure. Until the Secretary is satisfied that there is no longer any failure to comply with the provisions of this subchapter, as specified in clause (1) or clause (2), no further payments shall be made to the State under this subchapter or under the Federal programs specified in section 1413(a)(2) of this title within his jurisdiction to the extent that funds under such programs are available for the provision of assistance for the education of handicapped children, or payments by the State educational agency under this subchapter shall be limited to local educational agencies and intermediate educational units whose actions did not cause or were not involved in the failure, as the case may be. Any State educational agency, local educational agency, or intermediate educational unit in receipt of a notice pursuant to the first sentence of this subsection shall, by means of a public notice, take such measures as may be necessary to bring the pendency of an action pursuant to this subsection to the attention of the public within the jurisdiction of such agency or unit.

(b) Judicial review

(1) If any State is dissatisfied with the Secretary's final action with respect to its State plan submitted under section 1413 of this title, such State may, within sixty days after notice of such action, file with the United States court of appeals for the circuit in which such State is located a petition for review of that action. A copy of the petition shall be forthwith transmitted by the clerk of the court to the Secretary. The Secretary thereupon shall file in the court the record of the proceedings on which he based his action, as provided in section 2112 of title 28.

(2) The findings of fact by the Secretary, if supported by substantial evidence, shall be conclusive; but the court, for good cause shown, may remand the case to the Secretary to take further evidence, and the Secretary may thereupon make new or modified findings of fact that may modify his previous action, and shall file in the court the record of the further proceedings. Such new or modified findings of fact shall likewise be conclusive if supported by substantial evidence.

(3) Upon the filing of such petition, the court shall have jurisdiction to affirm the action of the Secretary or to set it aside, in whole or in part. The judgment of the court shall be subject to review by the Supreme Court of the United States upon certiorari or certification as provided in section 1254 of title 28.

(Pub. L. 91-230, title VI, § 616, as added Pub. L. 94-142, § 5(a), Nov. 29, 1975, 89 Stat. 789, and amended Pub. L. 98-199, § 3(b), Dec. 2, 1983, 97 Stat. 1358.)

AMENDMENTS

1983—Pub. L. 98-199 substituted "Secretary" for "Commissioner" wherever appearing in text and "Secretary's" for "Commissioner's" in subsec. (b)(1).

EFFECTIVE DATE OF 1983 AMENDMENT

Amendment by Pub. L. 98-199 effective Dec. 2, 1983, see section 18 of Pub. L. 98-199, set out as a note under section 1401 of this title.

EFFECTIVE DATE

Section effective Oct. 1, 1977, see section 8 of Pub. L. 94-142, set out as an Effective Date of 1975 Amendment note under section 1411 of this title.

TRANSFER OF FUNCTIONS

"Secretary", meaning the Secretary of Education, was substituted for "Commissioner" in text and "Secretary's" was substituted for "Commissioner's" in subsec. (b)(1) pursuant to sections 301(a)(1) and 507 of Pub. L. 96-88, which are classified to sections 344(a)(1) and 3507 of this title and which transferred all functions of the Commissioner of Education to the Secretary of Education.

SECTION REFERRED TO IN OTHER SECTIONS

This section is referred to in sections 1411, 1414 of this title.

§ 1417. Administration

(a) Duties of Secretary

(1) In carrying out his duties under this subchapter, the Secretary shall
(A) cooperate with, and furnish all technical assistance necessary, directly or by grant or contract, to the States in matters relating to the education of handicapped children and the execution of the provisions of this subchapter;
(B) provide such short-term training programs and institutes as are necessary;
(C) disseminate information, and otherwise promote the education of all handicapped children within the States; and
(D) assure that each State shall, within one year after November 29, 1975, provide certification of the actual number of handicapped children receiving special education and related services in such State.
(2) As soon as practicable after November 29, 1975, the Secretary shall, by regulation, prescribe a uniform financial report to be utilized by State educational agencies in submitting State plans under this subchapter in order to assure equity among the States.

(b) Rules and regulations

In carrying out the provisions of this subchapter, the Secretary shall issue, not later than January 1, 1977, amend, and revoke such rules and regulations as may be necessary. No other less formal method of implementing such provisions is authorized.

(c) Protection of rights and privacy of parents and students

The Secretary shall take appropriate action, in accordance with the provisions of section 1232g of this title, to assure the protection of the confidentiality of any personally identifiable data, information, and records collected or maintained by the Secretary and by State and local educational agencies pursuant to the provisions of this subchapter.

(d) Hiring of qualified personnel

The Secretary is authorized to hire qualified personnel necessary to conduct data collection and evaluation activities required by subsections (b), (c) and (d) of section 1418 of this title and to carry out his duties under subsection (a)(1) of this section without regard to the provisions of title 5 relating to appointments in the competitive service and without regard to chapter 51 and subchapter III of chapter 53 of such title relating to classification and general schedule pay rates except that no more than twenty such personnel shall be employed at any time.

(Pub. L. 91-230, title VI, § 617, as added Pub. L. 94-142, § 5(a), Nov. 29, 1975, 89 Stat. 791, and amended Pub. L. 98-199, § 3(b), Dec. 2, 1983, 97 Stat. 1358.)

REFERENCES IN TEXT

Section 1418 of this title, referred to in subsec. (d), was amended generally by Pub. L. 98-199, § 8, Dec. 2, 1983, 97 Stat. 1360, and, as so amended, the subject matter of subsecs. (b), (c), and (d) of that section is generally contained in subsecs. (b) and (f).

CODIFICATION

In subsec. (b), the words "(and the Secretary, in carrying out the provisions of subsection (c) of this section)", preceding "shall issue", have been omitted as redundant in view of the amendment by Pub. L. 98-199 substituting "the Secretary" for "the Commissioner" following "of this subchapter,".

AMENDMENTS

1983—Pub. L. 98-199 substituting "Secretary" for "Commissioner" wherever appearing.

EFFECTIVE DATE OF 1983 AMENDMENT

Amendment by Pub. L. 98-199 effective Dec. 2, 1983, see section 18 of Pub. L. 98-199, set out as a note under section 1401 of this title.

EFFECTIVE DATE

Section effective Oct. 1, 1977, except for subsecs. (a)(1)(D) and (b), which are effective Nov. 29, 1975, see section 8 of Pub. L. 94-142, set out as an Effective Date of 1975 Amendment note under section 1411 of this title.

TRANSFER OF FUNCTIONS

"Secretary", meaning the Secretary of Education, was substituted for "Commissioner" in text pursuant to sections 301(a)(1) and 507 of Pub. L. 96-88, which are classified to sections 3441(a)(1) and 3507 of this title and which transferred all functions of the Commissioner of Education to the Secretary of Education.

SECTION REFERRED TO IN OTHER SECTIONS

This section is referred to in sections 1412 to 1414 of this title.

§ 1418. Evaluation

(a) Duties of Secretary

The Secretary shall directly or by grant, contract, or cooperative agreement, collect data and conduct studies, investigations, and evaluations—
(1) to assess progress in the implementation of this chapter, the impact, and the effectiveness of State and local efforts to provide free appropriate public education to all handicapped children and youth; and
(2) to provide Congress with information relevant to policymaking and provide Federal, State, and local educational agencies with information relevant to program management, administration, and effectiveness with respect to such education.

(b) Collection of data on education of handicapped children and youth; additional information

In carrying out the responsibilities under this section, the Secretary, on at least an annual basis, shall obtain data concerning programs and projects assisted under this chapter, and under other Federal laws relating to the education of handicapped children and youth, and such additional information, from State and local educational agencies and other appropriate sources, as is necessary for the implementation of this chapter including—
(1) the number of handicapped children and youth in each State receiving a free appropriate public education (special education and related services) by disability category and by age group (3-5, 6-11, 12-17, and 18-21);
(2) the number of handicapped children and youth in each State who are participating in regular educational programs, by disability category (consistent with the requirements of section 1412(5)(b) and section 1414(a)(1)(C)(iv) of this title), and the number of handicapped children and youth in separate classes, separate schools or facilities, or public or private residential facilities, or who have been otherwise removed from the regular education environment;
(3) the number of handicapped children and youth exiting the educational system each year through program completion or otherwise, by disability category and age, and anticipated services for the next year;
(4) the amount of Federal, State, and local funds expended in each State specifically for special education and related services (which may be based upon a sampling of data from State agencies including State and local educational agencies);

(5) the number and type of personnel that are employed in the provision of special education and related services to handicapped children and youth by disability category served, and the estimated number and type of additional personnel by disability category needed to adequately carry out the policy established by this chapter; and

(6) a description of the special education and related services needed to fully implement the[2] chapter throughout each State, including estimates of the number of handicapped children and youth within each disability by age group (3-5, 6-11, 12-17, and 18-21) in need of improved services and the type of programs and services in need of improvement.

(c) Evaluations studies by grant, contract, or cooperative agreement

The Secretary shall, by grant, contract, or cooperative agreement, provide for evaluation studies to determine the impact of this chapter. Each such evaluation shall include recommendations for improvement of the programs under this chapter. The Secretary shall, not later than July 1 of each year, submit to the appropriate committees of each House of the Congress and publish in the Federal Register proposed evaluation priorities for review and comment.

(d) Cooperative agreements with State educational agencies

(1) The Secretary is authorized to enter into cooperative agreements with State educational agencies to carry out studies to assess the impact and effectiveness of programs assisted under the[2] chapter.

(2) Such agreements shall—

(A) provide for the payment of not to exceed 60 per centum of the total cost of studies conducted by a participating State educational agency to assess the impact and effectiveness of programs assisted under the[2] chapter; and

(B) be developed in consultation with the State Advisory Panel established under this chapter, the local educational agencies, and others involved in or concerned with the education of handicapped children and youth.

(3) The Secretary shall provide technical assistance to participating State Educational agencies in the implementation of the study design, analysis, and reporting procedures.

(4) In addition, the Secretary shall disseminate information from such studies to State educational agencies, and as appropriate, others involved in, or concerned with the education of handicapped children and youth.

(e) Specifically mandated studies

(1) At least one study shall be a longitudinal study of a sample of handicapped students, encompassing the full range of handicapping conditions, examining their educational progress while in special education and their occupational, educational, and independent living status after graduating from secondary school or otherwise leaving special education.

(2) At least one study shall focus on obtaining and compiling current information available through State educational agencies and local educa-

tional agencies and other service providers, regarding State and local expenditures for educational services for handicapped students (including special education and related services), and gather information needed in order to calculate a range of per pupil expenditures by handicapping condition.

(f) Annual report

(1) Not later than one hundred and twenty days after the close of each fiscal year, the Secretary shall publish and disseminate an annual report on the progress being made toward the provision of a free appropriate public education to all handicapped children and youth. The annual report is to be transmitted to the appropriate committees of each House of Congress and the National Advisory Committee on the Education of Handicapped Children and Youth, and published and disseminated in sufficient quantities to the education community at large and to other interest parties.

(2) The Secretary shall include in each annual report—

(A) an index and summary of each evaluation activity and results of studies conducted under subsection (c) of this section:

(B) a compilation and analysis of data gathered under subsection (b) of this section;

(C) a description of findings and determinations resulting from monitoring reviews of State implementation of this subchapter;

(D) an analysis and evaluation of the participation of handicapped children and youth in vocational education programs and services;

(E) an analysis and evaluation of the effectiveness of procedures undertaken by each State educational agency, local educational agency, and intermediate educational unit to ensure that handicapped children and youth receive special education and related services in the least restrictive environment commensurate with their needs and to improve programs of instruction for handicapped children and youth in day or residential facilities; and

(F) any recommendations for change in the provisions of this chapter or any other Federal law providing support for the education of handicapped children and youth.

(3) In the annual report for fiscal year 1985 (published in 1986) and for every third year thereafter, the Secretary shall include in the annual report—

(A) an index of current projects funded under subchapters III through VI of this chapter; and

(B) data reported under sections 1421, 1422, 1423, 1426, 1434, 1441, and 1453 of this title.

(g) Authorization of appropriations

There are authorized to be appropriated $3,100,000 for fiscal year 1984, $3,270,000 for fiscal year 1985, and $3,440,000 for fiscal year 1986 to carry out the provisions of this section.

(Pub. L. 91-230, title VI, § 618, as added Pub. L. 94-142, § 5(a), Nov. 29, 1975, 89 Stat. 791, and amended Pub. L. 98-199, §§ 3(b), 8, Dec. 2, 1983, 97 Stat. 1358, 1360.)

AMENDMENTS

1983—Pub. L. 98-199, § 8, amended section generally. Prior to the amendment, subsec. (a) required the Secretary to measure and evaluate the impact of the program authorized under this subchapter and the effectiveness of State efforts to assure the free appropriate public education of all handicapped children; subsec. (b) required the Secretary to conduct, directly or by grant or contract, such studies, investigations, and evaluations as are necessary to assure effective implementation of this subchapter, and in carrying out his responsibilities under this section, to (1), through the National Center for Education Statistics, provide to the appropriate committees of each House of the Congress and to the general public at least annually, and shall update at least annually, programmatic information concerning programs and projects assisted under this subchapter and other Federal programs supporting the education of handicapped children, and such information from State and local educational agencies and other appropriate sources necessary for the implementation of this subchapter, including— (A) the number of handicapped children in each State, within each disability, who require special education and related services; (B) the number of handicapped children in each State, within each disability, receiving a free appropriate public education and the number of handicapped children who need and are not receiving a free appropriate public education in each such State; (C) the number of handicapped children in each State, within each disability, who are participating in regular educational programs, consistent with the requirements of section 1412(5)(B) and section 1414(a)(1)(C)(iv) of this title, and the number of handicapped children who have been placed in separate classes or separate school facilities, or who have been otherwise removed from the regular education environment; (D) the number of handicapped children who are enrolled in public or private institutions in each State and who are receiving a free appropriate public education, and the number of handicapped children who are in such institutions and who are not receiving a free appropriate public education; (E) the amount of Federal, State, and local expenditures in each State specifically available for special education and related services; and (F) the number of personnel, by disability category, employed in the education of handicapped children, and the estimated number of additional personnel needed to adequately carry out the policy established by this chapter; and (2) provide for the evaluation of programs and projects assisted under this subchapter through (A) the development of effective methods and procedures for evaluation; (B) the testing and validation of such evaluation methods and procedures; and (C) conducting actual evaluation studies designed to test the effectiveness of such programs and projects; subsec. (c) required the Secretary in developing and furnishing information under subclause (E) of clause (1) of subsection (b) of this section, to base such information upon a sampling of data available from State agencies, including the State educational agencies, and local educational agencies; subsec. (d) required the Secretary (1), not later than one hundred twenty days after the close of each fiscal year, to transmit to the appropriate committees of each House of the Congress a report on the progress being made toward the provision of free appropriate public education to all handicapped children, including a detailed description of all evaluation activities conducted under subsection (b) of this section, and (2) to include in each such report (A) an analysis and evaluation of the effectiveness of procedures undertaken by each State educational agency, local educational agency, and intermediate educational unit to assure that handicapped children receive special education and related services in the least restrictive environment commensurate with their needs and to improve programs of instruction for handicapped children in day or residential facilities; (B) any recommendations for change in the provisions of this subchapter, or any other Federal law providing support for the education of handicapped children; and (C) an evaluation of the effectiveness of the procedures undertaken by each such agency or unit to prevent erroneous classification of children as eligible to be counted under section 1411 of this title, including actions undertaken by the Secretary to carry out provisions of this chapter relating to such erroneous classification, and, in order to carry out such analyses and evaluations, to conduct a statistically valid survey for assessing the effectiveness of individualized educational programs; and subsec. (e) authorized to be appropriated for each fiscal year such sums as may be necessary to carry out the provisions of this section.

Subsec. (a) to (d). Publ L. 98-199, § 3(b), substituted "Secretary" for "Commissioner" wherever appearing.

EFFECTIVE DATE OF 1983 AMENDMENT

Amendment by Pub. L. 98-199 effective Dec. 2, 1983, see section 18 of Pub. L. 98-199, set out as a note under section 1401 of this title.

EFFECTIVE DATE

Section effective Oct. 1, 1977, except for subsec. (a), which is effective Nov. 29, 1975, see section 8 of Pub. L. 94-142, set out as an Effective Date of 1975 Amendment note under section 1411 of this title.

TRANSFER OF FUNCTIONS

"Secretary", meaning the Secretary of Education, was substituted for "Commissioner" in subsecs. (a) to (d) pursuant to sections 301(a)(1) and 507 of Pub. L. 96-88, which are classified to sections 3441(a)(1) and 3507 of this title and which transferred all functions of the Commissioner of Education to the Secretary of Education.

LIMITATION ON AUTHORIZATION OF APPROPRIATIONS FOR FISCAL YEARS 1982 AND 1983

Pub. L. 97-35, title VI, § 602(a)(2), Aug. 13, 1981, 95 Stat. 483, provided that: "There is authorized to be appropriated to carry out section 618 of such Act [this section] $2,300,000 for each of the fiscal years 1982 and 1983."

SECTION REFERRED TO IN OTHER SECTIONS

This section is referred to in sections 1413, 1417, 1421, 1422, 1423, 1426, 1434, 1441 of this title.

§ 1419. Incentive grants

(a) Authority to make grants

The Secretary shall make a grant to any State which—
  (1) has met the eligibility requirements of section 1412 of this title;
  (2) has a State plan approved under section 1413 of this title; and
  (3) provides special education and related services to handicapped children aged three to five, inclusive, who are counted for the purposes of section 1411(a)(1)(A) of this title.

The maximum amount of the grant for each fiscal year which a State may receive under this section shall be $300 for each such child in that State.

(b) Application

Each State which—
  (1) has met the eligibility requirements of section 1412 of this title,

(2) has a State plan approved under section 1413 of this title, and

(3) desires to receive a grant under this section,

shall make an application to the Secretary at such time, in such manner, and containing or accompanied by such information, as the Secretary may reasonably require.

(c) Payment

The Secretary shall pay to each State having an application approved under subsection (b) of this section the amount to which the State is entitled under this section, which amount shall be used for the purpose of providing the services specified in clause (3) of subsection (a) of this section, and for providing special education and related services for handicapped children from birth to three years of age.

(d) Ratable reduction or increase of payments

If the sums appropriated for any fiscal year for making payments to States under this section are not sufficient to pay in full the maximum amounts which all States may receive under this subchapter for such fiscal year, the maximum amounts which all States may receive under this subchapter for such fiscal year shall be ratably reduced. In case additional funds become available for making such payments for any fiscal year during which the preceding sentence is applicable, such reduced amounts shall be increased on the same basis as they were reduced.

(e) Authorization of appropriations

In addition to the sums necessary to pay the entitlements under section 1411 of this title, there are authorized to be appropriated for each fiscal year such sums as may be necessary to carry out the provisions of this section.

(Pub. L. 91-230, title VI, § 619, as added Pub. L. 94-142, § 5(a), Nov. 29, 1975, 89 Stat. 793, and amended Pub. L. 98-199, §§ 3(b), 9, Dec. 2, 1983, 97 Stat. 1358, 1363.)

AMENDMENTS

1983—Subsecs. (a), (b). Pub. L. 98-199, § 3(b), substituted "Secretary" for "Commissioner".

Subsec. (c). Pub. L. 98-199, §§ 3(b), 9, authorized use of payments for providing special education and related services for handicapped children from birth to three years of age and substituted "Secretary" for "Commissioner".

EFFECTIVE DATE OF 1983 AMENDMENT

Amendment by Pub. L. 98-199 effective Dec. 2, 1983, see section 18 of Pub. L. 98-199, set out as a note under section 1401 of this title.

EFFECTIVE DATE

Section effective Oct. 1, 1977, see section 8 of Pub. L. 94-142, set out as an Effective Date of 1975 Amendment note under section 1411 of this title.

TRANSFER OF FUNCTIONS

"Secretary", meaning the Secretary of Education, was substituted for "Commissioner" in subsecs. (a) to (c) pursuant to sections 301(a)(1) and 507 of Pub. L. 96-88, which are classified to sections 3441(a)(1) and 3507 of this title and which transferred all functions of the Commissioner of Education to the Secretary of Education.

LIMITATION ON AUTHORIZATION OF APPROPRIATIONS FOR FISCAL YEARS 1982 AND 1983

Pub. L. 97-35, title VI, § 602(a)(3), Aug. 13, 1981, 95 Stat. 483, provided that: "There is authorized to be appropriated to carry out section 619 of such Act [this section] $25,000,000 for each of the fiscal years 1982 and 1983."

SECTION REFERRED TO IN OTHER SECTIONS

This section is referred to in sections 1411, 1423 of this title.

§ 1420. Payments

(a) Payments to States; distribution by States to local educational agencies and intermediate educational units

The Secretary shall make payments to each State in amounts which the State educational agency of such State is eligible to receive under this subchapter. Any State educational agency receiving payments under this subsection shall distribute payments to the local educational agencies and intermediate educational units of such State in amounts which such agencies and units are eligible to receive under this subchapter after the State educational agency has approved applications of such agencies or units for payments in accordance with section 1414(b) of this title.

(b) Advances, reimbursements, and installments

Payments under this subchapter may be made in advance or by way of reimbursement and in such installments as the Secretary may determine necessary.

(Pub. L. 91-230, title VI, § 620, as added Pub. L. 94-142, § 5(a), Nov. 29, 1975, 89 Stat. 793, and amended Pub. L. 98-199, § 3(b), Dec. 2, 1983, 97 Stat. 1358.)

AMENDMENTS

1983—Pub. L. 98-199 substituted "Secretary" for "Commissioner" wherever appearing.

EFFECTIVE DATE OF 1983 AMENDMENT

Amendment by Pub. L. 98-199 effective Dec. 2, 1983, see section 18 of Pub. L. 98-199, set out as a note under section 1401 of this title.

EFFECTIVE DATE

Section effective Oct. 1, 1977, see section 8 of Pub. L. 94-142, set out as an Effective Date of 1975 Amendment note under section 1411 of this title.

TRANSFER OF FUNCTIONS

"Secretary", meaning the Secretary of Education, was substituted for "Commissioner" in text pursuant to sections 301(a)(1) and 507 of Pub. L. 96-88, which are classified to sections 3441(a)(1) and 3507 of this title and which transferred all functions of the Commissioner of Education to the Secretary of Education.

SECTION REFERRED TO IN OTHER SECTIONS

This section is referred to in section 1414 of this title.

SUBCHAPTER III—CENTERS AND SERVICES TO MEET SPECIAL NEEDS OF THE HANDICAPPED

SUBCHAPTER REFERRED TO IN OTHER SECTIONS

This subchapter is referred to in sections 1401, 1418, 1443 of this title.

§ 1421. Regional resource centers

(a) Establishment; functions

The Secretary is authorized to make grants to, or to enter into contracts or cooperative agreements with, institutions of higher education, private nonprofit organizations, State educational agencies, or combinations of such agencies and institutions (which combinations may include one or more local educational agencies) within particular regions of the United States, to pay all or part of the cost of the establishment and operation of regional resource centers. Each regional resource center shall provide consultation, technical assistance, and training to State educational agencies and through such State agencies to local educational agencies. Each center established or operated under this section shall—

(1) assist in identifying and solving persistent problems in providing quality special education and related services for handicapped children and youth;

(2) assist in developing, identifying, and replicating successful programs and practices which will improve special education and related services to handicapped children and youth and their families;

(3) gather and disseminate information to all State educational agencies within the region and coordinate activities with other centers assisted under this section and other relevant projects conducted by the Department of Education; and

(4) assist in the improvement of information dissemination to and training activities for professionals and parents of handicapped children.

(b) Considerations governing approval of application

In determining whether to approve an application for a project under this section, the Secretary shall consider the need for such a center in the region to be served by the applicant and the capability of the applicant to fulfill the responsibilities under subsection (a) of this section.

(c) Annual report; summary of information

Each regional resource center shall report a summary of materials produced or developed and this information shall be included in the annual report to Congress required under section 1418 of this title.

(Pub. L. 91-230, title VI, § 621, Apr. 13, 1970, 84 Stat. 181; Pub. L. 98-199, §§ 3(b), 10, Dec. 2, 1983, 97 Stat. 1358, 1363.)

AMENDMENTS

1983—Pub. L. 98-199, § 10, amended section generally. Prior to amendment, section read:

"(a) The Secretary is authorized to make grants to or contracts with institutions of higher education, State educational agencies, or combinations of such agencies or institutions, which combinations may include one or more local educational agencies, within particular regions of the United States, to pay all or part of the cost of the establishment and operation of regional centers which will develop and apply the best methods of appraising the special educational needs of handicapped children referred to them and will provide other services to assist in meeting such needs. Centers established or operated under this section shall (1) provide testing and educational evaluation to determine the special educational needs of handicapped children referred to such centers, (2) develop educational programs to meet those needs, and (3) assist schools and other appropriate agencies, organizations, and institutions in providing such educational programs through services such as consultation (including, in appropriate cases, consultation with parents or teachers of handicapped children at such regional centers), periodic reexamination and reevaluation of special educational programs, and other technical services.

"(b) In determining whether to approve an application for a project under this section, the Secretary shall consider the need for such a center in the region to be served by the applicant and the capability of the applicant to develop and apply, with the assistance of funds under this section, new methods, techniques, devices, or facilities relating to educational evaluation or education of handicapped children."

Pub. L. 98-199, § 3(b), substituted "Secretary" for "Commissioner" wherever appearing.

EFFECTIVE DATE OF 1983 AMENDMENT

Amendment by Pub. L. 98-199 effective Dec. 2, 1983, with an exception for previously obligated funds and certain interim provisions for financial assistance, see section 18 of Pub. L. 98-199 set out as a note under section 1401 of this title.

TRANSFER OF FUNCTIONS

"Secretary", meaning the Secretary of Education, was substituted for "Commissioner" in text pursuant to sections 301(a)(1) and 507 of Pub. L. 96-88, which are classified to sections 3441(a)(1) and 3507 of this title and which transferred all functions of the Commissioner of Education to the Secretary of Education.

LIMITATION ON AUTHORIZATION OF APPROPRIATIONS FOR FISCAL YEARS 1982 AND 1983

Pub. L. 97-35, title VI, § 602(b)(1), (4), Aug. 13, 1981, 95 Stat. 483, provided that:

"(1) There is authorized to be appropriated to carry out section 621 of the Education of the Handicapped Act (relating to regional resource centers) [this section] $9,800,000 for each of the fiscal years 1982 and 1983.

"(4) There is authorized to be appropriated to carry out sections 621 and 624 of such Act (relating to projects for severely handicapped children) [sections 1421 and 1424 of this title] $5,000,000 for each of the fiscal years 1982 and 1983."

SECTION REFERRED TO IN OTHER SECTIONS

This section is referred to in sections 1418, 1427 of this title.

§ 1422. Services for deaf-blind children and youth

(a) Grant and contract authority; types and scope of programs; governing considerations

(1) The Secretary is authorized to make grants to, or to enter into cooperative agreements or contracts with, public or nonprofit private agencies, institutions, or organizations to assist State educational agencies to—

    (A) assure deaf-blind children and youth provision of special education and related services as well as vocational and transitional services; and

    (B) make available to deaf-blind youth upon attaining the year of twenty-two, programs and services to facilitate their transition from educational to other services.

(2) A grant, cooperative agreement, or contract pursuant to paragraph (1)(A) may be made only for programs providing (A) technical assistance to agencies, institutions, or organizations providing educational services to deaf-blind children or youth; (B) preservice or inservice training to paraprofessionals, professionals, or related services personnel preparing to serve, or serving, deaf-blind children or youth; (C) replication of successful innovative approaches to providing educational or related services to deaf-blind children and youth; and (D) facilitation of parental involvement in the education of their deaf-blind children and youth. Such programs may include—

    (i) the diagnosis and educational evaluation of children and youth at risk of being certified deaf-blind;

    (ii) programs of adjustment, education, and orientation for deaf-blind children and youth; and

    (iii) consultative, counseling, and training services for the families of deaf-blind children and youth.

(3) A grant, cooperative agreement, or contract pursuant to paragraph (1)(B) may be made only for programs providing (A) technical assistance to agencies, institutions, and organizations serving, or proposing to serve, deaf-blind individuals who have attained age twenty-two years; (B) training or inservice training to paraprofessionals or professionals serving, or preparing to serve, such individuals; and (C) assistance in the development or replication of successful innovative approaches to providing rehabilitative, semi-supervised, or independent living programs.

(4) In carrying out this subsection, the Secretary shall take into consideration the need for a center for deaf-blind children and youth in light of the general availability and quality of existing services for such children and youth in the part of the country involved.

(b) Contract authority for regional programs of technical assistance

The Secretary is also authorized to enter into a limited number of cooperative agreements or contracts to establish and support regional programs for the provision of technical assistance in the education of deaf-blind children and youth.

(c) Annual report to Secretary; examination of numbers and services and revision of numbers; annual report to Congress: summary of data

(1) Programs supported under this section shall report annually to the Secretary on (A) the numbers of deaf-blind children and youth served by age, severity, and nature of deaf-blindness; (B) the number of paraprofessionals, professionals, and family members directly served by each activity; and (C) the types of services provided.

(2) The Secretary shall examine the number of deaf-blind children and youth (A) reported under subparagraph (c)(1)(A) and by the States; (B) served by the programs under subchapter II of this chapter and subpart 2 of part B, title I, of the Elementary and Secondary Education Act of 1965 [20 U.S.C. 2771 et seq.] (as modified by chapter 1 of the Education Consolidation and Improvement Act of 1981 [20 U.S.C. 3801 et seq.]); and (C) the Deaf-Blind Registry of each State. The Secretary shall revise the count of deaf-blind children and youth to reflect the most accurate count.

(3) The Secretary shall summarize these data for submission in the annual report required under section 1418 of this title.

(d) Dissemination of materials and information concerning working practices

The Secretary shall disseminate materials and information concerning effective practices in working with deaf-blind children and youth.

(Pub. L. 91-230, title VI, § 622, Apr. 13, 1970, 83 Stat. 182; Pub. L. 98-199, §§ 3(b), 10, Dec. 2, 1983, 97 Stat. 1358, 1364.)

REFERENCES IN TEXT

The Elementary and Secondary Education Act of 1965, referred to in subsec. (c)(2), is Pub. L. 89-10, Apr. 11, 1965, 79 Stat. 27, as amended generally by Pub. L. 95-561, Nov. 1, 1978, 92 Stat. 2152. Subpart 2 of part B of title I of the 1965 Act is classified generally to subpart 2 (§ 2771 et seq.) of part B of subchapter I of chapter 47 of this title. For complete classification of this Act to the Code, see Short title note set out under section 2701 of this title and Tables.

The Education Consolidation and Improvement Act of 1981, referred to in subsec. (c)(2), is subtitle D [§§ 551 to 596] of title V of Pub. L. 97-35, Aug. 13, 1981, 95 Stat. 463, as amended. Chapter 1 of the Act is classified generally to subchapter 1 [§ 3801 et seq.] of chapter 51 of this title. For complete classification of this Act to the Code, see Short Title note set out under section 3801 of this title and Tables.

AMENDMENTS

1983—Pub. L. 98-199, § 10, amended section generally, substituting in subsec. (a) provisions for grant and contract authority for types and scope of certain programs for provisions containing Congressional declaration of policy in providing certain services for deaf-blind children through limited number of model centers; substituting in subsec. (b) provisions respecting contract authority for regional programs of technical assistance for provisions respecting grant and contract authority for establishment and operation of model centers for deaf-blind children; adding subsec. (c) and redesignating former subsec. (c) as subsec. (a)(4); and substituting in subsec. (d) provisions respecting dissemination of materials and information concerning working practices for provisions respecting necessary services to be provided by model centers.

Pub. L. 98-199, § 3(b), substituted "Secretary" for "Commissioner" wherever appearing.

EFFECTIVE DATE OF 1983 AMENDMENT

Amendment by Pub. L. 98-199 effective Dec. 2, 1983, with an exception for previously obligated funds and certain interim provisions for financial assistance, see section 18 of Pub. L. 98-199 set out as a note under section 1401 of this title.

TRANSFER OF FUNCTIONS

"Secretary", meaning the Secretary of Education, was substituted for "Commissioner" in subsecs. (b) to (d) pursuant to sections 301(a)(1) and 507 of Pub. L. 96-88, which are classified to sections 3441(a)(1) and 3507 of this title and which transferred all functions of the Commissioner of Education to the Secretary of Education.

LIMITATION ON AUTHORIZATION OF APPROPRIATIONS
FOR FISCAL YEARS 1982 AND 1983

Pub. L. 97-35, title VI, § 602(b)(2), Aug. 13, 1981, 95 Stat. 483, provided that: "There is authorized to be appropriated to carry out section 622 of such Act [this section] $16,000,000 for each of the fiscal years 1982 and 1983."

SECTION REFERRED TO IN OTHER SECTIONS

This section is referred to in sections 1418, 1427 of this title.

§ 1423. Experimental preschool and early education programs for handicapped children

(a) Authorization; special problems of handicapped; community coordination of programs; geographical dispersion; Federal share: non-Federal contributions; "handicapped children" defined

(1) The Secretary is authorized to arrange by contract, grant, or cooperative agreement with appropriate public agencies and private nonprofit organizations, for the development and operation of programs of experimental preschool and early education for handicapped children which the Secretary determines show promise of promoting a comprehensive and strengthened approach to the special problems of such children. Such programs shall include activities and services designed to (1) facilitate the intellectual, emotional, physical, mental, social, and language development of such children; (2) encourage the participation of the parents of such children in the development and operation of any such program; and (3) acquaint the community to be served by any such program with the problems and potentialities of such children.

(2) Programs authorized by this subsection shall be coordinated with similar programs in the schools operated or supported by State or local educational agencies of the community to be served.

(3) As much as is feasible, such programs shall be geographically dispersed throughout the Nation in urban as well as rural areas.

(4) No arrangement pursuant to this subsection shall provide for the payment of more than 90 per centum of the total annual costs of development, operation, and evaluation of any program. Non-Federal contributions may be in cash or in kind, fairly evaluated, including, but not limited to, plant, equipment, and services.

(5) For purposes of this subsection the term "handicapped children" includes children from birth through eight years of age.

(b) Special education and related services through comprehensive delivery system for handicapped children of certain age; types of grants; applications for grants; annual report: additional information

(1) Subject to paragraph (2), the Secretary is authorized to make a grant to each State through the State educational agency or other State agency to assist such State agency in planning, developing, and implementing a comprehensive delivery system for the provision of special education and related services to handicapped children from birth through five years of age.

(2) The Secretary shall make one of the following types of grants (authorized under paragraph (1)) to any State which submits an application which meets the requirements of this subsection:

(A) Planning grant

A grant for a maximum of two years for the purpose of assessing needs within the State and establishing a procedure and design for the development of a State plan which includes parent participation and training of professionals and others.

(B) Development grant

A grant for a maximum of three years for the purpose of developing a comprehensive State plan, and gaining approval of this plan from the State Board of Education, the Commissioner of Education, or other designated official of the appropriate State agency.

(C) Implementation grant

A grant for a maximum of three years for the purpose of implementing and evaluating the comprehensive State plan. A State must apply for annual renewal of such grant.

(3) Each State educational agency or other State agency desiring to receive a grant under this subsection shall submit an application at such time, in such manner, and accompanied by such information as the Secretary considers necessary. Each such application shall contain assurances and evidence that:

(A) The State agency receiving the grant will coordinate with other appropriate State agencies (including the State educational agency) in car-

(Pub. L. 91-230, title VI, § 623, Apr. 13, 1970, 84 Stat. 183; Pub. L. 98-199, §§ 3(b), 10, Dec. 2, 1983, 97 Stat. 1358, 1365.)

AMENDMENTS

1983—Pub. L. 98-199, § 10, amended section generally. Prior to amendment, section read:

"(a) The Secretary is authorized to arrange by contract, grant, or otherwise with appropriate public agencies and private nonprofit organizations, for the development and carrying out by such agencies and organizations of experimental preschool and early education programs for handicapped children which the Secretary determines show promise of promoting a comprehensive and strengthened approach to the special problems of such children. Such programs shall be distributed to the greatest extent possible throughout the Nation, and shall be carried out both in urban and in rural areas. Such programs shall include activities and services designed to (1) facilitate the intellectual, emotional, physical, mental, social, and language development of such children; (2) encourage the participation of the parents of such children in the development and operation of any such program; and (3) acquaint the community to be served by any such program with the problems and potentialities of such children.

"(b) Each arrangement for developing or carrying out a program authorized by this section shall provide for the effective coordination of each such program with similar programs in the schools of the community to be served by such a program.

"(c) No arrangement pursuant to this section shall provide for the payment of more than 90 per centum of the cost of developing, carrying out, or evaluating such a program. Non-Federal contributions may be in cash or in kind, fairly evaluated, including, but not limited to, plant, equipment, and services."

Subsec. (a). Pub. L. 98-199, § 3(b), substituted "Secretary" for "Commissioner" wherever appearing.

EFFECTIVE DATE OF 1983 AMENDMENT

Amendment by Pub. L. 98-199 effective Dec. 2, 1983, with an exception for previously obligated funds and certain interim provisions for financial assistance, see section 18 of Pub. L. 98-199 set out as a note under section 1401 of this title.

TRANSFER OF FUNCTIONS

"Secretary", meaning the Secretary of Education, was substituted for "Commissioner" in subsec. (a) pursuant to sections 301(a)(1) and 507 of Pub. L. 96-88, which are classified to sections 3441(a)(1) and 3507 of this title and which transferred all functions of the Commissioner of Education to the Secretary of Education.

LIMITATION ON AUTHORIZATION OF APPROPRIATIONS FOR FISCAL YEARS 1982 AND 1983

Pub. L. 97-35, title VI, § 602(b)(3), Aug. 13, 1981, 95 Stat. 483, provided that: "There is authorized to be appropriated to carry out section 623 of such Act [this section] $20,000,000 for each of the fiscal years 1982 and 1983."

SECTION REFERRED TO IN OTHER SECTIONS

This section is referred to in sections 1418, 1427 of this title.

§ 1424. Research, innovation, training, and dissemination activities in connection with model centers and services for the handicapped

(a) Grant and contract authority

The Secretary is authorized to make grants to, or to enter into contracts or cooperative agreements with such organizations or institutions, as are determined by the Secretary to be appropriate, consistent with the purposes of this subchapter, for—

(1) research to identify and meet the full range of special needs of handicapped children and youth;

(2) the development or demonstration of new, or improvements in existing, methods, approaches, or techniques which would contribute to

the adjustment and education of handicapped children and youth;
(3) training of personnel for programs specifically designed for handicapped children; and
(4) dissemination of materials and information about practices found effective in working with such children and youth.

(b) Coordination of activities with similar activities under other sections of this chapter

In making grants and contracts under this section, the Secretary shall ensure that the activities funded under such grants and contracts will be coordinated with similar activities funded from grants and contracts under other sections of this chapter.

(c) Needs of severely handicapped

In carrying out the provisions of this section the Secretary is authorized to address the needs of the severely handicapped.

(Pub. L. 91-230, title VI, § 624, Apr. 13, 1970, 84 Stat. 183; Pub. L. 98-199, §§ 3(b), 10, Dec. 2, 1983, 97 Stat. 1358, 1366.)

AMENDMENTS

1983—Pub. L. 98-199, § 10, amended section generally. Prior to amendment, subsec. (a) authorized the Secretary, either as part of any grant or contract under this subchapter, or by separate grant to, or contract with, an agency, organization, or institution operating a center or providing a service which meets such requirements as the Secretary determines to be appropriate, consistent with the purposes of this subchapter, to pay all or part of the cost of such activities as—(1) research to identify and meet the full range of special needs of handicapped children; (2) development or demonstration of new, or improvements in existing, methods, approaches, or techniques, which would contribute to the adjustment and education of such children; (3) training (either directly or otherwise) of professional and allied personnel engaged or preparing to engage in programs specifically designed for such children, including payment of stipends for trainees and allowances for travel and other expenses for them and their dependents; and (4) dissemination of materials and information about practices found effective in working with such children; and subsec. (b) required the Secretary, in making grants and contracts under this section, to insure that the activities funded under such grants and contracts be coordinated with similar activities funded from grants and contracts under other subchapters of this chapter.

Pub. L. 98-199, § 3(b), substituted "Secretary" for "Commissioner" wherever appearing.

EFFECTIVE DATE OF 1983 AMENDMENT

Amendment by Pub. L. 98-199 effective Dec. 2, 1983, with an exception for previously obligated funds and certain interim provisions for financial assistance, see section 18 of Pub. L. 98-199 set out as a note under section 1401 of this title.

TRANSFER OF FUNCTIONS

"Secretary", meaning the Secretary of Education, was substituted for "Commissioner" in text pursuant to sections 301(a)(1) and 507 of Pub. L. 96-88, which are classified to sections 3441(a)(1) and 507 of Pub. L. 96-88, which are classified to sections 3441(a)(1) and 3507 of this title and which transferred all functions of the Commissioner of Education to the Secretary of Education.

LIMITATION ON AUTHORIZATION OF APPROPRIATIONS FOR FISCAL YEARS 1982 AND 1983

Authorization to appropriate $5,000,000 for each of the fiscal years 1982 and 1983 to carry out sections 1421 and 1424 of this title (relating to projects for severely handicapped children), see section 602(b)(4) of Pub. L. 97-35, set out as a note under section 1421 of this title.

§ 1424a. Development, operation, and dissemination of specially designed model programs of postsecondary, vocational, technical, continuing, or adult education; grant and contract authority; priority of programs; "handicapped individual" defined

(a)(1) The Secretary is authorized to make grants to or enter into contracts with State educational agencies, institutions of higher education, junior and community colleges, vocational and technical institutions, and other appropriate nonprofit educational agencies for the development, operation, and dissemination of specially designed model programs of post-secondary, vocational, technical, continuing, or adult education for handicapped individuals.

(2) In making grants or contracts on a competitive basis under this section, the Secretary shall give priority consideration to the four regional centers for the deaf and to model programs for individuals with handicapping conditions other than deafness—

(A) for developing and adapting programs of postsecondary, vocational, technical, continuing, or adult education to meet the special needs of handicapped individuals; and

(B) for programs that coordinate, facilitate, and encourage education of handicapped individuals with their nonhandicapped peers.

(3) Of the sums made available for programs under this section, not less than $2,000,000 shall first be available for the four regional centers for the deaf.

(b) For the purposes of this section the term "handicapped individuals" means individuals who are mentally retarded, hard of hearing, deaf, speech or language impaired, visually handicapped, seriously emotionally disturbed, orthopedically impaired, or other health impaired individuals, or individuals with specific learning disabilities who by reason thereof require special education and related services.

(Pub. L. 91-230, title VI, § 625, as added Pub. L. 93-380, title VI, § 616, Aug, 21, 1974, 88 Stat. 584, and amended Pub. L. 98-199, §§ 3(b), 10, Dec. 2, 1983, 97 Stat. 1358, 1367.)

AMENDMENTS

1983—Pub. L. 98-199, § 10, amended section generally. Prior to amendment, subsec. (a) authorized the Secretary to make grants to or contracts with institutions of higher education, including junior and community colleges, vocational and technical institutions, and other appropriate nonprofit educational agencies for the development and operation of specially designed or modified programs of vocational, technical, postsecondary, or adult education for deaf or other handicapped persons; subsec. (b) required the Secretary in making grants or contracts authorized by this section, to give priority consideration to (1) programs serving multistate regions or large population centers; (2) programs adapting existing programs of vocational, technical, postsecondary, or adult education to the special needs of handicapped persons; and (3) programs designed to serve areas where a need for such services is clearly demonstrated; and subsec. (c), for purposes of this section, defined the term "handicapped persons" as meaning persons who are mentally retarded, hard of hearing, deaf, speech impaired, visually handicapped, emotionally disturbed, crippled, or in other ways health impaired and by reason thereof require special education programming and related services.

Subsec. (a), (b). Pub. L. 98-199, § 3(b), substituted "Secretary" for "Commissioner".

EFFECTIVE DATE OF 1983 AMENDMENT

Amendment by Pub. L. 98-199 effective Dec. 2, 1983, with an exception for previously obligated funds and certain interim provisions for financial assistance, see section 18 of Pub. L. 98-199 set out as a note under section 1401 of this title.

EFFECTIVE DATE

Section effective on and after sixtieth day after Aug. 21, 1974, see section 2(c) of Pub. L. 93-380, set out as an Effective Date of 1974 Amendment note under section 244 of this title.

TRANSFER OF FUNCTIONS

"Secretary", meaning the Secretary of Education, was substituted for "Commissioner" in subsecs. (a) and (b) pursuant to sections 301(a)(1) and 507 of Pub. L. 96-88, which are classified to sections 3441(a)(1) and 3507 of this title and which transferred all functions of the Commissioner of Education to the Secretary of Education

LIMITATION ON AUTHORIZATION OF APPROPRIATIONS
FOR FISCAL YEARS 1982 AND 1983

Pub. L. 97-35, title VI, § 602(b)(5), Aug. 13, 1981, 95 Stat. 483, provided that: "There is authorized to be appropriated to carry out section 625 of such Act [this section] $4,000,000 for each of the fiscal years 1982 and 1983."

SECTION REFERRED TO IN OTHER SECTIONS

This section is referred to in section 1427 of this title.

§ 1425. Secondary education and transitional services for handicapped youth

(a) Grant and contract authority; statement of purposes

The Secretary is authorized to make grants to, or enter into contracts with, institutions of higher education, State educational agencies, local educational agencies, or other appropriate public and private nonprofit institutions or agencies (including the State job training coordinating councils and service delivery area administrative entities established under the Job Training Partnership Act (Public Law 97-300— [29 U.S.C. 1501 et seq.]) to—

(1) strengthen and coordinate education, training, and related services for handicapped youth to assist in the transitional process to postsecondary education, vocational training, competitive employment, continuing education, or adult services; and

(2) stimulate the improvement and development of programs for secondary special education.

(b) Description of specific projects

Projects assisted under this section may include—

(1) developing strategies and techniques for transition to independent living, vocational training, postsecondary education, and competitive employment for handicapped youth;

(2) establishing demonstration models for services and programs which emphasize vocational training, transitional services, and placement for handicapped youth;

(3) conducting demographic studies which provide information on the numbers, age levels, types of handicapping conditions, and services required for handicapped youth in need of transitional programs;

(4) specially designed vocational programs to increase the potential for competitive employment for handicapped youth;

(5) research and development projects for exemplary service delivery models and the replication and dissemination of successful models;

(6) initiating cooperative models between educational agencies and adult service agencies, including vocational rehabilitation, mental health, mental retardation, public employment, and employers, which facilitate the planning and developing of transitional services for handicapped youth to postsecondary education, vocational training, employment, continuing education, and adult services; and

(7) developing appropriate procedures for evaluating vocational training, placement, and transitional services for handicapped youth.

(c) Coordination of noneducational agency applicant with State educational agency

For purposes of subsections (b)(a) and (b)(2) of this section, if an applicant is not an educational agency, such applicant shall coordinate with the State educational agency.

(d) Participation in planning, development, and implementation of projects

Projects funded under this section shall to the extent appropriate provide for the direct participation of handicapped students and the parents of handicapped students in the planning, development, and implementation of such projects.

(e) Coordination of educational programs with vocational rehabilitation projects

The Secretary, as appropriate, shall coordinate programs described under this section with projects developed under section 777a of title 29.

(Pub. L. 91-230, title VI, § 626, formerly § 625, Apr. 13, 1970, 84 Stat. 183, renumbered Pub. L. 93-380, title VI, § 616, Aug. 21, 1974, 88 Stat. 584, and amended Pub. L. 98-199, §§3(b), 10, Dec. 2, 1983, 97 Stat. 1358, 1367.)

REFERENCES IN TEXT

The Job Training Partnership Act, referred to in subsec. (a), is Pub. L. 97-300, Oct. 13, 1982, 96 Stat. 1322, which is classified generally to chapter 19 (§ 1501 et seq.) of Title 29, Labor. For complete classification of this Act to the Code, see Short Title note set out under section 1501 of Title 29 and Tables.

AMENDMENTS

1983—Pub. L. 98-199, § 10, amended section generally, substituting provisions respecting secondary education and transitional services for handicapped youth for provisions requiring evaluation of programs assisted under this subchapter. See section 1426 of this title.

Pub. L. 98-199, § 3(b), substituted "Secretary" for "Commissioner".

EFFECTIVE DATE OF 1983 AMENDMENT

Amendment by Pub. L. 98-199 effective Dec. 2, 1983, with an exception for previously obligated funds and certain interim provisions for financial assistance, see section 18 of Pub. L. 98-199 set out as a note under section 401 of this title.

TRANSFER OF FUNCTIONS

"Secretary", meaning the Secretary of Education, was substituted for "Commissioner" in text pursuant to sections 301(a)(1) and 507 of Pub. L. 96-88, which are classified to sections 3441(a)(1) and 3507 of this title and which transferred all functions of the Commissioner of Education to the Secretary of Education.

SECTION REFERRED TO IN OTHER SECTIONS

This section is referred to in section 1427 of this title; title 29 section 777a.

§ 1426. Program evaluations; submittal of analyses to Congressional committees

The Secretary shall conduct, either directly or by contract, a thorough and continuing evaluation of the effectiveness of each program assisted under this subchapter. Results of the evaluations shall be analyzed and submitted to the appropriate committees of each House of Congress together with the annual report under section 1418 of this title.

(As amended Pub. L. 98-199, § 10, Dec. 2, 1983, 97 Stat. 1368.)

PRIOR PROVISIONS

Provisions similar to those comprising this section were contained in Pub. L. 91-230, title VI, § 626, formerly § 625, Apr. 13, 1970, 84 Stat. 183, renumbered Pub. L. 93-380, title VI, § 616, Aug. 21, 1974, 88 Stat. 584, which is classified to section 1425 of this title, prior to general amendment of this subchapter by Pub. L. 98-199, § 10, Dec. 2, 1983, 97 Stat. 1363.

AMENDMENTS

1983—Pub. L. 98-199 amended section generally substituting provisions respecting program evaluations and submittance of results of analysis to Congressional committees for provisions authorizing appropriations. See section 1427 of this title.

1977—Pub. L. 95-49 authorized appropriations of $19,000,000 for fiscal year 1978, $19,000,000 for fiscal year 1979, $21,000,000 for fiscal year 1980, $24,000,000 for fiscal year 1981, and $25,000,000 for fiscal year 1982 to carry out the provisions of section 1421 of this title, authorized appropriations of $22,000,000 for fiscal year 1978, $24,000,000 for fiscal year 1979, $26,000,000 for fiscal year 1980, $29,000,000 for fiscal year 1981, and $32,000,000 for fiscal year 1982 to carry out the provisions of section 1422 of this title, authorized appropriations of $25,000,000 for fiscal year 1978, $25,000,000 for fiscal year 1979, $25,000,000 for fiscal year 1980, $20,000,000 for fiscal year 1981, and $20,000,000 for fiscal year 1982 to carry out the provisions of section 1423 of this title, and authorized appropriations of $10,000,000 for fiscal year 1978, $12,000,000 for fiscal year 1979, $14,000,000 for fiscal year 1980, $16,000,000 for fiscal year 1981, and $16,000,000 for fiscal year 1982 to carry out the provisions of section 1424a of this title.

1974—Pub. L. 93-380, § 617, substituted appropriations authorization for carrying out: section 1421 of this title of $12,500,000; $18,000,000; and $19,000,000 for fiscal years ending June 30, 1975, 1976, and 1977; section 1422 of this title of $15,000,000; $20,000,000; and $20,000,000 for fiscal years ending June 30, 1975, 1976, 1977; section 1423 of this title of $25,500,000; $36,000,000; and $38,000,000 for fiscal years ending June 30, 1975, 1976, and 1977; and section 1424a of this title of $1,000,000 for fiscal year ending June 30, 1975, and necessary sums for fiscal years ending June 30, 1976, and 1977 for prior authorization of $36,500,000; $51,500,000; and $66,500,000 for fiscal years ending June 30, 1971, 1972, and 1973, for carrying out this subchapter.

EFFECTIVE DATE OF 1983 AMENDMENT

Amendment by Pub. L. 98-199 effective Dec. 2, 1983, with an exception for previously obligated funds and certain interim provisions for financial assistance, see section 18 of Pub. L. 98-199 set out as a note under section 1401 of this title.

EFFECTIVE DATE OF 1977 AMENDMENT

Section 7 of Pub. L. 95-49 provided that: "The amendments made by sections 2, 3, 5, and 6 [amending sections 1426, 1436, 1444, and 1454 of this title] shall take effect on October 1, 1977."

EFFECTIVE DATE OF 1974 AMENDMENT

Amendment by Pub. L. 93-380 effective on and after sixtieth day after Aug. 21, 1974, see section 2(c) of Pub. L. 93-380, set out as an Effective Date of 1974 Amendment note under section 244 of this title.

SECTION REFERRED TO IN OTHER SECTIONS

This section is referred to in section 1418 of this title.

§ 1427. Authorization of appropriations

(a) There are authorized to be appropriated to carry out the provisions of section 1421 of this title, $5,700,000 for fiscal year 1984, $6,000,000 for fiscal year 1985, and $6,300,000 for fiscal year 1986.

(b) There are authorized to be appropriated to carry out the provisions of section 1422 of this title, $15,000,000 for fiscal year 1984, and for each of the two succeeding fiscal years.

(c) There are authorized to be appropriated to carry out the provisions of section 1423 of this title, $26,000,000 for fiscal year 1984, $27,100,000 for fiscal year 1985, and $28,300,000 for fiscal year 1986.

(d) There are authorized to be appropriated to carry out the provisions of subsection (c) of section 1424 of this title, $5,000,000 for fiscal year 1984, $5,300,000 for fiscal year 1985, and $5,600,000 for fiscal year 1986.

(e) There are authorized to be appropriated to carry out the provisions of section 1424a of this title, $5,000,000 for fiscal year 1984, $5,300,000 for fiscal year 1985, and $5,500,000 for fiscal year 1986.

(f) There are authorized to be appropriated to carry out the provisions of section 1425 of this title, $6,000,000 for fiscal year 1984, $6,330,000 for fiscal year 1985, and $6,660,000 for fiscal year 1986.

(Pub. L. 91-230, title VI, § 628, as added Pub. L. 98-199, § 10, Dec. 2, 1983, 97 Stat. 1368.)

PRIOR PROVISIONS

Provisions similar to those comprising this section were contained in Pub. L. 91-230, title VI, § 627, formerly § 626, Apr. 13, 1970, 84 Stat. 184, renumbered and amended Pub. L. 93-380, title VI, §§ 616, 617, Aug. 21, 1974, 88 Stat. 584; Pub. L. 95-49, § 2, June 17, 1977, 91 Stat. 230, which is classified to section 1426 of this title, prior to general amendment of this subchapter by Pub. L. 98-199, § 10, Dec. 2, 1983, 97 Stat. 1363.

EFFECTIVE DATE

Section effective Dec. 2, 1983, see section 18 of Pub. L. 98-199, set out as an Effective Date of 1983 Amendment note under section 1401 of this title.

SUBCHAPTER IV—TRAINING PERSONNEL FOR THE EDUCATION OF THE HANDICAPPED

SUBCHAPTER REFERRED TO IN OTHER SECTIONS

This subchapter is referred to in sections 1418, 1443 of this title.

§ 1431. Grants to institutions of higher education and other appropriate agencies for personnel training

(a) Careers in special education; personnel training standards; costs of courses, fellowships, and traineeships; contract authority for areas of personnel shortages

(1) The Secretary is authorized to make grants, which may include scholarships with necessary stipends and allowances, to institutions of higher education (including the university-affiliated facilities program under the Rehabilitation Act of 1973 [29 U.S.C. 701 et seq.] and the satellite network of the developmental disabilities program) and other appropriate nonprofit agencies to assist them in training personnel for careers in special education including—

(A) special education teaching, including speech, language, and hearing impaired, and adaptive physical education;

(B) related services to handicapped children and youth in educational settings;

(C) special education supervision and administration;

(D) special education research; and

(E) training of special education personnel and other personnel providing special services.

(2) The Secretary shall ensure that grants awarded to applicant institutions and agencies under this subsection meet State and professionally recognized standards for the training of special education and related services personnel.

(3) Grants under this subsection may be used by such institutions to assist in covering the cost of courses of training or study for such personnel and for establishing and maintaining fellowships or traineeships with such stipends and allowances as may be determined by the Secretary.

(4) The Secretary in carrying out the purposes of this subsection may reserve a sum not to exceed 5 per centum of the amount available for this subsection in each fiscal year for contracts to prepare personnel in areas where shortages exist, when a response to that need has not been adequately addressed by the grant process.

(b) Special projects for preservice training, regular educators, and inservice training of special education personnel

The Secretary is authorized to make grants to institutions of higher education and other appropriate nonprofit agencies to conduct special projects to develop and demonstrate new approaches for the preservice training purposes set forth in subsection (a) of this section, for regular educators, and for the inservice training of special education personnel, including classroom aides, related services personnel, and regular education personnel who serve handicapped children.

(c) Parent training and information programs

(1) The Secretary is authorized to make grants through a separate competition to private nonprofit organizations for the purpose of providing training and information to parents of handicapped children and volunteers who work with parents to enable such individuals to participate more effectively with professionals in meeting the educational needs of handicapped children. Such grants shall be designed to meet the unique training and information needs of parents of handicapped children, including those who are members of groups that have been traditionally underrepresented, living in the area to be served by the grant.

(2) In order to receive a grant under this subsection a private nonprofit organization shall—

(A) be governed by a board of directors on which a majority of the members are parents of handicapped children and which includes members who are professionals in the field of special education and related services who serve handicapped children and youth; or if the nonprofit private organization does not have such a board, such organization shall have a membership which represents the interests of individuals with handicapping conditions, and shall establish a special governing committee on which a majority of the members are parents of handicapped children and which includes members who are professionals in the fields of special education and related services, to operate the training and information program under this subsection:

(B) serve the parents of children with the full range of handicapping conditions under such grant program; and

(C) demonstrate the capacity and expertise to conduct effectively the training and information activities authorized under this subsection.

(3) The board of directors or special governing committee of a private nonprofit organization receiving a grant under this subsection shall meet at least once in each calendar quarter to review such parent training and information activities, and each such committee shall advise the governing board directly of its views and recommendations. Whenever a private nonprofit organization requests the renewal of a grant under this subsection, the board of directors or the special governing committee shall submit to the Secretary a written review of the parent training and information program conducted by that private nonprofit organization during the preceding fiscal year.

(4) The Secretary shall ensure that grants under this subsection will—

(A) be distributed geographically to the greatest extent possible throughout all the States; and

(B) be targeted to parents of handicapped children in both urban and rural areas, or on a State, or regional basis.

(5) Parent training and information programs assisted under this subsection shall assist parents to—

(A) better understand the nature and needs of the handicapping conditions of their child;

(B) provide followup support for their handicapped child's educational programs;

(C) communicate more effectively with special and regular educators, administrators, related services personnel, and other relevant professionals;

(D) participate in educational decisionmaking processes including the development of their handicapped child's individualized educational program;

(E) obtain information about the programs, services, and resources available to their handicapped child, and the degree to which the programs, services, and resources are appropriate; and

(F) understand the provisions for the education of handicapped children as specified under subchapter II of this chapter.

(6) Each private nonprofit organization operating a program receiving assistance under this subsection shall consult with appropriate agencies which serve or assist handicapped children and youth and are located in the jurisdictions served by the program.

(7) The Secretary shall provide technical assistance, by grant or contract, for establishing, developing, and coordinating parent training and information programs.

(Pub. L. 91-230, title VI, § 631, Apr. 13, 1970, 84 Stat. 184; Pub. L. 98-199, §§ 3(b), 11, Dec. 2, 1983, 97 Stat. 1358, 1369.)

REFERENCES IN TEXT

The Rehabilitation Act of 1973, referred to in subsec. (a)(1), is Pub. L. 93-112, Sept. 26, 1973, 87 Stat. 355, as amended, which is classified principally to chapter 16 (§ 701 et seq.) of Title 29. Labor. For complete classification of this Act to the Code, see Short Title note set out under section 701 of Title 29 and Tables.

AMENDMENTS

1983—Pub. L. 98-199, § 11, amended section generally. Prior to amendment, section authorized the Secretary to make grants to institutions of higher education and other appropriate nonprofit institutions of higher education and other appropriate nonprofit institutions or agencies to assist them (1) in providing training of professional personnel to conduct training of teachers and other specialists in fields related to the education of handicapped children; (2) in providing training for personnel engaged or preparing to engage in employment as teachers of handicapped children, as supervisors of such teachers, or as speech correctionists or other special personnel providing special services for the education of such children, or engaged or preparing to engage in research in fields related to the education of such children; and (3) in establishing and maintaining scholarships, with such stipends and allowances as may be determined by the Secretary, for training personnel engaged in or preparing to engage in employment as teachers of the handicapped or as related specialists and provided that grants under this section could be used by such institutions to assist in covering the cost of courses of training or study for such personnel and for establishing and maintaining fellowships or traineeships with such stipends and allowances as may be determined by the Secretary.

EFFECTIVE DATE OF 1983 AMENDMENT

Amendment by Pub. L. 98-199 effective Dec. 2, 1983, with an exception for previously obligated funds and certain interim provisions for financial assistance, see section 18 of Pub. L. 98-199 set out as a note under section 1401 of this title.

TRANSFER OF FUNCTIONS

"Secretary", meaning the Secretary of Education, was substituted for "Commissioner" in text pursuant to sections 301(a)(1) and 507 of Pub. L. 96-88, which are classified to sections 3441(a)(1) and 3507 of this title and which transferred all functions of the Commissioner of Education to the Secretary of Education.

LIMITATION ON AUTHORIZATION OF APPROPRIATIONS FOR FISCAL YEARS 1982 AND 1983

Pub. L. 97-35, title VI, § 602(b)(6), Aug. 13, 1981, 95 Stat. 483, provided that: "There is authorized to be appropriated to carry out sections 631, 632, and 634 of such Act [sections 1431, 1432, and 1434 of this title] $58,000,000 for each of the fiscal years 1982 and 1983."

SECTION REFERRED TO IN OTHER SECTIONS

This section is referred to in section 1435 of this title.

§ 1432. Grants to State educational agencies for traineeships

The Secretary shall make grants to State educational agencies to assist them in establishing and maintaining, directly or through grants to institutions of higher education, programs for the preservice and inservice training of teachers of handicapped children, or supervisors of such teachers.

(Pub. L. 91-230, title VI, § 632, Apr. 13, 1970, 84 Stat. 184; Pub. L. 98-199, §§ 3(b), 11, Dec. 2, 1983, 97 Stat. 1358, 1371.)

AMENDMENTS

1983—Pub. L. 98-199, § 11, amended section generally. Prior to amendment, section read: "The Secretary is authorized to make grants to State educational agencies to assist them in establishing and maintaining, directly or through grants to institutions of higher education, programs for training personnel engaged, or preparing to engage, in employment as teachers of handicapped children or as supervisors of such teachers. Such grants shall also be available to assist such institutions in meeting the cost of training such personnel."
Pub. L. 98-199, § 3(b), substituted "Secretary" for "Commissioner".

EFFECTIVE DATE OF 1983 AMENDMENT

Amendment by Pub. L. 98-199 effective Dec. 2, 1983, with an exception for previously obligated funds and certain interim provisions for financial assistance, see section 18 of Pub. L. 98-199 set out as a note under section 1401 of this title.

TRANSFER OF FUNCTIONS

"Secretary", meaning the Secretary of Education, was substituted for "Commissioner" in text pursuant to sections 301(a)(1) and 507 of Pub. L. 96-88, which are classified to sections 3441(a)(1) and 3507 of this title and which transferred all functions of the Commissioner of Education to the Secretary of Education.

LIMITATIONS ON AUTHORIZATION OF APPROPRIATIONS
FOR FISCAL YEARS 1982 AND 1983

Appropriations of $58,000,000 authorized to carry out sections 1431, 1432, and 1434 of this title for each of the fiscal years 1982 and 1983, see section 602(b)(6) of Pub. L. 97-35, set out as a note under section 1431 of this title.

§ 1433. Grants or contracts to improve recruiting of educational personnel and dissemination of information concerning educational opportunities for the handicapped

(a) National clearinghouse on education of handicapped; establishment; other support projects; statement of objectives

The Secretary is authorized to make a grant to or enter into a contract with a public agency or a nonprofit private organization or institution for a national clearinghouse on the education of the handicapped and to make grants or contracts with a public agency or a nonprofit private organization or institution for other support projects which may be deemed necessary by the Secretary to achieve the following objectives:

(1) to disseminate information and provide technical assistance on a national basis to parents, professionals, and other interested parties concerning—

(A) programs relating to the education of the handicapped under this chapter and under other Federal laws; and

(B) participation in such programs, including referral of individuals to appropriate national, State, and local agencies and organizations for further assistance;

(2) to encourage students and professional personnel to seek and obtain careers and employment in the various fields relating to the education of handicapped children and youth; and

(3) to provide information on available services and programs in postsecondary education for the handicapped.

(b) National clearinghouse on postsecondary education for handicapped; establishment; statement of purpose

In addition to the clearinghouse established under subsection (a) of this section, the Secretary shall make a grant or enter into a contract for a national clearinghouse on postsecondary education for handicapped individuals for the purpose of providing information on available services and programs in postsecondary education for the handicapped.

(c) Considerations governing awards; limitation of contracts with profitmaking organizations

(1) In awarding the grants and contracts under this section, the Secretary shall give particular attention to any demonstrated experience at the national level relevant to performance of the functions established in this section, and ability to conduct such projects, communicate with the intended consumers of information, and maintain the necessary communication with other agencies and organizations.

(2) The Secretary is authorized to make contracts with profitmaking organizations under this section only when necessary for materials or media access.

(Pub. L. 91-230, title VI, § 633, Apr. 13, 1970, 84 Stat. 184; Pub. L. 98-199, §§ 3(b), 11, Dec. 2, 1983, 97 Stat. 1358, 1371.)

AMENDMENTS

1983—Pub. L. 98-199, § 11, amended section generally. Prior to amendment, section authorized the Secretary to make grants to public or nonprofit private agencies, organizations, or institutions, or to enter into contracts with public or private agencies, organizations, or institutions, for projects for (1) encouraging students and professional personnel who work in various fields of education of handicapped children and youth through, among other ways, developing and distributing imaginative or innovative materials to assist in recruiting personnel for such careers, or (2) disseminating information about the programs, services, and resources for the education of handicapped children, or providing referral services to parents, teachers, and other persons especially interested in the handicapped.

Pub. L. 98-199, § 3(b), substituted "Secretary" for "Commissioner" in provisions preceding par. (1).

EFFECTIVE DATE OF 1983 AMENDMENT

Amendment by Pub. L. 98-199 effective Dec. 2, 1983, with an exception for previously obligated funds and certain interim provisions for financial assistance, see section 18 of Pub. L. 98-199 set out as a note under section 1401 of this title.

TRANSFER OF FUNCTIONS

"Secretary", meaning the Secretary of Education, was substituted for "Commissioner" in text pursuant to sections 301(a)(1) and 507 of Pub. L. 96-88, which are classified to sections 3441(a)(1) and 3507 of this title and which transferred all functions of the Commissioner of Education to the Secretary of Education.

LIMITATION ON AUTHORIZATION OF APPROPRIATIONS FOR FISCAL YEARS 1982 AND 1983

Pub. L. 97-35, title VI, § 602(b)(7), Aug. 13, 1981, 95 Stat. 483, provided that: "There is authorized to be appropriated to carry out section 633 of such Act [this section] $1,000,000 for each of the fiscal years 1982 and 1983."

SECTION REFERRED TO IN OTHER SECTIONS

This section is referred to in section 1435 of this title.

§ 1434. Reports to the Secretary

(a) Not more than sixty days after the end of any fiscal year, each recipient of a grant or contract under this subchapter during such fiscal year shall prepare and submit a report to the Secretary. Each such report shall be in such form and detail as the Secretary determines to be appropriate, and shall include—

(1) the number of individuals trained under the grant or contract, by category of training and level of training; and

(2) the number of individuals trained under the grant or contract receiving degrees and certification, by category and level of training.

(b) A summary of the data required by this section shall be included in the annual report of the Secretary under section 1418 of this title.

(Pub. L. 91-230, title VI, § 634, Apr. 13, 1970, 84 Stat. 185; Pub. L. 98-199, §§ 3(b), 11, Dec. 2, 1983, 97 Stat. 1358, 1372.)

PRIOR PROVISIONS

Provisions similar to those comprising this section were contained in Pub. L. 91-230, title VI, § 635, Apr. 13, 1970, 84 Stat. 185, which is classified to section 1435 of this title, prior to general amendment of this subchapter by Pub. L. 98-199, § 11, Dec. 2, 1983, 97 Stat. 1369.

AMENDMENTS

1983—Pub. L. 98-199, § 11, amended section generally, substituting provisions requiring reports to the Secretary for provisions respecting grants for training physical educators and recreation personnel for handicapped children.

Pub. L. 98-199, § 3(b), substituted "Secretary" for "Commissioner".

EFFECTIVE DATE OF 1983 AMENDMENT

Ammendment by Pub. L. 98-199 effective Dec. 2, 1983, with an exception for previously obligated funds and certain interim provisions for financial assistance, see section 18 of Pub. L. 98-199 set out as a note under section 1401 of this title.

TRANSFER OF FUNCTIONS

"Secretary", meaning the Secretary of Education, was substituted for "Commissioner" in text pursuant to sections 301(a)(1) and 507 of Pub. L. 96-88, which are classified to sections 3441(a)(1) and 3507 of this title and which transferred all functions of the Commissioner of Education to the Secretary of Education.

LIMITATION ON AUTHORIZATION OF APPROPRIATIONS FOR FISCAL YEARS 1982 AND 1983

Appropriations of $58,000,000 authorized to carry out sections 1431, 1432, and 1434 of this title for each of the fiscal years 1982 and 1983, see section 602(b)(6) of Pub. L. 97-35, set out as a note under section 1431 of this title.

SECTION REFERRED TO IN OTHER SECTIONS

This section is referred to in section 1418 of this title.

§ 1435. Authorization of appropriations

(a) There are authorized to be appropriated to carry out the provisions of this subchapter (other than section 1433 of this title) $58,000,000 for fiscal year 1984, $61,150,000 for fiscal year 1985, and $64,370,000 for fiscal year 1986. There are authorized to be appropriated to carry out the provisions of section 1433 of this title, $1,000,000 for fiscal year 1984, $1,050,000 for fiscal year 1985, and $1,110,000 for fiscal year 1986.

(b) Of the funds appropriated pursuant to subsection (a) of this section for any fiscal year, the Secretary shall reserve 10 per centum for activities under section 1431(c) of this title.

(Pub. L. 91-230, title VI, § 635, Apr. 13, 1970, 84 Stat. 185; Pub. L. 98-199, §§ 3(b), 11, Dec. 2, 1983, 97 Stat. 1358, 1372.)

PRIOR PROVISIONS

Provisions similar to those comprising this section were contained in Pub. L. 91-230, title VI, § 636, Apr. 13, 1970, 84 Stat. 185, as amended which was classified to section 1436 of this title, and was omitted from the Code in the general amendment of this subchapter by Pub. L. 98-199, § 11, Dec. 2, 1983, 97 Stat. 1369.

AMENDMENTS

1983—Pub. L. 98-199, § 11, amended section generally, substituting provision authorizing appropriations for provision requiring reports to Secretary.
Pub. L. 98-199, § 3(b), substituted "Secretary" for "Commissioner".

EFFECTIVE DATE OF 1983 AMENDMENT

Amendment by Pub. L. 98-199 effective Dec. 2, 1983, with an exception for previously obligated funds and certain interim provisions for financial assistance, see section 18 of Pub. L. 98-199 set out as a note under section 1401 of this title.

§ 1436. Omitted

CODIFICATION

Section, Pub. L. 91-230, title VI, § 636, Apr. 13, 1970, 84 Stat. 185; Pub. L. 93-380, title VI, § 618, Aug. 21, 1974, 88 Stat. 584; Pub. L. 95-49, § 3, June 17, 1977, 91 Stat. 230, authorized appropriations for the purposes of this subchapter, and was omitted in the general amendment of this subchapter by Pub. L. 98-199, § 11, Dec. 2, 1983, 97 Stat. 1369. See section 1435 of this title.

SUBCHAPTER V—RESEARCH IN THE EDUCATION OF THE HANDICAPPED

SUBCHAPTER REFERRED TO IN OTHER SECTIONS

This subchapter is referred to in sections 1418, 1443 of this title.

§ 1441. Research, surveys, and demonstrations projects to assist appropriate personnel and other persons in education of handicapped children and youth

(a) Grant and contract authority; statement of objectives; description of specific activities

The Secretary is authorized to make grants to, or enter into contracts or cooperative agreements with, State and local educational agencies, institutions of higher education, and other public agencies and nonprofit private organizations for research and related activities, to assist special education personnel, related services personnel, and other appropriate persons, including parents, in improving the education and related services for handicapped children and youth and to conduct research, surveys, or demonstrations relating to the education of handicapped children and youth. Research and related activities shall be designed to increase knowledge and understanding of handicapping conditions and teaching, learning, and education-related practices and services for handicapped children and youth. Research and related activities assisted under this section shall include, but not be limited to, the following:

(1) The development of new and improved techniques and devices for teaching handicapped children and youth.

(2) The development of curricula which meet the unique educational needs of handicapped children and youth.

(3) The application of new technologies and knowledge for the purpose of improving the instruction of handicapped children and youth.

(4) The development of program models and exemplary practices in areas of special education.

(5) The dissemination of information on research and related activities conducted under this subchapter to interested individuals and organizations.

(b) Qualifications of applicant

In carrying out this section the Secretary shall consider the special education experience of the applicant and the ability of the applicant to disseminate the findings of any grant or contract.

(c) Publication of research priorities in Federal Register

The Secretary shall publish proposed research priorities in the Federal Register every two years, not later than July 1, and shall allow a period of sixty days for public comments and suggestions. After analyzing and considering the public comments, the Secretary shall publish final research priorities in the Federal Register not later than thirty days after the close of the comment period.

(d) Reports of research projects; index of research projects for annual report; availability to interested parties

The Secretary shall provide an index (including the title of each research project and the name and address of the researching organization) of all research projects conducted in the prior fiscal year in the annual report described under section 1418 of this title. The Secretary shall make reports of research projects available to the education community at large and to other interested parties.

(e) Coordination of related research priorities; information respecting research priorities to Federal entities

The Secretary shall coordinate the research priorities established under this section with research priorities established by the National Institute of Handicapped Research and shall provide information concerning research priorities established under this section to the National Council on the Handicapped and to the National Advisory Committee on the Education of Handicapped Children.[1]

(Pub. L. 91-230, title VI, § 641, Apr. 13, 1970, 84 Stat. 185; Pub. L. 95-49, § 4, June 17, 1977, 91 Stat. 230; Pub. L. 98-199, § 3(b), 12, Dec. 2, 1983, 97 Stat. 1358, 1372.)

AMENDMENTS

1983—Pub. L. 98-199, § 12, amended section generally. Prior to amendment, section read: "The Secretary is authorized to make grants to States, State or local educational agencies, institutions of higher education, and other public or nonprofit private educational or research agencies and organizations, and to make contracts with States, State or local educational agencies, institutions of higher education, and other public or private educational or research agencies and organizations, for research and related purposes relating to physical education or recreation for handicapped children, and to conduct research, surveys, or demonstrations relating to physical education or recreation for handicapped children, including the development and conduct of model programs designed to meet the special educational needs of such children."

Pub. L. 98-199, § 3(b), substituted "Secretary" for "Commissioner".

1977—Pub. L. 95-49 added provisions calling for the development and conduct of model programs designed to meet the special educational needs of handicapped children.

EFFECTIVE DATE OF 1983 AMENDMENT

Amendment by Pub. L. 98-199 effective Dec. 2, 1983, with an exception for previously obligated funds and certain interim provisions for financial assistance, see section 18 of Pub. L. 98-199 set out as a note under section 1401 of this title.

TRANSFER OF FUNCTIONS

"Secretary", meaning the Secretary of Education, was substituted for "Commissioner" in text pursuant to sections 301(a)(1) and 507 of Pub. L. 96-88, which are classified to sections 3441(a)(1) and 3507 of this title and which transferred all functions of the Commissioner of Education to the Secretary of Education.

---

[1]Reproduced as in original. Probably should be "Children and Youth."

SECTION REFERRED TO IN OTHER SECTIONS

This section is referred to in section 1418 of this title.

§ 1442. Research and demonstration projects in physical education and recreation for handicapped children

The Secretary is authorized to make grants to States, State or local educational agencies, institutions of higher education, and other public or nonprofit private educational or research agencies and organizations, and to make contracts with States, State or local educational agencies, institutions of higher education, and other public or private educational or research agencies and organizations, for research and related purposes relating to physical education or recreation for handicapped children, and to conduct research, surveys, or demonstrations relating to physical education or recreation for handicapped children.

(Pub. L. 91-230, title VI, § 642, Apr. 13, 1970, 84 Stat. 185; Pub. L. 98-199, §§ 3(b), 12, Dec. 2, 1983, 97 Stat. 1358, 1373.)

AMENDMENTS

1983—Pub. L. 98-199, § 12, reenacted section without change.
Pub. L. 98-199, § 3(b), substituted "Secretary" for "Commissioner".

EFFECTIVE DATE OF 1983 AMENDMENT

Amendment by Pub. L. 98-199 effective Dec. 2, 1983, with an exception for previously obligated funds and certain interim provisions for financial assistance, see section 18, of Pub. L. 98-199 set out as a note under section 1401 of this title.

TRANSFER OF FUNCTIONS

"Secretary", meaning the Secretary of Education, was substituted for "Commissioner" in text pursuant to sections 301(a)(1) and 507 of Pub. L. 96-88, which are classified to sections 3441(a)(1) and 3507 of this title and which transferred all functions of the Commissioner of Education to the Secretary of Education.

§ 1443. Panels of experts

The Secretary shall from time to time appoint panels of experts who are competent to evaluate various types of proposals for projects under subchapters III, IV, V, and VI of this chapter, and shall secure the advice and recommendations of one such panel before making any grant or contract under subchapters III, IV, V, and VI of this chapter. The panels shall be composed of—

(1) individuals from the field of special education for the handicapped and other relevant disciplines who have significant expertise and experience in the content areas and age levels addressed in the proposals; and

(2) handicapped individuals and parents of handicapped individuals when appropriate.

(Pub. L. 91-230, title VI, § 643, Apr. 13, 1970, 84 Stat. 185; Pub. L. 98-199, §§ 3(b), 12, Dec. 2, 1983, 97 Stat. 1358, 1373.)

AMENDMENTS

1983—Pub. L. 98-199, § 12, amended section generally, substituting "proposals for projects under subchapter III, IV, V, and VI of this chapter" and "grant or contract under subchapters III, IV, V, and VI of this chapter" for "research or demonstration projects under this subchapter" and "grant under this subchapter", respectively, and added provisions respecting the composition of panels.

Pub. L. 98-199, § 3(b), substituted "Secretary" for "Commissioner".

EFFECTIVE DATE OF 1983 AMENDMENT

Amendment by Pub. L. 98-199 effective Dec. 2, 1983, with an exception for previously obligated funds and certain interim provisions for financial assistance, see section 18 of Pub. L. 98-199 set out as a note under section 1401 of this title.

TRANSFER OF FUNCTIONS

"Secretary", meaning the Secretary of Education, was substituted for "Commissioner" in text pursuant to sections 301(a)(1) and 507 of Pub. L. 96-88, which are classified to sections 3441(a)(1) and 3507 of this title and which transferred all functions of the Commissioner of Education to the Secretary of Education.

§ 1444. Authorization of appropriations

For purposes of carrying out this subchapter, there are authorized to be appropriated $20,000,000 for fiscal year 1984, $21,100,000 for fiscal year 1985, and $22,200,000 for fiscal year 1986.

(As amended Pub. L. 98-199, § 12, Dec. 2, 1983, 97 Stat. 1374.)

AMENDMENTS

1983—Pub. L. 98-199 amended section generally, substituting appropriations authorizations of $20,000,000, $21,100,000, and $22,200,000 for fiscal years 1984 through 1986, respectively, for prior authorizations of $20,000,000, $22,000,000, $24,000,000, $26,000,000, and $28,000,000 for fiscal years 1978 through 1982, respectively.

1977—Pub. L. 95-49 authorized the appropriation of $20,000,000 for fiscal year 1978, $22,000,000 for fiscal year 1979, $24,000,000 for fiscal year 1980, $26,000,000 for fiscal year 1981, and $28,000,000 for fiscal year 1982 for the purposes of carrying out this subchapter.

1974—Pub. L. 93-380 substituted appropriations authorization of $15,000,000; $20,000,000; and $20,000,000 for fiscal years ending June 30, 1975, 1976, and 1977, for prior authorization of $27,000,000; $35,500,000; and $45,000,000; for fiscal years ending June 30, 1971, 1972, and 1973.

EFFECTIVE DATE OF 1983 AMENDMENT

Amendment by Pub. L. 98-199 effective Dec. 2, 1983, with an exception for previously obligated funds and certain interim provisions for financial assistance, see section 18 of Pub. L. 98-199 set out as a note under section 1401 of this title.

EFFECTIVE DATE OF 1977 AMENDMENT

Amendment by Pub. L. 95-49 effective on Oct. 1, 1977, see section 7 of Pub. L.

95-49, set out as an Effective Date of 1977 Amendment note under section 1426 of this title.

EFFECTIVE DATE OF 1974 AMENDMENT

Amendment by Pub. L. 93-380 effective on an after sixtieth day after Aug. 21, 1974, see section 2(c) of Pub. L. 93-380, set out as an Effective Date of 1974 Amendment note under section 244 of this title.

LIMITATION ON AUTHORIZATION OF APPROPRIATIONS FOR FISCAL YEARS 1982 AND 1983

Pub. L. 97-35, title VI, § 602(b)(8), Aug. 13, 1981, 95 Stat. 483, provided that: "There is authorized to be appropriated to carry out part E of such Act [this subchapter] $20,000,000 for each of the fiscal years 1982 and 1983."

SUBCHAPTER VI—INSTRUCTIONAL MEDIA
FOR THE HANDICAPPED

SUBCHAPTER REFERRED TO IN OTHER SECTIONS

This subchapter is referred to in sections 1418, 1443 of this title.

§ 1451. Congressional statement of purposes

(a)[1] The purposes of this subchapter are to promote—
(1) the general welfare of deaf persons by (A) bringing to such persons understanding and appreciation of those films which play such an important part in the general and cultural advancement of hearing persons, (B) providing through these films enriched educational and cultural experiences through which deaf persons can be brought into better touch with the realities of their environment, and (C) providing a wholesome and rewarding experience which deaf persons may share together; and
(2) the educational advancement of handicapped persons by (A) carrying on research in the use of educational media for the handicapped, (B) producing and distributing educational media for the use of handicapped persons, their parents, their actual or potential employers, and other persons directly involved in work for the advancement of the handicapped, and (C) training persons in the use of educational media for the instruction of the handicapped.

(Pub. L. 91-230, title VI, § 651, Apr. 13, 1970, 84 Stat. 186.)

§ 1452. Captioned films and educational media for handicapped persons

(a) Establishment of loan service

The Secretary shall establish a loan service of captioned films and educational media for the purpose of making such materials available in the United States for nonprofit purposes to handicapped persons, parents of handicapped persons, and other persons directly involved in activities for the advancement of the handicapped in accordance with regulations.

(b) Authority of Secretary

The Secretary is authorized to—
(1) acquire films (or rights thereto) and other educational media by purchase, lease, or gift;
(2) acquire by lease or purchased[2] equipment necessary to the administration of this subchapter;
(3) provide, by grant or contract, for the captioning of films;
(4) provide, by grant or contract, for the distribution of captioned films and other educational media and equipment through State schools for the handicapped and such other agencies as the Secretary may deem appropriate to serve as local or regional centers for such distribution;
(5) provide, by grant or contract, for the conduct of research in the use of educational and training films and other educational media for the handi-

---

[1]Reproduced as in original. Enacted with no subsec. (b).

[2]Reproduced as in original.

capped, for the production and distribution of educational and training films and other educational media for the handicapped, for the production and distribution of educational and training films and other educational media for the handicapped and the training of persons in the use of such films and media, including the payment to those persons of such stipends (including allowances for travel and other expenses of such persons and their dependents) as he may determine, which shall be consistent with prevailing practices under comparable federally supported programs;

(6) utilize the facilities and services of other governmental agencies; and

(7) accept gifts, contributions, and voluntary and uncompensated services of individuals and organizations.

(Pub. L. 91-230, title VI, § 652, Apr. 13, 1970, 84 Stat. 186; Pub. L. 93-380, title VI, § 620(1), Aug. 21, 1974, 88 Stat. 585; Pub. L. 94-482, title V, § 501(h), Oct. 12, 1976, 90 Stat. 2237; Pub. L. 98-199, § 3(b), Dec. 2, 1983, 97 Stat. 1358.)

AMENDMENTS

1983—Pub. L. 98-199 substituted "Secretary" for "Commissioner" wherever appearing.

1976—Subsec. (b)(3) to (5). Pub. L. 94-482 substituted "grant or contract" for "grant and contract" wherever appearing therein.

1974—Subsec. (b)(3) to (5). Pub. L. 93-380 inserted after "provide" the words, "by grant and contract,".

EFFECTIVE DATE OF 1983 AMENDMENT

Amendment by Pub. L. 98-199 effective Dec. 2, 1983, see section 18 of Pub. L. 98-199, set out as a note under section 1401 of this title.

EFFECTIVE DATE OF 1976 AMENDMENT

Amendment by Pub. L. 94-482 effective 30 days after Oct. 12, 1976, except either as specifically otherwise provided or, if not so specifically otherwise provided, effective July 1, 1976, for those amendments providing for authorization of appropriations, see section 532 of Pub. L. 94-482, set out as an Effective Date of 1976 Amendment note under section 1001 of this title.

EFFECTIVE DATE OF 1974 AMENDMENT

Amendment by Pub. L. 93-380 effective on and after sixtieth day after Aug. 21, 1974, see section 2(c) of Pub. L. 93-380, set out as an Effective Date of 1974 Amendment note under section 244 of this title.

TRANSFER OF FUNCTIONS

"Secretary", meaning the Secretary of Education, was substituted for "Commissioner" in text pursuant to sections 301(a)(1) and 507 of Pub. L. 96-88, which are classified to sections 3441(a)(1) and 3507 of this title and which transferred all functions of the Commissioner of Education to the Secretary of Education.

§ 1453. Centers on educational media and materials for the handicapped

(a) Establishment and operation

The Secretary is authorized to enter into agreements with institutions of higher education, State and local educational agencies, or other appropriate nonprofit agencies, for the establishment and operation of centers on educational media and materials for the handicapped, which together will provide a comprehensive program of activities to facilitate the use of new educational technology in education programs for handicapped persons, including designing, developing, and adapting instructional materials, and such other activities consistent with the purposes of this subchapter as the Secretary may prescribe in such agreements. Any such agreement shall—

(1) provide that Federal funds paid to a center will be used solely for such purposes as are set forth in the agreement; and

(2) authorize the center involved, subject to prior approval by the Secretary, to contract with public and private agencies and organizations for demonstration projects.

(b) Preferences to qualified institutions and agencies

In considering proposals to enter into agreements under this section, the Secretary shall give preference to institutions and agencies—

(1) which have demonstrated the capabilities necessary for the development and evaluation of educational media for the handicapped; and

(2) which can serve the educational technology needs of the Model High School for the Deaf (established under Public Law 89-694) [20 U.S.C. 693 et seq.].

(c) Annual report to Congress

The Secretary shall make an annual report on activities carried out under this section which shall be transmitted to the Congress.

(Pub. L. 91-230, title VI, § 653, Apr. 13, 1970, 84 Stat. 187; Pub. L. 94-142, § 6(b), Nov. 29, 1975, 89 Stat. 795.)

REFERENCES IN TEXT

Public Law 89-694, referred to in subsec. (b)(2), is Pub. L. 89-694, Oct. 15, 1966, 80 Stat. 1027, known as the model Secondary School for the Deaf Act, which is classified to subchapter II (§ 693 et seq.) of chapter 20B of this title. For complete classification of this Act to the Code, see Short Title note set out under section 693 of this title and Tables.

AMENDMENTS

1975—Subsec. (a). Pub. L. 94-142 substituted provision for the establishment and operation of an unspecified number of centers on educational media nd materials for the handicapped and the agreements with institutions of higher education. State and local educational agencies, and other appropriate nonprofit agencies for the establishment of those centers for provisions authorizing the establishment of a single National Center on Educational Media and Materials for the Handicapped and the agreement with an institution of higher education for the establishment and tuition of higher education for the establishment and operation of that Center, and transferred to subsec. (c) provisions calling for an annual report to Congress.

Subsec. (b). Pub. L. 94-142 substituted references to "institutions and agencies" for references to "institutions".

Subsec. (c). Pub. L. 94-142 added subsec. (c), which incorporated therein provisions for an annual report to Congress formerly set out in subsec. (a).

EFFECTIVE DATE OF 1975 AMENDMENT

Amendment by Pub. L. 94-142 effective Nov. 29, 1975, see section 8(b) of Pub. L. 94-142, set out as an Effective Date of 1975 Amendment note under section 1411 of this title.

SECTION REFERRED TO IN OTHER SECTIONS

This section is referred to in section 1418 of this title.

§ 1454. Authorization of Appropriations

For the purposes of carrying out this subchapter, there are authorized to be appropriated $19,000,000 for fiscal year 1984, $20,000,000 for fiscal year 1985, and $21,100,000 for fiscal year 1985, and $21,100,000 for fiscal year 1986.

(As amended Pub. L. 98-199, § 13, Dec. 2, 1983, 97 Stat. 1374.)

AMENDMENTS

1983—Pub. L. 98-199 amended section generally, substituting appropriations authorizations of $19,000,000, $20,000,000, and $21,100,000 for fiscal years 1984 through 1986, respectively, for prior authorizations of $24,000,000, $25,000,000, $27,000,000 for fiscal years 1978 through 1980, respectively, and $29,000,000 for fiscal year 1981 and succeeding fiscal years.

1977—Pub. L. 95-49 raised the appropriation authorization for fiscal year 1978 from $22,000,000 to $24,000,000, for fiscal year 1979 from $22,000,000 to $25,000,000, for fiscal year 1980 from $22,000,000 to $27,000,000, and for fiscal year 1981 and each succeeding fiscal year thereafter from $22,000,000 to $29,000,000.

1974—Pub. L. 93-380 substituted appropriations authorization of $18,000,000; and $22,000,000 for fiscal years ending June 30, 1975, and 1976 and thereafter for prior authorization of $12,500,000; $15,000,000; and $20,000,000 for fiscal years ending June 30, 1971, 1972, and 1973 and thereafter.

EFFECTIVE DATE OF 1983 AMENDMENT

Amendment by Pub. L. 98-199 effective Dec. 2, 1983, see section 18 of Pub. L. 98-199, set out as a note under section 1401 of this title.

EFFECTIVE DATE OF 1977 AMENDMENT

Amendment by Pub. L. 95-49 effective on Oct. 1, 1977, see section 7 of Pub. L. 95-49, set out as an Effective Date of 1977 Amendment note under section 1426 of this title.

EFFECTIVE DATE OF 1974 AMENDMENT

Amendment by Pub. L. 93-380 effective on and after sixtieth day after Aug. 21, 1974, see section 2(c) of Pub. L. 93-380, set out as an Effective Date of 1974 Amendment note under section 244 of this title.

LIMITATION ON AUTHORIZATION OF APPROPRIATIONS
FOR FISCAL YEARS 1982 AND 1983

Pub. L. 97-35, title VI, § 602(b)(9), Aug. 13, 1981, 95 Stat. 483, provided that: "There is authorized to be appropriated to carry out part F of such Act [this subchapter] $19,000,000 for each of the fiscal years 1982 and 1983."

SUBCHAPTER VII—SPECIAL PROGRAMS FOR CHILDREN WITH SPECIFIC LEARNING DISABILITIES

§ 1461. Repealed. Pub. L. 98-199, § 14, Dec. 2, 1983, 97 Stat. 1374

Section, Pub. L. 91-230, title VI, § 661, Apr. 13, 1970, 84 Stat. 187; Pub. L. 93-380, title VI, § 621, Aug. 21, 1974, 88 Stat. 585; Pub. L. 98-199, § 3(b), Dec. 2, 1983, 97 Stat. 1358, related to research, training, and model centers respecting special programs for children with specific learning disabilities, providing in subsec. (a), Secretary's grant and contract authority, functions of model centers, and considerations governing making of contracts and grants; subsec. (b), other considerations in making awards, geographical distribution of training programs and trained personnel, and a model center in each State; and subsec. (c), appropriations authorization of $10, $20, and $20 million dollars for fiscal years ending June 30, 1975 through 1977, respectively.

EFFECTIVE DATE OF REPEAL

Section repealed effective Dec. 2, 1983, see section 18 of Pub. L. 98-199, set out as an Effective Date of 1983 Amendment note under section 1401 of this title.

APPENDIX B

U.S. SUPREME COURT CASES

Board of Education v. Rowley

U.S. Supreme Court, 458 U.S. 176, 102 S.Ct. 3034 (1982).

Syllabus*

The Education for All Handicapped Children Act of 1975 (Act) provides federal money to assist state and local agencies in educating handicapped children. To qualify for federal assistance, a State must demonstrate (through a detailed plan submitted for federal approval) that it has in effect a policy that assures all handicapped children the right to a "free appropriate public education," which must be tailored to the unique needs of the handicapped child by means of an "individualized educational program" (IEP). The IEP must be prepared (and reviewed at least annually) by school officials with participation by the child's parents or guardian. The Act also requires that a participating State provide specified administrative procedures by which the child's parents or guardian may challenge any change in the evaluation and education of the child. Any party aggrieved by the state administrative decisions is authorized to bring a civil action in either a state court or a federal district court. Respondents—a child with only minimal residual hearing who had been furnished by school authorities with a special hearing aid for use in the classroom and who was to receive additional instruction from tutors, and the child's parents—filed suit in Federal District Court to review New York administrative proceedings that had upheld the school administrators' denial of the parents' request that the child also be provided a qualified sign-language interpreter in all of her academic classes. Entering judgment for respondents, the District Court found that although the child performed better than the average child in her class and was advancing easily from grade to grade, she was not performing as well academically as she would without her handicap. Because of this disparity between the child's achievement and her potential, the court held that she was not receiving a "free appropriate public education," which the court defined as "an opportunity to achieve [her] full potential commensurate with the opportunity provided to other children." The Court of Appeals affirmed.

Held:

1. The Act's requirement of a "free appropriate public education" is satisfied when the State provides personalized instruction with sufficient support services to permit the handicapped child to benefit educationally from that instruction. Such instruction and services must be provided at public expense, must meet the State's educational standards, must approximate grade levels used in the State's regular education, and must comport with the child's IEP, as formulated in accordance with the Act's requirements. If the child is being educated in regular classrooms, as here, the IEP should be reasonably calculated to enable the child to achieve passing marks and advance from grade to grade.

(a) This interpretation is supported by the definitions contained in the Act, as well as by other provisions imposing procedural requirements and setting forth statutory findings and priorities for States to follow in extending educational services to handicapped children. The Act's language contains no express substantive standard prescribing the level of education to be accorded handicapped children.

---

*The syllabus constitutes no part of the opinion of the Court but has been prepared by the Reporter of Decisions for the convenience of the reader.

(b) The Act's legislative history shows that Congress sought to make public education available to handicapped children, but did not intend to impose upon the States any greater substantive educational standard than is necessary to make such access to public education meaningful. The Act's intent was more to open the door of public education to handicapped children by means of specialized educational services than to guarantee any particular substantive level of education once inside.

(c) While Congress sought to provide assistance to the States in carrying out their constitutional responsibilities to provide equal protection of the laws, it did not intend to achieve strict equality of opportunity or services for handicapped and nonhandicapped children, but rather sought primarily to identify and evaluate handicapped children, and to provide them with access to a free public education. The Act does not require a State to maximize the potential of each handicapped child commensurate with the opportunity provided nonhandicapped children.

2. In suits brought under the Act's judicial-review provisions, a court must first determine whether the State has complied with the statutory procedures, and must then determine whether the individualized program developed through such procedures is reasonably calculated to enable the child to receive educational benefits. If these requirements are met, the State has complied with the obligations imposed by Congress and the courts can require no more.

(a) Although the judicial-review provisions do not limit courts to ensuring that States have complied with the Act's procedural requirements, the Act's emphasis on procedural safeguards demonstrates the legislative conviction that adequate compliance with prescribed procedures will in most cases assure much, if not all, of what Congress wished in the way of substantive content in an IEP.

(b) The courts must be careful to avoid imposing their view of preferable educational methods upon the States. Once a court determines that the Act's requirements have been met, questions of methodology are for resolution by the States.

3. Entrusting a child's education to state and local agencies does not leave the child without protection. As demonstrated by this case, parents and guardians will not lack ardor in seeking to ensure that handicapped children receive all of the benefits to which they are entitled by the Act.

4. The Act does not require the provision of a sign-language interpreter here. Neither of the courts below found that there had been a failure to comply with the Act's procedures, and the findings of neither court will support a conclusion that the child's educational program failed to comply with the substantive requirements of the Act.

632 F. 2d 945, reversed and remanded.

REHNQUIST, J., delivered the opinion of the Court, in which BURGER, C.J., and POWELL, STEVENS, and O'CONNOR, JJ., joined. BLACKMUN, J., filed an opinion concurring in the judgment. WHITE, J., filed a dissenting opinion, in which BRENNAN and MARSHALL, JJ., joined.

JUSTICE REHNQUIST delivered the opinion of the Court.

This case presents a question of statutory interpretation. Petitioners contend that the Court of Appeals and the District Court misconstrued the requirements imposed by Congress upon States which receive federal funds under the Education for All Handicapped Children Act. We agree and reverse the judgement of the Court of Appeals.

I

The Education for All Handicapped Children Act of 1975 (Act), 20 U.S.C. § 1401 *et seq.*, provides federal money to assist state and local agencies in educating handicapped children, and conditions such funding upon a State's compliance with extensive goals and procedures. The Act represents an ambitious federal effort to promote the education of handicapped children, and was passed in response to Congress' perception that a majority of handicapped children in the United States "were either totally excluded from schools or [were] sitting idly in regular classrooms awaiting the time when they were old enough to 'drop out.' " H.R. Rep. No. 94-332, p. 2 (1975). The Act's evolution and major provisions shed light on the question of statutory interpretation which is at the heart of this case.

Congress first addressed the problem of educating the handicapped in 1966 when it amended the Elementary and Secondary Education Act of 1965 to establish a grant program "for the purpose of assisting the States in the initiation, expansion, and improvement of programs and projects . . . for the education of handicapped children." Pub. L. No. 89-750, § 161, 80 Stat. 1204 (1966). That program was repealed in 1970 by the Education for the Handicapped Act, Pub. L No. 91-230, 84 Stat. 175, Part B of which established a grant program similar in purpose to the repealed legislation. Neither the 1966 nor the 1970 legislation contained specific guidelines for state use of the grant money; both were aimed primarily at stimulating the States to develop educational resources and to train personnel for educating the handicapped.[1]

Dissatisfied with the progress being made under these earlier enactments, and spurred by two district court decisions holding that handicapped children should be given access to a public education,[2] Congress in 1974 greatly increased federal funding for education of the handicapped and for the first time required recipient States to adopt "a goal of providing full educational opportunities to all handicapped children." Pub. L. 93-380, 88 Stat. 579, 583 (1974) (the 1974 statute).

The 1974 statute was recognized as an interim measure only, adopted "in order to give the Congress an additional year in which to study what if any additional Federal assistance [was] required to enable the States to meet the needs of handicapped children." H.R. Rep. No. 94-332, *supra,* p. 4. The ensuing year of study produced the Education for All Handicapped Children Act of 1975.

In order to qualify for federal financial assistance under the Act, a State must demonstrate that it "has in effect a policy that assures all handicapped children the right to a free appropriate public education." 20 U. S. C. § 1412(1). That policy must be reflected in a state plan submitted to and

---

[1] See S. Rep. No. 94-168, p. 5 (1975); H.R. Rep. No. 94-332, pp. 2-3 (1975).

[2] Two cases, *Mills v. Board of Education of the District of Columbia,* 348 F. Supp. 866 (DC 1972), and *Pennsylvania Association for Retarded Children v. Commonwealth of Pennsylvania,* 334 F. Supp. 1257 (1971); 343 F. Supp. 279 (ED Pa 1972), were later identified as the most prominent of the cases contributing to Congress' enactment of the Act and the statutes which preceded it. H.R. Rep. No. 94-332, *supra,* at 3-4. Both decisions are discussed in Part III of this opinion, *infra.*

approved by the Commissioner of Education,[3] § 1413, which describes in detail the goals, programs, and timetables under which the State intends to educate handicapped children within its borders. §§ 1412, 1413. States receiving money under the Act must provide education to the handicapped by priority, first "to handicapped children who are not receiving an education" and second "to handicapped children . . . with the most severe handicaps who are receiving an inadequate education," § 1412(3), and "to the maximum extent appropriate" must educate handicapped children "with children who are not handicapped." § 1412(5).[4] The Act broadly defines "handicapped children" to include "mentally retarded, hard of hearing, deaf, speech impaired, visually handicapped, seriously emotionally disturbed, orthopedically impaired, [and] other health impaired children, [and] children with specific learning disabilities." § 1401(1).[5]

The "free appropriate public education" required by the Act is tailored to the unique needs of the handicapped child by means of an "individualized educational program" (IEP) § 1401(18). The IEP, which is prepared at a meeting between a qualified representative of the local educational agency, the child's teacher, the child's parents or guardian, and, where appropriate, the child, consists of a written document containing

"(A) a statement of the present levels of educational performance of the child, (B) a statement of annual goals, including short-term instructional objectives, (C) a statement of the specific educational services to be provided to such child, and the extent to which such child will be able to participate in regular educational programs, (D) the projected date for initiation and anticipated duration of such service, and (E) appropriate objective criteria and evaluation procedures and schedules for determining, on at least an annual basis, whether instructional objectives are being achieved." § 1401(19).

Local or regional educational agencies must review, and where appropriate revise, each child's IEP at least annually. § 1404(a)(5). See also §§ 1413(a)(11), 1414(a)(5).

In addition to the state plan and the IEP already described, the Act imposes extensive procedural requirements upon States receiving federal funds under its provisions. Parents or guardians of handicapped children

---

[3]All functions of the Commissioner of Education, formerly an officer in the Department of Health, Education, and Welfare, were transferred to the Secretary of Education in 1979 when Congress passed the Department of Education Organization Act, 20 U. S. C. § 3401 et seq. See 20 U. S. C. § 3441(a)(1).

[4]Despite this preference for "mainstreaming" handicapped children—educating them with nonhandicapped children—Congress recognized that regular classrooms simply would not be a suitable setting for the education of many handicapped children. The Act expressly acknowledges that "the nature or severity of the handicap [may be] such that education in regular classes with the use of supplementary aids and services cannot be achieved satisfactorily." § 1412(5). The Act thus provides for the education of some handicapped children in separate classes or institutional settings. See ibid.; § 1413(a)(4).

[5]In addition to covering a wide variety of handicapping conditions, the Act requires special educational services for children "regardless of the severity of their handicap." §§ 1412(2)(C), 1414(a)(1)(A).

must be notified of any proposed change in "the identification, evaluation, or educational placement of the child or the provision of a free appropriate public education to the child," and must be permitted to bring a complaint about "any matter relating to" such evaluation and education. § 1415(b)(1)(D) and (E).[6] Complaints brought by parents or guardians must be resolved at "an impartial due process hearing," and appeal to the State educational agency must be provided if the initial hearing is held at the local or regional level. § 1415(b)(2) and (c).[7]

Thereafter, "[a]ny party aggrieved by the findings and decisions" of the state administrative hearing has "the right to bring a civil action with respect to the complaint . . . in any State court of competent jurisdiction or in a district court of the United States without regard to the amount in controversy." § 1415(e)(2).

Thus, although the Act leaves to the States the primary responsibility for developing and executing educational programs for handicapped children, it imposes significant requirements to be followed in the discharge of that responsibility. Compliance is assured by provisions permitting the withholding of federal funds upon determination that a participating state or local agency has failed to satisfy the requirements of the Act, §§ 1414(b)(2)(A), 1416, and by the provision for judicial review. At present, all States except New Mexico receive federal funds under the portions of the Act at issue today. Brief for the United States as *Amicus Curiae* 2, n. 2.

II

This case arose in connection with the education of Amy Rowley, a deaf student at the Furnace Woods School in the Hendrick Hudson Central School District, Peekskill, New York. Amy has minimal residual hearing and is an excellent lipreader. During the year before she began attending Furnace

---

[6]The requirements that parents be permitted to file complaints regarding their child's education, and be present when the child's IEP is formulated, represent only two examples of Congress' effort to maximize parental involvement in the education of each handicapped child. In addition, the Act requires that parents be permitted "to examine all relevant records with respect to the identification, evaluation, and educational placement of the child, and . . . to obtain an independent educational evaluation of the child." § 1415(b)(1)(A). See also §§ 1412(4), 1414(a)(4). State educational policies and the state plan submitted to the Commissioner of Education must be formulated in "consultation with individuals involved in or concerned with the education of handicapped children, including handicapped individuals and parents or guardians of handicapped children." § 1412(7). See also § 1412(2)(E). Local agencies, which receive funds under the Act by applying to the state agency, must submit applications which assure that they have developed procedures for "the participation and consultation of the parents or guardian[s] of [handicapped] children" in local educational programs, § 1414(a)(1)(C)(iii), and the application itself, along with "all pertinent documents related to such application," must be made "available to parents, guardians, and other member of the general public." § 1414(a)(4).

[7]"Any party" to a state of local administrative hearing must "be accorded (1) the right to be accompanied and advised by counsel and by individuals with special knowledge or training with respect to the problems of handicapped children, (2) the right to present evidence and confront, cross examine, and compel the attendance of witnesses, (3) the right to a written or electronic verbatim record of such hearing, and (4) the right to written findings of fact and decision." § 1415(d).

Woods, a meeting between her parents and school administrators resulted in a decision to place her in a regular kindergarten class in order to determine what supplemental services would be necessary to her education. Several members of the school administration prepared for Amy's arrival by attending a course in sign-language interpretation, and a teletype machine was installed in the principal's office to facilitate communication with her parents who are also deaf. At the end of the trial period it was determined that Amy should remain in the kindergarten class, but that she should be provided with an FM hearing aid which would amplify words spoken into a wireless receiver by the teacher or fellow students during certain classroom activities. Amy successfully completed her kindergarten year.

As required by the Act, an IEP was prepared for Amy during the fall of her first-grade year. The IEP provided that Amy should be educated in a regular classroom at Furnace Woods, should continue to use the FM hearing aid, and should receive instruction from a tutor for the deaf for one hour each day and from a speech therapist for three hours each week. The Rowleys agreed with the IEP but insisted that Amy also be provided a qualified sign-language interpreter in all of her academic classes. Such an interpreter had been placed in Amy's kindergarten class for a two-week experimental period, but the interpreter had reported that Amy did not need his services at that time. The school administrators likewise concluded that Amy did not need such an interpreter in her first-grade classroom. They reached this conclusion after consulting the school district's Committee on the Handicapped, which had received expert evidence from Amy's parents on the importance of a sign-language interpreter, received testimony from Amy's teacher and other persons familiar with her academic and social progress, and visited a class for the deaf.

When their request for an interpreter was denied, the Rowleys demanded and received a hearing before an independent examiner. After receiving evidence from both sides, the examiner agreed with the administrators' determination that an interpreter was not necessary because "Amy was achieving educationally, academically, and socially" without such assistance. App. to Pet. for Cert. F-22. The examiner's decision was affirmed on appeal by the New York Commissioner of Education on the basis of substantial evidence in the record. *Id.,* at E-4. Pursuant to the Act's provision for judicial review, the Rowleys then brought an action in the United States District Court for the Southern District of New York, claiming that the administrators' denial of the sign-language interpreter constituted a denial of the "free appropriate public education" guaranteed by the Act.

The District Court found that Amy "is a remarkably well-adjusted child" who interacts and communicates well with her classmates and has "developed an extraordinary rapport" with her teachers. 483 F. Supp. 528, 531. It also found that "she performs better than the average child in her class and is advancing easily from grade to grade," *id.* at 534, but "that she understands considerably less of what goes on in class than she would if she were not deaf" and thus "is not learning as much, or performing as well academically, as she would without her handicap," *id.,* at 532. This disparity between Amy's achievement and her potential led the court to decide that she was not receiving a "free appropriate public education," which the court defined as "an opportunity to achieve [her] full potential commensurate with the opportunity provided to other children." *Id.,* at 534. According to the

District Court, such a standard "requires that the potential of the handicapped child be measured and compared to his or her performance, and that the remaining differential or 'shortfall' be compared to the shortfall experienced by non-handicapped children." *Ibid.* The District Court's definition arose from its assumption that the responsibility for "giv[ing] content to the requirement of an 'appropriate education' " had "been left entirely to the federal courts and the hearing officers." *Id.,* at 533.[8]

A divided panel of the United States Court of Appeals for the Second Circuit affirmed. The Court of Appeals "agree[d] with the [D]istrict [C]ourt's conclusions of law," and held that its "findings of fact [were] not clearly erroneous." 632 F. 2d 945, 947 (1980).

We granted certiorari to review the lower courts' interpretation of the Act. 454 U.S. 961 (1981). Such review requires us to consider two questions: What is meant by the Act's requirement of a "free appropriate public education?" And what is the role of state and federal courts in exercising the review granted by § 1415 of the Act? We consider these questions separately.[9]

III

A

This is the first case in which this Court has been called upon to interpret any provision of the Act. As noted previously, the District Court and the Court of Appeals concluded that "[t]he Act itself does not define 'appropriate education,'" 483 F. Supp., at 533, but leaves "to the courts and the hearing officers" the responsibility of "giv[ing] content to the requirement of an appropriate education." *Ibid.* See also 632 F. 2d, at 947. Petitioners contend that the definition of the phrase "free appropriate public education" used by the courts below overlooks the definition of that phrase actually found in the Act. Respondents agree that the Act defines "free appropriate public education," but contend that the statutory definition is not "functional" and thus "offers judges no guidance in their consideration of controversies involving the 'identification, evaluation, or educational placement of

---

[8]For reasons that are not revealed in the record, the District Court concluded that "[t]he Act itself does not define 'appropriate education.'" 483 F. Supp., at 533. In fact, the Act expressly defines the phrase "free appropriate public education," see § 1401(18), to which the District Court was referring. See 483 F. Supp., at 533. After overlooking the statutory definition, the District Court sought guidance not from regulations interpreting the Act, but from regulations promulgated under Section 504 of the Rehabilitation Act. See 483 F. Supp., at 533, citing 45 CFR § 84.33(b).

[9]The IEP which respondents challenged in the District Court was created for the 1978-1979 school year. Petitioners contend that the District Court erred in reviewing that IEP after the school year had ended and before the school administrators were able to develop another IEP for subsequent years. We disagree. Judicial review invariably takes more than nine months to complete, not to mention the time consumed during the preceding state administrative hearings. The District Court thus correctly ruled that it retained jurisdiction to grant relief because the alleged deficiencies in the IEP were capable of repetition as to the parties before it yet evading review. *Rowley* v. *The Board of Education of the Hendrick Hudson Central School District,* 483 F. Supp. 536, 538 (1980). See *Murphy* v. *Hunt,* 455 U.S. 478, 482 (1982); *Weinstein* v. *Bradford,* 423 U.S. 147, 149 (1975).

the child or the provision of a free appropriate public education.' " Brief for Respondents 28. The United States, appearing as *amicus curiae* on behalf of respondents, states that "[a]lthough the Act includes definitions of 'free appropriate public education' and other related terms, the statutory definitions do not adequately explain what is meant by 'appropriate.' " Brief for United States as *Amicus Curiae* 13.

We are loath to conclude that Congress failed to offer any assistance in defining the meaning of the principal substantive phrase used in the Act. It is beyond dispute that, contrary to the conclusions of the courts below, the Act does expressly define "free appropriate public education":

> "The term 'free appropriate public education' means *special education* and *related services* which (A) have been provided at public expense, under public supervision and direction, and without charge, (B) meet the standards of the State educational agency, (C) include an appropriate preschool, elementary, or secondary school education in the State involved, and (D) are provided in conformity with the individualized education program required under section 1414(a)(5) of this title." § 1401(18) (emphasis added).

"Special education," as referred to in this definition, means "specially designed instruction, at no cost to parents or guardians, to meet the unique needs of a handicapped child, including classroom instruction, instruction in physical education, home instruction, and instruction in hospitals and institutions." § 1401(16). "Related services" are defined as "transportation, and such developmental, corrective, and other supportive services . . . as may be required to assist a handicapped child to benefit from special education." § 1401(17).[10]

Like many statutory definitions, this one tends toward the cryptic rather than the comprehensive, but that is scarcely a reason for abandoning the quest for legislative intent. Whether or not the definition is a "functional" one as respondents contend it is not, it is the principal tool which Congress has given us for parsing the critical phrase of the Act. We think more must be made of it than either respondents or the United States seems willing to admit.

According to the definitions contained in the Act, a "free appropriate public education" consists of educational instruction specially designed to meet the unique needs of the handicapped child, supported by such services as are necessary to permit the child "to benefit" from the instruction. Almost as a checklist for adequacy under the Act, the definition also requires that such instruction and services be provided at public expense and under public supervision, meet the State's educational standards, approximate the grade levels used in the State's regular education, and comport with the child's IEP. Thus, if personalized instruction is being provided with sufficient supportive services to permit the child to benefit from the instruction, and the other items on the definitional checklist are satisfied, the child is receiving a "free appropriate public education" as defined by the Act.

---

[10]Examples of "related services" identified in the Act are "speech pathology and audiology, psychological services, physical and occupational therapy, recreation, and medical and counseling services, except that such medical services shall be for diagnostic and evaluation purposes only" § 1401(17).

Other portions of the statute also shed light upon congressional intent. Congress found that of the roughly eight million handicapped children in the United States at the time of enactment, one million were "excluded entirely from the public school system" and more than half were receiving an inappropriate education. Note to § 1401. In addition, as mentioned in Part I, the Act requires States to extend educational services first to those children who are receiving no education and second to those children who are receiving an "inadequate education." § 1412(3). When these express statutory findings and priorities are read together with the Act's extensive procedural requirements and its definition of "free appropriate public education," the face of the statute evinces a congressional intent to bring previously excluded handicapped children into the public education systems of the States and to require the States to adopt *procedures* which would result in individualized consideration of and instruction for each child.

Noticeably absent from the language of the statute is any substantive standard prescribing the level of education to be accorded handicapped children. Certainly the language of the statute contains no requirement like the one imposed by the lower courts—that States maximize the potential of handicapped children "commensurate with the opportunity provided to other children." 483 F. Supp., at 534. That standard was expounded by the District Court without reference to the statutory definitions or even to the legislative history of the Act. Although we find the statutory definition of "free appropriate public education" to be helpful in our interpretation of the Act, there remains the question of whether the legislative history indicates a congressional intent that such education meet some additional substantive standard. For an answer, we turn to that history.[11]

---

[11] The dissent, finding that "the standard of the courts below seems . . . to reflect the congressional purpose" of the Act, *post*, at 8, concludes that our answer to this question "is not a satisfactory one." *Id.*, at 5. Presumably, the dissent also agrees with the District Court's conclusion that "it has been left entirely to the courts and the hearing officers to give content to the requirement of an 'appropriate education.'" 483 F. Supp., at 533. It thus seems that the dissent would give the courts carte blanche to impose upon the States whatever burden their various judgments indicate should be imposed. Indeed, the dissent clearly characterizes the requirement of an "appropriate education" as open-ended, noting that "if there are limits not evident from the face of the statute on what may be considered an 'appropriate education,' they must be found in the purpose of the statute or its legislative history." *Post,* at 2. Not only are we unable to find any suggestion from the face of the statute that the requirement of an "appropriate private education" was to be limitless, but we also view the dissent's approach as contrary to the fundamental proposition that Congress, when exercising its spending power, can impose no burden upon the States unless it does so unambiguously. See *infra,* at 27, n. 26.

No one can doubt that this would have been an easier case if Congress had seen fit to provide a more comprehensive statutory definition of the phrase "free appropriate public education." But Congress did not do so, and "our problem is to construe what Congress has written. After all, Congress expresses its purpose by words. It is for us to ascertain—neither to add nor to subtract, neither to delete nor to distort." *62 Cases of Jam* v. *United States,* 340 U.S. 593, 596 (1951). We would be less than faithful to our obligation to construe what Congress has written if in this case we were to disregard the statutory language and legislative history of the Act by concluding that Congress had imposed upon the States a burden of unspecified proportions and weight, to be revealed only through case by case adjudication in the courts.

B

(i)

As suggested in Part I, federal support for education of the handicapped is a fairly recent development. Before passage of the Act some States had passed laws to improve the educational services afforded handicapped children,[12] but many of these children were excluded completely from any form of public education or were left to fend for themselves in classrooms designed for education of their nonhandicapped peers. The House Report begins by emphasizing this exclusion and misplacement, noting that millions of handicapped children "were either totally excluded from schools or [were] sitting idly in regular classrooms awaiting the time when they were old enough to 'drop out.'" H.R. Rep. No. 94-332, *supra*, at 2. See also S. Rep. No. 94-168, p. 8 (1975). One of the Act's two principal sponsors in the Senate urged its passage in similar terms:

"While much progress has been made in the last few years, we can take no solace in the progress until all handicapped children are, in fact, receiving an education. The most recent statistics provided by the Bureau of Education for the Handicapped estimate that . . . 1.75 million handicapped children do not receive any educational services, and 2.5 million handicapped children are not receiving an appropriate education." 121 Cong. Rec. 19486 (1975) (remarks of Sen. Williams).

This concern, stressed repeatedly throughout the legislative history,[13] confirms the impression conveyed by the language of the statute: By passing the Act, Congress sought primarily to make public education available to handicapped children. But in seeking to provide such access to public education, Congress did not impose upon the States any greater substantive educational standard than would be necessary to make such access meaningful. Indeed, Congress expressly "recognize[d] that in many instances the process of providing special education and related services to handicapped children is not guaranteed to produce any particular outcome." S. Rep. No. 94-168, *supra*, at 11. Thus, the intent of the Act was more to open the door of public education to handicapped children on appropriate terms than to guarantee any particular level of education once inside.

Both the House and the Senate reports attribute the impetus for the Act and its predecessors to two federal court judgments rendered in 1971 and 1972. As the Senate Report states, passage of the Act "followed a series of landmark court cases establishing in law the right to education for all handi-

---

[12]See H.R. Rep. No. 94-332, *supra,* at 10; Note, The Education of All Handicapped Children Act of 1975, Mich. J. L. Ref. 110, 119 (1976).

[13]See, e.g., 121 Cong. Rec. 19494 (1975) (remarks of Sen. Javits) ("all too often, our handicapped citizens have been denied the opportunity to receive an adequate education"); 121 Cong. Rec. 19502 (1975) (remarks of Sen. Cranston) (million of handicapped "children are largely excluded from educational opportunities that we give to our other children"); 121 Cong. rec. 23708 (1975) (remarks of Rep. Mink) ("handicapped children . . . are denied access to public schools because of a lack of trained personnel").

capped children." S. Rep. No. 94-168, *supra,* at 6.[14] The first case, *Pennsylvania Association for Retarded Children* v. *Commonwealth of Pennsylvania (PARC),* 334 F. Supp. 1257 (1971), 343 F. Supp. 279 (ED Pa 1972), was a suit on behalf of retarded children challenging the constitutionality of a Pennsylvania statute which acted to exclude them from public education and training. The case ended in a consent decree which enjoined the State from "deny[ing] to any mentally retarded child *access* to a free public program of education and training." 334 F. Supp., at 1258 (emphasis added).

PARC was followed by *Mills* v. *Board of Education of the District of Columbia,* 348 F. Supp. 866 (DC 1972), a case in which the plaintiff handicapped children had been excluded from the District of Columbia public schools. The court's judgment, quoted at page 6 of the Senate Report on the Act, provided

> "[t]hat no [handicapped] child eligible for a publicly supported education in the District of Columbia public schools shall be *excluded* from a regular school assignment by a rule, policy, or practice of the Board of Education of the District of Columbia or its agents unless such child is provided (a) *adequate* alternative educational services suited to the child's needs, which may include special education or tuition grants, and (b) a constitutionally adequate prior hearing and periodic review of the child's status, progress, and the *adequacy* of any educational alternative." 348 F. Supp., at 878 (emphasis added).

Mills and *PARC* both held that handicapped children must be given access to an adequate, publicly supported education. Neither case purports to require any particular substantive level of education.[15] Rather, like the language of the Act, the cases set forth extensive procedures to be followed in formulating personalized educational programs for handicapped children.

---

[14]Similarly, the Senate Report states that it was an "[i]ncreased awareness of the educational needs of handicapped children and landmark court decisions establishing the right to education for handicapped children [that] pointed to the necessity of an expanded federal role." S. Rep. No. 94-168, *supra,* at 5. See also H.R. Rep. No. 94-332, *supra,* at 2-3.

[15]The only substantive standard which can be implied from these cases comports with the standard implicit in the Act. *PARC* states that each child must receive "access to a free public program of education and training *appropriate to his learning capacities,"* 334 F. Supp., at 1258, and that further state action is required when it appears that "the needs of the mentally retarded child are not being *adequately* served," *id.,* at 1266. (Emphasis added.) *Mills* also speaks in terms of "adequate" educational services, 348 F. Supp., at 878, and sets a realistic standard of providing *some* educational services to each child when every need cannot be met.

"If sufficient funds are not available to finance all of the services and programs that are needed and desirable in the system then the available funds must be expended equitably in such a manner that no child is entirely excluded from a publicly supported education consistent with his needs and ability to benefit therefrom. The inadequacies of the District of Columbia Public School System whether occasioned by insufficient funding or administrative inefficiency, certainly cannot be permitted to bear more heavily on the 'exceptional' or handicapped child than on the normal child." *Id.,* at 876.

See 348 F. Supp., at 878-883; 334 F. Supp., at 1258-1267.[16] The fact that both *PARC* and *Mills* are discussed at length in the legislative reports[17] suggests that the principles which they established are the principles which, to a significant extent, guided the drafters of the Act. Indeed, immediately after discussing these cases the Senate Report describes the 1974 statute as having "incorporated the major principles of the right to education cases." S. Rep. No. 94-168, *supra,* at 8. Those principles in turn became the basis of the Act, which itself was designed to effectuate the purposes of the 1974 statute. H.R. Rep. No. 94-332, *supra,* at 5.[18]

That the Act imposes no clear obligation upon recipient States beyond the requirement that handicapped children receive some form of specialized education is perhaps best demonstrated by the fact the Congress, in explaining the need for the Act, equated an "appropriate education" to the receipt of some specialized educational services. The Senate Report states: [T]he most recent statistics provided by the Bureau of Education for the Handicapped estimate that of the more than 8 million children . . . with handicapping conditions requiring special education and related services, only 3.9 million such children are receiving an appropriate education." S. Rep. No.

---

[16]Like the Act, *PARC* required the State to "identify, locate, [and] evaluate" handicapped children 334 F. Supp., at 1267, to create for each child an individual educational program, *id.,* at 1265, and to hold a hearing "on any change in educational assignment," *id.,* 1266. *Mills* also required the preparation of an individual educational program for each child. In addition, *Mills* permitted the child's parents to inspect records relevant to the child's education, to obtain an independent educational evaluation of the child, to object to the IEP and receive a hearing before an independent hearing officer, to be represented by counsel at the hearing, and to have the right confront and cross-examine adverse witnesses, all of which are also permitted by the Act. 348 F. Supp., at 879-881. Like the Act, *Mills* also required that the education of handicapped children be conducted pursuant to an overall plan prepared by the District of Columbia, and established a policy of educating handicapped children with nonhandicapped children whenever possible. *Ibid.*

[17]*See S. Rep. No. 94-168, supra,* at 6-7; H.R. Rep. No. 94-332, *supra,* at 3-4.

[18]The 1974 statute "incorporated the major principles of the right to education cases," by "add[ing] important new provisions to the Education of the Handicapped Act which require the States to: establish a goal of providing full educational opportunities to all handicapped children; provide procedures for insuring that handicapped children and their parents or guardians are guaranteed procedural safeguards in decisions regarding identification, evaluation, and education placement of handicapped children; establish procedures to insure that, to the maximum extent appropriate, handicapped children . . . are educated with children who are not handicapped; . . . and establish procedures to insure that testing and evaluation materials and procedures utilized for the purposes of classification and placement of handicapped children will be selected and administered so as not to be racially or culturally discriminatory," S. Rep. No. 94-168, *supra,* at 8.

The House Report explains that the Act simply incorporated these purposes of the 1974 statute: the Act intended "primarily to amend . . . the Education of the Handicapped Act in order to provide permanent authorization and a comprehensive mechanism which will insure that those provisions enacted during the 93rd Congress [the 1974 statute] will result in maximum benefits for handicapped children and their families." H.R. Rep. No. 94-332, *supra,* at 5. Thus, the 1974 statute's purpose of providing handicapped children *access* to a public education became the purpose of the Act.

94-168, *supra,* at 8.[19] This statement, which reveals Congress' view that 3.9 million handicapped children were "receiving an appropriate education" in 1975, is followed immediately in the Senate Report by a table showing that 3.9 million handicapped children were "served" in 1975 and a slightly larger number were "unserved." A similar statement and table appear in the House Report. H.R. Rep. No. 94-332, *supra,* at 11-12.

It is evident from the legislative history that the characterization of handicapped children as "served" referred to children who were receiving some form of specialized educational services from the States, and that the characterization of children as "unserved" referred to those who were receiving no specialized educational services. For example, a letter sent to the United State Commissioner of Education by the House Committee on Education and Labor, signed by two key sponsors of the Act in the House, asked the Commissioner to identify the number of handicapped "children served" in each State. The letter asked for statistics on the number of children "being served" in various types of "special education program[s]" and the number of children who were not "receiving education services." Hearings on S. 6 before the Subcommittee on the Handicapped of the Senate Committee on Labor and Public Welfare, 94th Cong., 1st Sess., 205-207 (1975). Similarly, Senator Randolph, one of the Act's principal sponsors in the Senate, noted that roughly one-half of the handicapped children in the United States "are receiving special educational services." *Id.,* at 1.[20] By characterizing the 3.9

---

[19]These statistics appear repeatedly throughout the legislative history of the Act, demonstrating a virtual consensus among legislators that 3.9 million handicapped children were receiving and appropriate education in 1975. See, e.g., 121 Cong. Rec. 19486 (1975) (remarks of Sen. Williams); 121 Cong. Rec. 19504 (1975) (remarks of Sen. Schweicker); 121 Cong. Rec. 23702 (1975) (remarks of Rep. Madden); 121 Cong. Rec. 23702 (1975) (remarks of Rep. Brademas); 121 Cong. Rec. 23709 (1975) (remarks of Rep. Minish); 121 Cong. Rec. 37024 (1975) (remarks of Rep. Brademas); 121 Cong. Rec. 37027 (1975) (remarks of Rep. Gude); 121 Cong. Rec. 37417 (1975) (remarks of Sen. Javits); 121 Cong., Rec. 37420 (1975) (remarks of Sen. Hathaway).

[20]Senator Randolph stated: "only 55 percent of the school-aged handicapped children and 22 percent of the pre-school-aged handicapped children are receiving special educational services." Hearings on S. 6 before the Subcommittee on the Handicapped of the Senate Committee on Labor and Public Welfare, 94th Cong., 1st Sess., 1 (1975). Although the figures differ slightly in various parts of the legislative history, the general thrust of congressional calculations was that roughly one-half of the handicapped children in the United States were not receiving specialized educational services, and thus were not "served." See, e.g., 121 Cong. Rec. 19494 (1975) (remarks of Sen. Javits) ("only 50 percent of the Nation's handicapped children received proper education services"); 121 Cong. Rec. 19504 (1975) (remark of Sen. Humphrey) ("[a]lmost 3 million handicapped children, while in school, receive none of the special services that they require in order to make education a meaningful experience"); 121 Cong. Rec. 23706 (1975) (remarks of Rep. Quie) ("only 55 percent [of handicapped children] were receiving a public education"); 121 Cong. Rec. 233709 (1975) (remarks of Rep. Biaggi) ("[o]ver 3 million [handicapped] children in this country are receiving either below par education or none at all").

Statements similar to those appearing in the text, which equate "served" as it appears in the Senate Report to "receiving special educational services," appear throughout the legislative history. See, e.g. 121 Cong. Rec. 19492 (1975) (remarks of Sen. Williams); 121 Cong. Rec. 19494 (1975) (remarks of Sen. Javits); 121 Cong. Rec. 19496 (1975) (remarks of Sen. Stone); 121 Cong. Rec. 19504-19505 (1975) (remarks of Sen. Humphrey); 121 Cong. Rec. 23703 (1975) (remarks of Rep. Brademas); Hearings million handicapped children who were "served" as children who were "receiving an appropriate education," the Senate and House reports unmistakably disclose Congress' perception of the type of education required by the Act: an "appropriate education" is provided when personalized educational services are provided.[21]

(ii)

Respondents contend that "the goal of the Act is to provide each handicapped child with an equal educational opportunity." Brief for Respondents 35. We think, however, that the requirement that a State provide specialized educational services to handicapped children generates no additional requirement that the services so provided be sufficient to maximize each child's potential "commensurate with the opportunity provided other children." Respondents and the United States correctly note that Congress sought "to provide assistance to the States in carrying out their responsibilities under . . . the Constitution of the United States to provide equal protection of the laws." S. Rep. No. 94-168, *supra,* at 13.[22] But we do not think that such

---

on H.R. 7217 before the Subcommittee on Select Education of the Committee on Education and Labor of the House of Representatives, 94th Cong., 1st Sess., 91, 150, 153 (1975); Hearings on H.R. 4199 before the Select Subcommittee on Education of the Committee on Education and Labor of the House of Representatives, 93rd Cong., 1st Sess., 130, 139 (1973). See also 45 CFR § 121a.343(b) (1980).

[21]In seeking to read more into the Act than its language or legislative history will permit, the United States focuses upon the word "appropriate," arguing that "the statutory definitions do not adequately explain what [it means]." Brief for the United States as *Amicus Curiae* 13. Whatever Congress meant by an "appropriate" education, it is clear that it did not mean a potential-maximizing education.

The term as used in reference to education the handicapped appears to have originated in the *PARC* decision, where the District Court required that handicapped children be provided with "education and training appropriate to [their] learning capacities." 334 F. Supp., at 1258. The word appears again in the *Mills* decision, The district Court at one point referring to the need for "an appropriate educational program," 348 F. Supp., at 879, and at another point speaking of a "suitable publicly-supported education," *id.,* at 878. Both cases also refer to the need for an "adequate" education. See 334 F. Supp., at 1266; 348 F. Supp., at 878.

The use of "appropriate" in the language of the Act, although by no means definitive, suggests that Congress used the word as much to describe the settings in which handicapped children should be educated as to prescribe the substantive content or supportive services of their education. For example, § 1412(5) requires that handicapped children be educated in classrooms with nonhandicapped children "to the maximum extent appropriate." Similarly, § 1401(19) provides that, "whenever appropriate," handicapped children should attend and participate in the meeting at which their IEP is drafted. In addition, the definition of "free appropriate public education" itself states that instruction given handicapped children should be at an "appropriate preschool, elementary, or secondary school" level. § 1401(18)(C). The Act's use of the word "appropriate" thus seems to reflect Congress' recognition that some settings simply are not suitable environments for the participation of some handicapped children. At the very least, these statutory uses of the word refute the contention that Congress used "appropriate" as a term of art which concisely expresses the standard found by the lower courts.

[22]See also 121 Cong. Rec. 19492(1975) (remarks of Sen. Williams); 121 Cong. Rec. 19504 (1975) (remarks of Sen. Humphrey).

statements imply a congressional intent to achieve strict equality of opportunity or services.

The educational opportunities provided by our public school systems undoubtedly differ from student to student, depending upon a myriad of factors that might affect a particular student's ability to assimilate information presented in the classroom. The requirement that States provide "equal" educational opportunities would thus seem to present an entirely unworkable standard requiring impossible measurements and comparisons. Similarly, furnishing handicapped children with only such services as are available to nonhandicapped children would in all probability fall short of the statutory requirement of "free appropriate public education;" to require, on the other hand, the furnishing of every special service necessary to maximize each handicapped child's potential is, we think, further than Congress intended to go. Thus to speak in terms of "equal" services in one instance gives less than what is required by the Act and in another instance more. The theme of the Act is "free appropriate public education," a phrase which is too complex to be captured by the word "equal" whether one is speaking of opportunities or services.

The legislative conception of the requirements of equal protection was undoubtedly informed by the two district court decisions referred to above. But cases such as *Mills* and *PARC* held simply that handicapped children may not be excluded entirely from public education. In *Mills,* the District Court said:

> "If sufficient funds are not available to finance all of the services and programs that are needed and desirable in the system then the available funds must be expended equitably in such a manner that no child is entirely excluded from a publicly supported education consistent with his needs and ability to benefit therefrom." 348 F. Supp., at 876

The *PARC* Court used similar language, saying "[i]t is the commonwealth's obligation to place each mentally retarded child in a free, public program of education and training appropriate to the child's capacity. . . ." 334 F. Supp., at 1260. The right of access to free public education enunciated by these cases is significantly regardless of capacity. To the extent that Congress might have looked further than these cases which are mentioned in the legislative history, at the time of enactment of the Act this Court had held at least twice that the Equal Protection Clause of the Fourteenth Amendment does not require States to expend equal financial resources on the education of each child. *San Antonio School District* v. *Rodriguez,* 411 U. S. 1 (1975); *McInnis* v. *Shapiro,* 293 F. Supp. 327 (ND Ill. 1968), *aff'd sub nom, McInnis* v. *Ogilvie,* 394 U. S. 322 (1969).

In explaining the need for federal legislation, the House Report noted that "no congressional legislation, has required a precise guarantee for handicapped children, i.e. a basic floor of opportunity that would bring into compliance all school districts with the constitutional right of equal protection with respect to handicapped children." H.R. Rep. No. 94-332, *supra,* at 14. Assuming that the Act was designed to fill the need identified in the House Report—that is, to provide a "basic floor of opportunity" consistent with equal protection—neither the Act nor its history persuasively demonstrate that Congress thought that equal protection required anything more than equal access. Therefore, Congress' desire to provide specialized educational services, even in furtherance of "equality," cannot be read as imposing any particular substantive educational standard upon the States.

The District Court and the Court of Appeals thus erred when they held that the Act requires New York to maximize the potential of each handicapped child commensurate with the opportunity provided nonhandicapped children. Desirable though that goal might be, it is not the standard that Congress imposed upon States which receive funding under the Act. Rather, Congress sought primarily to identify and evaluate handicapped children, and to provide them with access to a free public education.

(iii)

Implicit in the congressional purpose of providing access to a "free appropriate public education" is the requirement that the education to which *access* is provided be sufficient to confer some educational benefit upon the handicapped child. It would do little good for Congress to spend millions of dollars in providing access to a public education only to have the handicapped child receive no benefit from that education. The statutory definition of "free appropriate public education," in addition to requiring that States provide each child with "specially designed instruction," expressly requires the provision of "such . . . supportive services . . . as may be required to assist a handicapped child to *benefit* from special education. § 1401(17) (emphasis added). We therefore conclude that the "basic floor of opportunity" provided by the Act consists of access to specialized instruction and related services which are individually designed to provide educational benefit to the handicapped child.[23]

---

[23]This view is supported by the congressional intention, frequently expressed in the legislative history, that handicapped children be enabled to achieve a reasonable degree of self sufficiency. After referring to statistics showing that many handicapped children were excluded from public education, the Senate Report states:

"The long range implications of these statistics are that public agencies and taxpayers will spend billions of dollars over the lifetimes of these individuals to maintain such persons as dependents and in a minimally acceptable lifestyle. With proper education services, many would be able to become productive citizens, contributing to society instead of being forced to remain burdens. Others, through such services, would increase their independence, thus reducing their dependence on society." S. Rep. No. 94-168, *supra,* at 9. See also H.R. Rep. No. 94-332, *supra,* at 11.

Similarly, one of the principal Senate sponsors of the Act stated that "providing appropriate educational services now means that many of these individuals will be able to become a contributing part of our society, and they will not have to depend on subsistence payments from public funds." 121 Cong. Rec. 19492 (1975) (remarks of Sen. Williams). See also 121 Cong. Rec. 25541 (1975) (remarks of Rep. Harkin); 121 Cong. Rec. 37024-37025 (1975) (remarks of Rep. Brademas); 121 Cong. Rec. 37027 (1975) (remarks of Rep. Gude); 121 Cong. Rec. 37410 (1975) (remarks of Sen. Randolph); 121 Cong. Rec. 37416 (1975) (Remarks of Sen. Williams).

The desire to provide handicapped children with an attainable degree of personal independence obviously anticipated that state educational programs would confer educational benefits upon such children. But at the same time, the goal of achieving some degree of self sufficiency in most cases is a good deal more modest than the potential-maximizing goal adopted by the lower courts.

Despite its frequent mention, we cannot conclude, as did the dissent in the Court of

The determination of when handicapped children are receiving suffic-ient educational benefits to satisfy the requirements of the Act presents a more difficult problem. The Act requires participating States to educate a wide spectrum of handicapped children, from the marginally hearing-im-paired to the profoundly retarded and palsied. It is clear that the benefits obtainable by children at one end of the spectrum will differ dramatically from those obtained by children at the other end, with infinite variations in between. One child may have little difficulty competing successfully in an academic setting with nonhandicapped children while another child may en-counter great difficulty in acquiring even the most basic of self-maintenance skills. We do not attempt today to establish any one test for determining the adequacy of educational benefits conferred upon all children covered by the Act. Because in this case we are presented with a handicapped child who is receiving substantial specialized instruction and related services, and who is performing above average in the regular classrooms of a public school sys-tem, we confine our analysis to that situation.

The Act requires participating States to educate handicapped children with nonhandicapped children whenever possible.[24] When that "mainstream-ing" preference of the Act has been met and a child is being educated in the regular classrooms of a public school system, the system itself monitors the educational progress of the child. Regular examinations are administered, grades are awarded, and yearly advancement to higher grade levels is permit-ted for those children who attain an adequate knowledge of the course mate-rial. The grading and advancement system thus constitutes an important factor in determining educational benefit. Children who graduate from our public school systems are considered by our society to have been "educated" at least to the grade level they have completed, and access to an "education" for handicapped children is precisely what Congress sought to provide in the Act.[25]

Appeals, the self sufficiency was itself the substantive standard which Congress im-posed upon the States. Because many mildly handicapped children will achieve self sufficiency without state assistance while personal independence for the severely handicapped may be an unreachable goal, "self sufficiency" as a substantive stan-dard is at once an inadequate protection and an overly demanding requirement. We thus view these references in the legislative history as evidence of Congress' intention that the services provided handicapped children be educationally beneficial, whatever the nature of severity of their handicap.

[24]Section 1412(5) of the Act requires that participating States establish "procedures to assure that, to the maximum extent appropriate, handicapped children, including children in public or private institutions or other care facilities, are educated with children who are not handicapped, and that special classes, separate schooling, or other removal of handicapped children from the regular educational environment occurs only when the nature of severity of the handicap is such that education in regular classes with the use of supplementary aids and services cannot be achieved satisfactorily."

[25]We do not hold today that every handicapped child who is advancing from grade to grade in a regular public school system is automatically receiving a "free appropri-ate public education." In this case, however, we find Amy's academic progress, when considered with the special services and professional consideration accorded by the Furnace Woods school administrators, to be dispositive.

C

When the language of the Act and its legislative history are considered together, the requirements imposed by Congress become tolerably clear. Insofar as a State is required to provide a handicapped child with a "free appropriate public education," we hold that it satisfies this requirement by providing personalized instruction with sufficient support services to permit the child to benefit educationally from that instruction. Such instruction and services must be provided at public expense, must meet the State's educational standards, must approximate the grade levels used in the State's regular education, and must comport with the child's IEP. In addition, the IEP, and therefore the personalized instruction, should be formulated in accordance with the requirements of the Act and, if the child is being educated in the regular classrooms of the public education system, should be reasonably calculated to enable the child to achieve passing marks and advance from grade to grade.[26]

IV

A

As mentioned in Part I, the Act permits "[a]ny party aggrieved by the findings and decision" of the state administrative hearings "to bring a civil action" in "any State court of competent jurisdiction or in a district court of the United States without regard to the amount in controversy." § 1415(e)(2). The complaint, and therefore the civil action, may concern "any matter relating to the identification, evaluation, or educational placement of the child, or the provision of a free appropriate public education to such child." § 1415(b)(1)(E). In reviewing the complaint, the Act provides that a court

---

[26]In defending the decisions of the District Court and the Court of Appeals, respondents and the United States rely upon isolated statements in the legislative history concerning the achievement of maximum potential, see H.R. Rep. No. 94-332, *supra*, at 13, as support for their contention that Congress intended to impose greater substantive requirements than we have found. These statements, however, are too thin a reed on which to base an interpretation of the Act which disregards both its language and the balance of its legislative history. "Passing references and isolated phrases are not controlling when analyzing a legislative history." *Department of State* v. *The Washington Post Co.,* 456 U.S. 595 (1982)

Moreover, even were we to agree that these statements evince a congressional intent to maximize each child's potential, we could not hold that Congress had successfully imposed that burden upon the States.

"[L]egislation enacted pursuant to the spending power is much in the nature of a contract: in return for federal funds, the States agree to comply with federally imposed conditions. The legitimacy of Congress' power to legislate under the spending power thus rests on whether the State voluntarily and knowingly accepts the terms of the 'contract.' . . . Accordingly, if Congress intends to impose a condition on the grant of federal moneys, it must do so unambiguously." *Pennhurst State School* v. *Halderman,* 451 U.S. 1, 17(1981).

As already demonstrated, the Act and its history impose no requirements on the States like those imposed by the District Court and the Court of Appeals. *A fortiori* Congress has not done so unambiguously, as required in the valid exercise of its spending power.

"shall receive the record of the [state] administrative proceeding, shall hear additional evidence at the request of a party, and, basing its decision on the preponderance of the evidence, shall grant such relief as the court determines is appropriate." § 1415(e)(2).

The parties disagree sharply over the meaning of these provisions, petitioners contending that courts are given only limited authority to review for state compliance with the Act's procedural requirements and no power to review the substance of the state program, and respondents contending that the Act requires courts to exercise *de novo* review over state educational decisions and policies. We find petitioners' contention unpersuasive, for Congress expressly rejected provisions that would have so severely restricted the role of reviewing courts. In substituting the current language of the statute for language that would have made state administrative findings conclusive if supported by substantial evidence, The Conference Committee explained that courts were to make "independent decision[s] based on a preponderance of the evidence." S. Cong. Rec. 37416 (1975) (remarks of Sen. Williams).

But although we find that this grant of authority is broader than claimed by petitioners, we think the fact that it is found in § 1415 of the Act, which is entitled "Procedural Safeguards," is not without significance. When the elaborate and highly specific procedural safeguards embodied in § 1415 are contrasted with the general and somewhat imprecise substantive admonitions contained in the Act, we think that the importance Congress attached to these procedural safeguards cannot be gainsaid. It seems to us no exaggeration to say that Congress placed every bit as much emphasis upon compliance with procedures giving parents and guardians a large measure of participation at every stage of the administrative process, see, e. g. § 1415(a)-(d), as it did upon the measurement of the resulting IEP against a substantive standard. We think that the Congressional emphasis upon full participation of concerned parties throughout the development of the IEP, as well as the requirements that state and local plans be submitted to the Commissioner for approval, demonstrate the legislative conviction that adequate compliance with the procedures prescribed would in most cases assure much if not all of what Congress wished in the way of substantive content in an IEP.

Thus the provision that a reviewing court base its decision on the "preponderance of the evidence" is by no means an invitation to the courts to substitute their own notions of sound educational policy for those of the school authorities which they review. The very importance which Congress has attached to compliance with certain procedures in the preparation of an IEP would be frustrated if a court were permitted simply to set state decisions at nought. The fact that § 1415(e) requires that the reviewing court "receive the records of the [state] administrative proceedings" carries with it the implied requirement that due weight shall be given to these proceedings. And we find nothing in the Act to suggest that merely because Congress was rather sketchy in establishing substantive requirements, as opposed to procedural requirements of the preparation of an IEP, it intended that reviewing courts should have a free hand to impose substantive standards of review which cannot be derived from the Act itself. In short, the statutory authorization to grant "such relief as the court determines is appropriate" cannot be read without reference to the obligations, largely procedural in nature, which are imposed upon recipient States by Congress.

Therefore, a court's inquiry in suits brought under § 1415(e)(2) is twofold. First, has the State complied with the procedures set forth in the Act?[27] And second, is the individualized educational program developed through the Act's procedures reasonably calculated to enable the child to receive educational benefits?[28] If these requirements are met, the State has complied with the obligations imposed by Congress and the Courts can require no more.

B

In assuring that the requirements of the Act have been met, courts must be careful to avoid imposing their view of preferable educational methods upon the States.[29] The primary responsibility for formulating the education to be accorded a handicapped child, and for choosing the educational method most suitable to the child's needs, was left by the Act to state and local educational agencies in cooperation with the parents or guardian of the child. The Act expressly charges States with the responsibility of "acquiring and disseminating to teachers and administrators of programs for handicapped children significant information derived from educational research, demonstration, and similar projects, and [of] adopting, where appropriate, promising educational practices and materials." § 1413(a)(3). In the face of such a clear statutory directive, it seems highly unlikely that Congress intended courts to overturn a State's choice of appropriate educational theories in a proceeding conducted pursuant to § 1415(e)(2).[30]

We previously have cautioned that courts lack the "specialized knowledge and experience" necessary to resolve "persistent and difficult questions of educational policy." *San Antonio School District* v. *Rodriguez,* 411 U. S. 1, 42 (1973). We think that Congress shared that view when it passed the Act. As already demonstrated, Congress' intention was not that the Act displace the primacy of States in the field of education, but that States receive funds to assist them in extending their educational systems to the handicapped.

---

[27]This inquiry will require a court not only to satisfy itself that the State has adopted the state plan, policies, and assurances required by the Act, but also to determine that the State has created an IEP for the child in question which conforms with the requirements of § 1401(19).

[28]When the handicapped child is being educated in the regular classrooms of a public school system, the achievement of passing marks and advancement from grade to grade will be one important factor in determining educational benefit. See Part III, *supra.*.

[29]In this case, for example, both the state hearing officer and the District Court were presented with evidence as to the best method for educating the deaf, a question long debated among scholars. See Large, Special Problems of the Deaf Under the Education for All Handicapped Children Act of 1975, 58 Washington U. L. Q. 213,229 (1980). The District Court accepted the testimony of respondents' experts that there was "a trend supported by studies showing the greater degree of success of students brought up in deaf households using [the method of communication used by the Rowleys]." 483 F. Supp., at 535.

[30]It is clear that Congress was aware of the States' traditional role in the formulation and execution of educational policy. "Historically, the States have had the primary responsibility for the education of children at the elementary and secondary level." 121 Cong. Rec. 19498 (1975) (remarks of Sen. Dole). See also *Epperson* v. *Arkansas,* 393 U. S. 97, 104 (1968) ("[b]y and large, public education in our Nation is committed to the control of state and local authorities").

Therefore, once a court determines that the requirements of the Act have been met, questions of methodology are for resolution by the States.

V

Entrusting a child's education to state and local agencies does not leave the child without protection. Congress sought to protect individual children by providing for parental involvement in the development of State plans and policies, *supra,* at 4-5 and n. 6, and in formulation of the child's individual educational program. As the Senate Report states:

> "The Committee recognizes that in many instances the process of providing special education and related services to handicapped children is not guaranteed to produce any particular outcome. By changing the language [of the provision relating to individualized educational programs] to emphasize the process of parent and child involvement and to provide a written record of reasonable expectations, the Committee intends to clarify that such individualized planning conferences are a way to provide parent involvement and protection to assure that appropriate services are provided to a handicapped child." S. Rep. No. 94-168, *supra,* at 11-12. See also S. Conf. Rep. No. 94-445, p. 30 (1975); 45 CFR § 121a.345 (1980).

As this very case demonstrates, parents and guardians will not lack ardor in seeking to ensure that handicapped children receive all of the benefits to which they are entitled by the Act.[31]

VI

Applying these principles to the facts of this case, we conclude that the Court of Appeals erred in affirming the decision of the District Court. Neither the District Court nor the Court of Appeals found that petitioners had failed to comply with the procedures of the Act, and the findings of neither court would support a conclusion that Amy's educational program failed to comply with the substantive requirements of the Act. On the contrary, the District Court found that the "evidence firmly establishes that Amy is receiving an 'adequate' education, since she performs better than the average child

---

[31]In addition to providing for extensive parental involvement in the formulation of state and local policies, as well as the preparation of individual educational programs, the Act ensures that States will receive the advice of experts in the field of educating handicapped children. As a condition for receiving federal funds under the Act, States must create "an advisory panel, appointed by the Governor or any other official authorized under State law to make such appointments, composed of individuals involved in or concerned with the education of handicapped children, including handicapped individuals, teachers, parents or guardians of handicapped children, State and local education officials, and administrators of programs for handicapped children, which (A) advises that State educational agency of unmet needs within the State in the education of handicapped children, [and] (B) comments publicly on any rules or regulations proposed for issuance by the State regarding the education of handicapped children." § 1413(a)(12).

in her class and is advancing easily from grade to grade." 483 F. Supp., at 534. In light of this finding, and of the fact that Amy was receiving personalized instruction and related services calculated by the Furnace Woods school administrators to meet her educational needs, the lower courts should not have concluded that the Act requires the provision of a sign-language interpreter. Accordingly, the decision of the Court of Appeals is reversed and the case is remanded for further proceedings consistent with this opinion.[32]

So ordered.

JUSTICE BLACKMUN, concurring in the judgment.

Although I reach the same result as the court does today, I read the legislative history and goals of the Education for All Handicapped Children Act differently. Congress unambiguously stated that it intended to "take a more active role under its responsibility for equal protection of the laws to guarantee that handicapped children are provided *equal educational opportunity.*" S. Rep. No 94-168, p. 9(1975) (emphasis added). See also 20 U.S.C. § 1412(2)(A)(i) (requiring States to establish plans with the "goal of providing full educational opportunity to all handicapped children").

As I have observed before, "[i]t seems plain to me that Congress, in enacting [this statute], intended to do more than merely set out politically self-serving but essentially meaningless language about what the [handicapped] deserve at the hands of state . . . authorities." *Pennhurst State School* v. *Halderman,* 451 U.S. 1, 32(1981) (opinion concurring in part and concurring in the judgment). The clarity of the legislative intent convinces me that the relevant question here is not, as the Court says, whether Amy Rowley's individualized education program was "reasonably calculated to enable [her] to receive educational benefits," *ante,* at 30, measured in part by whether or not she "achieve[s] passing marks and advance[s] from grade to grade," *ante,* at 27. Rather, the question is whether Amy's program, *viewed as a whole,* offered her an opportunity to understand and participate in the classroom that was substantially equal to that given her nonhandicapped classmates. This is a standard predicated on equal educational opportunity and equal access to the educational process, rather than upon Amy's achievement of any particular educational outcome.

In answering this question, I believe that the District Court and the Court of Appeals should have given greater deference than they did to the findings of the School District's impartial hearing officer and the State's Commissioner of Education, both of whom sustained petitioner's refusal to add a sign-language interpreter to Amy's individualized education program. Cf. 20 U.S.C. § 1415(e)(2) (requiring reviewing court to "receive the records of the administrative proceeding" before granting relief). I would suggest further that those courts focused too narrowly on the presence or absence of a particular service—a sign-language interpreter—rather than on the total package of services furnished to Amy by the School Board.

---

[32]Because the District Court declined to reach respondents' contention that petitioners had failed to comply with the Act's procedural requirements in developing Amy's IEP, 483 F. Supp., at 533, n. 8, the case must be remanded for further proceedings consistent with this opinion.

As the Court demonstrates, *ante* at 6-7, petitioner Board has provided Amy Rowley considerably more than "a teacher with a loud voice." See *post,* 4 (dissenting opinion). By concentrating on whether Amy was "learning as much, or performing as well academically, as she would without her handicap," 483 F Supp. 528, 532 (SDNY 1980), the District Court and the Court of Appeals paid too little attention to whether, on the entire record, respondent's individualized education program offered her an educational opportunity substantially equal to that provided her nonhandicapped classmates. Because I believe that standard has been satisfied here, I agree that the judgment of the Court of Appeals should be reversed.

JUSTICE WHITE, with whom JUSTICE BRENNAN and JUSTICE MARSHALL join, dissenting.

In order to reach its result in this case, the majority opinion contradicts itself, the language of the statute, and the legislative history. Both the majority's standard for a "free appropriate education" and its standard for judicial review disregard congressional intent.

I

The majority first turns its attention to the meaning of a "free appropriate public education." The Act provides:

> "The term 'free appropriate public education' means special education and related services which (A) have been provided at public expense, under public supervision and direction, and without charge, (B) meet the standards of the State educational agency, (C) include an appropriate preschool, elementary, or secondary school education in the State involved, and (D) are provided in conformity with the individualized education program required under section 1414(a)(5) of this title." 20 U.S.C. 1401(18).

The majority reads this statutory language as establishing a congressional intent limited to bringing "previously excluded handicapped children into the public education systems of the States and requiring the States to adopt *procedures* which would result in individualized consideration of and instruction for each child." *Ante,* at 12. In its attempt to constrict the definition of "appropriate" and the thrust of the Act, the majority opinion states, "Noticeably absent from the language of the statute is any substantive standard prescribing the level of education to be accorded handicapped children. Certainly the language of the statute contains no requirement like the one imposed by the lower courts—that States maximize the potential of handicapped children commensurate with opportunity provided to other children." *Ante,* at 12, quoting 483 F. Supp. at 534.

I agree that the language of the Act does not contain a substantive standard beyond requiring that the education offered must be "appropriate." However, if there are limits not evident from the face of the statute on what may be considered an "appropriate education," they must be found in the purpose of the statute or its legislative history. The Act itself announces it will provide a *"full* educational opportunity to all handicapped children." 20

U.S.C. § 1412(2)(A) (emphasis added). This goal is repeated throughout the legislative history, in statements too frequent to be "passing references and isolated phrases."[1] *Ante,* at 27, n. 26, quoting *Department of State* v. *Washington Post Co.,* 456 U.S. 596 (1982). These statements elucidate the meaning of "appropriate." According to the Senate Report, for example, the Act does "guarantee that handicapped children are provided *equal* educational opportunity." S. Rep. No. 94-168, at 9 (1975) (emphasis added). This promise appears throughout the legislative history. See 121 Cong. Rec. 19482-19483 (1975) (remarks of Sen. Randolph); *id.,* at 19504 (Sen. Humphrey); *id.,* at 19505 (Sen. Beall); *id.,* at 23704 (Rep. Brademas); *id.,* at 25538 (Rep. Cornell); *id.,* at 25540 (Rep. Grassley); *id.,* at 37025 (Rep. Perkins); *id.,* at 37030 (Rep. Mink); *id.,* at 37412 (Sen. Taft); *id.,* at 37413 (Sen. Williams); *id.,* at 37418-37419 (Sen. Cranston); *id.,* at 37419-37420 (Sen. Beall). Indeed, at times the purpose of the Act was described as tailoring each handicapped child's educational plan to enable the child "to achieve his or her maximum potential." H.R. Rep. No. 94-332, 94th Cong. 1st Sess. 13, 19 (1975), see 121 Cong. Rec. 23709 (1975). Sen. Stafford, one of the sponsors of the Act, declared, "We can all agree that the education [given a handicapped child] should be equivalent, at least, to the one those children who are not handicapped receive." 121 Cong. Rec. 19483 (1975). The legislative history thus directly supports the conclusion that the Act intends to give handicapped children an educational opportunity commensurate with that given other children.

The majority opinion announces a different substantive standard, that "Congress did not impose upon the States any greater substantive standard than would be necessary to make such access meaningful." *Ante,* at 13. While "meaningful" is no more enlightening than "appropriate," the Court purports to clarify itself. Because Amy was provided with *some* specialized instruction from which she obtained *some* benefit and because she passed from grade to grade, she was receiving a meaningful and therefore appropriate education.[2]

---

[1] The Court's opinion relies heavily on the statement, which occurs throughout the legislative history, that, at the time of enactment, one million of the roughly eight million handicapped children in the United States were excluded entirely from the public school system and more than half were receiving an inappropriate education. See, e.g., *ante,* at pp. 11, 18-19. But this statement was often linked to statements urging equal educational opportunity. See e.g., 121 Cong. Rec. 19502 (remarks of Sen. Cranston); *id.* at 23702 (remarks of Rep. Brademas). That is, Congress wanted not only to bring handicapped children into the schoolhouse, but also to benefit them once they had entered.

[2] As further support for its conclusion, the majority opinion turns to *Pennsylvania Association for Retarded Children* v. *Commonwealth of Pennsylvania* (PARC), 334 F. Supp. 1257 (1971), 343 F. Supp. 279 (ED Pa. 1972) and *Mills* v. *Board of Education of the District of Columbia,* 348 F. Supp. 866 (DDC 1972). That these decisions served as an impetus for the Act does not, however, establish them as the limits of the Act. In any case, the very language that the majority quotes from *Mills, ante* at 14-15, 21, sets a standard not of *some* education, but of educational opportunity equal to that of non-handicapped children.

Indeed, *Mills,* relying on decisions since called into question by this Court's opinion in *San Antonio School District* v. *Rodriguez,* 411 U.S. 1 (1973), states,

"In *Hobson* v. *Hansen* [269 F. Supp. 401 (DDC),] Judge Wright found that denying poor public school children educational opportunity equal to that available to

This falls far short of what the Act intended. The Act details as specifically as possible the kind of specialized education each handicapped child must receive. It would apparently satisfy the Court's standard of "access to specialized instruction and related services which are individually designed to provide educational benefit to the handicapped child," *ante,* at 24, for a deaf child such as Amy to be given a teacher with a loud voice, for she would benefit from the service. The Act requires more. It defines "special education" to mean "specifically designed instruction, at no cost to parents or guardians, to *meet the unique needs* of a handicapped child. . . ." § 1401(16) (emphasis added).[3] Providing a teacher with a loud voice would not meet Amy's needs and would not satisfy the Act. The basic floor of opportunity is instead, as the courts below recognized, intended to eliminate the effects of the handicap, at least to the extent that the child will be given an equal opportunity to learn if that is reasonably possible. Amy Rowley, without a sign language interpreter, comprehends less than half of what is said in the classroom—less than half of what normal children comprehend. This is hardly an equal opportunity to learn, even if Amy makes passing grades.

Despite its reliance on the use of "appropriate" in the definition of the Act, the majority opinion speculates that "Congress used the word as much to describe the settings in which the children should be educated as to prescribe the substantive content or supportive services of their education." *Ante,* at 20, n. 21. Of course, the word "appropriate" can be applied in many ways; at times in the Act, Congress used it to recommend mainstreaming handicapped children; at other points, it used the word to refer to the content of the individualized education. The issue before us is what standard the word "appropriate" incorporates when it is used to modify "education." the answer given by the Court is not a satisfactory one.

II

The Court's discussion of the standard for judicial review is as flawed as its discussion of a "free appropriate public education." According to the Court, a court can ask only whether the State has "complied with the procedures set forth in the Act" and whether the individualized education program is "reasonably calculated to enable the child to receive educational benefit." *Ante,* at 30, Both the language of the Act and the legislative history, however, demonstrate that Congress intended the courts to conduct a far more searching inquiry.

The majority assigns major significance to the review provision's being found in a section entitled "Procedural Safeguards." But where else would a

---

more affluent public school children was violative of the Due Process Clause of the Fifth Amendment. *A fortiori,* the defendants' conduct here, denying plaintiffs and their class not just an equal publicly supported education but all publicly supported education while providing such education to other children, is violative of the Due Process Clause." 348 F. Supp., at 875.

Whatever the effect of *Rodriguez* on the validity of this reasoning, the statement exposes the majority's mischaracterization of the opinion and thus of the assumptions of the legislature that passed the act.

[3] "Related services" are "transportation, and such developmental, corrective, and other supportive services . . . as may be required to assist a handicapped child to benefit from special education." § 1401(17).

provision for judicial review belong? The majority does acknowledge that the current language, specifying that a court "shall receive the record of the administrative proceeding, shall hear additional evidence at the request of a party, and basing its decision on the preponderance of the evidence, shall grant such relief as the court determines is appropriate," § 1415(e)(2), was substituted at Conference for language that would have restricted the role of the reviewing court much more sharply. It is clear enough to me that Congress decided to reduce substantially judicial deference to state administrative decisions.

The legislative history shows that judicial review is not limited to procedural matters and that the state educational agencies are given first, but not final, responsibility for the content of a handicapped child's education. The Conference Committee directs courts to make an "independent decision." S. Conf. Rep. No. 94-455, at 50. The deliberate change in the review provision is an unusually clear indication the Congress intended courts to undertake substantive review instead of relying on the conclusions of the state agency.

On the floor of the Senate, Senator Williams, the chief sponsor of the bill, committee chairman, and floor manager responsible for the legislation in the Senate, emphasized the breadth of the review provisions at both the administrative and judicial levels:

> "Any parent or guardian may present a complaint concerning *any matter* regarding the identification, evaluation, or educational placement of the child or the provision of a free appropriate public education to such a child. In this regard, Mr. President, I would like to stress that the language referring to 'free appropriate education' has been adopted to make clear that a complaint may involve matters such as questions respecting a child's individualized education program, questions of whether special education and related services are being provided without charge to the parents or guardians, questions relating to whether the services provided a child meet the standards of the State education agency, or *any other question* within the scope of the definition of 'free appropriate public education.' In addition, it should be clear that a parent or guardian may present a complaint alleging that a State or local education agency has refused to provide services to which a child may be entitled or alleging that the State or local educational agency has erroneously classified a child as a handicapped child when, in fact, that child is not a handicapped child." 121 Cong. Rec. 37415 (emphasis added).

There is no doubt that the state agency itself must make substantive decisions. The legislative history reveals that the courts are to consider, *de novo,* the same issues. Senator Williams explicitly stated that the civil action permitted under the Act encompasses all matters related to the original complaint. *Id.,* at 37416.

Thus, the Court's limitations on judicial review have no support in either the language of the Act or the legislative history. Congress did not envision that inquiry would end if a showing is made that the child is receiving passing marks and is advancing from grade to grade. Instead, it intended to permit a full and searching inquiry into any aspect of a handicapped child's education. The Court's standard, for example, would not permit a challenge to part of the IEP; the legislative history demonstrates beyond doubt that Congress intended such challenges to be possible, even if the plan as developed is reasonably calculated to give the child some benefits.

Parents can challenge the IEP for failing to supply the special education and related services needed by the individual handicapped child. That is what Rowleys did. As the Government observes, "courts called upon to review the content of an IEP, in accordance with 20 U.S.C. § 1415(e) inevitably are required to make a judgment on the basis of the evidence presented, concerning whether the educational methods proposed by the local school district are 'appropriate' for the handicapped child involved." Brief for United States as *Amicus Curiae* 13. The courts below, as they were required by the Act, did precisely that.

Under the judicial review provisions of the Act, neither the District Court nor the Court of Appeals was bound by the state's construction of what an "appropriate" education means in general or by what the state authorities considered to be an appropriate education for Amy Rowley. Because the standard of the courts below seems to me to reflect the congressional purpose and because their factual findings are not clearly erroneous, I respectfully dissent.

Smith v. Robinson

U.S. Supreme Court, 468 U.S. 992, 104 S.Ct. 3457 (1984).

Syllabus*

When the Superintendent of Schools in Cumberland, R. I., informed petitioner parents of petitioner child, who suffers from cerebral palsy, that the School Committee no longer would fund the child's placement in a special education program, the parents, in addition to appealing the Superintendent's decision to the School Committee and thereafter through the state administrative process, filed an action in Federal District Court against the School Committee and, subsequently, against certain state school officials. They asserted, at various points in the proceedings, claims for declaratory and injunctive relief based on state law, on the Education of the Handicapped Act (EHA), on § 504 of the Rehabilitation Act of 1973, and, with respect to certain federal constitutional claims, on 42 U. S. C. § 1983. The District Court held that the child was entitled, as a matter of state law, to a free appropriate special education paid for by the School Committee, and that it was therefore unnecessary and improper to reach petitioners' federal statutory and constitutional claims. By agreement between the parties, the court awarded attorney's fees against the School Committee. Petitioners then requested attorney's fees against the state defendants. The District Court held that petitioners were entitled to such fees for the hours spent in the state administrative process both before and after the date the state defendants were named as parties, reasoning that because petitioners were required to exhaust their EHA remedies before asserting their § 1983 and § 504 claims, they were entitled to fees for those procedures. The Court of Appeals reversed, holding that since the action and relief granted fell within the reach of the EHA, which establishes a comprehensive federal-state scheme for the provision of special education to handicapped children but does not provide for attorney's fees, the District Court had to look to 42 U. S. C. § 1988 and § 505 of the Rehabilitation Act for such fees. The Court of Appeals concluded that even if the unaddressed § 1983 claims were substantial enough to support federal jurisdiction so as generally to warrant an award of attorney's fees, nevertheless, given the comprehensiveness of the EHA, Congress could not have intended its omission of attorney's fees relief in that statute to be rectified by recourse to § 1988. The court disposed of the Rehabilitation Act basis for attorney's fees for similar reasons.

Held:
    1. Petitioners were not entitled to attorney's fees under § 1988. Pp. 12-22.
    (a) The fact that petitioners prevailed on their initial claim that the School Committee violated due process by refusing to grant petitioners a full hearing before terminating funding of petitioner child's special education program does not by itself entitle petitioners to attorney's fees for the subsequent administrative and judicial proceedings. That due process claim was entirely separate from the claims made in the subsequent proceedings, and was not sufficiently related to petitioners' ultimate success to support an award of fees for the entire proceeding. Pp. 14-15.
    (b) As to petitioners' claim that the child was being discriminated against on the basis of his handicapped condition, in violation of the Equal Protection Clause of the Fourteenth Amendment, it is apparent that Congress intended the

---

*The syllabus constitutes no part of the opinion of the Court but has been prepared by the Reporter of Decisions for the convenience of the reader.

EHA to be the exclusive avenue through which such a claim can be pursued. The EHA is a comprehensive scheme to aid the States in complying with their constitutional obligations to provide public education for the handicapped. Allowing a plaintiff to circumvent the EHA's administrative remedies by relying on § 1983 as a remedy for a substantial equal protection claim would be inconsistent with that scheme. Pp. 16-20.

(c) Even if petitioners' due process challenge to the partiality of the state hearing officer who reviewed the School Committee's decision might be maintained as an independent challenge, petitioners are not entitled to attorney's fees for such claim. That claim had no bearing on the substantive claim on which petitioners prevailed, that the School Board, as a matter of state and federal law, was required to pay for petitioner child's education. Where petitioners presented different claims for different relief, based on different facts and legal theories, and prevailed only on a nonfee claim, they are not entitled to a fee award simply because the other claim was a constitutional claim that could be asserted through § 1983. Pp. 20-22.

2. Nor were petitioners entitled to attorney's fees under § 505 of the Rehabilitation Act. Congress struck a careful balance in the EHA between clarifying and making enforceable the rights of handicapped children to a free appropriate public education and endeavoring to relieve the financial burden imposed on the agencies responsible to guarantee those rights. It could not have intended a handicapped child to upset that balance by relying on § 504 for otherwise unavailable damages or for an award of attorney's fees. Where, as here, whatever remedy might be provided under § 504—which prevents discrimination on the basis of a handicap in any program receiving federal financial assistance—is provided with more clarity and precision under the EHA, a plaintiff may not circumvent or enlarge on the remedies available under the EHA by resort to § 504. Pp. 22-28.

703 F. 2d 4, affirmed.

BLACKMUN, J., delivered the opinion of the Court, in which BURGER, C. J., and WHITE, POWELL, REHNQUIST, and O'CONNOR, JJ., joined. BRENNAN, J., filed a dissenting opinion, in which MARSHALL and STEVENS, JJ., joined.

JUSTICE BLACKMUN delivered the opinion of the Court.

This case presents questions regarding the award of attorney's fees in a proceeding to secure a "free appropriate public education" for a handicapped child. At various stages in the proceeding, petitioners asserted claims for relief based on state law, on the Education of the Handicapped Act (EHA), 84 Stat. 175, as amended, 20 U. S. C. §§ 1400 *et seq.*, on § 504 of the Rehabilitation Act of 1973, 87 Stat. 394, as amended, 29 U. S. C. § 794, and on the Due Process and Equal Protection Clauses of the Fourteenth Amendment to the United States Constitution. The United States Court of Appeals for the First Circuit concluded that because the proceeding, in essence, was one to enforce the provisions of the EHA, a statute that does not provide for the payment of attorney's fees, petitioners were not entitled to such fees. *Smith* v. *Cumberland School Committee*, 703 F. 2d 4 (1983). Petitioners insist that this Court's decision in *Maher* v. *Gagne*, 448 U. S. 122 (1980), compels a different conclusion.

I

The procedural history of the case is complicated, but it is significant to the resolution of the issues. Petitioner Thomas F. Smith, III (Tommy), suffers from cerebral palsy and a variety of physical and emotional handicaps. When this proceeding began in November 1976, Tommy was 8 years old. In the preceding December, the Cumberland School Committee had agreed to place Tommy in a day program at Emma Pendleton Bradley Hospital in East Providence, R. I., and Tommy began attending that program. In November 1976, however, the Superintendent of Schools informed Tommy's parents, who are the other petitioners here, that the School Committee no longer would fund Tommy's placement because, as it construed Rhode Island law, the responsibility for educating an emotionally disturbed child lay with the State's Divison of Mental Health, Retardation and Hospitals [MHRH]. App. 25-26.

Petitioners took an appeal from the decision of the Superintendent to the School Committee. In addition, petitioners filed a complaint under 42 U. S. C. § 1983 in the United States District Court for the District of Rhode Island against the members of the School Committee, asserting that due process required that the Committee comply with "Article IX—Procedural Safeguards" of the Regulations adopted by the State Board of Regents regarding Education of Handicapped Children [Regulations][1] and that Tommy's placement in his program be continued pending appeal of the Superintendent's decision.

In orders issued in December 1976 and January 1977, the District Court entered a temporary restraining order and then a preliminary injunction. The court agreed with petitioners that the Regulations required the School Committee to continue Tommy in his placement at Bradley Hospital pending appeal of the Superintendent's decision. The School Committee's failure to follow the Regulations, the court concluded, would constitute a deprivation of due process.

On May 10, 1978, petitioners filed a First Amended Complaint. App. 49. By that time, petitioners had completed the state administrative process. They had appealed the Superintendent's decision to the School Committee and then to the State Commissioner of Education, who delegated responsibility for conducting a hearing to an Associate Commissioner of Education.

---

[1]In November 1976, Rhode Island, through its Board of Regents for Education, was in the process of promulgating new regulations concerning the education of handicapped children. The old regulations, approved in 1963, had been issued by the State Department of Education and were entitled "Regulations—Education of Handicapped Children." Most of the new Regulations became effective October 1, 1977. Article IX of Section One, however, was made effective June 14, 1976. See Section One, Art. XII.

The Regulations were promulgated pursuant to R. I. Gen. Laws § 16-24-2 (1981). The immediately preceding section, § 16-24-1, sets out the duty of the local school committee to provide, for a child, "who is either mentally retarded or physically or emotionally handicapped to such an extent that normal educational growth and development is prevented," such type of special education "that will best satisfy the need of the handicapped child, as recommended and approved by the board of regents for education in accordance with its regulations." Section 16-24-1 has its origin in 1952 R. I. Pub. Laws, ch. 2905, § 1, and was in effect in November 1976.

Petitioners had moved that the Associate Commissioner recuse himself from conducting the review of the School Committee's decision, since he was an employee of the State Educational Agency and therefore not an impartial hearing officer. The Associate Commissioner denied the motion to recuse.

All the state officers agreed that, under R. I. Gen. Laws, Tit. 40, ch. 7 (1977), the responsibility for educating Tommy lay with MHRH.[2] The Associate Commissioner acknowledged petitioners' argument that since § 40.1-7-8 would require them to pay a portion of the cost of services provided to Tommy,[3] the statute conflicted with the EHA, but concluded that the problem was not within his jurisdiction to resolve.

In their First Amended Complaint, petitioners added as defendants the Commissioner of Education, the Associate Commissioner of Education, the Board of Regents for Education, and the Director of MHRH. They also specifically relied for the first time on the EHA, noting that at all times mentioned in the complaint, the State of Rhode Island had submitted a plan for state-administered programs of special education and related services and had received federal funds pursuant to the EHA.[4]

In the First Count of their Amended Complaint, petitioners challenged the fact that both the hearing before the School Committee and the hearing before the Associate Commissioner were conducted before examiners who were employees of the local or state education agency. They sought a declaratory judgment that the procedural safeguards contained in Article IX of the Regulations did not comply with the Due Process Clause of the Fourteenth Amendment or with the requirements of the EHA, 20 U. S. C. § 1415, and its accompanying regulations. They also sought an injunction prohibiting the Commissioner and Associate Commissioner from conducting any more hearings in review of decisions of the Rhode Island local education agencies (LEAs) unless and until the Board of Regents adopted regulations that con-

---

[2]Under § 40.1-7-3, enacted by 1971 R. I. Pub. Laws, ch. 89, art. 1, § 1, MHRH is charged "with the responsibility to promote the development of specialized services for the care and treatment of emotionally disturbed children and to cooperate to this end with all reputable agencies of a public or private character serving such children . . ."

[3]Section 40.1-7-8 provides: "The parents of children in the program, depending upon their resources, shall be obligated to participate in the costs of the care and treatment of their children in accordance with regulations to be promulgated by the director."

[4]The 1975 Amendment to the EHA, on which petitioners rely, became effective October 1, 1977. Prior to that date, the federal requirements governing States which, like Rhode Island, submitted state plans and received federal money for the education of handicapped children were found in the Education of the Handicapped Act, 84 Stat. 175, as amended in 1974, 88 Stat. 579. The obligations imposed on a State by that Act were to expend federal money on programs designed to benefit handicapped children. From August 1974 to September 30, 1977, the Act also required that parents be given minimal due process protections when the State proposed to change the educational placement of the child. 88 Stat. 582. The state hearing process in this case began on January 20, 1977, with a hearing before the School Committee. By the time petitioners' appeal progressed to the Associate Commissioner of Education on November 2, 1977, the 1975 Act was in effect. Unless otherwise indicated, future references to the "EHA" refer to the 1975 amendments to that Act.

formed to the requirements of § 1415 and its regulations. Finally, they sought reasonable attorney's fees and costs.

In the Second Count of their Amended Complaint, petitioners challenged the substance of the Associate Commissioner's decision. In their view, the decision violated Tommy's rights "under federal and state law to have his LEA provide a free, appropriate educational placement without regard to whether or not said placement can be made within the local school system." App. 61. They sought both a declaratory judgment that the School Committee, not MHRH, was responsible for providing Tommy a free appropriate education, and an injunction requiring the School Committee to provide Tommy such an education. They also asked for reasonable attorney's fees and costs.

On December 22, 1978, the District Court issued an opinion acknowledging confusion over whether, as a matter of state law, the School Committee or MHRH was responsible for funding and providing the necessary services for Tommy. App. 108. The court also noted that if the Associate Commissioner were correct that Tommy's education was governed by § 40.1-7, the state scheme would appear to be in conflict with the requirements of the EHA, since § 40.1-7 may require parental contribution and may not require MHRH to provide education at all if it would cause the Department to incur a deficit. At the request of the state defendants, the District Court certified to the Supreme Court of Rhode Island the state law questions whether the school committee was required to provide special education for a resident handicapped student if the local educational programs were inadequate, and whether the cost of such programs was the responsibility of the local school committee or of the MHRH.

On May 29, 1979, the District Court granted partial summary judgment for the defendants on petitioners' claim that they were denied due process by the requirement of the Regulations that they submit their dispute to the School Committee and by the Associate State Commissioner's refusal to recuse himself. The court noted that the School Committee's members were not "employees" of the local education agency, but elected officials, and determined that the provision of the EHA directing that no hearing shall be conducted by an employee of an agency or unit involved in the education or care of the child does not apply to hearings conducted by the state education agency.

On June 3, 1980, the Rhode Island Supreme Court issued an opinion answering the certified questions. *Smith* v. *Cumberland School Committee*, —— R. I. ——, 415 A. 2d 168. Noting the responsibility of the Board of Regents for Education to comply with the requirements of the EHA, the court determined that the primary obligation of financing a handicapped child's special education lay with the local School Committee. Whatever obligation § 40.1-7 imposes on MHRH to provide educational services is limited and complements, rather than supplants, the obligations of School Committees under § 16.24-1.

Petitioners thereafter filed their Second Amended and Supplemental Complaint. App. 152. In it they added to Count II claims for relief under the Equal Protection Clause of the Fourteenth Amendment and under § 504 of the Rehabilitation Act of 1973, as amended, 29 U. S. C. § 794. They also requested attorney's fees under 42 U. S. C. § 1988 and what was then 31 U. S. C. § 1244(e) (1976 ed.).[5]

On January 12, 1981, the District Court issued an order declaring petitioners' rights, entering a permanent injunction against the School Committee defendants, and approving an award of attorney's fees against those defendants. App. 172. The court ordered the School Committee to pay the full cost of Tommy's attendance at Harmony Hill School, Tommy's then-current placement. By agreement between petitioners and the School Committee and without prejudice to petitioners' claims against the other defendants, the court awarded attorney's fees in the amount of $8,000, pursuant to 42 U. S. C. § 1988 and the then 31 U. S. C. § 1244 (e).

On June 4, 1981, the District Court issued two orders, this time addressed to petitioners' claims against the state defendants. In the first order, App. 177, the court denied the state defendants' motion to dismiss. In the second order, *id.*, at 189, the court declared that Tommy is entitled to a free appropriate special education paid for by the Cumberland School Committee. The court noted that since Tommy was entitled to the relief he sought as a matter of state law, it was unnecessary and improper for the court to go further and reach petitioners' federal statutory and constitutional claims. Petitioners were given 14 days to move for an award of fees.

The Court of Appeals for the First Circuit affirmed in an unpublished *per curiam* opinion filed on January 11, 1982. It concluded that the Commissioner was not immune from injunctive relief and that petitioners' challenge to the District Court's award of summary judgment to respondents on their due process challenge was moot.

Petitioners requested fees and costs against the state defendants. *Id.*, at 195. On April 30, 1982, the District Court ruled orally that petitioners were entitled to fees and costs in the amount of $32,109 for the hours spent in the state administrative process both before and after the state defendants were named as parties to the federal litigation. App. to Pet. for Cert. A31-A58. Relying on *New York Gaslight Club, Inc.* v. *Carey*, 447 U. S. 54 (1980), and its own opinion in *Turillo* v. *Tyson*, 535 F. Supp. 577 (R. I. 1982), the court reasoned that because petitioners were required to exhaust their EHA remedies before bringing their § 1983 and § 504 claims, they were entitled to fees for those procedures. The court agreed with respondents that petitioners were not entitled to compensation for hours spent challenging the use of employees as hearing officers. No fees were awarded for hours spent obtaining the preliminary injunctive relief, as petitioners already had been compensated for that work by the school committee defendants. Finally, the court rejected the defendants' argument that fees should not be allowed because this was an action under the EHA, which does not provide for fees. In the court's view,

---

[5]By the time of the filing of petitioners' Second Amended Complaint on September 16, 1980, attorney's fees were available directly under the Rehabilitation Act. See Rehabilitation, Comprehensive Services, and Developmental Disabilities Amendments of 1978, § 120, 92 Stat. 2982, 29 U. S. C. § 794a. Instead of relying on that statute, however, petitioners relied on 31 U. S. C. § 1244(e) (1976 ed.) (now replaced by 31 U. S. C. § 6721(c)(2)), a statute that authorized a civil action to enforce § 504 of the Rehabilitation Act against any State or local government receiving federal funds under the State and Local Fiscal Assistance Act of 1972, 86 Stat. 919, as amended by the State and Local Fiscal Assistance Amendments of 1976, 90 Stat. 2341. Section § 1244(e) authorized an award of attorney's fees to a "prevailing party."

respondents had given insufficient weight to the fact that petitioners had alleged equal protection and § 1983 claims as well as the EHA claim. The court added that it found the equal protection claim petitioners included in their second amended complaint to be colorable and nonfrivolous. Petitioners thus were entitled to fees for prevailing in an action to enforce their § 1983 claim.

The Court of Appeals reversed. *Smith* v. *Cumberland School Committee*, 703 F. 2d 4 (CA1 1983). The court first noted that, under what is labelled the "American Rule," attorney's fees are available as a general matter only when statutory authority so provides. *Alyeska Pipeline Co.* v. *Wilderness Society*, 421 U. S. 240 (1975). Here the action and relief granted in this case fell within the reach of the EHA, a federal statute that establishes a comprehensive federal-state scheme for the provision of special education to handicapped children, but that does not provide for attorney's fees.[6] For fees, the District Court had to look to § 1988 and § 505 of the Rehabilitation Act.

As to the § 1988 claim, the court acknowledged the general rule that when the claim upon which a plaintiff actually prevails is accompanied by a "substantial," though undecided, § 1983 claim arising from the same nucleus of facts, a fee award is appropriate. *Maher* v. *Gagne*, 448 U. S. 122, 130-131 (1980). Here, petitioners' § 1983 claims arguably were at least substantial enough to support federal jurisdiction. *Ibid.* Even if the § 1983 claims were substantial, however, the Court of Appeals concluded that, given the comprehensiveness of the EHA, Congress could not have intended its omission of attorney's fees relief to be rectified by recourse to § 1988.

The Court of Appeals drew support for its conclusion from this Court's decision in *Middlesex County Sewage Auth.* v. *National Sea Clammers Assn.*, 453 U. S. 1 (1981). There the Court held that where Congress had provided comprehensive enforcement mechanisms for protection of a federal right and those mechanisms did not include a private right of action, a litigant could not obtain a private right of action by asserting his claim under § 1983. The Court of Appeals recognized that *Sea Clammers* might not logically preclude a § 1983 action for violation of the EHA, since the EHA expressly recognizes a private right of action, but it does support the more general proposition that when a statute creates a comprehensive remedial scheme, intentional "omissions" from that scheme should not be supplanted by the remedial apparatus of § 1983. In the view of the Court of Appeals, the fact that the § 1983 claims alleged here were based on independent constitutional violations rather than violations of the EHA was immaterial. The constitution claims alleged—a denial of due process and a denial of a free appropriate public education because of handicap—are factually identical to

---

[6]The District Court purported to award relief on the basis of state law. In light of the decision in *Pennhurst State School and Hospital* v. *Halderman*, 465 U. S. 89 (1984), that was improper. The propriety of the injunctive relief, however, is not at issue here. We think the Court of Appeals was correct in treating the relief as essentially awarded under the EHA, since petitioners had challenged the State Commissioner's construction of state law on the basis of their rights under the EHA, and since the question of state law on which petitioners prevailed was certified by the District Court in an effort to avoid a Supremacy Clause conflict with the EHA. It is clear that the EHA creates a right, enforceable in federal court, to the free appropriate public education required by the statute. *Board of Education* v. *Rowley*, 458 U. S. 176 (1982); 20 U. S. C. § 1415(e)(2).

the EHA claims. If a litigant could obtain fees simply by an incantation of § 1983, fees would become available in almost every case.[7]

The court disposed of the Rehabilitation Act basis for fees in a similar fashion. Even if Congress did not specifically intend to pre-empt § 504 claims with the EHA, the EHA's comprehensive remedial scheme entails a rejection of fee-shifting that properly limits the fees provision of the more general Rehabilitation Act.

Because of confusion in the circuits over the proper interplay among the various statutory and constitutional bases for relief in cases of this nature, and over the effect of that interplay on the provision of attorney's fees,[8] we granted certiorari, 464 U. S. 932 (1983).

II

Petitioners insist that the Court of Appeals simply ignored the guidance of this Court in *Mayer* v. *Gagne, supra*, that a prevailing party who asserts substantial but unaddressed constitutional claims is entitled to attorney's fees under 42 U. S. C. § 1988. They urge that the reliance of the Court of Appeals on *Sea Clammers* was misplaced. *Sea Clammers* had to do only with an effort to enlarge a statutory remedy by asserting a claim based on that statute under the "and laws" provision of § 1983.[9] In this case, petitioners made no effort to enlarge the remedies available under the EHA by asserting their claim through the "and laws" provision of § 1983. They presented separate constitutional claims, properly cognizable under § 1983. Since the claim on which they prevailed and their constitutional claims arose out of a "common nucleus of operative fact," *Mayer* v. *Gagne*, 448 U. S., at 132, n. 15, quoting

---

[7]The Court of Appeals added that it did not intend to indicate that the EHA in any way limits the scope of a handicapped child's constitutional rights. Claims not covered by the EHA should still be cognizable under § 1983, with fees available for such actions. The court noted, for instance, that to the extent petitioners' securing of a preliminary injunction fell outside any relief available under the EHA, attorney's fees might be appropriate for that relief. Because the award of fees against the School Committee for work done in obtaining the preliminary injunction was not challenged on appeal, the court had no occasion to decide the issue.

[8]See, *e. g., Quackenbush* v. *Johnson City School District*, 716 F. 2d 141 (CA2 1983) (§ 1983 remedy, including damages, available for claim that plaintiff was denied access to EHA procedures); *Department of Education* v. *Katherine D.*, 727 F. 2d 809 (CA 9 1983) (EHA precludes reliance on § 1983 or § 504); *Robert M.* v. *Benton*, 671 F. 2d 1104 (CA8 1982) (fees available under § 1988 because plaintiff made colorable due process as well as EHA challenges to use of state agency employee as hearing officer); *Hymes* v. *Harnett County Board of Education*, 664 F. 2d 410 (CA4 1981) (claims made under the EHA, § 504 and § 1983; fees available for due process relief not available under the EHA); *Anderson* v. *Thompson*, 658 F. 2d 1205 (CA7 1981) (EHA claim not assertable under § 1983; attorney's fees therefore not available).

[9]42 U. S. C. § 1983 provides a remedy for a deprivation, under color of state law, "of any rights, privileges, or immunities secured by the Constitution *and laws*" (emphasis added). In *Maine* v. *Thiboutot*, 448 U. S. 1 (1980), the Court held that § 1983 authorizes suits to redress violations by state officials of rights created by federal statutes as well as by the Federal Constitution and that fees are available under § 1988 for such statutory violations.

Sea Clammers excluded from the reach of *Thiboutot* cases in which Congress specifically foreclosed a remedy under § 1983. 453 U. S., at 19.

H. R. Rep. No. 94-1558, p. 4, n. 7 (1976), and since the constitutional claims were found by the District Court and assumed by the Court of Appeals to be substantial, petitioners urge that they are entitled to fees under § 1988. In addition, petitioners presented a substantial claim under § 504 of the Rehabilitation Act. Since § 505 of that Act authorizes attorney's fees in the same manner as does § 1988 and in fact incorporates the legislative history of § 1988, see 124 Cong. Rec. 30346 (1978) (remarks of Sen. Cranston), the reasoning of *Maher* applies to claims based on § 504. Petitioners therefore, it is claimed, are entitled to fees for substantial, though unaddressed, § 504 claims.

Respondents counter that petitioners simply are attempting to circumvent the lack of a provision for attorney's fees in the EHA by resorting to the pleading trick of adding surplus constitutional claims and similar claims under § 504 of the Rehabilitation Act. Whatever Congress' intent was in authorizing fees for substantial, unaddressed claims based on § 1988 or § 505, it could not have been to allow plaintiffs to receive an award of attorney's fees in a situation where Congress has made clear its intent that fees not be available.

Resolution of this dispute requires us to explore congressional intent, both in authorizing fees for substantial unaddressed constitutional claims and in setting out the elaborate substantive and procedural requirements of the EHA, with no indication that attorney's fees are available in an action to enforce those requirements. We turn first to petitioners' claim that they were entitled to fees under 42 U. S. C. § 1988 because they asserted substantial constitutional claims.

III

As the legislative history illustrates and as this Court has recognized, § 1988 is a broad grant of authority to courts to award attorney's fees to plaintiffs seeking to vindicate federal constitutional and statutory rights. *Maine* v. *Thiboutot*, 448 U. S. 1, 9 (1980); *Maher* v. *Gagne, supra; Hutto* v. *Finney*, 437 U. S. 678, 694 (1978); S. Rep. No. 94-1011, p. 4 (1976) (a prevailing plaintiff " 'should ordinarily recover an attorney's fee unless special circumstances would render such an award unjust,' " quoting *Newman* v. *Piggie Park Enterprises, Inc.*, 390 U. S. 400, 402 (1968). Congress did not intend to have that authority extinguished by the fact that the case was settled or resolved on a nonconstitutional ground. *Maher* v. *Gagne*, 448 U. S., at 132. As the Court also has recognized, however, the authority to award fees in a case where the plaintiff prevails on substantial constitutional claims is not without qualification. Due regard must be paid, not only to the fact that a plaintiff "prevailed," but also to the relationship between the claims on which effort was expended and the ultimate relief obtained. *Hensley* v. *Eckerhart*, 461 U. S. 424 (1983); *Blum* v. *Stenson*, 465 U. S. 886 (1984). Thus, for example, fees are not properly awarded for work done on a claim on which a plaintiff did not prevail and which involved distinctly different facts and legal theories from the claims on the basis of which relief was awarded. *Hensley* v. *Eckerhart*, 461 U. S., at 434-435, 440. Although, in most cases, there is no clear line between hours of work that contributed to a plaintiff's success and those that did not, district courts remain charged with the responsibility, imposed by Congress, of evaluating the award requested in light of the relationship between particular claims for which work is done and the plaintiff's success. *Id.*, at 436-437.

A similar analysis is appropriate in a case like this, where the prevailing plaintiffs rely on substantial, unaddressed constitutional claims as the basis for an award of attorney's fees. The fact that constitutional claims are made does not render automatic an award of fees for the entire proceeding. Congress' purpose in authorizing a fee award for an unaddressed constitutional claim was to avoid penalizing a litigant for the fact that courts are properly reluctant to resolve constitutional questions if a nonconstitutional claim is dispositive. H. R. Rep. No. 94-1558, p. 4, n. 7. That purpose does not alter the requirement that a claim for which fees are awarded be reasonably related to the plaintiff's ultimate success. It simply authorizes a district court to assume that the plaintiff has prevailed on his fee-generating claim and to award fees appropriate to that success.[10]

In light of the requirement that a claim for which fees are awarded be reasonably related to the plaintiff's ultimate success, it is clear that plaintiffs may not rely simply on the fact that substantial fee-generating claims were made during the course of the litigation. Closer examination of the nature of the claims and the relationship between those claims and petitioners' ultimate success is required.

Besides making a claim under the EHA, petitioners asserted at two different points in the proceedings that procedures employed by state officials denied them due process. They also claimed that Tommy was being discriminated against on the basis of his handicapping condition, in violation of the Equal Protection Clause of the Fourteenth Amendment.

A

The first due process claim may be disposed of briefly. Petitioners challenged the refusal of the School Board to grant them a full hearing before terminating Tommy's funding. Petitioners were awarded fees against the School Board for their efforts in obtaining an injunction to prevent that due process deprivation. The award was not challenged on appeal and we therefore assume that it was proper.

The fact that petitioners prevailed on their initial due process claim, however, by itself does not entitle them to fees for the subsequent administrative and judicial proceedings. The due process claim that entitled petitioners to an order maintaining Tommy's placement throughout the course of the subsequent proceedings is entirely separate from the claims petitioners made in those proceedings. Nor were those proceedings necessitated by the School Board's failings. Even if the School Board had complied with state regulations and had guaranteed Tommy's continued placement pending adminis-

---

[10]The legislative history also makes clear that the fact that a plaintiff has prevailed on one of two or more alternative bases for relief does not prevent an award of fees for the unaddressed claims, as long as those claims are reasonably related to the plaintiff's ultimate success. See S. Rep. No. 94-1011, p. 6 (1976), citing *Davis* v. *County of Los Angeles*, 8 EPD ¶9444 (CD Cal. 1974). See also *Hensley* v. *Eckerhart*, 461 U. S. 424, at 435. The same rule should apply when an unaddressed constitutional claim provides an alternative, but reasonably related, basis for the plaintiff's ultimate relief.

trative review of its decision, petitioners still would have had to avail themselves of the administrative process in order to obtain the permanent relief they wanted—an interpretation of state law that placed on the School Board the obligation to pay for Tommy's education. Petitioners' initial due process claim is not sufficiently related to their ultimate success to support an award of fees for the entire proceeding. We turn, therefore, to petitioners' other § 1983 claims.

As petitioners emphasize, their § 1983 claims were not based on alleged violations of the EHA,[11] but on independent claims of constitutional deprivations. As the Court of Appeals recognized, however, petitioners' constitutional claims, a denial of due process and a denial of a free appropriate public education as guaranteed by the Equal Protection Clause, are virtually identical to their EHA claims.[12] The question to be asked, therefore, is whether Congress intended that the EHA be the exclusive avenue through which a plaintiff may assert those claims.

B

We have little difficulty concluding that Congress intended the EHA to be the exclusive avenue through which a plaintiff may assert an equal protection claim to a publicly financed special education. The EHA is a comprehensive scheme set up by Congress to aid the States in complying with their constitutional obligations to provide public education for handicapped children. Both the provisions of the statute and its legislative history indicate that Congress intended handicapped children with constitutional claims to a free appropriate public education to pursue those claims through the carefully tailored administrative and judicial mechanism set out in the statute.

In the statement of findings with which the EHA begins, Congress noted that there were more than 8,000,000 handicapped children in the country, the special education needs of most of whom were not being fully met. 20 U. S. C. §§ 1400(b)(1), (2), and (3). Congress also recognized that in a series of "landmark court cases," the right to an equal education opportunity for handicapped children had been established. S. Rep. No. 94-168, p. 6 (1975). See also id., at 13 ("It is the intent of the Committee to establish and protect the right to education for all handicapped children and to provide assistance to the States in carrying out their responsibilities under State law and the Constitution of the United States to provide equal protection of the laws"). The EHA was an attempt to relieve the fiscal burden placed on States and

---

[11]Courts generally agree that the EHA may not be claimed as the basis for a § 1983 action. See, e. g., Quackenbush v. Johnson City School District, supra; Department of Education v. Katherine D., supra; Anderson v. Thompson, supra.

[12]The timing of the filing of petitioners' second amended complaint, after the Supreme Court of Rhode Island had ruled that petitioners were entitled to the relief they sought, reveals that the equal protection claim added nothing to petitioners' claims under the EHA and provides an alternative basis for denying attorney's fees on the basis of that claim. There is, of course, nothing wrong with seeking relief on the basis of certain statutes because those statutes provide for attorney's fees, or with amending a complaint to include claims that provide for attorney's fees. But where it is clear that the claims that provide for attorney's fees had nothing to do with a plaintiff's success, Hensley v. Eckerhart, supra, requires that fees not be awarded on the basis of those claims.

localities by their responsibility to provide education for all handicapped children. 20 U. S. C. §§ 1400(b)(8) and (9). At the same time, however, Congress made clear that the EHA is not simply a funding statute. The responsibility for providing the required education remains on the States. S. Rep. No. 94-168, at 22. And the Act establishes an enforceable substantive right to a free appropriate public education. See *Board of Education* v. *Rowley*, 458 U. S. 176 (1982). See also 121 Cong. Rec. 37417 (1975) (statement of Sen. Schweiker: "It can no longer be the policy of the Government to merely establish an unenforceable goal requiring all children to be in school. [The bill] takes positive necessary steps to insure that the rights of children and their families are protected").[13] Finally, the Act establishes an elaborate procedural mechanism to protect the rights of handicapped children. The procedures not only ensure that hearings conducted by the State are fair and adequate. They also effect Congress' intent that each child's individual educational needs be worked out through a process that begins on the local level and includes ongoing parental involvement, detailed procedural safeguards, and a right to judicial review. §§ 1412(4), 1414(a)(5), 1415. See also S. Rep. No. 94-168, at 11-12 (emphasizing the role of parental involvement in assuring that appropriate services are provided to a handicapped child); *id.*, at p. 22; Board of Education v. *Rowley*, 458 U. S., at 208-209.

In light of the comprehensive nature of the procedures and guarantees set out in the EHA and Congress' express efforts to place on local and state educational agencies the primary responsibility for developing a plan to accommodate the needs of each individual handicapped child, we find it difficult to believe that Congress also meant to leave undisturbed the ability of a handicapped child to go directly to court with an equal protection claim to a free appropriate public education.[14] Not only would such a result render su-

---

[13]Prior to 1975, federal provisions for the education of handicapped children were contained in the Education of the Handicapped Act, passed in 1970, 84 Stat. 175, and amended in 1974, 88 Stat. 579 (current version at 20 U. S. C. § 1400 *et seq.*). The Act then provided for grants to States to facilitate the development of programs for the education of handicapped children. § 611(a). The only requirements imposed on the States were that they use federal funds on programs designed to meet the special education needs of handicapped children, § 613(a), and that parents or guardians be guaranteed minimum procedural safeguards, including prior notice and an opportunity to be heard when a State proposed to change the educational placement of the child. § 614(d). See n. 4, *supra.*

[14]The District Court in this case relied on similar reasoning—that Congress could not have meant for a plaintiff to be able to circumvent the EHA administrative process—and concluded that a handicapped child asserting an equal protection claim to public education was required to exhaust his administrative remedies before making his § 1983 claim. See *Turillo* v. *Tyson*, 535 F. Supp. 577, 583 (R. I. 1982), cited in the District Court's oral decision of April 30, 1982, App. to Pet. for Cert. A40. Because exhaustion was required, the court, relying on *New York Gaslight Club, Inc.* v. *Carey*, 447 U. S. 54 (1980), concluded that attorney's fees were appropriate under § 1988 for work performed in the state administrative process.

The difference between *Carey* and this case is that in *Carey*, the statute that authorized fees, Title VII, also required a plaintiff to pursue available state administrative remedies. In contrast, nothing in § 1983 requires that a plaintiff exhaust his administrative remedies before bringing a § 1983 suit. See *Patsy* v. *Florida Board of Regents*, 457 U. S. 496 (1982). If § 1983 stood as an independent avenue of relief for petitioners, then they could go straight to court to assert it.

perfluous most of the detailed procedural protections outlined in the statute, but, more important, it would run counter to Congress' view that the needs of handicapped children are best accommodated by having the parents and the local education agency work together to formulate an individualized plan for each handicapped child's education. No federal district court presented with a constitutional claim to a public education can duplicate that process.

We do not lightly conclude that Congress intended to preclude reliance on § 1983 as a remedy for a substantial equal protection claim. Since 1871, when it was passed by Congress, § 1983 has stood as an independent safeguard against deprivations of federal constitutional and statutory rights. See *Patsy* v. *Florida Board of Regents*, 457 U. S. 496 (1982); *Mitchum* v. *Foster*, 407 U. S. 225, 242 (1972); *Monroe* v. *Pape*, 365 U. S. 167, 183 (1961). Nevertheless, § 1983 is a statutory remedy and Congress retains the authority to repeal it or replace it with an alternative remedy.[15] The crucial consideration is what Congress intended. See *Brown* v. *GSA*, 425 U. S. 820, 825-829 (1976); *Johnson* v. *Railway Express Agency*, 421 U. S. 454, 459 (1975); *Adickes* v. *S. H. Kress & Co.*, 398 U. S. 144, 151, n. 5 (1970).

In this case, we think Congress' intent is clear. Allowing a plaintiff to circumvent the EHA administrative remedies would be inconsistent with Congress' carefully tailored scheme. The legislative history gives no indication that Congress intended such a result.[16] Rather, it indicates that Congress perceived the EHA as the most effective vehicle for protecting the constitutional right of a handicapped child to a public education. We conclude, there-

---

[15]There is no issue here of Congress' ability to preclude the federal courts from granting a remedy for a constitutional deprivation. Even if Congress repealed all statutory remedies for constitutional violations, the power of federal courts to grant the relief necessary to protect against constitutional deprivations or to remedy the wrong done is presumed to be available in cases within their jurisdiction. See *Bell* v. *Hood*, 327 U. S. 678, 684 (1946); *Bivens* v. *Six Unknown Fed. Narcotics Agents*, 403 U. S. 388, 396 (1971); *id.*, at 400-406 (Harlan, J., concurring in judgment).

[16]Petitioners insist that regardless of the wisdom of requiring resort to available EHA remedies before a handicapped child may seek judicial review, Congress specifically indicated that it did not intend to limit the judicial remedies otherwise available to a handicapped child. If that were true, we would agree with petitioners that Congress' intent is controlling and that a § 1983 remedy remained availabe to them. See *Johnson* v. *Railway Express Agency*, 421 U. S. 454, 459 (1975). The sentence in the legislative history on which petitioners rely, however, is not the clear expression of congressional intent petitioners would like it to be.

The sentence on which petitioners rely is included in the Committee Report of the Senate's version of the EHA. S. Rep. No. 94-168, pp. 27-28 (1975). The Senate bill included a requirement, not in the Conference bill, see Senate Conference Report No. 94-455, pp. 39-40 (1975), that the States set up an entity for ensuring compliance with the EHA. The compliance entity would be authorized, *inter alia*, to receive complaints regarding alleged violations of the Act. The Committee added that it did "not intend the existence of such an entity to limit the right of individuals to seek redress of grievances through other avenues, such as bringing civil action in Federal or State courts to protect and enforce the rights of handicapped children under applicable law." S. Rep. No. 94-168, p. 26 (1975). In the context in which the statement was made, it appears to establish nothing more than that handicapped children retain a right to judicial review of their individual cases. It does not establish that they can choose whether to avail themselves of the EHA process or go straight to court with an equal protection claim.

fore, that where the EHA is available to a handicapped child asserting a right to a free appropriate public education, based either on the EHA or on the Equal Protection Clause of the Fourteenth Amendment, the EHA is the exclusive avenue through which the child and his parents or guardian can pursue their claim.

C

Petitioners also made a due process challenge to the partiality of the state hearing officer. The question whether this claim will support an award of attorney's fees has two aspects—whether the procedural safeguards set out in the EHA manifest Congress' intent to preclude resort to § 1983 on a due process challenge and, if not, whether petitioners are entitled to attorney's fees for their due process claim. We find it unnecessary to resolve the first question, because we are satisfied that even if an independent due process challenge may be maintained, petitioners are not entitled to attorney's fees for their particular claim.[17]

Petitioners' plea for injunctive relief was not made until after the administrative proceedings had ended. They did not seek an order requiring the Commissioner of Education to grant them a new hearing, but only a declaratory judgment that the state regulations did not comply with the requirements

---

[17]We note that the issue is not the same as that presented by a substantive equal protection claim to a free appropriate public education. The EHA does set out specific procedural safeguards that must be guaranteed by a State seeking funds under the Act. See 20 U. S. C. § 1415. And although some courts have concluded that the EHA does not authorize injunctive relief to remedy procedural deficiencies, see, *e. g., Hymes* v. *Harnett County Board of Education*, 664 F. 2d 410 (CA4 1981), other courts have construed the district courts' authority under § 1415(e)(2) to grant "appropriate relief" as including the authority to grant injunctive relief, either after an unsuccessful and allegedly unfair administrative proceeding, or prior to exhaustion of the state remedies if pursuing those remedies would be futile or inadequate. See, *e. g., Robert M.* v. *Benton*, 622 F. 2d 370 (CA8 1980); *Monahan* v. *Nebraska*, 491 F. Supp. 1074 (Neb. 1980), aff'd in part and vacated in part, 645 F. 2d 592 (CA8 1981); *Howard S.* v. *Friendwood Independent School District*, 454 F. Supp. 634 (SD Tex. 1978); *Armstrong* v. *Kline*, 476 F. Supp. 583, 601-602 (ED Pa. 1979), remanded on other grounds *sub nom. Battle* v. *Pennsylvania*, 629 F. 2d 269 (CA3 1980), cert. denied, 452 U. S. 968 (1981); *North* v. *District of Columbia Board of Education*, 471 F. Supp. 136 (D. C. 1979). See also 121 Cong. Rec. 37416 (1975) (remarks of Sen. Williams) ("exhaustion of the administrative procedures established under this part should not be required for any individual complainant filing a judicial action in cases where such exhaustion would be futile either as a legal or practical matter").

On the other hand, unlike an independent equal protection claim, maintenance of an independent due process challenge to state procedures would not be inconsistent with the EHA's comprehensive scheme. Under either the EHA or § 1983, a plaintiff would be entitled to bypass the administrative process by obtaining injunctive relief only on a showing that irreparable harm otherwise would result. See *Monahan* v. *Nebraska*, 645 F. 2d 592, 598-599 (CA8 1981). And, while Congress apparently has determined that local and state agencies should not be burdened with attorney's fees to litigants who succeed, through resort to the procedures outlined in the EHA, in requiring those agencies to provide free schooling, there is no indication that agencies should be exempt from a fee award where plaintiffs have had to resort to judicial relief to force the agencies to provide them the process they were constitutionally due.

of due process and the EHA, and an injunction prohibiting the Commissioner from conducting further hearings under those regulations. App. 59-60. That due process claim and the substantive claim on which petitioners ultimately prevailed involved entirely separate legal theories and, more important, would have warranted entirely different relief. According to their complaint, petitioners did not even seek relief for themselves on the due process claim, but sought only to protect the rights of others coming after them in the administrative process. The efforts petitioners subsequently expended in the judicial process addressed only the substantive question as to which agency, as a matter of state and federal law, was required to pay for Tommy's education. Whether or not the state procedures accorded petitioners the process they were due had no bearing on that substantive question.

We conclude that where, as here, petitioners have presented distinctly different claims for different relief, based on different facts and legal theories, and have prevailed only on a non-fee claim, they are not entitled to a fee award simply because the other claim was a constitutional claim that could be asserted through § 1983. We note that a contrary conclusion would mean that every EHA plaintiff who seeks judicial review after an adverse agency determination could ensure a fee award for successful judicial efforts simply by including in his substantive challenge a claim that the administrative process was unfair. If the court ignored the due process claim but granted substantive relief, the due process claim could be considered a substantial unaddressed constitutional claim and the plaintiff would be entitled to fees.[18] It is unlikely that Congress intended such a result.

IV

We turn, finally, to petitioners' claim that they were entitled to fees under § 505 of the Rehabilitation Act, because they asserted a substantial claim for relief under § 504 of that Act.

Much of our analysis of petitioners' equal protection claim is applicable here. The EHA is a comprehensive scheme designed by Congress as the most effective way to protect the right of a handicapped child to a free appropriate public education. We concluded above that in enacting the EHA, Congress was aware of, and intended to accommodate, the claims of handicapped children that the Equal Protection Clause required that they be ensured access to public education. We also concluded that Congress did not intend to have the EHA scheme circumvented by resort to the more general provisions of § 1983. We reach the same conclusion regarding petitioners' § 504 claim. The relationship between the EHA and § 504, however, requires a slightly different analysis from that required by petitioners' equal protection claim.

Section 504 and the EHA are different substantive statutes. While the

---

[18]Even if the court denied the due process claim, as here, it is arguable that the plaintiff would be entitled to have an appellate court determine whether the district court was correct in its ruling on the due process claim. In this case, the District Court ruled against petitioners on their due process claim and the Court of Appeals determined, on appeal from the District Court's award of substantive relief, that the issue was moot. Nevertheless, in considering the propriety of the District Court's award of fees, the Court of Appeals recognized that the due process claim was at least substantial enough to support federal jurisdiction. 703 F. 2d, at 7.

EHA guarantees a right to a free appropriate public education, § 504 simply prevents discrimination on the basis of handicap. But while the EHA is limited to handicapped children seeking access to public education, § 504 protects handicapped persons of all ages from discrimination in a variety of programs and activities receiving federal financial assistance.

Because both statutes are built around fundamental notions of equal access to state programs and facilities, their substantive requirements, as applied to the right of a handicapped child to a public education, have been interpreted to be strikingly similar. In regulations promulgated pursuant to § 504, the Secretary of Education[19] has interpreted § 504 as requiring a recipient of federal funds that operates a public elementary or secondary education program to provide a free appropriate public education to each qualified handicapped person in the recipient's jurisdiction. 34 CFR § 104.33(a) (1983).[20] The requirement extends to the provision of a public or private residential placement if necessary to provide a free appropriate public education. § 104.33(c)(3). The regulations also require that the recipient implement procedural safeguards, including notice, an opportunity for the parents or guardian to examine relevant records, an impartial hearing with opportunity for participation by the parents or guardian and representation by counsel, and a review procedure. § 104.36. The Secretary declined to require the exact EHA procedures, because those procedures might be inappropriate for some recipients not subject to the EHA, see 34 CFR, subtitle B, ch. 1, App. A, p. 371, but indicated that compliance with EHA procedures would satisfy § 104.36.

On the other hand, although both statutes begin with an equal protection premise that handicapped children must be given access to public education, it does not follow that the affirmative requirements imposed by the two statutes are the same. The significant difference between the two, as applied to special education claims, is that the substantive and procedural rights assumed to be guaranteed by both statutes are specifically required only by the EHA.

Section 504, 29 U. S. C. § 794, provides, in pertinent part, that:

"No otherwise qualified handicapped individual in the United States, . . . shall, solely by reason of his handicap, be excluded from the participation in, be denied the benefits of, or be subjected to discrimination under any program or activity receiving Federal financial assistance . . ."

In *Southeastern Community College* v. *Davis*, 442 U. S. 397 (1979), the Court emphasized that § 504 does not require affirmative action on behalf of handicapped persons, but only the absence of discrimination against those

---

[19]The regulations were promulgated by the Secretary of Health, Education, and Welfare (HEW). 42 Fed. Reg. 22676 (1977). The functions of the Secretary of HEW under the Rehabilitation Act and under the EHA were transferred in 1979 to the Secretary of Education under the Department of Education Organization Act, § 301(a), 93 Stat. 677, 20 U. S. C. § 3441(a).

[20]Regulations under § 504 and the EHA were being formulated at the same time. The § 504 regulations were effective June 3, 1977. 42 Fed. Reg., at 22676. The EHA regulations were effective October 1, 1977. *Id.*, at 42474. The Secretary of HEW and the Commissioner of Education emphasized the coordination of effort behind the two sets of regulations and the Department's intent that the § 504 regulations be consistent with the requirements of the EHA. See 41 Fed. Reg. 56967 (1976); 42 Fed. Reg., at 22677.

persons. 442 U. S., at 411-412. In light of *Davis*, courts construing § 504 as applied to the educational needs of handicapped children have expressed confusion about the extent to which § 504 requires special services necessary to make public education accessible to handicapped children.[21]

In the EHA, on the other hand, Congress specified the affirmative obligations imposed on States to ensure that equal access to a public education is not an empty guarantee, but offers some benefit to a handicapped child. Thus, the statute specifically requires "such . . . supportive services . . . as may be required to assist a handicapped child to benefit from special education," see *Board of Education* v. *Rowley*, 458 U. S., at 200, including, if the public facilities are inadequate for the needs of the child, "instruction in hospitals and institutions." 20 U. S. C. §§ 1401(16) and (17).

We need not decide the extent of the guarantee of a free appropriate public education Congress intended to impose under § 504. We note the uncertainty regarding the reach of § 504 to emphasize that it is only in the EHA that Congress specified the rights and remedies available to a handicapped child seeking access to public education. Even assuming that the reach of § 504 is coextensive with that of the EHA, there is no doubt that the remedies, rights, and procedures Congress set out in the EHA are the ones it intended to apply to a handicapped child's claim to a free appropriate public education. We are satisfied that Congress did not intend a handicapped child to be able to circumvent the requirements or supplement the remedies of the EHA by resort to the general antidiscrimination provision of § 504.

There is no suggestion that § 504 adds anything to petitioners' substantive right to a free appropriate public education.[22] The only elements added by § 504 are the possibility of circumventing EHA administrative procedures and going straight to court with a § 504 claim,[23] the possibility of a damages

---

[21]Courts generally have upheld the § 504 regulations on the grounds that they do not require extensive modification of existing programs and that States and localities generally provide nonhandicapped children with educational services appropriate to their needs. See *Phipps* v. *New Hanover County Board of Education*, 551 F. Supp. 732 (ED N. C. 1982). But see *Colin K.* v. *Schmidt*, 715 F. 2d 1, 9 (CA1 1983) (in light of *Davis*, requirement that a school system provide a private residential placement could not be imposed under § 504).

[22]Of course, if a State provided services beyond those required by the EHA, but discriminatorily denied those services to a handicapped child, § 504 would remain available to the child as an avenue of relief. In view of the substantial overlap between the two statutes and Congress' intent that efforts to accommodate educational needs be made first on the local level, the presumption in a case involving a claim arguably with the EHA should be that the plaintiff is required to exhaust EHA remedies, unless doing so would be futile.

[23]Lower courts appear to agree, however, that unless doing so would be futile, EHA administrative remedies must be exhausted before a § 504 claim for the same relief available under the EHA may be brought. See, *e. g., Riley* v. *Ambach*, 668 F. 2d 635 (CA2 1981); *Phipps* v. *New Hanover County Board of Education, supra; Harris* v. *Campbell*, 472 F. Supp. 51 (ED Va. 1979); *H. R.* v. *Hornbeck*, 524 F. Supp. 215 (Md. 1981).

award in cases where no such award is available under the EHA,[24] and attorney's fees. As discussed above, Congress' intent to place on local and state educational agencies the responsibility for determining the most appropriate educational plan for a handicapped child is clear. To the extent § 504 otherwise would allow a plaintiff to circumvent that state procedure, we are satisfied that the remedy conflicts with Congress' intent in the EHA.

Congress did not explain the absence of a provision for a damages remedy and attorney's fees in the EHA. Several references in the statute itself and in its legislative history, however, indicate that the omissions were in response to Congress' awareness of the financial burden already imposed on States by the responsibility of providing education for handicapped children. As noted above, one of the stated purposes of the statute was to relieve this financial burden. See 20 U. S. C. §§ 1400(b)(8) and (9). Discussions of the EHA by its proponents reflect Congress' intent to "make every resource, or as much as possible, available to the direct activities and the direct programs that are going to benefit the handicapped." 121 Cong. Rec. 19501 (1975) (remarks of Sen. Dole). See also id., at 37025 (procedural safeguards designed to further the congressional goal of ensuring full educational opportunity without overburdening the local school districts and state educational agencies) (remarks of Rep. Perkins); S. Rep. No. 94-168, p. 81 (minority views cognizant of financial burdens on localities). The Act appears to represent Congress' judgment that the best way to ensure a free appropriate public education for handicapped children is to clarify and make enforceable the rights of those children while at the same time endeavoring to relieve the financial burden imposed on the agencies responsible to guarantee those rights. Where § 504 adds nothing to the substantive rights of a handicapped child, we cannot believe that Congress intended to have the careful balance struck in the EHA upset by reliance on § 504 for otherwise unavailable damages or for an award of attorney's fees.

We emphasize the narrowness of our holding. We do not address a situation where the EHA is not available or where § 504 guarantees substantive rights greater than those available under the EHA. We hold only that where, as here, whatever remedy might be provided under § 504 is provided with more clarity and precision under the EHA, a plaintiff may not circumvent or enlarge on the remedies available under the EHA by resort to § 504.

In light of our conclusion that § 504 was not available to petitioners as an alternative basis for the relief they sought, we need not decide whether, as petitioners urge, § 505 authorizes attorney's fees for substantial, unaddressed § 504 claims or whether a Rehabilitation Act claim is entitled only to a "determination on the . . . claim for the purpose of awarding counsel fees." H. R. Rep. No. 94-1558, p. 4, n. 7 (1976).

---

[24]There is some confusion among the circuits as to the availability of a damages remedy under § 504 and under the EHA. Without expressing an opinion on the matter, we note that courts generally agree that damages are available under § 504, but are available under the EHA only in exceptional circumstances. See, e. g., Miener v. Missouri, 673 F. 2d 969, 978 (CA8 1982), cert. denied, 459 U. S. 909 (1983); Anderson v. Thompson, 658 F. 2d 1205 (CA7 1981); Monahan v. Nebraska, 491 F. Supp., at 1094; Hurry v. Jones, 560 F. Supp. 500 (R. I. 1983); Gregg B. v. Board of Education, 535 F. Supp. 1333, 1339-1340 (ED N. Y. 1982).

V

The judgment of the Court of Appeals is affirmed.

It is so ordered.

JUSTICE BRENNAN, with whom JUSTICE MARSHALL and JUSTICE STEVENS join, dissenting.

In this case we are called upon to analyze the interaction among five statutory provisions: § 1 of the Civil Rights Act of 1871, as amended, 42 U. S. C. § 1983; § 2 of the Civil Rights Attorney's Fees Awards Act of 1976, 42 U. S. C. § 1988; § 504 of the Rehabilitation Act of 1973, as amended, 29 U. S. C. § 794; § 505(b) of the Rehabilitation Act, 29 U. S. C. § 794a(b); and § 615(e)(2) of the Education of the Handicapped Act (EHA or Act), as added, 89 Stat. 789, 20 U. S. C. § 1415(e)(2).

Section 1983 provides:

"Every person who, under color of any statute, ordinance, regulation, custom, or usage, of any State or Territory, subjects, or causes to be subjected, any citizen of the United States or other person within the jurisdiction thereof to the deprivation of *any rights, privileges, or immunities secured by the Constitution* and laws, shall be liable to the party injured in an action at law, suit in equity, or other proper proceeding for redress." (Emphasis added).

And § 1988 provides that the prevailing party in an action prosecuted under § 1983 may be awarded reasonable attorney's fees. Similarly, §§ 504 and 505(b) of the Rehabilitation Act provide a cause of action and attorney's fees, respectively, to an individual who, "solely by reason of his handicap," has been "excluded from the participation in, . . . denied the benefits of, . . . [or] subjected to discrimination under any program or activity receiving Federal financial assistance." Finally, § 615(e)(2) of the EHA authorizes judicial review of the States' provision of "free appropriate public education" to handicapped children. Unlike 42 U. S. C. § 1983 and § 504 of the Rehabilitation Act, however, § 615(e)(2) has no counterpart in the EHA authorizing the award of attorney's fees to prevailing parties.

Petitioners challenge Rhode Island's discriminatory failure to afford Thomas F. Smith III access to certain educational programs made available to other handicapped children. As the Court recognizes, *ante*, at 12-13, 15, this challenge states a meritorious claim under the EHA and a substantial claim under the Equal Protection Clause of the Fourteenth Amendment. In addition, petitioners' claim appears to fall squarely within the terms of § 504 of the Rehabilitation Act. Consequently, if §§ 504 and 1983 are available as bases for petitioners' action, petitioners are entitled to recover reasonable attorney's fees under § 1988 and, at a minimum, to be given an opportunity to establish the meritoriousness of their § 504 claim. *Maher* v. *Gagne*, 448 U. S. 122 (1980); H. R. Rep. No. 94-1558, p. 4, n. 7 (1976); Brief for Petitioners 61-62, n. 26 (legislative history establishes that § 505(b) incorporates standards governing § 1988).[1]

To determine whether § 504 or § 1983 is available, each provision must be read together with the EHA.[2] As the Court demonstrates, in enacting the EHA, Congress surely intended that individuals with claims covered by that Act would pursue relief through the administrative channels that the Act established before seeking redress in court. See *ante*, at 16-20, 22-25. It would make little sense for Congress to have established such a detailed and comprehensive administrative system and yet allow individuals to bypass the system, at their option, by bringing suits directly to the courts under either § 504 or § 1983. To that extent, therefore, the statutes before us are in conflict with one another. Accordingly, our guide must be the familiar principle of statutory construction that conflicting statutes should be interpreted so as to give effect to each but to allow a later-enacted, more specific statute to amend an earlier, more general statute only to the extent of the repugnancy between the two statutes. *Watt* v. *Alaska*, 451 U. S. 259, 267 (1981); *Radzanower* v. *Touche Ross & Co.*, 426 U. S. 148, 153 (1976); *Morton* v. *Mancari*, 417 U. S. 535, 551 (1974). We must, therefore, construe the statutory provisions at issue here so as to promote the congressional intent underlying the EHA, which was enacted after §§ 504 and 1983 and which is addressed specifically to the problems facing handicapped school children. At the same time, however, we must preserve those aspects of §§ 504 and 1983 that are not in irreconcilable conflict with the EHA.

The natural resolution of the conflict between the EHA, on the one hand, and §§ 504 and 1983, on the other, is to require a plaintiff with a claim covered by the EHA to pursue relief through the administrative channels established by that Act before seeking redress in the courts under § 504 or § 1983. Under this resolution, the integrity of the EHA is preserved entirely, and yet §§ 504 and 1983 are also preserved to the extent that they do not undermine the EHA. Although the primary function of §§ 504 and 1983 is to provide direct access to the courts for certain types of claims, these provi-

---

[1] The Court holds that petitioners may not recover any fees for this lawsuit. That result is wrong, I believe, without regard to whether § 505(b) requires an unlitigated § 504 claim to be meritorious or merely "substantial." Even if petitioners must establish the meritoriousness, and not just the substantiality, of the unlitigated § 504 claim, affirmance of the Court of Appeals' judgment would be improper, for petitioners have been given no opportunity to establish that their § 504 claim has merit and because petitioners are entitled to fees under § 1988. Since I think petitioners are entitled to fees under § 1988, and since even my dissent from the Court's holding on § 505(b) does not depend on whether the substantiality standard applies to unlitigated § 504 claims, I do not address that question.

I also need not consider what effect petitioners' due process claim against respondents, *ante*, at 20-22, may have on petitioners' entitlement to fees. I dissent from the Court's holding because I believe that petitioners are entitled to fees under § 1988 and may be entitled to fees under § 505(b) of the Rehabilitation Act. Petitioners' due process claim might have a bearing on the amount of fees they should recover, but it does not deprive petitioners of all entitlement to a fee award.

[2] Some claims covered by the EHA are also grounded in the Constitution and hence could be pursued under § 1983. Others are nonconstitutional claims cognizable under § 504. Still others are nonconstitutional claims cognizable only under the EHA. This case is concerned only with claims that have as a substantive basis both the EHA and either the Constitution or § 504.

sions also operate, as this case demonstrates, to identify those types of causes of action for which Congress has authorized the award of attorney's fees to prevailing parties. Significantly, this function does not in any way conflict with the goals or operation of the EHA. There is no basis, therefore, for concluding that either § 504 or § 1983 is unavailable for this limited purpose.

The Court, however, has responded to the conflict among these statutes by restricting the applicability of §§ 504 and 1983 far more than is necessary to resolve their inconsistency. Indeed, the Court holds that both §§ 504 and 1983 are wholly unavailable to individuals seeking to secure their rights to a free appropriate public education, despite the fact that the terms and intent of Congress in enacting each of these provisions unquestionably extend to many of those claims. As a result, the Court finds that attorney's fees, which would otherwise be available to those individuals under §§ 505(b) and 1988, are now unavailable. Yet the Court recognizes that there is absolutely no indication in the language of the EHA or in the Act's legislative history that Congress meant to effect such a repeal, let alone any indication that Congress specifically intended to bar the recovery of attorney's fees for parties that prevail in this type of action. The Court's rationale for effectively repealing §§ 504, 505(b), 1983, and 1988 to the extent that they cover petitioners' claim is that the comprehensiveness and detail with which the EHA addresses the problem of providing schooling to handicapped children implies that Congress intended to repeal all other remedies that overlap with the EHA, even if they do not conflict with the EHA.[3]

Repeals by implication, however, are strongly disfavored. *St. Martin Lutheran Church* v. *South Dakota*, 451 U. S. 772, 788 (1981); *Morton* v. *Mancari, supra*, at 550; *Posadas* v. *National City Bank*, 296 U. S. 497, 503 (1936). And, as stated above, they are tolerated only to the extent necessary to resolve clear repugnancy between statutes. *Radzanower* v. *Touche Ross & Co. supra*, at 154; *Posadas* v. *National City Bank, supra*, at 503. The function that §§ 504 and 1983 perform of identifying those claims for which attorney's fees are authorized under §§ 505(b) and 1988 is not repugnant to the EHA. The Court therefore has erred in concluding that petitioners cannot obtain attorney's fees.

In cases like this, it is particularly important that the Court exercise restraint in concluding that one act of Congress implicitly repeals another, not only to avoid misconstruction of the law effecting the putative repeal, but also to preserve the intent of later Congresses that have already enacted laws that are dependent on the continued applicability of the law whose implicit repeal is in question. By failing to exercise such restraint here, and hence concluding that the EHA implicitly repealed, in part, §§ 504 and 1983, the Court has not only misconstrued the congressional intent underlying the EHA, it has also frustrated Congress' intent in enacting §§ 505(b) and 1988— each of which was enacted after the EHA and premised on a view of §§ 504 and 1983 that was significantly more expansive than that offered by the

---

[3]The Court at one point seems to indicate that Congress actually considered the question of withholding attorney's fees from prevailing parties in actions covered by the EHA. *Ante*, at 27. But at the time the EHA was enacted, neither § 505(b) of the Rehabilitation Act nor § 1988 had yet been enacted. In that context, congressional silence on the question of attorney's fees can only be interpreted to indicate that Congress did not consider the matter. Thus, this claim is particularly unpersuasive and, in fact, does not appear to constitute a significant basis of the Court's decision.

Court today. Although in enacting the EHA, Congress was silent with respect to the continued availability of §§ 504 and 1983 for claims that could be brought directly under the EHA, there can be no doubt that, at the time §§ 505(b) and 1988 were passed, Congress believed that the EHA had not eliminated these alternative remedies. The Congressional understanding at these later points certainly sheds light on Congress' earlier intent in enacting the EHA, but perhaps more importantly, it demonstrates the extent to which the Court's finding of an implicit repeal has undermined the congressional intent behind the enactment of §§ 505(b) and 1988.

The Department of Health, Education, and Welfare (HEW) promulgated regulations under § 504 of the Rehabilitation Act *after* the EHA was passed. Those regulations contained a lengthy subpart governing the provision of education to the handicapped stating: "A recipient that operates a public elementary or secondary education program shall provide a free appropriate public education to each qualified handicapped person who is in the recipient's jurisdiction, regardless of the nature or severity of the person's handicap." 42 Fed. Reg. 22676, 22682 (1977). Thus, the department charged with enforcing the Rehabilitation Act and the EHA did not understand the latter to repeal the former with respect to handicapped education.[4] And, of course, the interpretation of the Act by the agency responsible for its enforcement is entitled to great deference. *Griggs* v. *Duke Power Co.*, 401 U. S. 424, 434 (1971). Furthermore, Congress was very much aware of HEW's interpretation of the two acts. During oversight hearings on the Rehabilitation Act, held after the enactment of the EHA, representatives of HEW testified that the agency had recently promulgated regulations under § 504 and that those regulations addressed discrimination in the provision of education to handicapped children.[5] Hearings on Implementation of Section 504, Rehabilitation Act of 1973, before the Subcommittee on Select Education of the House Committee on Education and Labor, 95th Cong., 1st Sess., 296-297 (1977) (statement of David Tatel, Director, Office for Civil Rights, Department of Health, Education, and Welfare);[6] Hearings on the Rehabilitation of the Handicapped Programs, 1976, before the Subcommittee on the Handicapped of the Senate Committee on Labor and Public Welfare, 94th Cong., 2d Sess., 1498, 1499, 1508, 1539-1546 (1976) (statement of Martin H. Gerry, Director, Office for Civil Rights, Department of Health, Education, and Welfare). No

---

[4]As the Court notes, *ante*, at 1017, n. 20, the regulations promulgated under § 504 and the EHA were closely coordinated with one another. See 42 Fed. Reg. 22677 (1977).

[5]In addition, testimony was generally taken on the success of § 504 as applied to discrimination against handicapped children in the provision of publicly funded education. See, *e. g.* Hearings on Implementation of Section 504, Rehabilitation Act of 1973, before the Subcommittee on Select Education of the House Committee on Education and Labor, 95th Cong., 1st Sess., 263-265 (1977). (statement of Daniel Yohalem, Children's Defense Fund), 278-285 (statement of Edward E. Corbett, Jr., Maryland School for the Deaf).

[6]Mr. Tatel's testimony included the following:

"With regard to preschool, elementary, and secondary education institutions, the regulations require:

"—annual identification and location of unserved handicapped children;

"—free appropriate public education to each qualified handicapped child regardless of the nature or severity of the handicap (including coverage of nonmedical care,

member of the House or Senate committee raised any question regarding § 504's continued coverage of discrimination in education after the passage of the EHA.

Indeed, the Senate Report accompanying the bill that included § 505(b) of the Rehabilitation Act explicitly referred to, and approved, the regulations promulgated under § 504. The Report then went on to address the need for attorney's fees, referring to the rights that § 504 extended to handicapped individuals generally and intimating no exception for handicapped children seeking education. S. Rept. No. 95-890, p. 19-20.

Similarly, the House Report stated:

> "[t]he proposed amendment is not in any way unique. At present there are at least 90 separate attorney's fees provisions to promote enforcement of over 90 different Federal laws. In fact, disabled individuals are one of the very few minority groups in this country who have not been authorized by the Congress to seek attorney's fees. The amendment proposes to correct this omission and thereby assist handicapped individuals in securing the legal protection guaranteed them under title V of the Act. H. R. Rep. No. 95-1149, p. 21 (1978).

Neither the terms nor the logic of this statement admits of the possibility that Congress intended to exclude from the coverage of § 505(b) the claims of handicapped children seeking a free appropriate public education.

Finally, although Congress, in enacting § 1988, did not specifically refer to the applicability of § 1983 to constitutional claims by handicapped children seeking education, it clearly intended to authorize attorney's fees in all cases involving the deprivation of civil rights. Adopted in response to this Court's decision in *Alyeska Pipeline Service Co.* v. *Wilderness Society*, 421 U. S. 240 (1975), § 1988 was intended to close "anomalous gaps in our civil rights laws whereby awards of fees are . . . unavailable." S. Rep. No. 94-1011, p. 4 (1976). The Senate Report thus stated:

> "In many cases arising under our civil rights laws, the citizen who must sue to enforce the law has little or no money with which to hire a lawyer. If private citizens are to be able to assert their civil rights, and if those who violate the Nation's fundamental laws are not to proceed with impunity, then citizens must have the opportunity to recover what it costs them to vindicate these rights in court.

* * *

> "'Not to award counsel fees in cases such as this would be tantamount to repealing the Act itself by frustrating its basic purpose. ***

---

room and board where residential placement required);
   "—education of handicapped students to maximum extent possible;
   "—comparability of facilities (including services and activities provided therein) identifiable as being for handicapped persons;
   "—evaluation requirements to insure proper classification and placement of handicapped children and procedural safeguards;
   "—equal opportunity for participation of handicapped students in non-academic and extracurricular services and activities." *Id.*, at 296 (statement of David Tatel, Director, Office of Civil Rights, Department of Health, Education, and Welfare).

Without counsel fees the grant of Federal jurisdiction is but an empty gesture ***. *Hall* v. *Cole*, 412 U. S. 1 (1973), quoting 462 F. 2d 777, 780-81 (2d Cir. 1972).'

"The remedy of attorneys' fees has always been recognized as particularly appropriate in the civil rights area, and civil rights and attorneys' fees have always been closely interwoven." *Id.*, at 2-3.

It would be anomalous, to say the least, for Congress to have passed a provision as broad as § 1988, and to provide an equally broad explanation, and yet to leave a "gap" in its own coverage of the constitutional claims of handicapped children seeking a free appropriate public education.[7] See also H. R. Rep. No. 94-1558, pp. 4-5 (1976).

In sum, the Court's conclusion that the EHA repealed the availability of §§ 504 and 1983 to individuals seeking a free appropriate public education runs counter to well-established principles of statutory interpretation. It finds no support in the terms or legislative history of the EHA. And, most importantly, it undermines the intent of Congress in enacting both §§ 505(b) and 1988. Had this case arisen prior to the enactment of §§ 505(b) and 1988, Congress could have taken account of the Court's expansive interpretation of the EHA. Presumably, it would have either clarified the applicability of §§ 504 and 1983 to claims for a free appropriate public education, or it would have extended the coverage of §§ 505(b) and 1988 to certain claims brought under the EHA. But with today's decision coming as it does after Congress has spoken on the subject of attorney's fees, Congress will now have to take the time to revisit the matter. And until it does, the handicapped children of this country whose difficulties are compounded by discrimination and by other deprivations of constitutional rights will have to pay the costs. It is at best ironic that the Court has managed to impose this burden on handicapped children in the course of interpreting a statute wholly intended to promote the educational rights of those children.

---

[7]Moreover, Congress was fully aware of the possibility that the same claim in the civil rights area might have duplicative statutory remedies. For instance, one of the "gaps" that Congress sought to close in enacting § 1988 was the possibility that an individual could bring an employment discrimination suit under Title VII of the 1964 Civil Rights Act and receive attorney's fees, although another individual bringing the same suit under 42 U. S. C. § 1981 could not recover attorney's fees. S. Rep. No. 94-1011, p. 4 (1976). Congress' response to this situation was to ensure that attorney's fees would be available under either provision.

Irving Independent School District v. Tatro

U.S. Supreme Court, 468 U.S. 883, 104 S.Ct. 3371 (1984).

Syllabus*

Respondents' 8-year-old daughter was born with a defect known as spina bifida. As a result she suffers from orthopedic and speech impairments and a neurogenic bladder, which prevents her from emptying her bladder voluntarily. Consequently, she must be catheterized every three or four hours to avoid injury to her kidneys. To accomplish this, a procedure known as clean intermittent catheterization (CIC) was prescribed. This is a simple procedure that can be performed in a few minutes by a layperson with less than an hour's training. Since petitioner School District received federal funding under the Education of the Handicapped Act it was required to provide the child with "a free appropriate public education," which is defined in the Act to include "related services," which are defined in turn to include "supportive services (including . . . medical . . . services except that such medical services shall be for diagnostic and evaluation purposes only) as may be required to assist a handicapped child to benefit from special education." Pursuant to the Act, petitioner developed an individualized education program for the child, but the program made no provision for school personnel to administer CIC. After unsuccessfully pursuing administrative remedies to secure CIC services for the child during school hours, respondents brought an action against petitioner and others in Federal District Court, seeking injunctive relief, damages, and attorney's fees. Respondents invoked the Education of the Handicapped Act, arguing that CIC is one of the included "related services" under the statutory definition, and also invoked § 504 of the Rehabilitation Act of 1973, which forbids a person, by reason of a handicap, to be "excluded from the participation in, be denied the benefits of, or be subjected to discrimination under" any program receiving federal aid. After its initial denial of relief was reversed by the Court of Appeals, the District Court, on remand, held that CIC was a "related service" under the Education of the Handicapped Act, ordered that the child's education program be modified to include provision of CIC during school hours, and awarded compensatory damages against petitioner. The court further held that respondents had proved a violation of § 504 of the Rehabilitation Act, and awarded attorney's fees to respondents under § 505 of that Act. The Court of Appeals affirmed.

Held:

1. CIC is a "related service" under the Education of the Handicapped Act. Pp. 5-11.

(a) CIC services qualify as a "supportive servic[e] . . . required to assist a handicapped child to benefit from special education," within the meaning of the Act. Without CIC services available during the school day, respondents' child cannot attend school and thereby "benefit from special education." Such services are no less related to the effort to educate than are services that enable a child to reach, enter, or exit a school. Pp. 6-7.

(b) The provision of CIC is not subject to exclusion as a "medical service." The Department of Education regulations, which are entitled to deference, define "related services" for handicapped children to include "school health services," which are defined in turn as "services provided by a qualified school nurse or other qualified person," and define "medical services" as "ser-

---

*The syllabus constitutes no part of the opinion of the Court but has been prepared by the Reporter of Decisions for the convenience of the reader.

vices provided by a licensed physician." This definition of "medical services" is a reasonable interpretation of congressional intent to exclude physician's services as such and to impose an obligation to provide school nursing services. Pp. 7-11.

2. Section 504 of the Rehabilitation Act is inapplicable when relief is available under the Education of the Handicapped Act to remedy a denial of educational service, *Smith* v. *Robinson, post,* p. ——, and therefore respondents are not entitled to any relief under § 504, including recovery of attorney's fees. Pp. 11-12.

703 F. 2d 823, affirmed in part and reversed in part.

BURGER, C.J., delivered the opinion of the Court, in which WHITE, BLACKMUN, POWELL, REHNQUIST, and O'CONNOR, JJ., joined, and in all but Part III of which BRENNAN, MARSHALL, and STEVENS, JJ., joined. BRENNAN, J., filed an opinion concurring in part and dissenting in part, in which MARSHALL, J., joined. STEVENS, J., filed an opinion concurring in part and dissenting in part.

CHIEF JUSTICE BURGER delivered the opinion of the Court.

We granted certiorari to determine whether the Education of the Handicapped Act or the Rehabilitation Act of 1973 requires a school district to provide a handicapped child with clean intermittent catheterization during school hours.

I

Amber Tatro is an 8-year-old girl born with a defect known as spina bifida. As a result she suffers from orthopedic and speech impairments and a neurogenic bladder, which prevents her from emptying her bladder voluntarily. Consequently, she must be catheterized every three or four hours to avoid injury to her kidneys. In accordance with accepted medical practice, clean intermittent catheterization (CIC), a procedure involving the insertion of a catheter into the urethra to drain the bladder, has been prescribed. The procedure is a simple one that can be performed in a few minutes by a layperson with less than an hour's training. Amber's parents, babysitter, and teenage brother are all qualified to administer CIC, and Amber soon will be able to perform this procedure herself.

In 1979 petitioner Irving Independent School District agreed to provide special education for Amber, who was then three and one-half years old. In consultation with her parents, who are respondents here, petitioner developed an individualized education program for Amber under the requirements of the Education of the Handicapped Act, 84 Stat. 175, as amended significantly by the Education for All Handicapped Children Act of 1975, 89 Stat. 773, 20 U. S. C. §§ 1401(19), 1414(a)(5). The individualized education program provided that Amber would attend early childhood development classes and receive special services such as physical and occupational therapy. That program, however, made no provision for school personnel to administer CIC.

Respondents unsuccessfully pursued administrative remedies to secure

CIC services for Amber during school hours.[1] In October 1979 respondents brought the present action in District Court against petitioner, the State Board of Education, and others. See § 1415(e)(2). They sought an injunction ordering petitioner to provide Amber with CIC and sought damages and attorney's fees. First, respondents invoked the Education of the Handicapped Act. Because Texas received funding under that statute, petitioner was required to provide Amber with a "free appropriate public education," §§1412(1), 1414(a)(1)(C)(ii), which is defined to include "related services," § 1401(18). Respondents argued that CIC is one such "related service."[2] Second, respondents invoked § 504 of the Rehabilitation Act of 1973, 87 Stat. 394, as amended, 29 U. S. C. § 794, which forbids an individual, by reason of a handicap, to be "excluded from the participation in, be denied the benefits of, or be subjected to discrimination under" any program receiving federal aid.

The District Court denied respondents' request for a preliminary injunction. *Tatro* v. *Texas*, 481 F. Supp. 1224 (ND Tex. 1979). That court concluded that CIC was not a "related service" under the Education of the Handicapped Act because it did not serve a need arising from the effort to educate. It also held that § 504 of the Rehabilitation Act did not require "the setting up of governmental health care for people seeking to participate" in federally funded programs. *Id.*, at 1229.

The Court of Appeals reversed. *Tatro* v. *Texas*, 625 F. 2d 557 (CA5 1980) (*Tatro I*). First, it held that CIC was a "related service" under the Education of the Handicapped Act, 20 U. S. C. § 1401(17), because without the procedure Amber could not attend classes and benefit from special education. Second, it held that petitioner's refusal to provide CIC effectively excluded her from a federally funded educational program in violation of § 504 of the Rehabilitation Act. The Court of Appeals remanded for the District Court to develop a factual record and apply these legal principles.

On remand petitioner stressed the Education of the Handicapped Act's explicit provision that "medical services" could qualify as "related services" only when they served the purpose of diagnosis or evaluation. See n. 2, *supra*. The District Court held that under Texas law a nurse or other qualified person may administer CIC without engaging in the unauthorized practice of medicine, provided that a doctor prescribes and supervises the procedure. The District Court then held that, because a doctor was not needed to administer CIC, provision of the procedure was not a "medical service" for purposes of the Education of the Handicapped Act. Finding CIC to be a "related service" under that Act, the District Court ordered petitioner and the State Board of Education to modify Amber's individualized education program to include provision of CIC during school hours. It also awarded

---

[1]The Education of the Handicapped Act's procedures for administrative hearings are set out in 20 U. S. C. § 1415. In this case a hearing officer ruled that the Education of the Handicapped Act did require the school to provide CIC, and the Texas Commissioner of Education adopted the hearing officer's decision. The State Board of Education reversed, holding that the Act did not require petitioner to provide CIC.

[2]As discussed more fully later, the Education of the Handicapped Act defines "related services" to include "supportive services (including . . . medical and counseling services, except that such medical services shall be for diagnostic and evaluation purposes only) as may be required to assist a handicapped child to benefit from special education." 20 U. S. C. § 1401(17).

compensatory damages against petitioner.[3] *Tatro* v. *Texas*, 516 F. Supp. 968 (ND Tex. 1981).

On the authority of *Tatro I*, the District Court then held that respondents had proved a violation of § 504 of the Rehabilitation Act. Although the District Court did not rely on this holding to authorize any greater injunctive or compensatory relief, it did invoke the holding to award attorney's fees against petitioner and the State Board of Education.[4] 516 F. Supp., at 968; App. to Pet. for Cert. 55a-63a. The Rehabilitation Act, unlike the Education of the Handicapped Act, authorizes prevailing parties to recover attorney's fees. See 29 U. S. C. § 794a.

The Court of Appeals affirmed. *Tatro* v. *Texas*, 703 F. 2d 823 (CA5 1983) *(Tatro II)*. That court accepted the District Court's conclusion that state law permitted qualified persons to administer CIC without the physical presence of a doctor, and it affirmed the award of relief under the Education of the Handicapped Act. In affirming the award of attorney's fees based on a finding of liability under the Rehabilitation Act, the Court of Appeals held that no change of circumstances since *Tatro I* justified a different result.

We granted certiorari, 464 U. S. 1007 (1983), and we affirm in part and reverse in part.

II

This case poses two separate issues. The first is whether the Education of the Handicapped Act requires petitioner to provide CIC services to Amber. The second is whether § 504 of the Rehabilitation Act creates such an obligation. We first turn to the claim presented under the Education of the Handicapped Act.

States receiving funds under the Act are obliged to satisfy certain conditions. A primary condition is that the state implement a policy "that assures all handicapped children the right to a free appropriate public education." 20 U. S. C. § 1412(1). Each educational agency applying to a state for funding must provide assurances in turn that its program aims to provide "a free appropriate public education to all handicapped children." § 1414(a)(1)(C)(ii).

A "free appropriate public education" is explicitly defined as "special education and related services." § 1401(18).[5] The term "special education" means

---

[3]The District Court dismissed the claims against all defendants other than petitioner and the State Board, though it retained the members of the State Board "in their official capacities for the purpose of injunctive relief." 516 F. Supp., at 972-974.

[4]The District Court held that § 505 of the Rehabilitation Act, 29 U. S. C. § 794a, which authorizes attorney's fees as a part of a prevailing party's costs, abrogated the State Board's immunity under the Eleventh Amendment. See App. to Pet. for Cert. 56a-60a. The State Board did not petition for certiorari, and the Eleventh Amendment issue is not before us.

[5]Specifically, the "special education and related services" must

"(A) have been provided at public expense, under public supervision and direction, and without charge, (B) meet the standards of the State educational agency, (C) include an appropriate preschool, elementary, or secondary school education in the State involved, and (D) [be] provided in conformity with the individualized education program required under section 1414(a)(5) of this title." § 1401(18).

"specially designed instruction, at no cost to parents or guardians, to meet the unique needs of a handicapped child, including classroom instruction, instruction in physical education, home instruction, and instruction in hospitals and institutions." § 1401(16).

"Related service" are defined as

"transportation, and such developmental, corrective, and other *supportive services (including* speech pathology and audiology, psychological services, physical and occupational therapy, recreation, and *medical* and counseling *services, except that such medical services shall be for diagnostic and evaluation purposes only) as may be required to assist a handicapped child to benefit from special education*, and includes the early identification and assessment of handicapping conditions in children." § 1401(17)(emphasis added).

The issue in this case is whether CIC is a "related service" that petitioner is obliged to provide to Amber. We must answer two questions: first, whether CIC is a "supportive servic[e] . . . required to assist a handicapped child to benefit from special education"; and second, whether CIC is excluded from this definition as a "medical servic[e]" serving purposes other than diagnosis or evaluation.

A

The Court of Appeals was clearly correct in holding that CIC is a "supportive servic[e] . . . required to assist a handicapped child to benefit from special education."[6] It is clear on this record that, without having CIC services available during the school day, Amber cannot attend school and thereby "benefit from special education." CIC services therefore fall squarely within the definition of a "supportive service"[7]

As we have stated before, "Congress sought primarily to make public education available to handicapped children" and "to make such access

---

[6]Petitioner claims that courts deciding cases arising under the Education of the Handicapped Act are limited to inquiring whether a school district has followed the requirements of the state plan and has followed the Acts's procedural requirements. However, we held in *Board of Education of Hendrick Hudson Central School District v. Rowley*, 458 U. S. 176, 206, n. 27 (1982), that a court is required "not only to satisfy itself that the State has adopted the state plan, policies, and assurances required by the Act, but also to determine that the State has created an [individualized education plan] for the child in question which conforms with the requirements of § 1401(19) [defining such plans]." Judicial review is equally appropriate in this case, which presents the legal question of a school's substantive obligation under the "related services" requirement of § 1401(197).

[7]The Department of Education has agreed with this reasoning in an interpretive ruling that specifically found CIC to be a "related service." 46 Fed. Reg. 4912 (1981). Accord *Tokarcik* v. *Forest Hills School District*, 665 F. 2d 443 (CA3 1981), cert. denied sub nom. *Scanlon* v. *Tokarcik*, 458 U. S. 1121 (1982). The Secretary twice postponed temporarily the effective date of this interpretive ruling, see 46 Fed. Reg. 12495 (1981); *id.* at 18975, and later postponed it indefinitely, *id.* at 25614. But the Department presently does view CIC services as an allowable cost under Part B of the Act. *Ibid.*

meaningful." *Board of Education of Hendrick Hudson Central School District* v. *Rowley*, 458 U. S. 176, 192 (1982). A service that enables a handicapped child to remain at school during the day is an important means of providing the child with the meaningful access to education that Congress envisioned. The Act makes specific provision for services, like transportation, for example, that do no more than enable a child to be physically present in class, see 20 U. S. C. § 1401(17); and the Act specifically authorizes grants for schools to alter buildings and equipment to make them accessible to the handicapped, § 1406; see S. Rep, No. 94-168, p. 38 (1975); 121 Cong. Rec. 19483-19484 (1975) (remarks of Sen. Stafford). Services like CIC that permit a child to remain at school during the day are no less related to the effort to educate than are services that enable the child to reach, enter, or exit the school.

We hold that CIC services in this case qualify as a "supportive servic[e] . . . required to assist a handicapped child to benefit from special education."[8]

B

We also agree with the Court of Appeals that provision of CIC is not a "medical servic[e]," which a school is required to provide only for purposes of diagnosis or evaluation. See 20 U. S. C. § 1401(17). We begin with the regulations of the Department of Education, which are entitled to deference.[9] See, *e. g.*, *Blum* v. *Bacon*, 457 U. S. 132, 141 (1982). The regulations define "related services" for handicapped children to include "school health services," 34 CFR § 300.13(a)(1983), which are defined in turn as "services provided by a qualified school nurse or other qualified person," § 300.13(b)(10). "Medical services" are defined as "services provided by a licensed physician." § 300.13(b)(4).[10] Thus, the Secretary has determined that the services of a school nurse otherwise qualifying as a "related service" are not subject to exclusion as a "medical service," but that the services of a physician are excludable as such.

---

[8]The obligation to provide special education and related services is expressly phrased as a "conditio[n]" for a state to receive funds under the Act. See 20 U. S. C. § 1412; see also S. Rep. No. 94-168, p. 16 (1975). This refutes petitioner's contention that the Act did not "impos[e] an obligation on the States to spend state money to fund certain rights as a condition of receiving federal moneys" but "spoke merely in precatory terms," *Pennhurst State School and Hospital* v. *Halderman*, 451 U. S. 1, 18 (1981).

[9]The Secretary of Education is empowered to issue such regulations as may be necessary to carry out the provisions of the Act. 20 U. S. C. § 1417(b). This function was initially vested in the Commissioner of Education of the Department of Health, Education, and Welfare, who promulgated the regulations in question. This function was transferred to the Secretary of Education when Congress created that position, see Department of Education Organization Act. §§ 301(a)(1), (2)(H), 93 Stat. 677, 20 U. S. C. §§ 3441(a)(1), (2)(H).

[10]The regulations actually define only those "medical services" that *are* owed to handicapped children: "services provided by a licensed physician to determine a child's medically related handicapping condition which results in the child's need for special education and related services." 34 CFR § 300.13(b)(4) (1983). Presumably this means that "medical services" *not* owed under the statute are those "services by a licensed physician" that serve other purposes.

This definition of "medical services" is a reasonable interpretation of congressional intent. Although Congress devoted little discussion to the "medical services" exclusion, the Secretary could reasonably have concluded that it was designed to spare schools from an obligation to provide a service that might well prove unduly expensive and beyond the range of their competence.[11] From this understanding of congressional purpose, the Secretary could reasonably have concluded that Congress intended to impose the obligation to provide school nursing services.

Congress plainly required schools to hire various specially trained personnel to help handicapped children, such as "trained occupational therapists, speech therapists, psychologists, social workers and other appropriately trained personnel." S. Rep. No. 94-168, *supra*, at 33. School nurses have long been a part of the educational system, and the Secretary could therefore reasonably conclude that school nursing services are not the sort of burden that Congress intended to exclude as a "medical service." By limiting the "medical services" exclusion to the services of a physician or hospital, both far more expensive, the Secretary has given a permissible construction to the provision.

Petitioner's contrary interpretation of the "medical services" exclusion is unconvincing. In petitioner's view, CIC is a "medical service," even though it may be provided by a nurse or trained layperson; that conclusion rests on its reading of Texas law that confines CIC to uses in accordance with a physician's prescription and under a physician's ultimate supervision. Aside from conflicting with the Secretary's reasonable interpretation of congressional intent, however, such a rule would be anomalous. Nurses in petitioner's school district are authorized to dispense oral medications and administer emergency injections in accordance with a physician's prescription. This kind of service for nonhandicapped children is difficult to distinguish from the provision of CIC to the handicapped.[12] It would be strange indeed if Congress, in attempting to extend special services to handicapped children, were unwilling to guarantee them services of a kind that are routinely provided to the nonhandicapped.

To keep in perspective the obligation to provide services that relate to both the health and educational needs of handicapped students, we note several limitations that should minimize the burden petitioner fears. First, to be entitled to related services, a child must be handicapped so as to require

---

[11]Children with serious medical needs are still entitled to an education. For example, the Act specifically includes instruction in hospitals and at home within the definition of "special education." See 20 U. S. C. § 1401(16).

[12]Petitioner attempts to distinguish the administration of prescription drugs from the administration of CIC on the ground that Texas law expressly limits the liability of school personnel performing the former, see Tex. Educ. Code Ann. § 21.914(c) (Supp. 1984), but not the latter. This distinction, however, bears no relation to whether CIC is a "related service." The introduction of handicapped children into a school creates numerous new possibilities for injury and liability. Many of these risks are more serious than that posed by CIC, which the courts below found is a safe procedure even when performed by a 9-year-old girl. Congress assumed that states receiving the generous grants under the Act were up to the job of managing these new risks. Whether petitioner decides to purchase more liability insurance or to persuade the state to extend the limitation on liability, the risks posed by CIC should not prove to be a large burden.

special education. See 20 U. S. C. § 1401(1); 34 CFR § 300.5 (1983). In the absence of a handicap that requires special education, the need for what otherwise might qualify as a related service does not create an obligation under the Act. See 34 CFR § 300.14, Comment (1) (1983).

Second, only those services necessary to aid a handicapped child to benefit from special education must be provided, regardless how easily a school nurse or layperson could furnish them. For example, if a particular medication or treatment may appropriately be administered to a handicapped child other than during the school day, a school is not required to provide nursing services to administer it.

Third, the regulations state that school nursing services must be provided only if they can be performed by a nurse or other qualified person, not if they must be performed by a physician. See 34 CFR §§/300.13(a), (b)(4), (b)(10) (1983). It bears mentioning that here not even the services of a nurse are required; as is conceded, a layperson with minimal training is qualified to provide CIC. See also, *e. g., Department of Education of Hawaii* v. *Katherine D.*, 727 F. 2d 809 (CA9 1983).

Finally, we note that respondents are not asking petitioner to provide *equipment* that Amber needs for CIC. Tr. of Oral Arg. 18-19. They seek only the *services* of a qualified person at the school.

We conclude that provision of CIC to Amber is not subject to exclusion as a "medical service," and we affirm the Court of Appeals' holding that CIC is a "related service" under the Education of the Handicapped Act.[13]

III

Respondents sought relief not only under the Education of the Handicapped Act but under § 504 of the Rehabilitation Act as well. After finding petitioner liable to provide CIC under the former, the District Court proceeded to hold that petitioner was similarly liable under § 504 and that respondents were therefore entitled to attorney's fees under § 505 of the Rehabilitation Act, 29 U. S. C. § 794a. We hold today, in *Smith* v. *Robinson,* 468 U. S. 992 (1984), that § 504 is inapplicable when relief is available under the Education of the Handicapped Act to remedy a denial of educational services. Respondents are therefore not entitled to relief under § 504, and we reverse the Court of Appeals' holding that respondents are entitled to recover attorney's fees. In all other respects, the judgment of the Court of Appeals is affirmed.

It is so ordered.

---

[13]We need not address respondents' claim that CIC, in addition to being a "related service," is a "supplementary ai[d] and servic[e]" that petitioner must provide to enable Amber to attend classes with nonhandicapped students under the Act's "mainstreaming" directive. See 20 U. S. C. § 1412(5)(B). Respondents have not sought an order prohibiting petitioner from educating Amber with handicapped children alone. Indeed, any request for such an order might not present a live controversy. Amber's present individualized education program provides for regular public school classes with nonhandicapped children. And petitioner has admitted that it would be far more costly to pay for Amber's instruction and CIC services at a private school, or to arrange for home tutoring, than to provide CIC at the regular public school placement provided in her current individualized education program. Tr. of Oral Arg. 12.

JUSTICE BRENNAN, with whom JUSTICE MARSHALL joins, concurring in part and dissenting in part.

I join all but Part III of the Court's opinion. For the reasons stated in my dissenting opinion in *Smith* v. *Robinson, post*, at 992, I would affirm the award of attorney's fees to the respondents.

JUSTICE STEVENS, concurring in part and dissenting in part.

The petition for certiorari did not challenge the award of attorney's fees. It contested only the award of relief on the merits to respondents. Inasmuch as the judgment on the merits is supported by the Court's interpretation of the Education of the Handicapped Act, there is no need to express any opinion concerning the Rehabilitation Act of 1973.* Accordingly, while I join Parts I and II of the Court's opinion, I do not join Part III.

---

*The "Statement of the Questions Presented" in the petition for certiorari reads as follows:

"1. Whether 'medical treatment' such as clean intermittent catheterization is a 'related service' required under the Education for All Handicapped Children Act and, therefore, required to be provided to the minor respondent.

"2. Is a public school required to provide and perform the medical treatment prescribed by the physician of a handicapped child by the Education of All Handicapped Children Act or the Rehabilitation Act of 1973?

"3. Whether the Fifth Circuit Court of Appeals misconstrued the opinions of this Court in *Southeastern Community College, Pennhurst State School & Hospital* v. *Halderman*, and *State Board of Education* v. *Rowley.*" Pet. for Cert. i.

Because the Court does not hold that the Court of Appeals answered any of these questions incorrectly, it is not justified in reversing in part the judgment of that court.

Burlington School Committee v. Department of Education of Massachusetts

U.S. Supreme Court, 105 S.Ct. 1996 (1985).

Syllabus*

The Education of the Handicapped Act requires participating state and local educational agencies to assure that handicapped children and their parents are guaranteed procedural safeguards with respect to the provision of free appropriate public education for such children. These procedures include the parents' right to participate in the development of an "individualized education program" (IEP) for the child and to challenge in administrative and court proceedings a proposed IEP with which they disagree. With respect to judicial review, the Act in 20 U. S. C. § 1415(e)(2) authorizes the reviewing court to "grant such relief as the court determines is appropriate." Section 1415(e)(3) provides that during the pendency of any review proceedings, unless the state or local educational agency and the parents otherwise agree, "the child shall remain in the then current educational placement of such child." Respondent father of a handicapped child rejected petitioner town's proposed IEP for the 1979-1980 school year calling for placement of the child in a certain public school, and sought review by respondent Massachusetts Department of Education's Bureau of Special Education Appeals (BSEA). Meanwhile, the father, at his own expense, enrolled the child in a state-approved private school for special education. The BSEA thereafter decided that the town's proposed IEP was inappropriate and that the private school was better suited for the child's educational needs, and ordered the town to pay the child's expenses at the private school for the 1979-1980 school year. The town then sought review in Federal District Court. Ultimately, after the town in the meantime had agreed to pay for the child's private-school placement for the 1980-1981 school year but refused to reimburse the father for the 1979-1980 school year as ordered by the BSEA, the court overturned the BSEA's decision, holding that the appropriate 1979-1980 placement was the one proposed in the IEP and that the town was not responsible for the costs at the private school for the 1979-1980 through 1981-1982 school years. The Court of Appeals, remanding, held that the father's unilateral change of the child's placement during the pendency of the administrative proceedings would not be a bar to reimbursement if such change were held to be appropriate.

Held:

1. The grant of authority to a reviewing court under § 1415(e)(2) includes the power to order school authorities to reimburse parents for their expenditures on private special education for a child if the court ultimately determines that such placement, rather than a proposed IEP, is proper under the Act. The ordinary meaning of the language in § 1415(e)(2) directing the court to "grant such relief as [it] determines is appropriate" confers broad discretion on the court. To deny such reimbursement would mean that the child's right to a free appropriate public education, the parents' right to participate fully in developing a proper IEP, and all of the procedural safeguards of the Act would be less than complete. Pp. 9-11.

---

*The syllabus constitutes no part of the opinion of the Court but has been prepared by the Reporter of Decisions for the convenience of the reader.

2. A parental violation of § 1415(e)(3) by changing the "then current educational placement" of their child during the pendency of proceedings to review a challenged proposed IEP does not constitute a waiver of the parents' right to reimbursement for expenses of the private placement. Otherwise, the parents would be forced to leave the child in what may turn out to be an inappropriate educational placement or to obtain the appropriate placement only by sacrificing any claim for reimbursement. But if the courts ultimately determine that the proposed IEP was appropriate, the parents would be barred from obtaining reimbursement for any interim period in which their child's placement violated § 1415(e)(3). Pp. 11-14.

736 F. 2d 773, affirmed.

REHNQUIST, J., delivered the opinion for a unanimous Court.

JUSTICE REHNQUIST delivered the opinion of the Court.

The Education of the Handicapped Act (Act), 84 Stat. 175, as amended, 20 U. S. C. § 1401 *et seq.*, requires participating state and local educational agencies "to assure that handicapped children and their parents or guardians are guaranteed procedural safeguards with respect to the provision of free appropriate public education" to such handicapped children. § 1415(a). These procedures include the right of the parents to participate in the development of an "individualized education program" (IEP) for the child and to challenge in administrative and court proceedings a proposed IEP with which they disagree. §§ 1401(19), 1415(b),(d),(e). Where as in the present case review of a contested IEP takes years to run its course—years critical to the child's development—important practical questions arise concerning interim placement of the child and financial responsibility for that placement. This case requires us to address some of those questions.

Michael Panico, the son of respondent Robert Panico, was a first grader in the public school system of petitioner Town of Burlington, Massachusetts, when he began experiencing serious difficulties in school. It later became evident that he had "specific learning disabilities" and thus was "handicapped" within the meaning of the Act, 20 U. S. C. § 1401(1). This entitled him to receive at public expense specially designed instruction to meet his unique needs, as well as related transportation. §§ 1401(16), 1401(17). The negotiations and other proceedings between the Town and the Panicos, thus far spanning more than 8 years, are too involved to relate in full detail; the following are the parts relevant to the issues on which we granted certiorari.

In the spring of 1979, Michael attended the third grade of the Memorial School, a public school in Burlington, Mass., under an IEP calling for individual tutoring by a reading specialist for one hour a day and individual and group counselling. Michael's continued poor performance and the fact that Memorial School encompassed only grades K through 3 led to much discussion between his parents and Town school officials about his difficulties and his future schooling. Apparently the course of these discussions did not run smoothly; the upshot was that the Panicos and the Town agreed that Michael was generally of above average to superior intelligence, but had special educational needs calling for a placement in a school other than Memorial. They disagreed over the source and exact nature of Michael's learning difficulties, the Town believing the source to be emotional and the parents believing it to be neurological.

In late June, the Town presented the Panicos with a proposed IEP for Michael for the 1979-1980 academic year. It called for placing Michael in a highly structured class of six children with special academic and social needs, located at another Town public school, the Pine Glen School. On July 3, Michael's father rejected the proposed IEP and sought review under § 1415(b)(2) by respondent Massachusetts Department of Education's Bureau of Special Education Appeals (BSEA). A hearing was initially scheduled for August 8, but was apparently postponed in favor of a mediation session on August 17. The mediation efforts proved unsuccessful.

Meanwhile the Panicos received the results of the latest expert evaluation of Michael by specialists at Massachusetts General Hospital, who opined that Michael's "emotional difficulties are secondary to a rather severe learning disorder characterized by perceptual difficulties" and recommended "a highly specialized setting for children with learning handicaps . . . such as the Carroll School," a state approved private school for special education located in Lincoln, Mass. App. 26, 31. Believing that the Town's proposed placement of Michael at the Pine Glen school was inappropriate in light of Michael's needs, Mr. Panico enrolled Michael in the Carroll School in mid-August at his own expense, and Michael started there in September.

The BSEA held several hearings during the fall of 1979, and in January 1980 the hearing officer decided that the Town's proposed placement at the Pine Glen School was inappropriate and that the Carroll School was "the least restrictive adequate program within the record" for Michael's educational needs. The hearing officer ordered the Town to pay for Michael's tuition and transportation to the Carroll School for the 1979-1980 school year, including reimbursing the Panicos for their expenditures on these items for the school year to date.

The Town sought judicial review of the State's administrative decision in the United States District Court for the District of Massachusetts pursuant to 20 U. S. C. § 1415(e)(2) and a parallel state statute, naming Mr. Panico and the State Department of Education as defendants. In November 1980, the District Court granted summary judgment against the Town on the state-law claim under a "substantial evidence" standard of review, entering a final judgment on this claim under Federal Rule of Civil Procedure 54(b). The Court also set the federal claim for future trial. The Court of Appeals vacated the judgment on the state-law claim, holding that review under the state statute was pre-empted by § 1415(e)(2), which establishes a "preponderance of the evidence" standard of review and which permits the reviewing court to hear additional evidence.

In the meantime, the Town had refused to comply with the BSEA order, the District Court had denied a stay of that order, and the Panicos and the State had moved for preliminary injunctive relief. The State also had threatened outside of the judicial proceedings to freeze all of the Town's special education assistance unless it complied with the BSEA order. Apparently in response to this threat, the Town agreed in February 1981 to pay for Michael's Carroll School placement and related transportation for the 1980-1981 term, none of which had yet been paid, and to continue paying for these expenses until the case was decided. But the Town persisted in refusing to reimburse Mr. Panico for the expenses of the 1979-1980 school year. When the Court of Appeals disposed of the state claim, it also held that under this status quo none of the parties could show irreparable injury and thus none was entitled to a preliminary injunction. The court reasoned that the Town had not shown that Mr. Panico would not be able to repay the tuition and related costs borne by the Town if he ultimately lost on the merits, and Mr. Panico had not shown that he would be irreparably harmed if not reimbursed immediately for past payments which might ultimately be determined to be the Town's responsibility.

On remand, the District Court entered an extensive pretrial order on the Town's federal claim. In denying the Town summary judgment, it ruled that 20 U. S. C. § 1415(e)(3) did not bar reimbursement despite the Town's insistence that the Panicos violated that provision by changing Michael's placement to the Carroll School during the pendency of the administrative proceedings. The court reasoned that § 1415(e)(3) concerned the physical placement of the child and not the right to tuition reimbursement or to procedural review of a contested IEP. The court also dealt with the problem that no IEP had been developed for the 1980-1981 or 1981-1982 school years. It held that its power under § 1415(e)(A) to grant "appropriate" relief upon reviewing the contested IEP for the 1979-1980 school year included the power to grant relief for subsequent school years despite the lack of IEPs for those years. In this connection, however, the court interpreted the statute to place the burden of proof on the Town to upset the BSEA decision that the IEP was inappropriate for 1979-1980 and on the Panicos and the State to show that the relief for subsequent terms was appropriate.

After a 4-day trial, the District Court in August 1982 overturned the BSEA decision, holding that the appropriate 1979-1980 placement for Michael was the one proposed by the town in the IEP and that the parents had failed to show that this placement would not also have been appropriate for subsequent years. Accordingly, the court concluded that the Town was "not responsible for the cost of Michael's education at the Carroll School for the academic years 1979-80 through 1981-82."

In contesting the Town's proposed form of judgment embodying the court's conclusion, Mr. Panico argued that, despite finally losing on the merits of the IEP in August 1982, he should be reimbursed for his expenditures in 1979-1980, that the Town should finish paying for the recently completed 1981-1982 term, and that he should not be required to reimburse the Town for its payments to date, apparently because the school terms in question fell within the pendency of the administrative and judicial review contemplated by § 1415(e)(2). The case was transferred to another District Judge and consolidated with two other cases to resolve similar issues concerning the reimbursement for expenditures during the pendency of review proceedings.

In a decision on the consolidated case, the court rejected Mr. Panico's argument that the Carroll School was the "current educational placement" during the pendency of the review proceedings and thus that under § 1415(e)(3) the Town was obligated to maintain that placement. *Doe* v. *Anrig*, 561 F. Supp. 121 (1983). The court reasoned that the Panicos' unilateral action in placing Michael at the Carroll School without the Town's consent could not "confer thereon the imprimatur of continued placement," *id.*, at 129, n. 5, even though strictly speaking there was no actual placement in effect during the summer of 1979 because all parties agreed Michael was finished with the Memorial School and the Town itself proposed in the IEP to transfer him to a new school in the fall.

The District Court next rejected an argument, apparently grounded at least in part on a state regulation, that the Panicos were entitled to rely on the BSEA decision upholding their placement contrary to the IEP, regardless of whether that decision were ultimately reversed by a court. With respect to the payments made by the Town after the BSEA decision, under the State's threat to cut off funding, the court criticized the State for resorting to extra-judicial pressure to enforce a decision subject to further review. Because this "was not a case where the town was legally obliged under section 1415(e)(3) to continue payments preserving the status quo," the State's coercion could not be viewed as "the basis for a final decision on liability" and it could only be "regarded as other than wrongful . . . on the assumption that the payments were to be returned if the order was ultimately reversed." *Id.*, at 130. The court entered a judgment ordering the Panicos to reimburse the Town for its payments for Michael's Carroll placement and related transportation in 1980-1981 and 1981-1982. The Panicos appealed.

In a broad opinion, most of which we do not review, the Court of Appeals for the First Circuit remanded the case a second time. 736 F. 2d 773 (1984). The court ruled, among other things, that the District Court erred in conducting a full trial *de novo*, that it gave insufficient weight to the BSEA findings, and that in other respects it did not properly evaluate the IEP. The court also considered several questions about the availability of reimbursement for interim placement. The Town argued that § 1415(e)(3) bars the Panicos from any reimbursement relief, even if on remand they were to prevail on the merits of the IEP, because of their unilateral change of Michael's placement during the pendency of the § 1415(e)(2) proceedings. The court held that such unilateral parental change of placement would not be "a bar to reimbursement of the parents if their actions are held to be appropriate at final judgment." *Id.*, at 799. In dictum the court suggested, however, that a lack of parental consultation with the Town or "attempt to achieve a negotiated compromise and agreement on a private placement," as contemplated by the Act, "may be taken into account in a district court's computation of an award of equitable reimbursement." *Ibid.* To guide the District Court on remand, the court stated that "whether to order reimbursement, and at what amount, is a question determined by balancing the equities." *Id.*, at 801. The court also held that the Panicos' reliance on the BSEA decision would estop the Town from obtaining reimbursement "for the period of reliance and requires that where parents have paid the bill for the period, they must be reimbursed." *Ibid.*

The Town filed a petition for a writ of certiorari in this Court challenging the decision of the Court of Appeals on numerous issues, including the scope of judicial review of the administrative decision and the relevance to the merits of an IEP of violations by local school authorities of the Act's procedural requirements. We granted certiorari, 469 U. S. — (1984), only to consider the following two issues: whether the potential relief available under § 1415(e)(2) includes reimbursement to parents for private school tuition and related expenses, and whether § 1415(e)(3) bars such reimbursement to parents who reject a proposed IEP and place a child in a private school without the consent of local school authorities. We express no opinion on any of the many other views stated by the Court of Appeals.

Congress stated the purpose of the Act in these words:

"to assure that all handicapped children have available to them . . . a free appropriate public education which emphasizes special education and related services designed to meet their unique needs [and] to assure that the rights of handicapped children and their parents or guardians are protected." 20 U. S. C. § 1400(c).

The Act defines a "free appropriate public education" to mean:

"special education and related services which (A) have been provided at public expense, under public supervision and direction, and without charge, (B) meet the standards of the State educational agency, (C) include an appropriate preschool, elementary, or secondary school education in the State involved, and (D) are provided in conformity with [an] individualized education program." 20 U. S. C. § 1401(18).

To accomplish this ambitious objective, the Act provides federal money to state and local educational agencies that undertake to implement the substantive and procedural requirements of the Act. See *Hendrick Hudson District Bd. of Education* v. *Rowley*, 458 U. S. 176, 179-184 (1982).

The *modus operandi* of the Act is the already mentioned "individualized educational program." The IEP is in brief a comprehensive statement of the educational needs of a handicapped child and the specially designed instruction and related services to be employed to meet those needs. § 1401(19). The IEP is to be developed jointly by a school official qualified in special education, the child's teacher, the parents or guardian, and, where appropriate, the child. In several places, the Act emphasizes the participation of the parents in developing the child's educational program and assessing its effectiveness. See §§ 1400(c), 1401(19), 1412(7), 1415(b)(1)(A), (C), (D), (E), and 1415(b)(2); 34 CFR § 300.345 (1984).

Apparently recognizing that this cooperative approach would not always produce a consensus between the school officials and the parents, and that in any disputes the school officials would have a natural advantage, Congress incorporated an elaborate set of what it labeled "procedural safeguards" to insure the full participation of the parents and proper resolution of substantive disagreements. Section 1415(b) entitles the parents "to examine all relevant records with respect to the identification, evaluation, and educational placement of the child," to obtain an independent educational evaluation of the child, to notice of any decision to initiate or change the identification, evaluation, or educational placement of the child, and to present complaints with respect to any of the above. The parents are further entitled to "an impartial due process hearing," which in the instant case was the BSEA hearing, to resolve their complaints.

The Act also provides for judicial review in state or federal court to "[a]ny party aggrieved by the findings and decision" made after the due process hearing. The Act confers on the reviewing court the following authority:

"[T]he court shall receive the records of the administrative proceedings, shall hear additional evidence at the request of a party, and, basing its decision of the preponderance of the evidence, shall grant such relief as the court determines is appropriate." § 1415(e)(2).

The first question on which we granted certiorari requires us to decide whether this grant of authority includes the power to order school authorities to reimburse parents for their expenditures on private special education for a child if the court ultimately determines that such placement, rather than a proposed IEP, is proper under the Act.

We conclude that the Act authorizes such reimbursement. The statute directs the court to "grant such relief as [it] determines is appropriate." The ordinary meaning of these words confers broad discretion on the court. The type of relief is not further specified, except that it must be "appropriate." Absent other reference, the only possible interpretation is that the relief is to be "appropriate" in light of the purpose of the Act. As already noted, this is principally to provide handicapped children with "a free appropriate public education which emphasizes special education and related services designed to meet their unique needs." The Act contemplates that such education will be provided where possible in regular public schools, with the child participating as much as possible in the same activities as nonhandicapped children, but the Act also provides for placement in private schools at public expense where this is not possible. See § 1412(5); 34 CFR §§ 300.132, 300.227, 300.307(b), 300.347 (1984). In a case where a court determines that a private placement desired by the parents was proper under the Act and that an IEP calling for placement in a public school was inappropriate, it seems clear beyond cavil that "appropriate" relief would include a prospective injunction directing the school officials to develop and implement at public expense an IEP placing the child in a private school.

If the administrative and judicial review under the Act could be completed in a matter of weeks, rather than years, it would be difficult to imagine a case in which such prospective injunctive relief would not be sufficient. As this case so vividly demonstrates, however, the review process is ponderous. A final judicial decision on the merits of an IEP will in most instances come a year or more after the school term covered by that IEP has passed. In the meantime, the parents who disagree with the proposed IEP are faced with a choice: go along with the IEP to the detriment of their child if it turns out to be inappropriate or pay for what they consider to be the appropriate placement. If they choose the latter course, which conscientious parents who have adequate means and who are reasonably confident of their assessment normally would, it would be an empty victory to have a court tell them several years later that they were right but that these expenditures could not in a proper case be reimbursed by the school officials. If that were the case, the child's right to a *free* appropriate public education, the parents' right to participate fully in developing a proper IEP, and all of the procedural safeguards would be less than complete. Because Congress undoubtedly did not intend this result, we are confident that by empowering the court to grant "appropriate" relief Congress meant to include retroactive reimbursement to parents as an available remedy in a proper case.

In this Court, the Town repeatedly characterizes reimbursement as "damages," but that simply is not the case. Reimbursement merely requires the Town to belatedly pay expenses that it should have paid all along and would have borne in the first instance had it developed a proper IEP. Such a *post-hoc* determination of financial responsibility was contemplated in the legislative history:

> "If a parent contends that he or she has been forced, at that parent's own expense, to seek private schooling for the child because an appropriate program does not exist within the local educational agency responsible for the child's education and the local educational agency disagrees, that disagreement and *the question of who remains financially responsible* is a matter to which the due process procedures established under [the predecessor to § 1415] appl[y]." S. Rep. No. 94-168, p. 32 (1975) (emphasis added).

See 34 CFR § 300.403(b)(1984) (disagreements and question of financial responsibility subject to the due process procedures).

Regardless of the availability of reimbursement as a form of relief in a proper case, the Town maintains that the Panicos have waived any right they otherwise might have to reimbursement because they violated § 1415(e)(3), which provides:

> "During the pendency of any proceedings conducted pursuant to [§ 1415], unless the State or local educational agency and the parents or guardian otherwise agree, the child shall remain in the then current educational placement of such child. . . ."

We need not resolve the academic question of what Michael's "then current placement" was in the summer of 1979, when both the Town and the parents had agreed that a new school was in order. For the purposes of our decision, we assume that the Pine Glen School, proposed in the IEP, was Michael's current placement and, therefore, that the Panicos did "change" his placement after they had rejected the IEP and had set the administrative review in motion. In so doing, the Panicos contravened the conditional command of § 1415(e)(3) that "the child shall remain in the then current educational placement."

As an initial matter, we note that the section calls for agreement by *either* the *State or* the *local educational agency.* The BSEA's decision in favor of the Panicos and the Carroll School placement would seem to constitute agreement by the State to the change of placement. The decision was issued in January 1980, so from then on the Panicos were no longer in violation of § 1415(e)(3). This conclusion, however, does not entirely resolve the instant dispute because the Panicos are also seeking reimbursement for Michael's expenses during the fall of 1979, prior to the State's concurrence in the Carroll School placement.

We do not agree with the Town that a parental violation of § 1415(e)(3) constitutes a waiver of reimbursement. The provision says nothing about financial responsibility, waiver, or parental right to reimbursement at the conclusion of judicial proceedings. Moreover, if the provision is interpreted to cut off parental rights to reimbursement, the principal purpose of the Act will in many cases be defeated in the same way as if reimbursement were never available. As in this case, parents will often notice a child's learning difficulties while the child is in a regular public school program. If the school officials disagree with the need for special education of the adequacy of the public school's program to meet the child's needs, it is unlikely they will agree to an interim private school placement while the review process runs its course. Thus, under the Town's reading of § 1415(e)(3), the parents are forced to leave the child in what may turn out to be an inappropriate educational placement or to obtain the appropriate placement only by sacrificing any claim for reimbursement. The Act was intended to give handicapped children both an appropriate education and a free one; it should not be interpreted to defeat one or the other of those objectives.

The legislative history supports this interpretation, favoring a proper interim placement pending the resolution of disagreements over the IEP:

> "The conferees are cognizant that an impartial due process hearing may be required to assure that the rights of the child have been completely protected. We did feel, however, that the placement, or change of placement should not be unnecessarily delayed while long and tedious administrative appeals were being exhausted. Thus the conference adopted a flexible approach to try to meet the needs of both the child and the State." 121 Cong. Rec. 37412 (1975) (Sen. Stafford).

We think at least one purpose of § 1415(e)(3) was to prevent school officials from removing a child from the regular public school classroom over the parents' objection pending completion of the review proceedings. As we observed in *Rowley*, 458 U. S., at 192, the impetus for the Act came from two federal court decisions, *Pennsylvania Assn. for Retarded Children* v. *Commonwealth*, 334 F. Supp. 1257 (ED Pa. 1971), and 343 F. Supp. 279 (1972), and *Mills* v. *Board of Education of District of Columbia*, 348 F. Supp. 866 (DC 1972), which arose from the efforts of parents of handicapped children to prevent the exclusion or expulsion of their children from the public schools. Congress was concerned about the apparently widespread practice of relegating handicapped children to private institutions or warehousing them in special classes. See § 1400(4); 34 CFR § 300.347(a) (1984). We also note that § 1415(e)(3) is located in a section detailing procedural safeguards which are largely for the benefit of the parents and the child.

This is not to say that § 1415(e)(3) has no effect on parents. While we doubt that this provision would authorize a court to order parents to leave their child in a particular placement, we think it operates in such a way that parents who unilaterally change their child's placement during the pendency of review proceedings, without the consent of state or local school officials, do so at their own financial risk. If the courts ultimately determine that the IEP proposed by the school officials was appropriate, the parents would be barred from obtaining reimbursement for any interim period in which their child's placement violated § 1415(e)(3). This conclusion is supported by the agency's interpretation of the Act's application to private placements by the parents:

> "(a) If a handicapped child has available a free appropriate public education and the parents choose to place the child in a private school or facility, the public agency is not required by this part to pay for the child's education at the private school or facility. . . .
> "(b) Disagreements between a parent and a public agency regarding the availability of a program appropriate for the child, and the

question of financial responsibility, are subject to the due process procedures under [§ 1415]." 34 CFR § 300.403 (1984).

We thus resolve the questions on which we granted certiorari; because the case is here in an interlocutory posture, we do not consider the estoppel ruling below or the specific equitable factors identified by the Court of Appeals for granting relief. We do think that the court was correct in concluding that "such relief as the court determines is appropriate," within the meaning of § 1415(e)(2), means that equitable considerations are relevant in fashioning relief.

The judgment of the Court of Appeals is

Affirmed.

APPENDIX C
TABLE OF CASES

INDEX